LIBRARY OF NEW TESTAMENT STUDIES
609

Formerly the Journal for the Study of the New Testament Supplement series

Editor
Chris Keith

Editorial Board
Dale C. Allison, John M.G. Barclay, Lynn H. Cohick, R. Alan Culpepper, Craig A. Evans, Robert Fowler, Simon J. Gathercole, Juan Hernandez Jr., John S. Kloppenborg, Michael Labahn, Love L. Sechrest, Robert Wall, Catrin H. Williams, Britanny Wilson

The *Proskynesis* of Jesus in the New Testament

A Study on the Significance of Jesus as an Object of προσκυνέω in the New Testament Writings

Ray M. Lozano

LONDON • NEW YORK • OXFORD • NEW DELHI • SYDNEY

T&T CLARK
Bloomsbury Publishing Plc
50 Bedford Square, London, WC1B 3DP, UK
1385 Broadway, New York, NY 10018, USA

BLOOMSBURY, T&T CLARK and the T&T Clark logo
are trademarks of Bloomsbury Publishing Plc

First published in Great Britain in 2020
Paperback edition first published 2021

Copyright © Ray M. Lozano, 2020

Ray M. Lozano has asserted his right under the Copyright,
Designs and Patents Act, 1988, to be identified as Author of this work.

For legal purposes the Acknowledgements on p. vii constitute
an extension of this copyright page.

Cover design: Eleanor Rose
Cover image © Vince Cavataio/Getty Images

All rights reserved. No part of this publication may be reproduced or
transmitted in any form or by any means, electronic or mechanical,
including photocopying, recording, or any information storage or retrieval
system, without prior permission in writing from the publishers.

Bloomsbury Publishing Plc does not have any control over, or responsibility for,
any third-party websites referred to or in this book. All internet addresses given
in this book were correct at the time of going to press. The author and publisher
regret any inconvenience caused if addresses have changed or sites have
ceased to exist, but can accept no responsibility for any such changes.

A catalogue record for this book is available from the British Library.

Library of Congress Cataloging-in-Publication Data
Names: Lozano, Ray M., author.
Title: The proskynesis of Jesus in the New Testament: a study on the significance of
Jesus as an object of proskuneo in the New Testament writings / by Ray M. Lozano.
Description: 1 [edition]. | New York: T&T Clark, 2019. |
Series: Library of New Testament studies; volume 609 |
Includes bibliographical references and index.
Identifiers: LCCN 2019016134 | ISBN 9780567688149 (hardback) |
ISBN 9780567688170 (epub)
Subjects: LCSH: Jesus Christ–Divinity. | God (Christianity)–Worship and love. |
Posture in worship. | Bible. Gospels–Criticism, interpretation, etc. |
Bible. New Testament–Criticism, interpretation, etc.
Classification: LCC BT216.3 .L69 2019 | DDC 232/.8–dc23
LC record available at https://lccn.loc.gov/2019016134

ISBN: HB: 978-0-5676-8814-9
PB: 978-0-5677-0146-6
ePDF: 978-0-5676-8815-6
eBook: 978-0-5676-8817-0

Series: Library of New Testament Studies, 2513-8790, volume 609

Typeset by Deanta Global Publishing Services, Chennai, India

To find out more about our authors and books visit
www.bloomsbury.com and sign up for our newsletters.

Contents

Acknowledgments	vii
Introduction	1
A. Justification for this study	2
B. Approach of this study	7
C. Outline of this study	10
1 Προσκυνέω in the Cultural Context of the NT Writings	13
A. Προσκυνέω in Greco-Roman literature	13
B. Προσκυνέω in the OT and in early Jewish literature	21
C. Conclusion	33
2 The Προσκύνησις of Jesus in the Gospel of Mark	35
A. The Προσκύνησις of Jesus by the Gerasene demoniac	35
B. The Προσκύνησις of Jesus by the Roman soldiers	37
C. The significance of the Προσκύνησις of Jesus in Mark	37
D. Conclusion	50
3 The Προσκύνησις of Jesus in the Gospel of Matthew	51
A. The Προσκύνησις of God	52
B. The Προσκύνησις of Jesus	53
1. By the magi at Jesus's birth	53
2. By various suppliants throughout Jesus's earthly ministry	55
3. By the disciples at Jesus's theophanic walk upon the sea	56
4. By the women and the disciples at Jesus's resurrection appearances	59
C. The significance of the Προσκύνησις of Jesus in Matthew	64
D. Conclusion	81
4 The Προσκύνησις of Jesus in the Gospel of Luke and the Book of Acts	83
A. The Προσκύνησις of God	83
B. The Προσκύνησις of false gods	84
C. The Προσκύνησις of Peter	85
D. The Προσκύνησις of Jesus by the disciples at his ascension	89
E. The significance of the Προσκύνησις of Jesus in Luke-Acts	93
F. Conclusion	99

5	The Προσκύνησις of Jesus in the Gospel of John	101
	A. The Προσκύνησις of God	101
	B. The Προσκύνησις of Jesus by the formerly blind man	106
	C. The significance of the Προσκύνησις of Jesus in John	109
	D. Conclusion	115
6	The Προσκύνησις of Jesus in the Epistle to the Hebrews	117
	A. The Προσκύνησις of Jesus by the angels	117
	B. The significance of the Προσκύνησις of Jesus in Hebrews	124
	C. Conclusion	139
7	The Προσκύνησις of Jesus in the Book of Revelation	141
	A. The Προσκύνησις of God	141
	B. The Προσκύνησις of evil figures	144
	C. The Προσκύνησις of angels	147
	D. The Προσκύνησις of the Philadelphian Christians	150
	E. The Προσκύνησις of Jesus by heavenly beings	151
	F. The significance of the Προσκύνησις of Jesus in Revelation	161
	G. Conclusion	167
Conclusion		169
	A. Summary of findings	169
	B. Significant points of commonality	172
	C. Final overall assessment	174
Bibliography		177
Index of Authors		199
Index of References		206

Acknowledgments

I am deeply grateful for the many people who came alongside me and supported me in various ways throughout my PhD studies at the University of Edinburgh. I am especially thankful for my supervisor, Professor Larry Hurtado, who not only provided helpful guidance and feedback every step of the way but also saw me through the struggles of coming up with a new research topic when my original project had to be abandoned so late in my studies (even having on hand a few alternative research topics to explore!). To my examiners, Professor Grant Macaskill and Professor Paul Foster, many thanks are due for their encouraging comments and helpful suggestions in the assessment of my work. I would also like to thank Professor Helen Bond for her involvement in the early stages of my research, and for the many opportunities to attend and host receptions for various stimulating CSCO events.

Although I became much more of a hermit in my studies than I would have liked to have been, I was still fortunate to be blessed with many lifelong friendships made with fellow PhD students and faculty at New College, with colleagues at Prestonfield House, and with church family at Duncan Street Baptist Church. I am especially thankful for my family back home in California. I could not have made it without their constant support, prayers, and the many late-night Skype chats.

Lastly, I am most grateful to my Lord and Savior, Jesus Christ, to whom this work is ultimately dedicated.

Introduction

An intriguing literary feature of a number of NT writings that has received very little adequate, comprehensive scholarly attention is the depiction of Jesus as a recipient of προσκύνησις—that is, as an object of the Greek verb προσκυνέω.[1] In the broadest, most basic sense of the term, προσκυνέω signifies reverence directed toward a superior, typically through prostration. More specific instances of the use of the term reveal its capacity to run the reverential gamut, from designating a simple respectful greeting of an elder, to designating homage paid to a king, to designating cultic worship of a deity. An initial overview of the sixty occurrences of προσκυνέω[2] in the NT already gives the impression that there does indeed appear to be something quite significant in those numerous instances where it is Jesus who is made the object of προσκυνέω. The term is frequently used for the worship of Israel's God (twenty-six times)[3] and for idolatrous or blasphemous worship of false gods, idols, Satan, demons, and "the beast" along with its image (fourteen times).[4] There are only a few instances where the term is used for some kind of reverence of humans (three times)[5] or angels (two times).[6] But, interestingly, on three of these occasions, the human and the angels consider themselves unworthy recipients of such reverence and therefore reject it, and on one occasion, the human appears to be a parabolic figure for God. All other NT uses of προσκυνέω have Jesus as the object (fifteen [or more likely, sixteen] times),[7] in which he is not only consistently portrayed freely accepting such reverence but even doing so in a number of overtly striking scenes where he appears to be "more than human."[8] Could it be that in the NT's numerous depictions of Jesus as an object of προσκυνέω—a term that is otherwise frequently used in the NT for worship of divine figures and is even occasionally used for reverence rejected by humans and angels—he is portrayed as a divine figure and/or a legitimate recipient of divine worship?

---

[1]   Throughout this work, I frequently use phrases such as "render προσκύνησις to," "give προσκύνησις to," "do προσκύνησις before," and so forth to render προσκυνέω (e.g., ὁ δοῦλος προσεκύνησεν τὸν βασιλέα = The servant rendered/gave/did προσκύνησις to/before the king) before arriving at a more specific reverential nuance for each instance.
[2]   Note also one occurrence of προσκυνητής ("one who renders προσκύνησις") in John 4:23.
[3]   Matt 4:10; Luke 4:8; John 4:20–24 (9x); 12:20; Acts 8:27; 24:11; 1 Cor 14:25; Heb 11:21; Rev 4:10; 5:14; 7:11; 11:1, 16; 14:7; 15:4; 19:4, 10; 22:9. So too is προσκυνητής in John 4:23.
[4]   Matt 4:9; Luke 4:7; Acts 7:43; Rev 9:20; 13:4 (2x), 8, 12, 15; 14:9, 11; 16:2; 19:20; 20:4.
[5]   Matt 18:26; Acts 10:25; Rev 3:9.
[6]   Rev 19:10; 22:8.
[7]   Mark 5:6; 15:19; Matt 2:2, 8, 11; 8:2; 9:18; 14:33; 15:25; 20:20; 28:9, 17; Luke 24:52; John 9:38; Heb 1:6. I will argue that Rev 5:14 should also be included here.
[8]   I occasionally refer to the "more-than-human" character of Jesus throughout my discussion. By this, I mean that Jesus is described behaving, speaking, and/or being perceived in ways more characteristic of supernatural beings. In each case, I go on to explain whether Jesus is being presented as angel-like, godlike, or Yahweh-like.

A. Justification for this study

As we have already suggested, there is surprisingly little substantial scholarly discussion of this NT phenomenon as a whole. Moreover, the few who have offered brief assessments of NT προσκυνέω usage come to very different conclusions regarding its christological significance. For some, the NT usage suggests Jesus is portrayed as divine in his reception of προσκύνησις. In his contribution to the προσκυνέω entry in *Theological Dictionary of the New Testament*, Heinrich Greeven rather boldly stated, "When the NT uses προσκυνεῖν, the object is always something—truly or supposedly—divine."[9] Along with the frequent use of προσκυνέω in the much stronger sense of worship reserved for God,[10] Greeven drew attention to the Gospel of Matthew's redaction of Markan material, whereby those who are described prostrate before Jesus in more generic terms in the Gospel of Mark (e.g., γονυπετῶν [Mark 1:40]; πίπτει πρὸς τοὺς πόδας [Mark 5:22]) are more suggestively characterized as rendering προσκύνησις to Jesus in the Gospel of Matthew (cf. Matt 8:2; 9:18; etc.).[11] These are made to represent unwitting acknowledgments of the Jesus whose divinity is elsewhere more clearly perceived when he receives προσκύνησις as the Son of God (Matt 14:33; cf. John 9:38) and the risen Lord (Matt 28:9, 17; Luke 24:52).[12] C. F. D. Moule held a similar view of the significance of the προσκύνησις of Jesus, which he briefly discussed in an excursus on προσκυνέω in the NT at the end of his work *The Origin of Christology*.[13] Although Moule did not go as far as Greeven did in positing divine-recipient significance in every instance of προσκυνέω (noting Matt 18:26 and Rev 3:9), he did essentially stand on common ground with Greeven in his other assessments, and therefore concluded that "proskunein was, indeed, for the most part reserved for worship of a divine being" and that "broadly speaking . . . Jesus *is* represented as receiving the highest honours."[14]

Others, however, such as J. Lionel North, come to the exact opposite conclusion: "We have nothing here . . . that requires us to conclude that Jesus is regarded as divine because he is worshipped" (i.e., the object of προσκυνέω).[15] North concedes that προσκυνέω is frequently used in the NT to designate that which is ultimately legitimately restricted to God (Matt 4:9–10; Acts 10:25; Revelation passages; etc.) but so can it be used for that reverence which is properly directed to mere humans (Matt 18:26; Rev 3:9).[16] He explains that all προσκύνησις of Jesus passages can be categorized in one of three ways—προσκύνησις after a miracle expressing wonder and gratitude (Matt 14:33; 28:9, 17; Luke 24:52; John 9:38), προσκύνησις before a miracle expressing petition (Mark 5:6; Matt 8:2; 9:18; 15:25; 20:20), and προσκύνησις expressing homage (Mark 15:19; Matt 2:11; Heb 1:6)—none of which requires that Jesus is regarded as

---

[9] Heinrich Greeven, "προσκυνέω, προσκυνητής," *TDNT* 6:763.
[10] Greeven, *TDNT* 6:764–65.
[11] Greeven, *TDNT* 6:763.
[12] Greeven, *TDNT* 6:764.
[13] C. F. D. Moule, *The Origin of Christology* (Cambridge: Cambridge University Press, 1977), 175–76.
[14] Moule, *Origin*, 176 (italics his).
[15] J. Lionel North, "Jesus and Worship, God and Sacrifice," in *Early Jewish and Christian Monotheism* (ed. Loren T. Stuckenbruck and Wendy E. S. North; JSNTSup 263; London: T&T Clark, 2004), 189.
[16] North, "Jesus," 188.

divine in his reception of προσκύνησις.[17] In North's view, as the title of his article "Jesus and Worship, God and Sacrifice" in *Early Jewish and Christian Monotheism* suggests, there is a substantial difference between προσκύνησις (what he calls "worship") and sacrifice, the latter alone belonging exclusively to God, and thus being the only true test of divinity.[18] By contrast, since προσκύνησις could legitimately be given to both God and humans, one cannot infer the divinity of Jesus from passages depicting his reception of προσκύνησις.[19]

Still others seem to take a view that lies somewhere between the two extreme positions above. In his work *Did the First Christians Worship Jesus?*, James Dunn includes in his discussion a survey of the NT's worship language, beginning with the use of προσκυνέω.[20] On the one hand, Dunn highlights a number of passages where the προσκύνησις of Jesus appears to be little more than appropriate reverence given to a human authority figure (Mark 15:19; Matt 8:2; 9:18; 15:25; 20:20; cf. Matt 18:26; Rev 3:9).[21] On the other hand, he points to a few passages where the προσκύνησις of Jesus goes well beyond this sense (Matt 28:9, 17; Luke 24:52; Heb 1:6)[22] and to one passage where Jesus does appear to be worshiped alongside God (Rev 5:14).[23] In the end, Dunn concludes that "the use of *proskynein* in the sense of offering worship to Jesus seems to be rather limited."[24]

None of these discussions are particularly satisfying as they are all far too brief to address adequately the issue at hand. Indeed, conclusions are reached (and widely diverging ones at that) from mere two- to five-page discussions on sixty uses of προσκυνέω spread across several NT works! The broad sweeping claims of Greeven and North are particularly suspect. With regard to Greeven, is it really the case that in *all* uses of προσκυνέω, the object is truly or supposedly divine? Is it not pressing the text of Rev 3:9 to suggest, as Greeven did, that προσκύνησις rendered to the Philadelphian Christians (or perhaps to their representative angel) is actually indirectly rendered to Jesus?[25] With regard to North, can all προσκύνησις of Jesus

---

[17] North, "Jesus," 188–89.
[18] North, "Jesus," 189–202.
[19] For a similar view, see James F. McGrath, *The Only True God: Early Christian Monotheism in Its Jewish Context* (Chicago: University of Illinois Press, 2009), 7–8, 18–19.
[20] James D. G. Dunn, *Did the First Christians Worship Jesus? The New Testament Evidence* (London: SPCK, 2010), 8–12.
[21] Dunn, *First*, 9–10.
[22] See also Dunn, *First*, 10, n. 9, where he says that Matt 14:33; Mark 5:6; John 9:38 "may have fuller significance for the Evangelists."
[23] Dunn, *First*, 11–12.
[24] Dunn, *First*, 12. Cf. Karen H. Jobes, "Distinguishing the Meaning of Greek Verbs in the Semantic Domain for Worship," *Filologia Neotestamentaria* 4 (1991): 183–91. Although Jobes does not attempt a comprehensive analysis of προσκυνέω in the NT (this is not her primary focus), she considers προσκυνέω to have basically three senses in the NT: entreaty, political homage, and worship. With respect to Jesus, she only highlights specific examples of the first sense (Matt 20:20) and the second sense (Matt 2:11). It is not clear if she thinks of the third sense as applicable to Jesus when she says that "the actions and attitudes referred to by this verb are always evaluated positively with [sic] used with respect to God and Jesus and always condemned when directed toward angels, Satan, demons or pagan deity" (187).
[25] Greeven, *TDNT* 6:765 and n. 66.

passages be so easily dismissed as insignificant for Jesus's divine status on the basis that he is not also a recipient of sacrifice? Can προσκυνέω really be ruled out entirely as representing a type of honor reserved for deity when numerous passages so strongly censure the προσκύνησις of false gods with no mention whatsoever of sacrifice?[26] Is it not more reasonable to conclude from such evidence that προσκυνέω *in certain contexts* can represent a type of honor that acknowledges a deity as such, while *in other contexts* it represents some other type of reverence determinable by its own context? Concerning North's analysis of the προσκύνησις of Jesus passages themselves, one might question, for instance, whether his classification of the προσκύνησις of Jesus in the sea-walking account (Matt 14:33) and in the resurrection accounts (Matt 28:9, 17; Luke 24:52) as wonder in response to a miracle is adequate. In addition, one might also question if the προσκύνησις Jesus receives from the angels (Heb 1:6) is really "on a par" with the προσκύνησις he receives from the magi (Matt 2:11).[27] Dunn himself admits that the angels' προσκύνησις of Jesus in Heb 1:6 is "very striking," rightly drawing attention to the christological application of Deut 32:43 here, which originally calls for the angels to render προσκύνησις to God.[28] Still, the question remains, just how striking is this depiction? The lack of thorough examination of this passage, and of all προσκύνησις of Jesus passages (and indeed of all προσκύνησις passages in the NT), ultimately leaves these and other key questions largely unanswered. To my knowledge, the only comprehensive, detailed study related to this subject is Johannes Horst's 1932 monograph entitled *Proskynein: Zur Anbetung im Urchristentum nach ihrer religionsgeschichtlichen Eigenart*.[29] Building from the first half of his study, which is devoted to a thorough *religionsgeschichtliche* investigation of the use of προσκυνέω and of the gestures and attitudes associated with the term leading into and around the time of the early Christian era, Horst turns his attention in the second half of his work to the NT environment and the NT use of προσκυνέω. He argued that as the wider pagan world was not only continuing in their worship of many gods through προσκύνησις but was even more and more embracing such worship of humans as gods, particularly seen in the rise of Hellenistic ruler cult and the imperial cult,[30] Jews and even more so Christians in response had taken more restrictive measures. Jewish writings continue to reject idolatrous προσκύνησις (e.g., Philo, *Decal.* 64; Josephus, *Ant.* 3.91), including προσκύνησις of humans as gods (e.g., Philo, *Legat.* 116),[31] and accordingly evince aversion to προσκύνησις of humans in general.[32] Yet they also allow

---

[26] See, for example, LXX Lev 26:1; Judg 2:2; 3 Kgdms 19:18; Pss 80:10; 96:7; 105:19; Isa 2:8; 44:15–19; Mic 5:12; Zeph 1:5; Jdt 8:18; Ep Jer 5; *Let. Aris.* 135–37; Josephus, *Ant.* 8.317; 10.69; *T. Zeb.* 9:5; and so on.

[27] North, "Jesus," 189.

[28] Dunn, *First*, 11.

[29] Johannes Horst, *Proskynein: Zur Anbetung im Urchristentum nach ihrer religionsgeschichtlichen Eigenart* (NTF 3/2; Gütersloh: Bertelsmann, 1932).

[30] Horst, *Proskynein*, 95–111.

[31] Horst, *Proskynein*, 112–13, 117–19.

[32] See Horst's discussion of Josephus's avoidance of depicting Jews rendering προσκύνησις to any human when he writes contemporary history (*Proskynein*, 126–27), and the impact Greek Esther's rejection of προσκύνησις of humans on religious grounds may have had on this (*Proskynein*, 121–27).

something of an excessive worshipful regard through the use of προσκυνέω for the Law, the Temple, and holy days (e.g., Philo, *Mos.* 2.23, 40; Josephus, *J.W.* 5.402).[33] In the NT writings, Christians are shown to go even further in their restriction of προσκύνησις for that which is due to God alone. With one exception (Rev 3:9), προσκυνέω is never approvingly used weakly for mere reverence of humans. It is otherwise consistently reserved for worship that is due to God, and thus is not to be given to any other, be it false gods, blasphemous opponents of God, or even angelic and human servants of God.

With regard to the προσκύνησις of Jesus, it is also clear that Horst maintained his contention that such instances do not undermine the view that the NT writers understood προσκύνησις to be reserved for God alone. In Horst's view, προσκύνησις of Jesus is either "unwelcome" when it comes too close to the kind of exaggerated and idolatrous worship of humans characteristic of pagans, which the earthly Jesus rejects (Matt 15:22–26; 20:20–23; Mark 15:19; cf. Mark 10:17–18),[34] or "welcome" when it is associated with an acknowledgment of the power of God at work in Jesus and/or an acknowledgment of Jesus as the Son of God or as risen Lord (Matt 8:2; 9:18; 14:33; 28:9, 17; cf. John 9:38; Heb 1:6; etc.), which is ultimately to be understood as worship of God in Jesus.[35] Thus, while Horst in a sense conceded the character of worship in most instances of προσκύνησις shown to Jesus, it is not ultimately because Jesus himself is so worshiped, but rather because God is worshiped in/through Jesus.

Yet it appears that what led Horst to this judgment by and large had less to do with a careful consideration of the way each NT author portrays the προσκύνησις of Jesus, both within its immediate literary context and within the wider context of the entire literary work, and much more to do with reading such texts informed by what may certainly be considered in more recent times a debatable understanding of early high Christology. Horst largely took as a given that early Christians did not—and indeed, as self-professed monotheists, could not—worship or acknowledge Jesus as divine.[36] The terms he assumes for this understanding, however, are problematic:

> Da die Anbetung Jesu im Urchristentum von vornherein neben dem strengen Monotheismus steht, liegt sie auf einer ganz andern Ebene als auf der hellenistisch-religiösen Denkens. Es handelt sich hier in keiner Weise um die Apotheose eines Kultheros. Die strenge Ablehnung der ganzen Tendenzen dieser Art von Menschenvergötterung durch das Neue Testament lässt es unmöglich erscheinen, dass Christus irgendwie als ein zweiter Gott neben dem einen Gott angebetet sein könnte. Darum sind die Zeugnisse einer Anbetung Jesu überhaupt so sparsam.[37]

Horst allowed for only two options in considering the possibility of early Christian worship or acknowledgment of Jesus as divine. Either Christians did worship Jesus as

---

[33] Horst, *Proskynein*, 120–21.
[34] Horst, *Proskynein*, 190–92, 236 (see also 185, 225, 229–30).
[35] Horst, *Proskynein*, 186–87, 191–92, 236 (see also 220–21, 223, 227, 233, 250, 281, 292–93).
[36] Horst, *Proskynein*, 185–94.
[37] Horst, *Proskynein*, 188–89.

divine, which could only mean for Horst that they had adopted a pagan polytheistic stance and regarded Jesus as a second god next to the God of Israel, or they upheld a Jewish monotheistic stance, which could only mean for him that they could not have worshiped Jesus as divine given their affirmation of the exclusive worship of the God of Israel. Since, then, early Christians were certainly monotheists, worshiping the God of Israel alone (e.g., 1 Cor 8:4, 6; Mark 12:28–30), and had rejected the treatment of humans as divine (e.g., 2 Thess 2:4; Acts 12:21–23),[38] they could not have worshiped Jesus as a divine figure. At best, as already noted above, even the more profound instances of Jesus receiving προσκύνησις, for example as the Son of God and as the risen Lord, are instances of worship directed to God in Jesus.[39]

There is, however, a third option, which Horst (and most scholars in his time) did not consider, and which has won wide support in more recent scholarship—namely, that early Christians both regarded Jesus as a divine figure alongside the God of Israel worthy of divine worship and understood this within a Jewish monotheistic framework.[40] Ironically, a key text to which Horst referred in support of his position (1 Cor 8:6 [see above]) is now considered by many to be one of the earliest pieces of evidence for the Christian affirmation of the divinity of Jesus conceived in Jewish monotheistic terms, as Paul here reworks the Shema to include Jesus alongside God.[41] Could it be, then, that a number of the προσκύνησις of Jesus passages, which Horst acknowledged as having the character of worship, but which he was in the end compelled to interpret as acts of worship of God in Jesus, are better understood as

---

[38] Horst, *Proskynein*, 185–86.
[39] Horst, *Proskynein*, 186–87.
[40] Most notable and influential in establishing this perspective are Martin Hengel (*The Son of God: The Origin of Christology and the History of Jewish-Hellenistic Religion* [trans. John Bowden; Philadelphia: Fortress, 1976]; *Studies in Early Christology* [Edinburgh: T&T Clark, 1995]); Larry W. Hurtado (*One God, One Lord: Early Christian Devotion and Ancient Jewish Monotheism* [2nd ed.; Edinburgh: T&T Clark, 1998]; *Lord Jesus Christ: Devotion to Jesus in Earliest Christianity* [Grand Rapids: Eerdmans, 2003]); and Richard Bauckham ("The Worship of Jesus in Apocalyptic Christianity," NTS 27 [1981]: 322–41; *Jesus and the God of Israel: God Crucified and Other Studies on the New Testament's Christology of Divine Identity* [Grand Rapids: Eerdmans, 2008]). See also Andrew Chester, "High Christology—Whence, When and Why?" *Early Christianity* 2 (2011): 38, who notes that this perspective has become "the clear (though not unanimous) scholarly consensus." Cf. Christopher Rowland, *The Open Heaven: A Study of Apocalyptic in Judaism and Early Christianity* (London: SPCK, 1982); Jarl E. Fossum, *The Name of God and the Angel of the Lord: Samaritan and Jewish Concepts of Intermediation and the Origin of Gnosticism* (WUNT 36; Tübingen: Mohr Siebeck, 1985), who argue for the presence of binitarian patterns already within pre-Christian Judaism. See, however, Hurtado's critique of this view (*One*, 85–90).

For discussion and defense of Greco-Roman Judaism as "monotheistic" (despite some objections to the appropriateness of this label [Peter Hayman, "Monotheism—A Misused Word in Jewish Studies?" *JJS* 42 (1991): 1–15; Paula Fredriksen, "Mandatory Retirement: Ideas in the Study of Christian Origins Whose Time Has Come to Go," in *Israel's God and Rebecca's Children: Christology and Community in Early Judaism and Christianity. Essays in Honor of Larry W. Hurtado and Alan F. Segal* (ed. David B. Capes et al.; Waco, TX: Baylor University Press, 2007), 35–38]), see Larry W. Hurtado, "First-Century Jewish Monotheism," *JSNT* 71 (1998): 3–26; Richard Bauckham, "Biblical Theology and the Problems of Monotheism," in *Out of Egypt: Biblical Theology and Biblical Interpretation* (ed. Craig Bartholomew et al.; SHS 5; Milton Keynes: Paternoster, 2004), 187–232. See also Paul A. Rainbow, "Monotheism and Christology in 1 Corinthians 8.4-6" (PhD diss., Oxford University, 1987).

[41] Bauckham, *Jesus*, 210–18; Hurtado, *Lord*, 114; Chester, "High," 35–37.

worship or acknowledgment of Jesus himself as divine? We submit that this possibility, which is not adequately taken into consideration in the only detailed NT προσκυνέω study to date, warrants a fresh reexamination of the NT material.

In sum, since these treatments of the significance of the προσκύνησις of Jesus in the NT writings are far too brief, differ radically from one another in their conclusions, and/or do not adequately engage a number of important issues in high Christology discussions, a new comprehensive study is in order. There are, of course, a number of studies and commentaries that give attention (some more, some less) to the προσκύνησις of Jesus in a single NT work, with which we will interact in relevant chapters. Yet even in such narrowly focused studies, we will often find a number of opportunities to challenge views, refine analyses, and offer new insights, so that this study is not a mere summary of work that has already been done.

B. Approach of this study

The two main defects in most discussions of the significance of the προσκύνησις of Jesus in the NT writings are (1) a lack of close examination of both the προσκύνησις of Jesus passages themselves and their place in the larger NT work in which they appear and (2) inadequate explanations of the possible implications for a high or divine Christology.

Thus, in order to remedy this problem, we conduct our study by offering a more detailed exegetical and literary-critical analysis of such NT works and their προσκύνησις of Jesus passages, and by giving more thoughtful attention to how this relates to the high/divine Christology question. Yet as we have already begun to indicate, it is the term προσκυνέω itself that also poses challenges to interpreters since it can be used for various degrees of reverence directed to various types of figures. Therefore, our examination will be guided by a number of key factors that ought to be taken into consideration where relevant in order to ascertain the significance of the προσκύνησις of Jesus (and of other figures) in each NT passage and in every NT work as a whole. They include the following:

- **Status/character of the one receiving προσκύνησις:** Is the one who receives προσκύνησις a low-ranking or high-ranking figure? Is the figure human, angelic, divine, and so on? Is the figure an ally or an adversary? Is the figure associated with the people of God or with the larger pagan world?
- **Status/character of the one rendering προσκύνησις:** Is the one who renders προσκύνησις a low-ranking or high-ranking figure? Is the figure human, angelic, divine, and so on? Is the figure an ally or an adversary? Is the figure associated with the people of God or with the larger pagan world?
- **Speech accompanying προσκύνησις:** Does the one who renders προσκύνησις speak words of gratitude, voice a request, acknowledge the status of the recipient of προσκύνησις, and so on? Does the one who receives προσκύνησις say anything indicative of his/her status?

- **Activity accompanying προσκύνησις**: Does the one who renders προσκύνησις also offer tributary gifts as to a king, offer cultic service as to a god, and so on? Does the one who receives προσκύνησις do anything indicative of his/her status?
- **Setting of προσκύνησις**: Does προσκύνησις occur in a cultic sanctuary, in a royal court, on earth, in heaven, and so on?
- **Occasion of προσκύνησις**: Does one do προσκύνησις because he/she is in the presence of a superior figure, because he/she has received a benefit from the figure, because he/she hopes to appease the figure, and so on?
- **Response to προσκύνησις**: Does the one who receives προσκύνησις approve or reject such reverence? Does the one expected to render προσκύνησις to another approve or reject the opportunity to do so? Does a third party or author approve or reject the προσκύνησις of another?
- **Relevant backgrounds or parallels to προσκύνησις**: Is an instance of προσκύνησις further illuminated by any relevant background material? Does an instance of προσκύνησις resemble or parallel other accounts or depictions of figures receiving a similar kind of reverence?
- **Authorial use of προσκυνέω**: Does the author reveal any tendencies or patterns of usage of προσκυνέω? Does the author use προσκυνέω in such a way that it is differentiated from his use of other prostration or reverence/worship terms? Does the author make any relevant intratextual or intertextual connections in his προσκυνέω passages that impact how they are to be interpreted? How are the author's προσκυνέω passages to be understood both in their immediate literary contexts and in the wider literary context of his entire work?

It is surprising how often a number of these factors are either inadequately taken into consideration or are overlooked entirely, both in the comprehensive treatments of the προσκύνησις of Jesus in the NT as well as in narrower treatments of the προσκύνησις of Jesus in individual NT works. For example, North includes Mark 5:6 among the instances of προσκύνησις of Jesus before a miracle expressing petition (cf. Matt 8:2; 9:18; 15:25; etc.)[42] without adequately taking consideration of the potentially significant difference between Mark 5:6 and the Matthean passages with regard to the status/character of the one rendering προσκύνησις. One could make a case that while these Matthean passages portray humans coming before Jesus in προσκύνησις, Mark 5:6 is unique in that it presents a demonic being from the supernatural realm (rather than the human host) coming before Jesus in προσκύνησις. This may indeed be highly significant since, unlike the Gospel of Matthew, the Gospel of Mark has these human suppliants prostrate before Jesus, but it is not specifically said that they render προσκύνησις to him as the demon does, which could also suggest that authorial use of προσκυνέω is another key factor to take into consideration. Is it appropriate simply to equate Mark 5:6 with Matt 8:2; 9:18; 15:25 as North does when the Gospel of Mark uniquely portrays the demonic, who are often said to have special insight into Jesus's true identity (Mark 1:24, 34; 3:11–12; these do not appear in the Gospel of Matthew), rendering προσκύνησις to Jesus?

---

[42] North, "Jesus," 189.

Consider also the angels' προσκύνησις of Jesus ("the Son") in Heb 1:6. Besides, once again, the questionable suggestion of simply equating an instance of supernatural beings rendering προσκύνησις to Jesus with humans rendering προσκύνησις to Jesus (Matt 2:11) without argument,[43] another key factor to take into consideration here is the setting of προσκύνησις. Both Horst and North assume Jesus is in the earthly realm when he receives προσκύνησις from the angels (though they differ over whether this occurs at Jesus's parousia [Horst] or at his incarnation [North]),[44] but it is far more likely that Jesus is in the heavenly realm seated alongside God as he receives προσκύνησις from the angels.[45] If so, this is certainly a passage to which much more attention and discussion should be given than the brief treatments of Horst, North, and Dunn.[46]

We could also note how often attention is drawn to Jesus's reception of προσκύνησις as, for example, the Son of God or as the risen Lord, yet without explaining what it means for Jesus to be reverenced as such or without taking due consideration of how this is understood according to each NT author. Greeven noted such instances (e.g., Matt 14:33; 28:9, 17; Luke 24:52) but did not discuss their significance.[47] Horst, as we noted above, understood all such instances as worship of God in Jesus: "Hier ist die Proskynese als Überwältigtwerden von der Macht und Herrlichkeit des einen unsichtbaren Gottes selbst zu verstehen, der in Christus angebetet wird."[48] Again, in Horst's view, this is because it was impossible for Jesus himself to have been worshiped by his early followers. But Horst gave very little attention to the NT passages themselves and to how the individual NT authors present the προσκύνησις of Jesus as Son of God and risen Lord in their own way and on their own terms. For instance, no real attention is given to the highly significant act of Jesus walking on the sea and delivering others from the sea's perils in Matt 14:22–33, an act which is arguably no mere miracle among miracles, but which wider background perusal reveals was thought to have been possible for deity alone. Nor is any mention made of Jesus's final words as risen Lord in Matt 28:18–20, where Jesus speaks of having Yahweh-like cosmic authority, of assuring Yahweh-like perpetual presence, and of placing himself alongside the Father and the Holy Spirit as the Son in whose name converts to the community of faith are to be baptized.[49] Horst thereby fails to take due consideration of a number of key factors

---

[43] North, "Jesus," 189.
[44] Horst, *Proskynein*, 249–50; North, "Jesus," 189. Dunn makes no mention of the event or setting in view (*First*, 11). Surprisingly, neither Greeven (*TDNT* 6:765) nor Moule (*Origin*, 176) say much of anything about Heb 1:6.
[45] See discussion in Chapter 6.
[46] One provides only a couple of paragraphs of discussion (Horst, *Proskynein*, 249–50); the other two provide only a couple of sentences of discussion (North, "Jesus," 189; Dunn, *First*, 11).
[47] Greeven, *TDNT* 6:764.
[48] Horst, *Proskynein*, 186.
[49] With regard to the προσκύνησις of Jesus as risen Lord in Luke 24:52, although Horst doubted that προσκυνήσαντες αὐτὸν was original to the Gospel of Luke, he was nevertheless content to refer his readers to his discussion of Matt 28:17, since, as he put it, the προσκύνησις of Jesus as the risen Lord in both instances would still have "die gleiche Bedeutung" (*Proskynein*, 244). But this ignores the fact the Gospel of Matthew and the Gospel of Luke relate the resurrection account in their own unique ways. The depiction of the risen Jesus as a recipient of προσκύνησις within the resurrection accounts must first be interpreted on each Gospel writer's own terms.

in assessing these two passages, including relevant speech and activity accompanying προσκύνησις, and relevant backgrounds/parallels to προσκύνησις. These are weighty passages, and one ought to give much more attention to them (and to others like them) before too hastily concluding that the προσκύνησις Jesus receives in such passages is not really directed to him, but to God in/through Jesus.

Although we could certainly highlight many more examples, these are sufficient for supporting our contention that any adequate treatment of the significance of the προσκύνησις of Jesus in the NT writings ought to take careful consideration of these key factors in the interpretation process. This is how we will analyze the NT material. We will give careful attention to the details of the various individual προσκύνησις passages (noting, for example, the status/character of those receiving and rendering προσκύνησις, any relevant speech and/or activity accompanying προσκύνησις, a relevant setting in which προσκύνησις occurs, etc.), as well as to relevant backgrounds and parallels that shed further light on these passages and to the various linguistic and literary features of the NT writing that direct the reader to interpret such passages on the NT author's own terms.

C. Outline of this study

We begin our study with a brief overview of προσκυνέω in the biblical, early Jewish, and Greco-Roman literature roughly contemporary with the NT to get a sense of the various uses of the term at the time (Chapter 1). The rest of the study is devoted to a thorough examination of the προσκύνησις of Jesus (i.e., Jesus as an object of προσκυνέω) and of its significance within the confines of each NT writing that this phenomenon appears, which are the Gospel of Mark: Mark 5:6; 15:19 (Chapter 2), the Gospel of Matthew: Matt 2:2, 8, 11; 8:2; 9:18; 14:33; 15:25; 20:20; 28:9, 17 (Chapter 3), the Gospel of Luke and the book of Acts: Luke 24:52 (Chapter 4), the Gospel of John: John 9:38 (Chapter 5), the Epistle to the Hebrews: Heb 1:6 (Chapter 6), and, as we will argue, the book of Revelation: Rev 5:14 (Chapter 7).[50] In each of these chapters, with the key factors discussed above guiding our analysis, the standard procedure will be first to examine those passages where προσκυνέω is used for reverence of figures other than Jesus, if there are such instances, then to examine those passages

---

[50] Since the issue of the identities of the author(s) or final editor(s) of these works is not critical to our discussion, I refer to the author of the Gospel of Mark as "Mark," the author of the Gospel of Matthew as "Matthew," and so on simply for convenience without thereby making any claims regarding authorial identity. I also accept the common view of the Gospel of Luke and the book of Acts as forming two volumes of a unified work of common authorship (Luke-Acts), and accordingly devote a single chapter to the προσκύνησις of Jesus within this two-volume work. I leave aside the need to determine whether or not the Gospel of John and the book of Revelation share common authorship, since in this particular case, each work and the use of προσκυνέω within them can be adequately treated on their own terms without relating one work to the other. I also note in advance here that all translations of the NT are my own.

where προσκυνέω is used for reverence of Jesus, and finally to determine the overall significance of the προσκύνησις of Jesus in the NT work, particularly as it relates to ongoing scholarly discussions of the possibility of a divine Christology in first-century Christianity. Lastly, we will conclude our investigation with a summary of our findings, highlight significant points of commonality shared between the NT writings in their presentation of Jesus as a recipient of προσκύνησις, and offer a final overall assessment of the NT depiction of Jesus as one who frequently and rather uniquely receives προσκύνησις.

1

Προσκυνέω in the Cultural Context of the NT Writings

The goal of this chapter is to provide a brief overview of the use of προσκυνέω in literature roughly contemporary with the NT as a way of establishing the general parameters and patterns of usage. Since the term is used in the NT writings for reverence or worship of personal beings (i.e., gods, humans, angels, etc.), we limit our focus here to similar instances. We begin with a discussion of the use of προσκυνέω in Greco-Roman literature before turning our attention to its use in OT writings and early Jewish literature.

A. Προσκυνέω in Greco-Roman literature

In pagan literature, we see quite a broad and diverse range of figures as objects of προσκυνέω, from the supreme deities down to mortal humans and various other divine and semi-divine beings that span the human-divine continuum. Quite frequently, προσκυνέω is used for worship of the many gods in the Greco-Roman world, including the principal deities in the Greco-Roman pantheon (Zeus/Jupiter, Poseidon/Neptune, etc.), various lower-level gods (Pan, the nymphs, nature deities, etc.), and chief gods of the larger pagan world (Ahura Mazdā, Isis, etc.). Here, the strongest reverential/worshipful senses of the term are most clearly seen, as those who render προσκύνησις to the gods often do so at/before cultic sites and objects and/or in association with cultic activities. It is said, for instance, that Chilonis did προσκύνησις before Poseidon's altar (προσκυνήσασα τὸν βωμὸν τοῦ θεοῦ [Plutarch, *Ag. Cleom.* 18.2]). The announcement to the people of Thessaly that Artemis has come to bless the city leads them to offer her προσκύνησις and honor her with sacrifices (πάντων δὲ προσκυνούντων καὶ τιμώντων τὴν θεὸν θυσίαις [Diodorus Siculus, *Hist.* 4.51.3]). Plutarch describes Camillus's supplication of Jupiter and of the gods as an expression of both prayer and προσκύνησις (ταῦτ᾽ εἰπών, καθάπερ ἐστὶ Ῥωμαίοις ἔθος ἐπευξαμένοις καὶ προσκυνήσασιν [*Cam.* 5.6–7]).[1]

---

[1] See also Plutarch, *Art.* 23.5; *Mulier. virt.* 258B; Babrius, Fable 119; Chariton, *Chaer.* 1.1.5; 2.2.7; 3.6.3; 8.4.10; Achilles Tatius, *Leuc. Clit.* 8.8.8.

So too are various other lower-level gods and foreign deities depicted as objects of worship through reception of προσκύνησις. In *Daphnis and Chloe*, Daphnis is portrayed as doing προσκύνησις before the statues of the nymphs and the statue of Pan, praying to them for Chloe's safe return with a promise to sacrifice to them if she is returned to him (τὰ ἀγάλματα τῶν Νυμφῶν προσεκύνει καὶ ἐπηγγέλλετο σωθείσης Χλόης θύσειν τῶν αἰγῶν τὴν ἀρίστην / δραμὼν δὲ καὶ ἐπὶ τὴν πίτυν ἔνθα τὸ τοῦ Πανὸς ἄγαλμα ἵδρυτο ... κἀκεῖνον προσεκύνει καὶ ηὔχετο ὑπὲρ τῆς Χλόης καὶ τράγον θύσειν ἐπηγγέλλετο [Longus, *Daphn.* 2.24.1–2]). The Tyrian Ousoos consecrates two pillars to Fire and Wind, rendering προσκύνησις to them and offering libations of animal blood to them (ἀνιεῶρσαι δὲ δύο στήλας Πυρὶ καὶ Πνεύματι, καὶ προσκυνῆσαι αἷμά τε σπένδειν αὐταῖς ἐξ ὧν ἤγρευε θηρίων [Philo of Byblos, *FGH* 790 frg. 2.10]). It is said that Dicaearchus treated Impiety and Lawlessness like divinities as he would customarily set up altars to them, offer sacrifices to them, and render προσκύνησις to them (δύο κατεσκεύαζε βωμούς, τὸν μὲν Ἀσεβείας, τὸν δὲ Παρανομίας, καὶ ἐπὶ τούτοις ἔθυε καὶ τούτους προσεκύνει καθάπερ ἂν εἰ δαίμονας [Polybius, 18.54.10]). In *Anthia and Habrocomes*, when the virgin Anthia tells Psammis that he will have to reckon with the Egyptian goddess Isis if he violates her, he takes heed of her words, renders προσκύνησις to Isis, and leaves Anthia alone (πείθεται Ψάμμις καὶ τὴν θεὸν προσεκύνει καὶ Ἀνθίας ἀπέχεται [Xenophon of Ephesus, *Anth. Habr.* 3.11.4–5]).[2]

There are numerous instances where προσκυνέω is used for worship of the gods in general, as when Plutarch notes that the Pythagoreans do not allow one to do προσκύνησις and pray to the gods while cursorily passing by (ὡς γάρ φασι τοὺς Πυθαγορικοὺς οὐκ ἐᾶν ἐκ παρόδου προσκυνεῖν καὶ προσεύχεσθαι τοῖς θεοῖς [Plutarch, *Num.* 14.2]), when he mentions the practice of Romans who cover their heads when they offer προσκύνησις to the gods (Διὰ τί τοὺς θεοὺς προσκυνοῦντες ἐπικαλύπτονται τὴν κεφαλήν [*Quaest. rom.* 266C]), and when he notes that Alexander the Great taught foreigners to give προσκύνησις to the Greek gods (ὢ θαυμαστῆς φιλοσοφίας, δι᾽ ἣν Ἰνδοὶ θεοὺς Ἑλληνικοὺς προσκυνοῦσι [*Alex. fort.* 328C]).[3] This last example in particular shows how προσκυνέω can be used in a more abstract sense for worship. While the term is commonly understood to be a form of reverence/worship expressed concretely, often through prostration in this period,[4] as can be seen, for example, when it is said that Callirhoe rendered προσκύνησις to Aphrodite, taking hold of the feet of her cult statue (προσκυνήσασα δὲ ἡ Καλλιρόη καὶ τῶν ποδῶν λαβομένη τῆς

---

[2] See also Plutarch, *Amat.* 771D–E; *Art.* 15.5; 29.6–7; *Quaest. rom.* 266F–267A; Philo of Byblos, *FGH* 790 frg. 2.6; Chariton, *Chaer.* 3.8.6; Longus, *Daphn.* 2.2.4–5; 3.28.1; Xenophon of Ephesus, *Anth. Habr.* 5.11.4.

[3] See also Polybius 32.15.7; Posidonius, *FGH* 87 frg. 15*.5; Plutarch, *Marc.* 6.5–6; *Num.* 14.3–5; *Quaest. rom.* 270D; *Superst.* 170E; Epictetus, *Diatr.* 1.4.31; 4.1.103–05.

[4] It may also be that a kissing gesture—which is undoubtedly the gesture that the term originally signified in its earliest usage (προσκυνέω being a compound word formed from πρός ["toward"] and κυνέω ["to kiss"])—is implied in addition to or instead of the gesture of prostration. In Jewish (and Christian) literature, προσκυνέω is more closely associated with prostration than with kissing as it is almost exclusively used to render OT Hebrew and Aramaic prostration terms (הׁשתחוה and סגד, respectively) in the LXX (although cf. 3 Kgdms 19:18, where προσκυνέω renders נׁשק ["to kiss"]), and it is frequently linked with other terms suggestive of prostration (κύπτω; πίπτω; προσπίπτω; [ἐπὶ πρόσωπον] ἐπὶ τῆς γῆς; τοῖς ποσίν; etc.). See Horst, *Proskynein*, 14–32, 44–67.

Ἀφροδίτης [Chariton, *Chaer.* 2.2.7]), this is not the sense of the passage above. The point here is not that Alexander introduced these foreigners to a particular gesture of reverence/worship but more generally that he taught them to reverence/worship gods that were formerly unknown to them.

Moving from one end of the spectrum to the other, we see that προσκυνέω is also often used in Greco-Roman literature for homage or deference paid to human superiors. Such reverence is given to both low-ranking authority figures, such as masters, patrons, and fathers, and high-ranking authority figures, such as military leaders, kings, and queens. In many cases, the human superior does not necessarily receive προσκύνησις as a divine figure. For instance, following Herodotus's observation, Strabo describes how Persians customarily render προσκύνησις to a person of significantly greater social status:

> When they meet people on the streets, they approach and kiss those with whom they are acquainted and who are of equal rank, and to those of lower rank they offer the cheek and in that way receive the kiss; but those of still lower rank merely make obeisance (οἱ δ' ἔτι ταπεινότεροι προσκυνοῦσι μόνον). (Strabo 15.3.20, Jones)

Thus, in the case where the social disparity between the inferior and the superior individual is most pronounced, those of inferior rank do προσκύνησις to their superior. Such high-ranking individuals would certainly include noblemen, royal associates, those in high office, and the wealthy.[5] Lucian often portrays the rich and the powerful receiving προσκύνησις from others. The Athenian Timon recalls how his fellow citizens used to cringe and do προσκύνησις before him when he was rich (ἐπειδὴ πένης διὰ ταῦτα ἐγενόμην, οὐκέτι οὐδὲ γνωρίζομαι πρὸς αὐτῶν οὐδὲ προσβλέπουσιν οἱ τέως ὑποπτήσσοντες καὶ προσκυνοῦντες [*Tim.* 5]). The Athenian Adimantus fantasizes about being wealthy and receiving προσκύνησις from his friends as they ask him for favors (φίλων πρόσοδοι καὶ δεήσεις καὶ τὸ ἅπαντας ὑποπτήσσειν καὶ προσκυνεῖν [*Nav.* 22]).[6] A number of first- and second-century C.E. papyri letters similarly show how common it was to use προσκυνέω to express deep respect for a human superior. For instance, a slave writes of her desire to be present with her master so that she could render προσκύνησις to him (ὤφελον εἰ ἐδυνάμεθα πέτασθαι καὶ ἐλθεῖν καὶ προσκυνῆσαί σε [*P.Giess.* 17.11–12 = *SelPap* I, 115]) and a shipmaster regretfully informs a chief magistrate that he has been detained and is unable to greet him with προσκύνησις (ἐπὶ ἐγὼ οὐ πάρειμει προσκυνῆσαί σε τὸν τιμιώτατον [*P.Giess.* 11.12–15 = *SelPap* II, 423]).[7]

---

[5] Amélie Kuhrt, "The Achaemenid Persian Empire (c. 550–c. 330 BCE): Continuities, Adaptations, Transformations," in *Empires: Perspectives from Archaeology and History* (ed. Susan E. Alcock et al.; Cambridge: Cambridge University Press, 2001), 113.

[6] See also Diodorus Siculus 1.83.4; Lucian, *Nigr.* 21; *Gall.* 9; 14; *Sat.* 29; Chariton, *Chaer.* 5.2.3; 5.3.11; 6.7.5.

[7] See also *BGU* 423.11–16 = *SelPap* I, 112; *CPR* 19.5–8 = *NewDocs* I, 16; *BGU* 615.6–9; *P.Mich.* 465.4, 33; 473.4; 474.6; *SB* 9636.6; *P.Giess.* 22.5–6; 77.8–9.

Moving up the ranks, προσκύνησις is also shown to military leaders. After proposing terms of peace, the Roman general Sulla expected King Mithridates to give προσκύνησις to him for allowing him to live (ὃν ἐγὼ προσκυνήσειν ἐνόμιζον, εἰ τὴν δεξιὰν αὐτῷ καταλείποιμι χεῖρα), when instead the king boldly rejects the general's terms (Plutarch, *Sull.* 23.3). The son of the Armenian emperor Tigranes the Great, seeking a treaty with the Roman general Pompey, does προσκύνησις before him as his superior in barbarian fashion (ὁ δὲ Τιγράνης ἦλθε, καὶ τὸν Πομπήιον ὡς κρείττονα βαρβαρικῶς προσεκύνησεν [Appian, *Hist. rom.* 12.104]). And the Roman general Scipio Africanus receives προσκύνησις from Iberian prisoners of war, both initially as an expression of gratitude for their freedom (οὗτοι μὲν οὖν ἅμα δακρύοντες καὶ χαίροντες ἐπὶ τῷ παραδόξῳ τῆς σωτηρίας, προσκυνήσαντες τὸν στρατηγὸν διελύθησας) and later in recognition of him as king (προσκυνησάντων αὐτὸν καὶ προσφωνησάντων βασιλέα [Polybius 10.17.8; 10.38.3; cf. 10.40.3]).[8] Indeed, kings and queens in particular, the highest ranking human authority figures, are frequently portrayed receiving προσκύνησις. It is said that a "friend" of the Parthian king, though fed scraps tossed to him on the ground and frequently dragged away to be scourged, nevertheless does προσκύνησις before his tormentor as his benefactor (τὸν τιμωρησάμενον ὡς εὐεργέτην ἐπὶ τὸ ἔδαφος πρηνὴς προσπεσὼν προσκυνεῖ [Posidonius, *FGH* 87 frg. 5]). Sillaces does προσκύνησις as he appears before the Parthian king Orodes II to deliver the head of the Roman general Crassus (Σιλλάκης ἐπιστὰς τῷ ἀνδρῶνι καὶ προσκυνήσας προὔβαλεν εἰς μέσον τοῦ Κράσσου τὴν κεφαλήν [Plutarch, *Crass.* 33.2]). It is said that a barbarian mistook the Athenian Callias for a king because of his appearance and rendered προσκύνησις to him (Τούτῳ γάρ τις, ὡς ἔοικε, τῶν βαρβάρων προσέπεσεν οἰηθεὶς βασιλέα διὰ τὴν κόμην καὶ τὸ στρόφιον εἶναι· προσκυνήσας [Plutarch, *Arist.* 5.6]). Persian monarchs are often depicted receiving προσκύνησις. Ariamenes renders προσκύνησις to his brother, Xerxes I, the king, as he seats him upon the royal throne (Ἀριαμένης δ' εὐθὺς ἀναπηδήσας προσεκύνησε τὸν ἀδελφὸν καὶ λαβόμενος τῆς δεξιᾶς εἰς τὸν θρόνον ἐκάθισε τὸν βασίλειον [Plutarch, *Frat. amor.* 488F]). As Cyrus the Younger charges in battle, those around clear a path and give προσκύνησις to him (οἱ μὲν ἐξίσταντο προσκυνοῦντες [Plutarch, *Art.* 11.3]). Both Artaxerxes II and his queen Statira are many times portrayed receiving προσκύνησις in Chariton's *Chaereas and Callirhoe* (*Chaer.* 5.2.2; 5.3.3; 5.4.8; 5.8.9; 6.7.3, 5; 7.5.15; 8.5.5, 12).[9]

In all the instances discussed thus far of προσκύνησις directed toward humans, the sense is that such reverence is shown either as a respectful greeting of a human superior, as an expression of gratitude for a benefit, as a way of humbly approaching in seeking a favor, and/or as an acknowledgment of the human superior's authority. Moreover, the sense is that προσκύνησις is being rendered to humans *as* humans. Yet, by way of transition, in this last case of προσκύνησις shown to Persian kings, we may see something of the sense in which such humans who are considered to have a special

---

[8] See also Plutarch, *Crass.* 31.1; *Flam.* 21.7; *Sull.* 22.5.
[9] See also Plutarch, *Art.* 13.2; *Them.* 28.1; 29.2; Arrian, *Anab.* 4.11.9; Lucian, *Cat.* 11; *Dial. mort.* 3(2).2; *Nav.* 30; 37–38; Polyaenus, *Strat.* 7.10.1.

connection with the gods are thereby thought to receive προσκύνησις as divine figures. The Persians themselves regarded their king as one who ruled under divine sanction, but they did not view him as a god,[10] nor was the gesture of προσκύνησις performed before their king an acknowledgment of his divinity.[11] Yet a passage from Plutarch suggests that some Greeks may have interpreted the Persian gesture of προσκύνησις before the Great King as a recognition of his divinity.[12] When the Athenian Themistocles desires to speak with the Persian king, Plutarch reports that the chiliarch Artabanus explains to him that one must first offer προσκύνησις to the king as the image of god if he has any hope of having an audience with him:

> Now you Hellenes are said to admire liberty and equality above all things; but in our eyes, among many fair customs, this is the fairest of all, to honor the King, and to pay obeisance to him as the image of that god who is the preserver of all things (τιμᾶν βασιλέα, καὶ προσκυνεῖν ὡς εἰκόνα θεοῦ τοῦ τὰ πάντα σώζοντος). (Plutarch, *Them.* 27.3, Perrin)

Plutarch elsewhere indicates, as is also hinted at here, that Greeks viewed προσκύνησις before a human as degrading and undermining their status as freemen. Thus, the Theban Ismenias deliberately drops his ring before Artaxerxes II and stoops down to pick it up, thereby giving the mere appearance of rendering προσκύνησις to the Persian king (Ἰσμηνίας δὲ προσκυνῆσαι κελευόμενος ἐξέβαλε πρὸ αὐτοῦ χαμᾶζε τὸν δακτύλιον, εἶτα κύψας ἀνείλετο καὶ παρέσχε δόξαν προσκυνοῦντος), and his companion Pelopidas simply resists any impulse to do προσκύνησις before the king and thereby, as Plutarch comments, "did nothing to disgrace himself" (ἀλλ᾽ οὗτος μὲν οὐδὲν αἰσχρὸν ἐποίησεν [*Art.* 22.4]).[13] It may be, then, that such reverence toward men was dually objectionable, as earlier sources similarly object that Greeks refuse to bow in προσκύνησις to others both because it is degrading to prostrate oneself before mortal men (οὔτε γὰρ σφίσι ἐν νόμῳ εἶναι ἄνθρωπον προσκυνέειν [Herodotus, *Hist.* 7.136]) and because such reverence is reserved for the gods alone (οὐδένα γὰρ ἄνθρωπον δεσπότην ἀλλὰ τοὺς θεοὺς προσκυνεῖτε [Xenophon, *Anab.* 3.2.13]).

---

[10] Pierre Briant, *From Cyrus to Alexander: A History of the Persian Empire* (trans. Peter T. Daniels; Winona Lake, IN: Eisenbrauns, 2002), 240–41; Maria Brosius, *The Persians: An Introduction* (London: Routledge, 2006), 31–32. Lloyd Llewelyn-Jones, *King and Court in Ancient Persia 559 to 331 BCE* (Edinburgh: Edinburgh University Press, 2013), 19–21, stresses the close relationship between the Persian king and his gods but is clear that "Persian kings were not gods."
[11] Richard N. Frye, "Gestures of Deference to Royalty in Ancient Iran," *IA* 9 (1972): 102–3.
[12] Cf. Zenobius 5.25; Isocrates, *Paneg.* 151. For a similar view from a Roman perspective, see Curtius 8.5.11. However, it is not clear that *all* Greeks and Romans interpreted obeisance to the Persian king in this way. For the view that προσκύνησις of the Persian king was generally understood as a secular act, see A. S. F. Gow, "Notes on the *Persae* of Aeschylus," *JHS* 48 (1928): 134–35, and A. B. Bosworth, *A Historical Commentary on Arrian's History of Alexander* (vol. 2; Oxford: Oxford University Press, 1995), 69.
[13] Cf. Lucian, *Nav.* 37–38, where Samippus says if he were king, all would render προσκύνησις to him with the exception of his companions, who, in accordance with Greek custom, would acknowledge him as sole commander.

In other instances, we similarly find that those regarded as having a special connection or association with the gods are thereby thought to be worthy of προσκύνησις, perhaps even as divine figures. In some instances, such reverence may perhaps amount to little more than excessive flattery, as, for example, when King Prusias II ingratiates himself with the Roman senate when he places his hands to the ground, does προσκύνησις before them, and hails them as savior gods (καθεὶς τὰς χεῖρας ἀμφοτέρας προσεκύνησε τὸν οὐδὸν καὶ τοὺς καθημένους, ἐπιφθεγξάμενος "χαίρετε, θεοὶ σωτῆρες" [Polybius 30.18.5]).[14] In other instances, however, we have what is perceived to be a closer connection between divine manifestations/activity and the human associated with such. For example, In Iranian territory, native barbarians do προσκύνησις before the Roman general Lucullus when the flooded Euphrates unexpectedly tamed itself to allow an easy passage for him (προσεκύνουν τὸν Λούκουλλον, ὡς ὀλιγάκις τούτου συμβεβηκότος πρότερον, ἐκείνῳ δ' ἑκουσίως χειροήθη καὶ πρᾷον αὐτὸν ἐνδιδόντος τοῦ ποταμοῦ [Plutarch, *Luc.* 24.5]), and the Roman Sertorius receives προσκύνησις from Iberians as one having supernatural power (ἐξέπληξε τοὺς βαρβάρους καὶ προσεκυνεῖτο, καὶ πάντες αὐτῷ προσέφευγον ὡς δαιμονιωτέραν ἰσχὺν ἔχοντι) when he leads them to believe that the goddess Diana foretold future events to him through his white fawn (Polyaenus, *Strat.* 8.22).

In the larger pagan world, it was widely acknowledged that exceptional human figures whose character and accomplishments far surpassed those of ordinary humans were considered to be divine and worthy of divine worship. Philo of Byblos speaks of the way the ancients considered their great human benefactors to be worthy of προσκύνησις as divinities:

> The most ancient of the barbarians, especially the Phoenicians and the Egyptians, from whom the remainder [of mankind] received [their ideas], considered as the greatest gods those who discovered things useful for life or who, in some way, benefited the peoples. Considering them as benefactors and as the causes of many good things, [these ancients] worshipped them as divinities (ὡς θεοὺς προσεκύνουν). (Philo of Byblos, *FGH* 790 frg. 1.29, Baumgarten)

Not surprisingly then, we find numerous examples in pagan literature of such human figures who are clearly portrayed as divine and/or worthy of divine worship, including through reception of προσκύνησις. A number of human figures in Greek and Roman mythology achieved godlike status and are depicted receiving προσκύνησις as gods. For instance, it is said that a man prays to Heracles for help, to whom he truly gave προσκύνησις and honored above all the gods (τῷ δ' Ἡρακλεῖ προσηύχεθ', ὃν μόνον πάντων θεῶν ἀληθῶς προσεκύνει τε κἄτιμα [Babrius, Fable 20]). In the well-known tale of Rome's legendary founder Romulus and his mysterious disappearance, when some reported that he had been taken up into heaven to become a god (ἀνηρπασμένον εἰς θεοὺς καὶ θεὸν εὐμενῆ γενησόμενον αὐτοῖς), many believed and rendered him προσκύνησις (τοὺς μὲν οὖν πολλοὺς ταῦτα πειθομένους καὶ χαίροντας ἀπαλλάττεσθαι μετ'

---

[14] See also Galen, *Protr.* 1.8 K; Plutarch, *Pomp.* 27.3; *Comp. Thes. Rom.* 6.4; Dio Chrysostom, *Or.* 32.50.

ἐλπίδων ἀγαθῶν προσκυνοῦντας [Plutarch, *Rom.* 27.7-8]).[15] In their novels, both Chariton and Xenophon portray their lead characters as having such exceptional beauty that they are often likened to and even mistaken for gods, with other characters so overwhelmed by their divine resemblances that they often respond with προσκύνησις (*Chaer.* 1.1.16; 3.2.14; 3.9.1; 4.1.9; 5.3.9; *Anth. Habr.* 1.1.3; 1.2.7; 1.12.1).

It is not just mythical and fictional human figures who are portrayed receiving προσκύνησις as divine beings—historical human figures are as well. Diodorus Siculus records that the Ethiopians give προσκύνησις to their king as to a god, being divinely entrusted with sovereignty (εὐθὺς δὲ καὶ προσκυνεῖ καὶ τιμᾷ καθάπερ θεόν, ὡς ὑπὸ τῆς τοῦ δαιμονίου προνοίας ἐγκεχειρισμένης αὐτῷ τῆς ἀρχῆς [*Hist.* 3.5.1])[16] and, even more strongly, that the Egyptians render προσκύνησις to their kings as those who truly are gods and share in the divine nature (Αἰγύπτιοι τοὺς ἑαυτῶν βασιλεῖς προσκυνεῖν τε καὶ τιμᾶν ὡς πρὸς ἀλήθειαν ὄντας θεούς ... τοὺς βουλομένους τε καὶ δυναμένους τὰ μέγιστ᾽ εὐεργετεῖν ἡγούμενοι θείας μετέχειν φύσεως [*Hist.* 1.90.3]).[17] It is said that Alexander the Great established cultic worship for his companion Hephaestion after his death, with temples, altars, offerings, and festivals instituted in his honor. So dear was Hephaestion to Alexander that, as Lucian states, there was no greater offense to Alexander than to refuse to worship and give προσκύνησις to Hephaestion (Παρὰ δὲ Ἀλεξάνδρῳ μεγίστη ποτὲ πασῶν ἦν διαβολή, εἰ λέγοιτο τις μὴ σέβειν μηδὲ προσκυνεῖν τὸν Ἡφαιστίωνα [*Cal.* 17]).

So too are the Roman emperors said to have received divine worship in part through reception of προσκύνησις. Lucian affirms that the emperor is duly rewarded with "praise, universal fame, reverence (i.e., προσκύνησις) for his benefactions, statues and temples and shrines" (ἔπαινοι καὶ ἡ παρὰ πᾶσιν εὔκλεια καὶ τὸ ἐπὶ ταῖς εὐεργεσίαις προσκυνεῖσθαι, καὶ εἰκόνες δὲ καὶ νεῷ καὶ τεμένη), all fitting for one so devoted to the common weal and its progress (*Apol.* 13). Epictetus says of Roman emperors, "We worship these persons as gods (ὡς θεοὺς αὐτοὺς προσκυνοῦμεν); for we consider that what has power to confer the greatest advantage is divine" (*Diatr.* 4.1.60).[18]

Finally, we come to a particular figure in Greek history whose associations with προσκύνησις sparked controversy: Alexander the Great. In an incident commonly referred to as "the προσκύνησις affair," the Macedonian ruler Alexander, seeking προσκύνησις for himself, attempted to impose this gesture of obeisance upon his Greek and Macedonian subjects in Bactra in 327 B.C.E. But the plan met with

---

[15] See also Diodorus Siculus, *Hist.* 3.71.5; Plutarch, *Gen. Socr.* 590B; Pausanias, *Descr.* 4.27.2; Artemidorus, *Onir.* 2.37.

[16] In line with Diodorus's description of ancient Ethiopian kingship here, Ulrich Braukämper, "Kingship, divine," *EAE* 3:401, explains, "the ruler is not regarded as an immediate incarnation of a god" but, rather, "after his installation the incumbent becomes a vehicle or shrine of a god, a royal ancestor or a cultural hero."

[17] On the divinity of the Egyptian king, see David P. Silverman, "The Nature of Egyptian Kingship," in *Ancient Egyptian Kingship* (Probleme der Ägyptologie 9; Leiden: Brill, 1995), 69–87.

[18] On worship of Roman emperors as divine figures, see esp. S. R. F. Price, *Rituals and Power: The Roman Imperial Cult in Asia Minor* (Cambridge: Cambridge University Press, 1984). For other later instances of προσκύνησις of Roman emperors recorded in Dio Cassius (third century C.E.), see p. 156 below.

resistance, and the matter was ultimately dropped. It is interesting to note the different reflections and interpretations of this event in the ancient sources. Plutarch's account (*Alex.* 54.2–4) appears to be free of any indications that προσκύνησις of Alexander was seen as a form of divine worship. Indeed, other passages in the *Life of Alexander* seem to support this. Elsewhere, it is suggested that Alexander intended προσκύνησις to be a step toward culturally acclimating Macedonians to Persian lifestyles (*Alex.* 45.1), and the Macedonian Cleitus contrasts freemen like himself with barbarians and slaves who offer προσκύνησις to the Persian-clad Alexander (*Alex.* 51.3). It seems that in Plutarch's account, Alexander desired to establish social uniformity between his Persian and Greek subjects by enforcing a common court ceremonial and that Greeks objected to this because it undermined their status as freemen. However, in Arrian's account (*Anab.* 4.10.5–12.5), the idea of offering προσκύνησις to Alexander clearly includes associations with divine worship.[19] When some among Alexander's subjects reason that since Alexander will certainly be honored as a god in death, then he should also receive such divine recognition in his life through προσκύνησις (*Anab.* 4.10.7), Callisthenes objects by stating that of all the honors appropriate to gods and that distinguish them from men, "the most important distinction concerns the matter of obeisance" (ἀτὰρ οὐχ ἥκιστα τῷ τῆς προσκυνήσεως νόμῳ). He goes on to explain that while men are appropriately greeted with a direct kiss, what is divine is far above men and cannot be touched, and so is appropriately honored with προσκύνησις (τὸ θεῖον δέ, ὅτι ἄνω που ἱδρυμένον καὶ οὐδὲ ψαῦσαι αὐτοῦ θέμις, ἐπὶ τῷδε ἄρα τῇ προσκυνήσει γεραίρεται [*Anab.* 4.11.3]). In Arrian's account, Callisthenes treats προσκύνησις as a form of divine worship inappropriate for a mortal like Alexander.

Although scholars remain divided over whether or not Alexander achieved (or aimed to achieve) divine recognition in his own lifetime,[20] it is clear that he was treated like a divine figure after death. Diodorus Siculus reports that following a dream in which Alexander appeared to General Eumenes as one continuing to rule from beyond the grave, Eumenes and the other generals set up a golden throne furnished with Alexander's royal insignia, burned incense to Alexander, and offered προσκύνησις to him as a god (καὶ κειμένης ἐσχάρας ἐχούσης πῦρ ἐπέθυον ἐκ κιβωτίου χρυσοῦ πάντες οἱ ἡγεμόνες τόν τε λιβανωτὸν καὶ τῶν ἄλλων εὐωδιῶν τὰ πολυτελέστατα καὶ προσεκύνουν ὡς θεὸν τὸν Ἀλέξανδρον [*Hist.* 18.61.1]).

Certainly, more could be said regarding the use of προσκυνέω in Greco-Roman literature,[21] but the foregoing suffices as a representation of its use with regard to reverence/worship of gods, mere humans, and godlike humans.

---

[19] See similarly Curtius 8.5.5–21.
[20] See, for example, discussions in W. W. Tarn, *Alexander the Great, II: Sources and Studies* (Cambridge: Cambridge University Press, 1948), 362–69; J. P. V. D. Balsdon, "The 'Divinity' of Alexander," *Historia* 1 (1950): 376–77; Robin Lane Fox, *Alexander the Great* (London: Allen Lane, 1973), 321–24; A. B. Bosworth, *Conquest and Empire: The Reign of Alexander the Great* (Cambridge: Cambridge University Press, 1988), 284–87; E. Badian, "Alexander the Great between Two Thrones and Heaven: Variations on an Old Theme," in *Alexander the Great: A Reader* (ed. Ian Worthington; 1st ed.; London: Routledge, 2003), 253–54.
[21] For instance, various places and objects (typically sacred) are also frequently objects of προσκυνέω (see, for example, Plutarch, *Exil.* 607A; Lucian, *Ver. hist.* 1.7; *Tyr.* 19), the sense being that even such places and objects associated with the divine should be regarded reverently.

B. Προσκυνέω in the OT and in early Jewish literature

Just as προσκυνέω is frequently used in Greco-Roman literature for worship of the gods, so too is this the case in the OT and early Jewish literature.[22] Not surprisingly, however, the term is generally used positively when its object is the God of Israel, Yahweh, and negatively when all other so-called gods are its object, because Yahweh is the one true God for Jews, and thus is alone considered worthy of such worship. The strongest senses of the term are again clear in the προσκύνησις of both Yahweh and false gods as such worship often takes place at/before cultic sites and objects and/ or in association with cultic activities. For instance, David goes to God's sanctuary and renders προσκύνησις to him (εἰσῆλθεν εἰς τὸν οἶκον τοῦ θεοῦ καὶ προσεκύνησεν αὐτῷ [2 Kgdms 12:20]),[23] as does Sennacherib go to Nisroch's sanctuary where he renders προσκύνησις to his god (ἐγένετο αὐτοῦ προσκυνοῦντος ἐν οἴκῳ Νεσεραχ θεοῦ αὐτοῦ [4 Kgdms 19:37]).[24] Elkanah both offers προσκύνησις and sacrifices to God (ἀνέβαινεν ὁ ἄνθρωπος ... προσκυνεῖν καὶ θύειν τῷ κυρίῳ θεῷ σαβαωθ [1 Kgdms 1:3]),[25] as does Amaziah offer προσκύνησις and sacrifices to foreign gods (ἤνεγκεν πρὸς αὐτοὺς τοὺς θεοὺς υἱῶν Σηιρ ... καὶ ἐναντίον αὐτῶν προσεκύνει καὶ αὐτοῖς αὐτὸς ἔθυεν [2 Chr 25:14]).[26] Along with associating προσκύνησις with sacrifice, προσκύνησις of God is also linked with various types of praise (e.g., blessing, hymn singing, and thanksgiving), and, to a lesser extent, petitionary prayer.[27] At other times, προσκυνέω is unaccompanied by other worship terms, and yet the sense is clearly

---

[22] All citation references and translations of texts of the LXX and Old Testament Pseudepigrapha are from *A New English Translation of the Septuagint: And the Other Greek Translations Traditionally Included under That Title* (ed. Albert Pietersma and Benjamin G. Wright; Oxford: Oxford University Press, 2007), and *The Old Testament Pseudepigrapha* (ed. James H. Charlesworth; 2 vols.; Garden City, NY: Doubleday, 1983–1985), unless otherwise noted.

Although it may be that some or all of the pseudepigraphal works cited here (namely, the *Testaments of the Twelve Patriarchs*, the *Testament of Abraham*, *Joseph and Aseneth*, the *Apocalypse of Moses*, and *3 Baruch*) are later Christian works, or perhaps Jewish works with some Christian interpolations (along with the introductions to these works in *OTP*, see also discussions in James R. Davila, *The Provenance of the Pseudepigrapha: Jewish, Christian, or Other?* [Leiden: Brill, 2005]), we can safely include them in the discussion here since the use of προσκυνέω in these works does not radically diverge from the usage in the LXX, Philo, or Josephus (although see the somewhat unique passage *Jos. Asen.* 15:11-12x discussed below), with the notable exception of clearly Christian passages (see p. 34 below).

[23] See also 4 Kgdms 18:22; Pss 5:7; 28:2; 95:9; 98:5; 131:7; Jer 33:2; Ezek 46:2-3; Josephus, *Ant.* 8.225–28; 10.29; 11.87; 13.54; *J.W.* 2.341; 5.99; and so on.

[24] See also Lev 26:1; 4 Kgdms 5:18; Ps 105:19; Isa 2:8; 44:15; 46:6; Dan 3:5-7; Mic 5:13; Philo, *Mos.* 1.276; *Decal.* 76; Josephus, *Ant.* 3.91; 10.213; *T. Zeb.* 9:5; and so on.

[25] See also Deut 26:10; 4 Kgdms 17:36; Jdt 16:18; Josephus, *Ant.* 8.118; *J.W.* 2.414; and so on.

[26] See also Exod 32:8; Num 25:2; 4 Kgdms 17:35; Jer 1:16; Philo, *Mos.* 2.165; Josephus, *Ant.* 9.135; and so on. Note also the frequent pairing of προσκυνέω with the cultic worship term λατρεύω for both the worship of God (Dan 3:95; 6:27; *1 En.* 10:21) and false gods (Exod 20:5; Deut 4:19; Josh 23:7; 4 Kgdms 21:21; Dan 3:12-18; etc.).

[27] Προσκύνησις with: αἰνέω (2 Chr 7:3; 20:18-19; Sir 50:17-18); εὐλογέω (Gen 24:48; 1 Chr 29:20; Job 1:20-21; 1 Macc 4:55; Josephus, *Ant.* 8.119; cf. Jdt 13:17); ᾄδω/ὑμνέω/ψάλλω (2 Chr 29:28-30; Ps 65:4; Josephus, *Ant.* 7.95; 9.11, 269; *T. Ab.* 20:12-13 [A]; cf. Philo, *Spec.* 2.199); εὐχαριστέω (Josephus, *Ant.* 7.95; 9.11; cf. Exod 4:31; Judg 7:15); petitionary prayer (Jdt 6:18-19; *Apoc. Mos.* 33:5; cf. Isa 44:17).

that those who render προσκύνησις to God engage in cultic worship, as when Saul requests that Samuel accompany him in offering προσκύνησις to God (ἀνάστρεψον μετ᾽ ἐμοῦ, καὶ προσκυνήσω κυρίῳ τῷ θεῷ σου [1 Kgdms 15:25]).[28] Not only humans but heavenly beings are also said to give προσκύνησις to God (e.g., σοὶ προσκυνοῦσιν αἱ στρατιαὶ τῶν οὐρανῶν [Neh 9:6]).[29] God's people are even identified as those who worship him and are devoted to him through προσκύνησις, as opposed to other gods (e.g., οὐκ ἐβουλήθησαν ἀκολουθῆσαι τοῖς θεοῖς τῶν πατέρων αὐτῶν, οἳ ἐγένοντο ἐν γῇ Χαλδαίων· καὶ ἐξέβησαν ἐξ ὁδοῦ τῶν γονέων αὐτῶν καὶ προσεκύνησαν τῷ θεῷ τοῦ οὐρανοῦ [Jdt 5:7–8]).[30] Finally, a time is anticipated when all will join God's people in rendering προσκύνησις to him (e.g., ἥξει πᾶσα σὰρξ ἐνώπιόν μου προσκυνῆσαι ἐν Ιερουσαλημ, εἶπεν κύριος [Isa 66:23]).[31]

There are occasional instances where προσκυνέω appears with angelic figures as its object. The general sense in such instances is that those who encounter these otherworldly beings are overwhelmed with awe (and perhaps fear as well), which moves the human to fall prostrate in reverence. When the angel of the Lord suddenly appears to Balaam, for example, he immediately falls face down in προσκύνησις (ὁρᾷ τὸν ἄγγελον κυρίου ἀνθεστηκότα ἐν τῇ ὁδῷ καὶ τὴν μάχαιραν ἐσπασμένην ἐν τῇ χειρὶ αὐτοῦ καὶ κύψας προσεκύνησεν τῷ προσώπῳ αὐτοῦ [Num 22:31]). Joshua similarly falls face down in reverence before the "commander-in-chief of the force of the Lord," whom he likely takes to be a heavenly being (Josh 5:14).[32] In the pseudepigraphal writings, when Abraham's son, Isaac, immediately perceives the heavenly nature of their mysterious visitor (the archangel Michael), he runs to him and falls at the feet of "the incorporeal one" in προσκύνησις (ἔδραμεν Ἰσαάκ, καὶ προσεκύνησεν αὐτὸν καὶ προσέπεσεν τοῖς ποσὶν τοῦ ἀσωμάτου [T. Ab. 3:6 (A)]).[33] In one case, it is a lower-ranking angel (rather than a human) who renders προσκύνησις to the higher-ranking commander Michael (ἦλθεν Μιχαήλ, καὶ συνήντησεν αὐτῷ ὁ ἄγγελος ὁ ὢν μετ᾽ ἐμοῦ, καὶ προσεκύνησεν αὐτόν, καὶ εἶπεν·Χαίροις, ὁ ἐμὸς ἀρχιστράτηγος καὶ παντὸς τοῦ ἡμετέρου τάγματος [3 Bar. 11:6]). In a rather striking case, Aseneth not only falls face down at the feet of an angelic figure in προσκύνησις (ἔπεσεν ἐπὶ τοὺς πόδας αὐτοῦ καὶ προσεκύνησεν αὐτῷ ἐπὶ πρόσωπον εἰς τὴν γῆν [Jos. Asen. 15:11])[34] but then proceeds to bless both the Lord God and the angel for her deliverance, and asks for the angel's name that she may hymn and glorify him forever (Jos. Asen. 15:12–12x). Unlike Aseneth's first two prostrations before the angel in which προσκυνέω is absent

---

[28] See also 1 Kgdms 1:19; 15:30–31; 2 Kgdms 15:32.
[29] See also Ps 96:7; T. Ab. 4:4–6 [B]; Apoc. Mos. 7:2; 17:1; 27:5; 33:5; cf. Deut 32:43.
[30] See also Ep Jer 5; Josephus, Ant. 10.263; 11.3.
[31] See also Pss 21:28; 85:9; Zeph 2:11; Zech 14:16–17.
[32] Although LXX Josh 5:14 lacks προσκυνέω which typically renders חוה‎השת (cf. Josh 5:14 [MT]), it is present in the Greek translations of Aquila, Symmachus and Theodotion (Greeven, TDNT 6:760, n. 23).
[33] Cf. the original Genesis account (Gen 18–19). Here, it may be that when Abraham and Lot greet their supernatural visitors with προσκύνησις (Gen 18:2; 19:1), they unwittingly reverence them in a more fitting way than they realize (cf. also LXX^A Judg 6:19).
[34] From a reconstruction of the longer form of Joseph and Aseneth in Christoph Burchard, Gesammelte Studien zu Joseph und Aseneth (SVTP 13; Leiden: Brill, 1996).

and the emphasis is on her initial fear from the overwhelming appearance of the angel (ἔπεσεν ἐπὶ πρόσωπον ἐπὶ τὴν τέφραν [14:3]; ἔπεσεν ἐπὶ πρόσωπον . . . καὶ ἐφοβήθη Ἀσενὲθ φόβον μέγαν καὶ ἐτρόμαξε πάντα τὰ μέλη αὐτῆς [14:10]), in her prostration with προσκύνησις in 15:11, the context shows the emphasis is clearly on her desire to reverence/worship the angel.[35]

This last example in particular seems to move significantly beyond a mere show of awed reverence toward a heavenly figure and could perhaps be indicative of a view of angels as worthy of a kind of cultic worship comparable to that typically reserved for God. Indeed, according to some scholars, there is a wealth of evidence supporting the emergence of the worship of angels within early Jewish circles. Often highlighted as relevant data are the following: (1) praise of angels (e.g., Tob 11:14; *Jos. Asen.* 15:11–12x); (2) invocation of angels (e.g., *T. Levi* 5:5; *PGM*); (3) possible allusions to angel worship (e.g., Col 2:18; Heb 1:5–2:18); (4) depictions of angels refusing to be reverenced/worshiped (e.g., *Apoc. Zeph.* 6:11–15; Rev 19:10; 22:8–9; *Ascen. Isa.* 7:21); (5) accusations of Jewish worship of angels (e.g., Aristides, *Apol.* 14.4; *Kerygma Petrou* [in Clement of Alexandria, *Strom.* 6.5.41]); and (6) later rabbinic prohibitions against various forms of angel worship (e.g., *t. Hul.* 2:18; *j. Ber.* 9:13a–b).[36] Some have gone so far as to conclude that such evidence is likely indicative of the existence of angel cults within Judaism.[37] More recent scholarship, however, has rightly objected that the evidence is insufficient for such a strong conclusion.[38] Instead, it is more likely that the evidence is indicative of some forms of "angel veneration," that is, reverential attitudes and behaviors toward angels welcomed among some Jewish groups that others may

---

[35] Cf. many other texts that depict humans prostrate in their encounters with angelic figures, yet without the use of προσκυνέω (Judg 13:20; 1 Chr 21:16; Dan 8:17; 10:9–10; Tob 12:16; 4 Macc 4:10–11; *T. Ab.* 9:1 [A]), where the emphasis in such instances is almost always on a kind of involuntary prostration from fear rather than voluntary prostration in reverence. For example, Manoah and his wife "fell on their face to the ground" (ἔπεσαν ἐπὶ πρόσωπον αὐτῶν ἐπὶ τὴν γῆν) after witnessing the angel's mysterious ascent, but Manoah's concern that they would surely die as a result of this angelic encounter suggests the prostration was triggered by fear (Judg 13:20–22). These passages often note the humans' fear and/or the angel's comforting words to not be afraid.

[36] See Peter Schäfer, *Rivalität zwischen Engeln und Menschen: Untersuchungen zur rabbinischen Engelvorstellung* (SJ 8; Berlin: de Gruyter, 1975), 67–72, who identifies prohibitions against four types of angel worship in rabbinic literature: images, offerings, invocations, and veneration.

[37] Wilhelm Bousset, *Die Religion des Judentums im späthellenistischen Zeitalter* (HNT 21; Tübingen: Mohr Siebeck, 1926), 329–31; Erwin R. Goodenough, *Jewish Symbols in the Greco-Roman Period* (13 vols.; Bollingen Series 37; New York: Pantheon, 1953–1968), 2:145–46; Schäfer, *Rivalität*, 67–74; Marcel Simon, *Verus Israel: A Study of the Relations between Christians and Jews in the Roman Empire (135–425)* (trans. Henry McKeating; LLJC; Oxford: Oxford University Press, 1986), 345–47; Andrew Chester, *Messiah and Exaltation: Jewish Messianic and Visionary Traditions and New Testament Christology* (WUNT 207; Tübingen: Mohr Siebeck, 2007), 109–13.

[38] Hurtado, *One*, 28–34; Clinton E. Arnold, *The Colossian Syncretism: The Interface between Christianity and Folk Belief at Colossae* (WUNT 2/77; Tübingen: Mohr Siebeck, 1995), 20–89; Peter R. Carrell, *Jesus and the Angels: Angelology and the Christology of the Apocalypse of John* (SNTSMS 95; Cambridge: Cambridge University Press, 1997), 73–75; Darrell D. Hannah, *Michael and Christ: Michael Traditions and Angel Christology in Early Christianity* (WUNT 2/109; Tübingen: Mohr Siebeck, 1999), 104–11.

have regarded as potential or real threats to monotheistic faith and the worship of God alone.[39]

With regard to the praise and προσκύνησις of the angel in *Jos. Asen.* 15:11–12x, it is not entirely clear whether this is an example of "angel veneration"[40] or is instead conceived as the type of unambiguous worship typically reserved for God alone which is in the end depicted as either acceptably[41] or unacceptably[42] given to angels. Other instances where not just angels (e.g., Tob 11:14) but even humans (e.g., 1 Sam 25:32–33; Tob 11:17; Jdt 13:17–18; *1 En.* 40:4–5) are blessed alongside God in praise may at first make the same here appear somewhat less striking, yet the basis for such praise (salvation of Aseneth's soul) does seem to give it more weight. Aseneth's desire to know the angel's name in order to hymn (ὑμνήσω) and glorify (δοξάσω) the angel forever also seems quite weighty and comparable to divine worship. The angel's response to this in 15:12x is understood differently. Some take his refusal to divulge his name to signify a rejection of Aseneth's desire to worship him,[43] while others counter that the explicit reason given for keeping the name secret is that it is too lofty to be uttered.[44] The latter, however, does not necessarily preclude the former. Indeed, in the end, the fact remains that the angel does not give Aseneth his name, thereby effectively preventing her from worshiping him *by name* as she desired, and so some reserve could very well be intended here.

In general then, it seems best to conclude that while such instances of προσκύνησις of angels certainly reflect a form of reverential regard that Jews had for these celestial beings, there is little clear evidence to suggest from these literary depictions that they were thought to be worthy of the kind of cultic worship reserved for deities.

Προσκυνέω is also frequently used for reverence shown to humans of various rank and status. Such reverence shown to lower-ranking social superiors is occasionally attested, as when Joseph's sons greet their grandfather Jacob by prostrating themselves in προσκύνησις before him (προσεκύνησαν αὐτῷ ἐπὶ πρόσωπον ἐπὶ τῆς γῆς [Gen 48:12]), or when Moses greets his father-in-law, Jethro, with προσκύνησις (ἐξῆλθεν δὲ Μωυσῆς εἰς συνάντησιν τῷ γαμβρῷ αὐτοῦ καὶ προσεκύνησεν αὐτῷ καὶ ἐφίλησεν αὐτόν, καὶ ἠσπάσαντο ἀλλήλους [Exod 18:7]), or again when Ruth prostrates herself in προσκύνησις before Boaz, a prominent figure in the community, as a gesture of gratitude for allowing her to glean from his field (ἔπεσεν ἐπὶ πρόσωπον αὐτῆς καὶ προσεκύνησεν ἐπὶ τὴν γῆν καὶ εἶπεν πρὸς αὐτόν Τί ὅτι εὗρον χάριν ἐν ὀφθαλμοῖς σου [Ruth 2:10]). Moving up the ranks, there are also instances where various men and women of a more widely recognized stature and repute receive προσκύνησις. Following the tenth plague of Egypt, Moses expects Pharaoh's servants to render προσκύνησις to

---

[39] See esp. Loren T. Stuckenbruck, *Angel Veneration and Christology: A Study in Early Judaism and in the Christology of the Apocalypse of John* (WUNT 2/70; Tübingen: Mohr Siebeck, 1995), 51–203.
[40] Stuckenbruck, *Angel,* 168–70, 200–1.
[41] Chester, *Messiah,* 112–13.
[42] Hurtado, *One,* xi, 81, 84.
[43] Hurtado, *One,* xi, 81, 84.
[44] Chester, *Messiah,* 112; cf. Stuckenbruck, *Angel,* 170. Chester posits that this angel bears the divine name, but this is far from clear.

him as they urge him to take the Israelites with him and leave Egypt (καταβήσονται πάντες οἱ παῖδές σου οὗτοι πρός με καὶ προσκυνήσουσίν με λέγοντες Ἔξελθε σὺ καὶ πᾶς ὁ λαός σου, οὗ σὺ ἀφηγῇ [Exod 11:8]). A "faithful priest" will receive προσκύνησις from Eli's descendants who seek provisions from him (ἔσται ὁ περισσεύων ἐν οἴκῳ σου ἥξει προσκυνεῖν αὐτῷ ὀβολοῦ ἀργυρίου λέγων Παράρριψόν με ἐπὶ μίαν τῶν ἱερατειῶν σου φαγεῖν ἄρτον [1 Kgdms 2:36]). The prophet Elisha receives προσκύνησις from a prophetic guild that acknowledges him as Elijah's successor (εἶδον αὐτὸν οἱ υἱοὶ τῶν προφητῶν οἱ ἐν Ιεριχω ἐξ ἐναντίας καὶ εἶπον Ἐπαναπέπαυται τὸ πνεῦμα Ηλιου ἐπὶ Ελισαιε·καὶ ἦλθον εἰς συναντὴν αὐτοῦ καὶ προσεκύνησαν αὐτῷ ἐπὶ τὴν γῆν [4 Kgdms 2:15]) and from a Shunammite woman who falls in προσκύνησις as a gesture of gratitude for bringing her son back to life (εἰσῆλθεν ἡ γυνὴ καὶ ἔπεσεν ἐπὶ τοὺς πόδας αὐτοῦ καὶ προσεκύνησεν ἐπὶ τὴν γῆν καὶ ἔλαβεν τὸν υἱὸν αὐτῆς [4 Kgdms 4:37]). Judith receives προσκύνησις for her key role in bringing an end to Israel's oppressor (προσέπεσεν τοῖς ποσὶν Ιουδιθ καὶ προσεκύνησεν τῷ προσώπῳ αὐτῆς καὶ εἶπεν Εὐλογημένη σὺ ἐν παντὶ σκηνώματι Ιουδα καὶ ἐν παντὶ ἔθνει [Jdt 14:7]). In the pseudepigraphal works, the stature of OT patriarchs is reflected in part by the προσκύνησις they receive, as when Death greets Abraham with προσκύνησις, whom he acknowledges as "true friend of the Most High God" (ἰδὼν αὐτὸν ὁ θάνατος προσεκύνησεν αὐτὸν λέγων· Χαίροις, τίμιε Ἀβραάμ, δικαία ψυχή, φίλε γνήσιε τοῦ θεοῦ τοῦ ὑψίστου, καὶ τῶν ἁγίων ἀγγέλων ὁμόσκηνε [T. Ab. 16:9 (A)]), and when Aseneth greets Jacob with προσκύνησις, who is described in angelomorphic terms (οἱ τένοντες αὐτοῦ καὶ οἱ ὦμοι αὐτοῦ καὶ οἱ βραχίονες ὡς ἀγγέλου . . . καὶ εἶδεν αὐτὸν Ἀσενὲθ καὶ ἐθαμβήθη καὶ προσεκύνησεν αὐτῷ ἐπὶ πρόσωπον ἐπὶ τὴν γῆν [Jos. Asen. 22:7–8]).

Προσκύνησις is also shown to higher-ranking social superiors, such as officials, military commanders, and governors. Joseph renders προσκύνησις to Pentephris, third in rank of Pharaoh's officers (εἰσαχθεὶς προσεκύνησα τῷ ἀρχιευνούχῳ·τρίτος γὰρ ἦν ἐν ἀξίᾳ παρὰ τῷ Φαραώ [T. Jos. 13:5]). Chousi renders προσκύνησις to David's military commander Joab (εἶπεν Ιωαβ τῷ Χουσι βαδίσας ἀνάγγειλον τῷ βασιλεῖ ὅσα εἶδες·καὶ προσεκύνησεν Χουσι τῷ Ιωαβ καὶ ἐξῆλθεν [2 Kgdms 18:21]), as does Judith to Nebuchadnezzar's military commander Holofernes (πεσοῦσα ἐπὶ πρόσωπον προσεκύνησεν αὐτῷ [Jdt 10:23]). Joseph, whom Pharaoh appoints to be second-in-command in Egypt, is frequently reverenced with προσκύνησις (Gen 42:6; 43:26, 28).[45] There are numerous instances of kings and queens reverenced with προσκύνησις. Even as David is being hunted by King Saul, he shows great loyalty to him as God's appointed ruler by prostrating himself in προσκύνησις before Saul when he had the opportunity to take his life (ἀνέστη Δαυιδ ὀπίσω αὐτοῦ ἐκ τοῦ σπηλαίου, καὶ ἐβόησεν Δαυιδ ὀπίσω Σαουλ λέγων Κύριε βασιλεῦ· καὶ ἐπέβλεψεν Σαουλ εἰς τὰ ὀπίσω αὐτοῦ, καὶ ἔκυψεν Δαυιδ ἐπὶ πρόσωπον αὐτοῦ ἐπὶ τὴν γῆν καὶ προσεκύνησεν αὐτῷ [1 Kgdms 24:9]). David himself is frequently a recipient of προσκύνησις when he becomes Israel's

---

[45] See also Philo, Ios. 164; T. Zeb. 3:6–7; Jos. Asen. 5:10; 22:4.

king (2 Kgdms 9:6; 14:4; 3 Kgdms 1:16; etc.),[46] as are King Solomon, Queen Bathsheba, King Joash, and other royal figures (3 Kgdms 1:53; 2:13; 2 Chr 24:17).[47]

In all such instances of προσκύνησις directed toward humans mentioned above, the reverence is done as a way of greeting a human superior, expressing gratitude for a benefit, expressing supplication, and/or acknowledging the human superior's authority.

There are a few instances, however, where προσκύνησις of a human could perhaps be taken as worship that acknowledges or treats the human as a divine figure. First to be considered is Saul's προσκύνησις of the prophet Samuel in his postmortem spiritual form. When Saul consults a medium to conjure up Samuel from the dead, the medium exclaims that she sees "gods" (θεοὺς) ascending from the earth (1 Kgdms 28:13) and goes on to describe the numinous figure's clothing as that characteristic of Samuel, which leads Saul to perceive Samuel's presence and to fall face down in προσκύνησις before him (ἔγνω Σαουλ ὅτι Σαμουηλ οὗτος, καὶ ἔκυψεν ἐπὶ πρόσωπον αὐτοῦ ἐπὶ τὴν γῆν καὶ προσεκύνησεν αὐτῷ [1 Kgdms 28:14]). While there is certainly a sense in which Samuel receives προσκύνησις as an otherworldly being here, this does not necessarily mean such reverence is analogous to the worship of God. Even the association of Samuel's appearance with an ascending of θεοὺς should probably not be given too much weight since this is the medium's description. It is not at all clear that Saul shares the same perspective on Samuel's perceived godlike character.[48]

A second case to consider is Nebuchadnezzar's προσκύνησις of Daniel. When Daniel interprets Nebuchadnezzar's dream, Nebuchadnezzar falls in προσκύνησις before Daniel and commands for cultic offerings to be given to him (Ναβουχοδονοσορ ὁ βασιλεὺς πεσὼν ἐπὶ πρόσωπον χαμαὶ προσεκύνησε τῷ Δανιηλ καὶ ἐπέταξε θυσίας καὶ σπονδὰς ποιῆσαι αὐτῷ [Dan 2:46]). On the one hand, the association of προσκύνησις with cultic offerings makes it clear that divine worship is in view and that such worship is indeed directed to Daniel himself.[49] On the other hand, although nothing is said of Daniel's refusal of such worship (which is somewhat surprising), since Daniel himself gives all praise and credit to God for revealing Nebuchadnezzar's dream and its interpretation (2:19–23, 26–30), and since it is clear elsewhere in Daniel that man is not to be exalted above God (Dan 4; 5:17–23) and that God alone is to be worshiped (Dan 3; cf. 6:25–27), it is probably reasonable to infer from this that the lack

---

[46] See also 2 Kgdms 9:8; 14:22, 33; 16:4; 18:28; 24:20; 3 Kgdms 1:16, 23, 31.

[47] See also Pss 44:13; 71:11; Josephus, *Ant.* 6.285; 20.28, 56, 65; and so on.

[48] Cf. Josephus's retelling of the account where he has the medium describing Samuel's appearance as τῷ θεῷ τινα τὴν μορφὴν ὅμοιον (*Ant.* 6.333), which is likely indicative of Josephus's desire to move away from attributing divine status to Samuel's spirit (see Christopher T. Begg, *Judean Antiquities, Books 5–7* [vol. 4 of *Flavius Josephus: Translation and Commentary*; ed. Steve Mason; Leiden: Brill, 2004], 191, n. 1219).

[49] Contra Carol A. Newsom and Brennan W. Breed, *Daniel: A Commentary* (OTL; Louisville: Westminster John Knox, 2014), 84, who argue unconvincingly that Nebuchadnezzar's praise of God immediately following (Dan 2:47) indicates all worship is in reality given to God. Appeal to Alexander's προσκύνησις of the Jewish high priest, which Alexander later explains was really directed to God (Josephus, *Ant.* 11.331–33), is not as close and relevant a parallel as is often supposed. The high priest is not presented with cultic offerings as Daniel is. Moreover, Alexander explicitly states that he did not ultimately reverence the high priest but rather his God, but Nebuchadnezzar makes no such statement denying reverence of Daniel.

of objection from Daniel does not necessarily mean such divine worship of humans is endorsed. Rather, the author may have allowed the worship of Daniel to stand without direct criticism because it is a powerful image of a Gentile king acknowledging a Jew whom he perceives to have an exceptionally close association with the divine (cf. 5:11–12; 6:3).[50]

A third case to consider is Alexander the Great's προσκύνησις before the Jewish high priest Jaddus in Josephus's *Jewish Antiquities*. It has recently been argued that when Alexander comes to Jerusalem and meets the high priest, he worships him as Israel's god's "idol," the visual image and embodiment of Yahweh himself.[51] Certain key details thought to point in this direction include (1) the high priest's garments (11.331), which evoke the image of the divine-warrior Yahweh; (2) the festive welcome of Alexander's advent with the presence of the high priest (11.327–31), who takes the place of the cult statue(s) brought out by the welcoming city; and (3) Alexander's dream of a figure resembling the high priest who encourages him in his exploits (11.334–35), a role played by gods in epiphanic dream stories.[52] Yet each of these points is contestable. While some traditions ascribe divine-warrior significance to the priestly garments, in Josephus's discussions of the priestly garments elsewhere (*Ant.* 3.151–78), he explicitly states that the articles of clothing represent the universe (3.180; cf. Philo, *Mos.* 2.117–35; *Spec.* 1.84–87, 93–97), thereby attributing cosmic significance (priest as embodiment of the world), not divine significance (priest as embodiment of Yahweh) to the garments. It is not at all clear that the high priest Jaddus is made to fill the role that the cult statue plays in a typical advent story since priests were already commonly present as part of the welcoming party in an advent.[53] And while it is intriguing that Alexander sees a figure in the form of the high priest when it is often divine beings encountered in epiphanic dream stories, the implications for the high priest's divinity do not necessarily follow from this any more than it does in an analogous account of the god Asclepius appearing to a man in a dream in the form of the merely mortal consul L. Petronius Sabinus.[54] Besides these concerns, it should also be noted that Josephus not only verbally distinguishes between the "προσκύνησις,"

---

[50] B. A. Mastin's attempt to tone down and render unremarkable Nebuchadnezzar's worship of Daniel ("Daniel 2:46 and the Hellenistic World," *ZAW* 85 [1973]: 80–93) weakens the force of what is likely intended to be a striking image. Josephus also allows Nebuchadnezzar's divine worship of Daniel to stand without objection (*Ant.* 10.211–12). As Paul Spilsbury argues, since one of Josephus's aims is to commend the Jews as a virtuous and pious people to his Gentile audience, he incorporates pagan views of exemplary Jews such as Daniel (and Moses) as divinities to boost the image of the Jew without necessarily fully endorsing such opinions (*The Image of the Jew in Flavius Josephus' Paraphrase of the Bible* [TSAJ 69; Tübingen: Mohr Siebeck, 1998], 109–10).

[51] Crispin H. T. Fletcher-Louis, "Alexander the Great's Worship of the High Priest," in *Early Jewish and Christian Monotheism* (ed. L. T. Stuckenbruck; W. E. S. North; JSNTSup 263; London: T&T Clark, 2004), 71–102.

[52] Fletcher-Louis, "Alexander," 86–91. On the account as a combination of advent story and epiphany story, see Shaye J. D. Cohen, "Alexander the Great and Jaddus the High Priest according to Josephus," *AJSR* 7–8 (1982–1983): 44–55.

[53] Cohen, "Alexander," 45.

[54] See Cohen, "Alexander," 52, n. 31, for this example. Note also the possibility in Josephus's story, as Cohen states here, that "Alexander sees an *angel* with the features of Jaddus" (italics mine).

which Alexander is said to have rendered to the divine name on the high priest's miter, and the "greeting," which is said to be given to the high priest himself (προσεκύνησεν τὸ ὄνομα καὶ τὸν ἀρχιερέα πρῶτος ἠσπάσατο [11.331]), but also has Alexander go on to explain to his general, Parmenion, who is shocked by Alexander's apparent προσκύνησις of the high priest, that he did not render προσκύνησις to him but to the God who so honored him to be high priest ("οὐ τοῦτον," εἶπεν, "προσεκύνησα, τὸν δὲ θεόν οὗ τὴν ἀρχιερωσύνην οὗτος τετίμηται" [11.333]).[55] Far from a view of the high priest as Yahweh's idol who receives divine worship through προσκύνησις, it is God himself whom Josephus very suggestively describes receiving προσκύνησις from him to whom all men everywhere else rendered προσκύνησις as the most godlike ruler among them.

Finally, we consider the προσκύνησις of Israel's king. We have already briefly noted numerous instances above, and there seems to be little indication that προσκύνησις in such cases is anything more than a customary gesture of respect and obeisance appropriate for a human sovereign. Yet we also noted from the use of προσκυνέω in Greco-Roman literature that some kings in the ancient world were thought to have had special relationships with the gods (e.g., Ethiopian kings), even to have been gods incarnate (e.g., Egyptian kings), and therefore, as Diodorus Siculus states, to have received προσκύνησις as gods in some sense (*Hist.* 1.90.3; 3.5.1). Is it possible that Israel's kings were worshiped as divine figures? Some OT passages may suggest that they were in some sense regarded as divine. A number of biblical psalms speak of the king in extraordinary terms: he is seated at God's right hand, is granted exceptionally long life, has a name that is to endure forever, is designated as God's son, and is even addressed as "god."[56] Of particular interest for the issue of the προσκύνησις of Israel's king is a passage we have yet to mention: 1 Chr 29:20. Here, King David calls on the assembly to bless God, and in response the people bless God and bow their knees in προσκύνησις before both God and the king (κάμψαντες τὰ γόνατα προσεκύνησαν τῷ κυρίῳ καὶ τῷ βασιλεῖ). While some scholars are content

---

[55] Fletcher-Louis attempts unconvincingly to get around the plain sense of these. Concerning the first, he argues that since Josephus understands the high priest not only to bear the divine name but also to be "called the most honored of revered names" (*J.W.* 4.164), that is, the divine name, the high priest is included as a recipient of Alexander's προσκύνησις ("Alexander," 88–89). But the "name" he is called in *J.W.* 4.164 could simply be "high priest." Fletcher-Louis dismisses this suggestion since there is no other evidence of the title "high priest" being described this way but neither is there other evidence of the high priest being called the divine name. Concerning the second, Fletcher-Louis claims Alexander was denying reverence of the person Jaddus but not of his priestly office ("Alexander," 94). But this fails as an adequate response to Parmenion, who is confounded that Alexander would do προσκύνησις to any human, no matter his office. Notice Parmenion is explicitly said to question Alexander's προσκύνησις of "τὸν Ἰουδαίων ἀρχιερέα," meaning he does have in mind the priestly office and not merely the person when he protests. It makes more sense that Alexander is defending his προσκύνησις of Israel's God and that this explanation would satisfy Parmenion.

Elsewhere, Josephus does use προσκυνέω with the high priests as objects (*J.W.* 4.324), but the sense here is that of the esteem they once held, which is contrasted with the abusive treatment they were currently receiving (cf. *J.W.* 4.262).

[56] Pss 109:1; 20:5; 71:17; 2:7; 88:28; 44:7–8. Two of these psalms also speak of the προσκύνησις of the king by other rulers and nations (Pss 44:13; 71:11).

simply to regard the reverence paid to the king here as honor befitting a human sovereign,[57] others take this passage as evidence that Israelites worshiped their kings as divine figures.[58]

Did the Israelites, then, consider their kings to be divine? A number of scholars affiliated with the so-called Myth and Ritual school would answer in the affirmative.[59] In their view, a common pattern of myth and ritual practice, which included the central feature of the divine king impersonating (even incarnating) the deity in key ritual ceremonies, was widespread in the ancient Near East and undoubtedly had an influence on Hebrew belief and practice, including conceptions of kingship. Thus, it is suggested that just as other ancient Near Eastern societies considered their kings to be divine, so too had Israel embraced this common Eastern conception of the king's divinity.

However, many scholars have taken issue with the Myth and Ritual school, with regard to both its general views of a uniform cultural pattern and its specific views on Israel's divine-kingship ideology. They protest that Myth and Ritual advocates tend to over-exaggerate superficial similarities between Eastern religions and to minimize significant differences between them in their attempts to validate their theory of a uniform cultural pattern. These dissenters are left with the impression that this school has merely imposed its preconceived notions of a supposed cultural pattern upon the evidence and in the end are unconvinced of any alleged pattern prevalent among Eastern cultures.[60] With regard to kingship, Henri Frankfort observed significant differences between the royal ideologies of ancient Near Eastern states: the Egyptian king was god incarnate, the Mesopotamian king was a chosen servant of the gods, and

---

[57] For example, Larry W. Hurtado, "The Binitarian Shape of Early Christian Worship," in *The Jewish Roots of Christological Monotheism: Papers from the St. Andrews Conference on the Historical Origins of the Worship of Jesus* (ed. Carey C. Newman et al.; JSJSup 63; Leiden: Brill, 1999), 190; Horst, *Proskynein*, 54, n. 2.

[58] For example, Margaret Barker, "The High Priest and the Worship of Jesus," in *The Jewish Roots of Christological Monotheism: Papers from the St. Andrews Conference on the Historical Origins of the Worship of Jesus* (ed. Carey C. Newman et al.; Leiden: Brill, 1999), 94–95; Crispin H. T. Fletcher-Louis, "The Worship of Divine Humanity as God's Image and the Worship of Jesus," in *The Jewish Roots of Christological Monotheism: Papers from the St. Andrews Conference on the Historical Origins of the Worship of Jesus* (ed. Carey C. Newman et al.; Leiden: Brill, 1999), 113, n. 3.

[59] See *Myth and Ritual: Essays on the Myth and Ritual of the Hebrews in Relation to the Culture Pattern of the Ancient East* (ed. Samuel H. Hooke; London: Oxford University Press, 1933). See also Ivan Engnell, *Studies in Divine Kingship in the Ancient Near East* (Uppsala: Almqvist & Wiksell, 1943); Geo Widengren, *Sakrales Königtum im Alten Testament und im Judentum* (Stuttgart: Kohlhammer, 1955).

[60] See Henri Frankfort, *The Problem of Similarity in Ancient Near Eastern Religions* (Oxford: Clarendon, 1951), 6–8; Samuel G. F. Brandon, "The Myth and Ritual Position Critically Considered," in *Myth, Ritual, and Kingship: Essays on the Theory and Practice of Kingship in the Ancient Near East and in Israel* (ed. Samuel H. Hooke; Oxford: Clarendon, 1958), 266–74; Jean de Fraine, *L'aspect religieux de la royauté israélite: L'institution monarchique dans l'Ancien Testament et dans les textes mésopotamiens* (AnBib 3; Rome: Pontificio Istituto Biblico, 1954), 34–54; Karl-Heinz Bernhardt, *Das Problem der altorientalischen Königsideologie im Alten Testament: unter besonderer Berücksichtigung der Geschichte der Psalmenexegese dargestellt und kritisch gewürdigt* (VTSup 8; Leiden: Brill, 1961), 57–66.

the Israelite king was different from both of these types of kings.[61] Others agree that Israel's kingship ideology was significantly different from those of its neighbors and that it should not be characterized as a type of divine kingship. C. R. North noted that Israel's denunciation of foreign kings for their divine pretensions (Isa 14:12-15; 31:3; Ezek 28:1-10; Dan 11:36) speaks against a divine-kingship ideology for Israel itself.[62] He acknowledged that there are some OT passages that use language that closely associates Israel's king with Yahweh but that nothing of it suggests the king himself was actually regarded as divine.[63] Furthermore, he was insistent that if there was such a thing as a divine-kingship ideology at any point in Israel's history, it must be adequately demonstrated rather than cursorily conjectured, as is so often the case among divine-kingship proponents.[64] Martin Noth's assessment of the evidence led him to conclude that Israel may have been aware of, and even appropriated language from, Eastern societies that treated the king as a divine figure but that it had ultimately rejected true divine-king ideology.[65] Likewise, John Day concedes that Israel appears to have been influenced by its neighbors in describing the king in divine terms but states clearly, "In general, contrary to the old Myth and Ritual School, it seems that the Israelites did not regard the king as divine."[66] For these and other reasons, many scholars reject the notion of the divinity of Israel's kings.[67]

If it is unlikely that Israel's kings were considered divine, it is also unlikely that the προσκύνησις of the king in 1 Chr 29:20 is to be understood as an instance of divine worship of the king. Although it is somewhat striking that the one verb προσεκύνησαν takes both τῷ κυρίῳ and τῷ βασιλεῖ as its objects, this does not necessarily mean that

---

[61] Henri Frankfort, *Kingship and the Gods: A Study of Ancient Near Eastern Religion as the Integration of Society and Nature* (Chicago: University of Chicago Press, 1948), 337.
[62] C. R. North, "The Religious Aspects of Hebrew Kingship," *ZAW* 50 (1932): 21-22.
[63] North, "Religious," 22-31. He explains, for instance, that when various texts speak of the long life of the king, "it is not the king *qua* king who is immortal, but the dynasty." Similarly, for texts that speak of the divine sonship of the king, "it is not the king *qua* individual who is as a son to Yahweh, but the king *qua* Davidic" ("Religious," 24-26).
[64] North, "Religious," 31-37.
[65] Martin Noth, "Gott, König, Volk im Alten Testament: Eine methodologische Auseinandersetzung mit einer gegenwärtigen Forschungsrichtung," *ZTK* 47 (1950): 185-86.
[66] John Day, "The Canaanite Inheritance of the Israelite Monarchy," in *King and Messiah in Israel and the Ancient Near East: Proceedings of the Oxford Old Testament Seminar* (ed. John Day; JSOTSup 270; Sheffield: Sheffield Academic, 1998), 81-85. Day explains here that divine language applied to Israel's king is not necessarily an indication of the king's divinity. Thus, the king is indeed described as a "son of God," but this is by adoption, not by birth (Ps 2:7). Similarly, although the more natural way of reading MT Ps 45:7 is as an address of the king as "god," it is still best to regard this ascription in hyperbolic terms.
[67] See also Fraine, *L'aspect*, 263-84; Bernhardt, *Problem*, 303-4; David J. A. Clines, *On the Way to the Postmodern: Old Testament Essays, 1967-1998* (vol. 2; JSOTSup 293; Sheffield: Sheffield Academic, 1998), 690-700. Some scholars take a more intermediate position on Israelite kingship ideology. Sigmund Mowinckel, *He That Cometh: The Messiah Concept in the Old Testament and Later Judaism* (trans. G. W. Anderson; Grand Rapids: Eerdmans, 2005), 56-89, rejects the extremist views of the Myth and Ritual school in identifying Israel's king with Yahweh but holds that the king was nevertheless, in some qualified sense, divine. According to Aubrey R. Johnson, *Sacral Kingship in Ancient Israel* (Cardiff: University of Wales Press, 1967), 13-31 [esp. pp. 30-31, n. 1], Israel's king was the cultic leader of the people and shared a close, unique relationship to Yahweh but was not a divine being.

God and king are reverenced in the same sense.[68] Indeed, Josephus's phrasing of the account suggests a distinction could ultimately be made between the reverence shown to God on the one hand and that shown to the king on the other, for, while he retains the term προσκυνέω to describe the reverence of God, he prefers the term εὐχαριστέω to describe the reverence of the king:

> [King David] commanded the multitude also to bless God. And so they fell upon the ground and prostrated themselves (προσεκύνησαν); and they also gave thanks (εὐχαρίστησαν) to David for all the blessings they had enjoyed since he had succeeded to the throne. (Josephus, *Ant.* 7.381, Marcus)

By contrast, it seems to be in the case of those humans in the larger pagan world who were acknowledged and treated as godlike beings (and/or who indulged themselves in such divine pretensions) that we see προσκυνέω used pejoratively for a kind of worship that so acknowledges or treats the human as a divine figure. Thus, along with the censure of divine worship through προσκύνησις of idols,[69] natural elements,[70] and animals,[71] belong a few instances of the censure of divine worship through προσκύνησις of humans.

In the *Letter of Aristeas*, the Jewish high priest Eleazar decries the Greek euhemeristic practice of making images of men who have benefited mankind by their discoveries and offering προσκύνησις to them as deified beings (ἀγάλματα γὰρ ποιήσαντες ἐκ λίθων καὶ ξύλων, εἰκόνας φασὶν εἶναι τῶν ἐξευρόντων τι πρὸς τὸ ζῆν αὐτοῖς χρήσιμον, οἷς προσκυνοῦσι ... καὶ γὰρ ἔτι καὶ νῦν εὑρεματικώτεροι καὶ πολυμαθέστεροι τῶν ἀνθρώπων τῶν πρίν εἰσι πολλοί, καὶ οὐκ ἄν φθάνοιεν αὐτοὺς προσκυνοῦντες [*Let. Aris.* 135–37]).

Also significant is Philo's allegorical interpretation of Joseph's two dreams where he envisions himself receiving προσκύνησις (Gen 37:5-11) in his work *On Dreams* (*Somn.* 2.78–154). The two dreams are interpreted separately, and while both interpretations present the Joseph who desires προσκύνησις as a type of contemporary tyrannical ruler figure, the second dream and its interpretation concerns a more blasphemous type of tyrant. While the first type of arrogant ruler (represented by Joseph's upright sheaf which receives προσκύνησις from other sheaves) is faulted for making himself superior over his fellow man and tyrannizing him (2.78–92), the second type (represented by Joseph receiving προσκύνησις from the sun, moon, and stars) is castigated for exalting himself not only above men but even above the natural and celestial elements (2.110–32). Philo recalls his own experience of dealing with such a ruler in Egypt who tried to

---

[68] Cf. 1 Kgdms 12:18; *Sib. Or.* 2:60; Ign. *Smyrn.* 9:1, where one verb governs two objects (one divine, the other human) without the implication that the two recipients thereby receive reverence in the same sense.
[69] Exod 20:5; 32:8; Lev 26:1; Num 25:2; 4 Kgdms 21:21; Ps 96:7; Isa 2:8; 46:6; Jer 1:16; Dan 3:5; Mic 5:13; Jdt 8:18; Ep Jer 5; Bel 4; Philo, *Mos.* 2.165; *Decal.* 76; Josephus, *Ant.* 3.91; 8.248; 10.69; *T. Zeb* 9:5; and so on.
[70] Deut 4:19; 17:3; Jer 8:2; Ezek 8:16; Philo, *Decal.* 64; *Spec.* 1.15.
[71] *Let. Aris.* 138; *Sib. Or.* 3:30; Philo, *Contempl.* 9.

do away with the Sabbath. When this ruler was met with resistance from the Jews, he reasoned that just as they would certainly forego Sabbath observance in the event of a natural disaster, so should they do the same in response to one like him who wields supernatural power comparable to these forces (2.123–29). With such words, in Philo's estimation, this man "dared to liken to the All-blessed his all-miserable self," and thus, Philo explains, he would not be surprised were the man to accuse the heavenly bodies of neglecting to render προσκύνησις to him should the seasons act contrary to his desires (ὥσπερ τὸν εἰωθότα δασμὸν οὐκ ἐνεγκόντας τοὺς ἀστέρας αἰτιάσεται, τιμᾶσθαι μονονοῦ καὶ προσκυνεῖσθαι δικαιῶν ὑπὸ τῶν οὐρανίων τἀπίγεια καὶ περιττότερον ἑαυτόν [2.130–32]).

In his work *On the Embassy to Gaius*, Philo notes the introduction of προσκύνησις into Italy, performed before the tyrannical emperor Gaius Caligula (ἔνιοι δὲ καὶ τὸ βαρβαρικὸν ἔθος εἰς Ἰταλίαν ἤγαγον, τὴν προσκύνησιν, τὸ εὐγενὲς τῆς Ῥωμαϊκῆς ἐλευθερίας παραχαράττοντες [*Legat.* 116]). On the one hand, προσκύνησις is certainly understood here in secular terms as Philo describes it as a "barbarian practice" and "a degradation of the high tradition of Roman freedom." On the other hand, that it appears in the context of Philo's extensive criticism of Gaius's divine pretensions (74–118) as a form of flattery that no doubt further stoked the flames of Gaius's exalted view of himself likely suggests that Philo also considered such reverence in this case to be sacrilegious. Gaius's megalomania had risen to blasphemous heights, but whereas the rest of the world exacerbated this problem with the flattery of προσκύνησις, the Jews alone, Philo claims, opposed him and instead remained resolute in their acknowledgment of the only God (114–16).

A final instance[72] that may have the repudiation of divine worship of humans through προσκύνησις in mind is Mordecai's refusal to render προσκύνησις to Haman. When the Persian king promotes Haman to be second-in-command and orders his officials to give προσκύνησις to him, Mordecai alone refuses to do so (πάντες οἱ ἐν τῇ αὐλῇ προσεκύνουν αὐτῷ, οὕτως γὰρ προσέταξεν ὁ βασιλεὺς ποιῆσαι·ὁ δὲ Μαρδοχαῖος οὐ προσεκύνει αὐτῷ [Esth 3:2]). Although in the Hebrew version, the most likely explanation for Mordecai's refusal to reverence Haman has to do with the long-standing ancestral rivalry between them as Jews (Mordecai) and Amalekites (Haman),[73] additional material appearing only in the Greek version reveals a different, religiously grounded explanation is ultimately offered for the refusal as seen in Mordecai's prayer to God:

> You know all things; you know, O Lord, that it was not in insolence nor pride nor for any love of glory that I did this, namely, to refuse to do obeisance (προσκυνεῖν) to this prideful Haman, for I would have been willing to kiss the soles of his feet

---

[72] Since we are only discussing the use of προσκυνέω in this chapter, no mention is made here of the reverence of the Enochic Son of Man in the *Similitudes of Enoch*, the reverence of Moses in the *Exagoge* of Ezekiel the Tragedian, or the reverence of Adam in the *Life of Adam and Eve*. These will be discussed in subsequent chapters in relation to the προσκύνησις of Jesus where relevant.

[73] Carey A. Moore, *Esther: Introduction, Translation, and Notes* (AB 7B; Garden City, NY: Doubleday, 1971), 36–37; Michael V. Fox, *Character and Ideology in the Book of Esther* (Columbia: University of South Carolina Press, 1991), 44–45.

for Israel's safety! But I did this so that I might not set human glory above divine glory, and I will not do obeisance (προσκυνήσω) to anyone but you, my Lord, and I will not do these things in pride. (LXX Add Esth C 5–7)

It has recently been argued that this religiously grounded defense of Mordecai's refusal to render προσκύνησις to Haman in Add Esth C was formulated as a subtle critique of Hellenistic ruler cult.[74] Since the date of the Greek additions (second to first centuries B.C.E.)[75] places Mordecai's prayer in Add Esth C within the reigns of the Ptolemaic and Seleucid kings who were recipients of cultic worship, this could very well form the background to this religiously expressed Jewish protest against προσκύνησις rendered to human ruler figures "so that [one] might not set human glory above divine glory." This explanation, however, does face some difficulties. For example, if ruler cult is being opposed, one might expect the Persian king, rather than the subordinate Haman, to be the more likely prototype of the Hellenistic ruler and the more likely target for critique. Yet he is described in glorious, almost godlike terms (Add Esth D), and there is no criticism, correction, or diminution of this lofty description of the king.[76] It may also be that a religiously based rationale was added simply to offer a more reasonable justification for Mordecai's refusal since it nearly led to the annihilation of the Jews. In any case, whether or not the passage was conceived as a direct response to ruler cult, it undoubtedly remains, in some way, a reflection of Jewish scruples over the propriety of showing a form of deference to humans which could perhaps compromise one's devotion to God.[77]

C. Conclusion

In both Greco-Roman literature and Jewish literature, προσκυνέω is generally used to express reverence or worship given to various figures of various rank and status. In both types of literature, προσκύνησις is generally shown as a customary greeting, an expression of gratitude or supplication, and/or an acknowledgment of the authority and superiority of the one reverenced/worshiped. In both types of literature, the character of προσκύνησις in any particular case is clarified by various key factors,

---

[74] Beate Ego, "Mordecai's Refusal of Proskynesis before Haman according to the Septuagint: Traditio-historical and Literal Aspects," in *Deuterocanonical Additions of the Old Testament Books: Selected Studies* (ed. Géza G. Xeravits and József Zsengellér; vol. 5 of *Deuterocanonical and Cognate Literature Studies*, ed. Friedrich V. Reiterer et al.; Berlin: de Gruyter, 2010), 16–26.

[75] Carey A. Moore, *Daniel, Esther, and Jeremiah: The Additions. A New Translation with Introduction and Commentary* (AB 44; Garden City, NY: Doubleday, 1977), 165–67.

[76] *Pace* Ego, "Mordecai's," 25–26, who sees the reference to the king as "an angel of God" as a diminution of the preceding godlike characterization of the king.

[77] We briefly note here other uses of προσκυνέω, for example, reverence of the things of God, such as God's Temple (Philo, *Legat.* 310; Josephus, *J.W.* 4.262; 5.381, 402; 6.123), God's Scriptures (*Let. Aris.* 177; Philo, *Mos.* 2.40; Josephus, *Ant.* 12.114), and God's holy days (Philo, *Mos.* 2.23). Note also the way Philo's metaphorical uses employ cultic and/or royal imagery (*Conf.* 49; *Somn.* 2.140; *Decal.* 4–9; *Spec.* 1.24; *Prov.* 2.19).

including the status of the figure reverenced/worshiped, accompanying acts and/or statements, relevant setting, and so on.

Yet while in Greco-Roman literature, the polytheistic character of such usage is reflected in the many gods and godlike humans being depicted as worthy recipients of a kind of worship through προσκύνησις that acknowledges and/or treats the figure as divine, this is not characteristic of Jewish literature. In the latter, the God of Israel is presented as the only legitimate recipient of such worship. Other so-called gods may receive such worship, but the general understanding is that they receive it illegitimately. In the rare cases where it might initially appear as though a human or angelic figure is depicted as a legitimate recipient of such worship, a closer examination of such instances ultimately suggests otherwise.

Yet interestingly, we find in some of the pseudepigraphal writings surveyed above that there is a descendant of Judah who is worthy of προσκύνησις since he will die for humans in wars visible and invisible, and will be an eternal king (*T. Reu.* 6:12); that the saints will one day render προσκύνησις to the king of heaven, who appeared on earth in the form of a man and as God in the flesh (*T. Benj.* 10:7–8); and that glory, honor, and προσκύνησις are due to the Father, the Son, and the Holy Spirit (*T. Ab.* 14:9 [B]). These are, clearly, later Christian passages that offer an exalted portrait of Christ Jesus in his reception of προσκύνησις much like other later Christian writings do (e.g., *Mart. Pol.* 17:3; *Ascen. Isa.* 9:27–32 [cf. Greek Legend 2:25, 40]; Justin, *Dial.* 63–64; *2 Apol.* 13:4). As we now turn our attention to the προσκύνησις of Jesus in the NT writings, we consider whether these depictions of an exalted Jesus receiving προσκύνησις in later Christian passages and writings might already be similarly present in the earliest Christian writings.

2

The Προσκύνησις of Jesus in the Gospel of Mark

In the Gospel of Mark, various acts of kneeling and prostration before Jesus during his earthly ministry signify his high regard among many of his contemporaries. Among those described approaching Jesus with such humble reverential postures are a leper seeking to be healed of his leprosy (Mark 1:40),[1] a synagogue official seeking healing for his terminally ill daughter (5:22), a woman seeking to be healed of her long-term hemorrhage (5:33), a Syrophoenician woman seeking an exorcism for her demon-possessed daughter (7:25), and a man seeking wisdom on inheriting eternal life (10:17). It is clear from the contexts that Jesus typically receives such reverence as a powerful healer and a wise teacher. Yet while in such instances, Mark uses a variety of synonymous terms and phrases to depict the humble posture of these suppliants (γονυπετῶν; πίπτει πρὸς τοὺς πόδας; προσέπεσεν; προσέπεσεν πρὸς τοὺς πόδας; γονυπετήσας), in two unique instances, he uses προσκυνέω for a demoniac's reverence of Jesus (5:6) and for a group of Roman soldiers' mock obeisance of Jesus (15:19), neither of which appears to be akin to the examples above of reverence of Jesus as healer and teacher. Through a careful examination of these two προσκύνησις passages in Mark, I will argue that there are indeed distinctive nuances in the reverence extended to Jesus through Mark's use of προσκυνέω—particularly, that Jesus is reverenced as a mighty sovereign—and that Mark may even be using this term as one small part of his larger christological portrait of Jesus as a transcendent figure uniquely related to God.

A. The Προσκύνησις of Jesus by the Gerasene demoniac

When Jesus enters into Gentile territory in Mark 5, he is confronted by a demon-possessed man who sees Jesus from afar, runs to him, and renders him προσκύνησις (καὶ ἰδὼν τὸν Ἰησοῦν ἀπὸ μακρόθεν ἔδραμεν καὶ προσεκύνησεν αὐτῷ[2] [5:6]). This demoniac's plight is described in great detail: he lives among the tombs, cries aloud day and night, gashes himself with stones, and frequently breaks through the chains by

---

[1] Here, however, the relevant term of reverence (γονυπετῶν) is textually uncertain, present in some key manuscripts (ℵ A C) but lacking in others (B D W).
[2] αὐτῷ: ℵ D K W et al. / αὐτόν: A B C L et al.

which others attempted to subdue him (5:3–5). Much like Jesus's encounter with the demon-possessed man in the Capernaum synagogue (1:21–28), in 5:7, the Gerasene demoniac questions Jesus's involvement with him (τί ἐμοὶ καὶ σοί [cf. 1:24]), addresses Jesus with a lofty title, "Son of the Most High God" (cf. 1:24, where the demoniac calls Jesus "the Holy One of God"), and begs Jesus not to torment him (cf. 1:24, where the demoniac asks Jesus, "Have you come to destroy us?"). Yet here, Jesus's exchange with the demonic goes much further than his prior demonic encounter. He asks for the demon's name, and the demon replies, "Legion is my name, for we are many" (5:9). It becomes clear from this response and from what follows that the man is possessed by a multitude of demons. The demonic horde urges Jesus not to expel them from the region but rather to send them into the nearby herd of pigs (5:10–12). When Jesus grants this request, the demons come out of the man and enter the pigs, which rush into the sea and drown (5:13). The account concludes with the polar responses to the incident—the residents urge Jesus to leave while the healed demoniac urges Jesus to let him accompany him—and the former demoniac's proclamation of the incident in the wider Gentile regions (5:14–20).

It is not immediately clear here if it is the man or the demon within him who is responsible for the act of προσκύνησις. On the one hand, since it is slightly odd that the demoniac would willingly run toward Jesus only to express a desire to be left alone, it is possible that such conflicted behavior is an indication of an internal struggle between the demons who seek to avoid Jesus and the man who seeks help from Jesus to be delivered from the demonic. This may suggest that it is the man who runs to Jesus and does προσκύνησις before him, much like the suppliants mentioned above who similarly assume humble postures in seeking his help.[3] On the other hand, all other actions (5:3–5) and speech (5:7–12) are clearly attributable to the demonic, thus emphasizing the dominance, if not the complete control, of these demons over the man.[4] While it may seem somewhat paradoxical for the demons to behave both aggressively and defensively toward Jesus, it is perhaps not very different from other details in this interaction, such as the demons' offensive maneuver of "adjuring" (ὁρκίζω) Jesus,[5] which is, however, filled out by a defensive plea to not be tormented (5:7).[6] And although the προσκύνησις of the Gerasene demoniac may be likened to the lowly postures of various suppliants in Mark, the overall portrayal more closely corresponds to Mark's general summary of Jesus's encounters with demonic spirits in 3:11. Here it is stated that whenever the demons saw Jesus, they would fall down before

---

[3] Robert H. Stein seems to prefer this interpretive option (*Mark* [BECNT; Grand Rapids: Baker Academic, 2008], 253).

[4] Joel Marcus notes how Mark's description of this demon-possessed man as being ἄνθρωπος ἐν πνεύματι ἀκαθάρτῳ (lit. "a man *in* an unclean spirit"; cf. 1:23) suggests "the man has been swallowed up by his possessing spirit" (*Mark 1-8: A New Translation with Introduction and Commentary* [AB 27; New York: Doubleday, 2000], 342).

[5] Commentators often note that ὁρκίζω is being used here in a technical exorcistic sense (see, for example, Marcus, *Mark*, 344). Ironically, it is here the demon rather than the exorcist who employs such terminology in an effort to gain control over Jesus (cf. R. T. France, *The Gospel of Mark: A Commentary on the Greek Text* [NIGTC; Grand Rapids: Eerdmans, 2002], 228).

[6] See also Marcus, *Mark*, 350–51; France, *Mark*, 227–28.

him and cry out, "You are the Son of God!"[7] In Mark 5, we see a more specific instance of this general description as the Gerasene demoniac similarly falls in προσκύνησις before Jesus (5:6) and acknowledges his divine sonship (5:7). It is best to conclude, then, that this act of προσκύνησις before Jesus is initiated by the demon(s).[8]

In view of the dialogue that takes place between Jesus and the demonic spirits, it is clear that they concede Jesus's superiority over them. They must plead with Jesus that he would not torment them, that he would not send them out of the region, and that he would grant them permission to find alternative hosts. Whatever futile attempts they may make to gain an upper hand or to negotiate terms with Jesus, they are ultimately subject to his will. In stark contrast to the man whom the demons inhabit, whose self-destructive behavior and preternatural strength underscore the demons' overwhelming power over him and over all who unsuccessfully tried to restrain him, the demons prove to be utterly impotent in their dealings with Jesus. Thus, the demons' προσκύνησις before Jesus is correspondingly an expression of their recognition of his unique superiority over them.

B. The Προσκύνησις of Jesus by the Roman soldiers

Following Jesus's hearing before Pilate (15:1–15) and leading into his execution (15:21–32), Jesus is subjected to ridicule and mistreatment at the hands of Pilate's soldiers (15:16–20). As is clear from both the wider context and the immediate context, the focus is on Jesus's regal status as "King of the Jews" (15:2, 9, 12, 18, 26, 32), a seditious claim in Jesus's case as far as Rome and its governing authorities are concerned. It is this treasonous claim that results in his conviction and crucifixion, and that here incites the soldiers' derision. In mock fashion, they dress him up in the garb of royalty by clothing him in purple and setting a crown of thorns on his head (15:17), hail him as King of the Jews (15:18), and kneel in προσκύνησις before him (τιθέντες τὰ γόνατα προσεκύνουν αὐτῷ), all the while beating him and spitting on him (15:19). Although done in sport, the soldiers' προσκύνησις of Jesus is clearly intended as a gesture of homage befitting a kingly figure.

C. The significance of the Προσκύνησις of Jesus in Mark

While some have noted this distinctive use of προσκυνέω for the reverence of Jesus in Mark, there are different views regarding its precise significance. One possibility, put forward by Johannes Horst, is that προσκυνέω is being used pejoratively as a reflection

---

[7] The lack of mention of human hosts in 3:11, while certainly implied, makes it abundantly clear that the activity described here is ultimately attributed to demons.

[8] So also Adela Yarbro Collins, *Mark: A Commentary* (Hermeneia; Minneapolis: Fortress, 2007), 267; Ben Witherington, *The Gospel of Mark: A Socio-Rhetorical Commentary* (Grand Rapids: Eerdmans, 2001), 181; Horst, *Proskynein*, 239. Many commentators seem less inclined to specify clearly whether the Gerasene demoniac's προσκύνησις is ultimately initiated by the man or the demon(s).

of "heidnisch-hellenistischer Religionsübung." Such pagan reverence extended to Jesus is unwelcome and is largely differentiated from those instances where Mark uses other terms, such as πίπτω and προσπίπτω, for the appropriate reverence given to Jesus by those who genuinely seek God's help through him.[9] However, while the προσκύνησις by the Gerasene demoniac and the soldiers is certainly not equivalent to the positive examples of deference motivated by true faith in Jesus, it is not clear that it is cast in the kind of thoroughly negative light that Horst attributed to it. For instance, in the case of the προσκύνησις by the Gerasene demoniac, the fact that Mark stresses elsewhere that the demons know who Jesus is (1:24, 34; 3:11–12) suggests the προσκύνησις this figure extends to Jesus correspondingly reflects the right response to the person of Jesus and is therefore in some sense to be understood positively.

Another more likely possibility is that Mark exploits the political connotations associated with the term. This is clearly demonstrable in the case of 15:19 and may indeed be so in the case of 5:6 as well, as a number of interpreters contend that the Gerasene demoniac account is filled with political and military imagery. One of the most commonly noted elements to this effect is the name "Legion" (λεγιών) attributed to the demon(s). As a loanword from the Latin *legio* (a term for a Roman military unit numbering upward of six thousand soldiers),[10] λεγιών may very well have militaristic overtones here. Others have further argued for militaristic nuances to several terms, including ἀποστέλλω (5:10), ἀγέλη (5:11, 13), ἐπιτρέπω (5:13), and ὁρμάω (5:13).[11] Hence, Jesus is portrayed as a military superior over the demonic "troops" (ἀγέλη), who request not to be "dispatched" (ἀποστείλῃ) from the region, and who subsequently submit to Jesus's "military order" (ἐπέτρεψεν) as they "charge" (ὥρμησεν) into the sea. Also along these lines, some consider the demons' request not to be sent out from the region to be uncharacteristic of exorcisms, suggesting instead that such language evokes the political image of a struggle to maintain territorial occupation.[12] The demoniac's προσκύνησις of Jesus, then, may likewise be politically charged and may suggest the demons' subjection to Jesus as a ruler figure.

The significance of such militaristic and political imagery, however, is a disputed issue among scholars. Many find in these and other clues an anti-Roman polemic.[13] Λεγιών, it is argued, is a highly specific term connoting not just military might and massiveness in general, but that of the Romans, signaling an unmistakable

---

[9] Horst, *Proskynein*, 240.
[10] Herbert Preisker, "λεγιών," *TDNT* 4:68.
[11] J. Duncan M. Derrett, "Contributions to the Study of the Gerasene Demoniac," *JSNT* 3 (1979): 5–6.
[12] Joshua Garroway, "The Invasion of a Mustard Seed: A Reading of Mark 5.1-20," *JSNT* 32 (2009): 64.
[13] Ched Myers, *Binding the Strong Man: A Political Reading of Mark's Story of Jesus* (Maryknoll, NY: Orbis Books, 1988), 190–94; Gerd Theissen, *The Gospels in Context: Social and Political History in the Synoptic Tradition* (Edinburgh: T&T Clark, 1992), 109–11; Richard A. Horsley, *Hearing the Whole Story: The Politics of Plot in Mark's Gospel* (Louisville: Westminster John Knox, 2001), 140–48; Richard Dormandy, "The Expulsion of Legion: A Political Reading of Mark 5:1-20," *ExpTim* 111 (2000): 335–37; Stephen D. Moore, *Empire and Apocalypse: Postcolonialism and the New Testament* (BMW 12; Sheffield: Sheffield Phoenix, 2006), 24–29; Garroway, "Invasion," 60–68; Hans Leander, *Discourses of Empire: The Gospel of Mark from a Postcolonial Perspective* (SemeiaSt 71; Atlanta: Society of Biblical Literature, 2013), 201–19 (see also pp. 201–02, n. 1, where Leander provides a fuller list of proponents).

identification of the demonic forces with Roman imperial power.¹⁴ The presence of swine is often seen as a link to the tenth legion, Legio X Fretensis, stationed in the Decapolis region at the time, as it had on its standards an image of a wild boar.¹⁵ The possessed man's deranged, unruly behavior is interpreted either as representing Rome's oppressive forces¹⁶ or as being triggered by it.¹⁷ Thus, it is ultimately the Romans who symbolically confront Jesus and who strive to remain in the region, yet in the end they are overpowered and driven out by Jesus. If the demonic legion represents Rome, then it may be that here in 5:6 and later in 15:19, Mark's portrayal of both Legion and the Roman auxiliary soldiers rendering προσκύνησις to Jesus conveys the message that Jesus is the true emperor over against Caesar.¹⁸

Others, while affirming some measure of military and political nuancing to the Gerasene demoniac account, remain largely unconvinced of any Markan opposition to Rome.¹⁹ The contention that the high specificity of the term λεγιών at the time was such that it could only be understood as a reference to the Roman military is perhaps too overconfident. Although minimal, there is nevertheless some evidence contemporary with and even prior to Mark's Gospel that the term could be used for ideas associated with the Roman legion, such as numerousness and military might, without specifically denoting the Roman legion itself.²⁰ It is often noted as well that the general lack of clear opposition to Rome elsewhere in Mark speaks against an anti-Roman polemic in Mark's Gerasene demoniac account.²¹

However one decides the place of Rome here, it is important that the spiritual aspects of this account not be relegated to the periphery.²² The initial description of the demoniac as one whom "no one was able to bind" (οὐδεὶς ἐδύνατο αὐτὸν δῆσαι [5:3]; see also δεδέσθαι [5:4]), and whom "no one was strong enough" (οὐδεὶς ἴσχυεν) to subdue (5:4), is reminiscent of 3:27, where Jesus speaks parabolically of binding

---

[14] Garroway, "Invasion," 60–63; Leander, *Discourses*, 203–6.
[15] Theissen, *Gospels*, 110; Leander, *Discourses*, 206–7; Garroway, "Invasion," 65.
[16] Leander, *Discourses*, 215; Garroway, "Invasion," 64.
[17] Myers, *Binding*, 192–93; Horsley, *Hearing*, 140, 144–45.
[18] On this and Mark's use of προσκυνέω as a technical term for political homage rendered to the Roman emperor, see esp. Thomas Witulski, "Jesus und der Kaiser: Das Ritual der *Proskynesis*," in *Christ and the Emperor: The Gospel Evidence* (BTS 20; Leuven: Peeters, 2014), 104–35.
[19] Robert H. Gundry, *Mark: A Commentary on His Apology for the Cross* (Grand Rapids: Eerdmans, 1993), 260–61; Witherington, *Mark*, 183; Collins, *Mark*, 269–70; Stein, *Mark*, 255; Graham H. Twelftree, *In the Name of Jesus: Exorcism among Early Christians* (Grand Rapids: Baker Academic, 2007), 108–11; Elizabeth E. Shively, "Characterizing the Non-Human: Satan in the Gospel of Mark," in *Character Studies and the Gospel of Mark* (ed. Christopher W. Skinner and Matthew Ryan Hauge; LNTS 483; London: Bloomsbury T&T Clark, 2014), 143; Christopher M. Tuckett, "Christ and the Emperor: Some Reflections on Method and Methodological Issues Illustrated from the Gospel of Mark," in *Christ and the Emperor: The Gospel Evidence* (BTS 20; Leuven: Peeters, 2014), 187–89, 198.
[20] See, for example, the use of the Latin *legio* in Pliny the Elder (23/24–79 C.E.) for "legions (i.e., large numbers) of slaves" (*Nat.* 33.26) and in Plautus (ca. 254–184 B.C.E.) for "legions" (i.e., large numbers) of supporters (*Cas.* 50), noted by Twelftree, *Name*, 108–09.
[21] See Collins, *Mark*, 269; Shively, "Characterizing," 143; Tuckett, "Christ," 200–01.
[22] See Gregory David Wiebe, "The Demonic Phenomena of Mark's 'Legion': Evaluating Postcolonial Understandings of Demon Possession," in *Exegesis in the Making: Postcolonialism and New Testament Studies* (ed. Anna Runesson; BibInt 103; Leiden: Brill, 2011), 186–212.

the strong man, Satan: "But no one is able (δύναται οὐδεὶς) to enter the house of the strong man (ἰσχυροῦ) and plunder his goods, unless he first binds the strong man (τὸν ἰσχυρὸν δήσῃ)." These linguistic and thematic links indicate that in Mark's view, Satan is the ultimate source of the Gerasene demoniac's power.[23] Moreover, this strong man parable appears in the context of an accusation regarding the satanic source of Jesus's exorcistic powers, which Jesus dismisses in his depiction of Satan as a ruler over a kingdom (3:24; cf. 3:22, where Satan/Beelzebul is called "ruler of the demons") whom he comes to overpower (3:22–27). Here, we see Mark's overall understanding of the nature of Jesus's exorcisms, and while it is cast in political and military terms—as Jesus is depicted waging war with Satan, the ruler of demons, and plundering his goods—there is no clear, specific reference to Rome. It may be, then, that the military and political language in the Gerasene demoniac account is due more to Mark's conception of Jesus involved in a cosmic war with Satan and his army of demons than to an anti-Roman polemic.[24] Thus, while the legion of demons display the power of their commander, Satan, the strong man whom no ordinary human is strong enough to bind, they are no match for Jesus, the stronger one (cf. 1:7) who shows through his exorcisms that he is capable of binding the strong man Satan and plundering his goods (i.e., delivering humans from demonic possession).[25]

It may very well be, then, that, as in 15:19, the Gerasene demoniac's προσκύνησις of Jesus is cast in political terms, as the army of demons within the human host sees in Jesus a hostile invader of its dominion capable of destroying it. But since it is ultimately the demonic realm that submits to Jesus in προσκύνησις, Jesus is depicted not merely as one who rivals Caesar as true ruler[26] but as one who rivals Satan, the ruler of the demons, a far more formidable superpower. This also intensifies the contrast between the two scenes of προσκύνησις directed to Jesus—whereas mere humans presumptuously scoff at the idea of Jesus's competition with the Roman emperor in their mock obeisance, supernatural entities show by their obeisance that they take seriously the threat Jesus poses to them and to their ruler, Satan.

So too is the contrast between the titles ascribed to Jesus in the act of προσκύνησις noteworthy. Whereas the soldiers jokingly kneel in προσκύνησις before Jesus as "King of the Jews" (15:18–19), the demons do προσκύνησις before Jesus as "Son of the Most High God" (5:6–7; cf. 3:11). This latter designation is quite striking, especially in view of the fact that whereas the vast majority of human characters in Mark acknowledge and/or address Jesus by various, often only partially adequate titles (though in some

---

[23] Marcus, *Mark*, 343.
[24] Even granting a reference to Rome, since several Jewish and Christian texts describe spiritual forces aligned with, and even controlling, earthly adversaries, hence posing the greater threat (Dan 10:13, 20–21; 1QS III, 20ff; 1QM *passim*; *1 En.* 54:4–6; *Jub.* 10:1–11; 48:1–19; *T. Sim.* 6:6; *T. Dan* 5:10–11; Eph 6:12; Rev 13:1–18; 16:13–14; 19:11–20:3; 20:7–10), it is more likely that Mark as well identifies and stresses spiritual forces as the ultimate threat. Cf. Rikki E. Watts, *Isaiah's New Exodus in Mark* (Grand Rapids: Baker Academic, 2000), 163.
[25] Cf. Shively, "Characterizing," 142–43.
[26] Cf. Witulski, "Jesus," 134–35.

instances wholly inadequate),[27] the acknowledgment of Jesus as God's Son is, apart from one climactic exception (15:39), attributed solely to those who belong to the supernatural realm.[28] Thus, along with God himself who affirms Jesus as his Son (1:11; 9:7), the demons, who as Mark points out know who Jesus is (1:24, 34; 3:11–12), also perceive this mysterious aspect of his identity (3:11–12; 5:7).[29] What does it mean for Jesus to be the Son of God in Mark, and what is it that the demons know about Jesus as the Son of God that presumably compels them to respond with προσκύνησις?

Following what William Wrede appears to have advocated in primitive form, Rudolf Bultmann and others understood Jesus's divine sonship in Mark in terms of the so-called Hellenistic concept of the *theios anēr* ("divine man").[30] It is as a typical *theios anēr*, so the explanation goes, that Jesus is able to perform miracles, impart great wisdom, foretell the future, and so on. In Mark, Jesus is transformed from a mere human being into this supernatural "divine-man" figure when he receives the Spirit at his baptism, thus becoming at that moment, as the divine voice declares, the Son of God.[31] As Wrede explained, it is as this transformed superhuman Son of God that the demons come to recognize Jesus: "The object of [the demons'] knowledge is equally supernatural; it is not the human Jesus as such, but the supernatural Jesus equipped with the *pneuma*—the Son of God."[32] The use of προσκυνέω for the Gerasene demoniac's reverence of Jesus as the Son of the Most High God may thus be reflective of the demons' special insight into Jesus's supernatural character.

Yet a number of scholars have taken issue with this notion of a *theios anēr* concept, arguing that the evidence does not support the kind of well-defined specificity that its proponents seem to attribute to it, leading to serious doubts regarding its usefulness as a category for explaining Mark's Christology, including his Son-of-God concept.[33]

---

[27] For example, Teacher (4:38; 5:35; 9:17, 38; 10:17, 20, 35; 12:14, 19, 32; 13:1); Rabbi (9:5; 10:51; 11:21; 14:45); King of the Jews/Israel (15:9, 12, 18, 26, 32 [all mock]); Christ (8:29; 15:32 [mock]); Sir/Lord (7:28); Son of David (10:47, 48); Prophet, Elijah, or John the Baptist (6:14–16; 8:28).

[28] And, quite possibly, to the evangelist himself (1:1), depending on the authenticity of the longer reading of the Gospel's incipit (Ἀρχὴ τοῦ εὐαγγελίου Ἰησοῦ Χριστοῦ [υἱοῦ θεοῦ]). For a recent defense of this longer reading, see Tommy Wasserman, "The 'Son of God' Was in the Beginning (Mark 1:1)," *JTS* 62 (2011): 20–50.

[29] Jesus himself is also aware of his divine sonship (8:38; 12:6; 13:32; 14:61–62).

[30] Rudolf Bultmann, *Theology of the New Testament* (trans. Kendrick Grobel; vol. 1; London: SCM, 1952), 129–31; Siegfried Schulz, *Die Stunde der Botschaft: Einführung in die Theologie der vier Evangelisten* (Hamburg: Furche, 1967), 54–59, 64–79; Ferdinand Hahn, *The Titles of Jesus in Christology: Their History in Early Christianity* (trans. Harold Knight and George Ogg; London: Lutterworth, 1969), 288–99. Cf. William Wrede, *The Messianic Secret* (trans. J. C. G. Greig; Cambridge: James Clark, 1971; 1st Germ. ed., 1901), 72–79.

[31] Wrede, *Messianic*, 73; Bultmann, *Theology*, 131; Schulz, *Stunde*, 55; Hahn, *Titles*, 338–39.

[32] Wrede, *Messianic*, 25.

[33] Wülfing von Martitz, "υἱός," *TDNT* 8:338–40; Carl R. Holladay, *Theios Aner in Hellenistic-Judaism: A Critique of the Use of This Category in New Testament Christology* (SBLDS 40; Missoula, MT: Scholars Press, 1977); Otto Betz, "The Concept of the So-Called 'Divine-Man' in Mark's Christology," in *Studies in New Testament and Early Christian Literature: Essays in Honor of Allen P. Wikgren* (ed. David E. Aune; NovTSup 33; Leiden: Brill, 1972), 229–40; Jack Dean Kingsbury, "The 'Divine Man' as the Key to Mark's Christology—The End of an Era?" *Int* 35 (1981): 243–57; Hengel, *Son*, 31.

Other scholars interpret Jesus's divine sonship against a Jewish background. For some, the emphasis is placed on Jesus as the suffering, righteous, and obedient son.[34] Just as the people of Israel were called to obedience to God as his son(s) (e.g., Deut 14:1ff; 32:18–20; Isa 1:2; Jer 3:19; Mal 1:6; cf. Sir 4:10) even in the face of suffering (Wis 2:12–20), so Jesus proves to be God's true son in this respect. Lewis Hay pointed out that in the many passages in Mark where Jesus's divine sonship is concerned, it is frequently tied to his faithful obedience to God even to the point of suffering and death. For instance, the one declared to be God's Son at his transfiguration (9:7) obediently submits to God's will to suffer and die (9:9);[35] Jesus parabolically refers to himself as God's obedient Son put to death by the wicked tenants of God's vineyard (12:1–9); and at the crucifixion, the centurion affirms Jesus's divine sonship as he fulfills God's will to be subject to death (15:39).[36]

For others, the emphasis is placed on Jesus's royal messianic status.[37] The OT spoke of the king of Israel as God's son (2 Sam 7:14; Pss 2:7; cf. 89:26–27). Such texts and the divine sonship language contained within them were interpreted messianically in both Jewish and Christian circles.[38] So too in Mark, then, at Jesus's baptism (as well as at his transfiguration [cf. Mark 9:7]), when the divine voice says to him in the words of the royal psalm (Ps 2:7), "You are my Son" (Mark 1:11), the likely implication is that this language is being applied to Jesus to convey his messianic status.[39] Also, the fact that this designation for Jesus is placed in apposition to χριστός (1:1; 14:62)—much like the way the titles "Son of David" and "King of the Jews/Israel" are also directly linked with χριστός (12:35; 15:32)—signifies that they all function as messianic titles.[40] It is again possible as well to see in Jesus's royal messianic identity as the Son of God an implicit challenge to the Roman emperor's claims to be the sovereign of the world as *divi filius* or θεοῦ υἱός.[41]

---

[34] Lewis S. Hay, "The Son-of-God Christology in Mark," *JBR* 32 (1964): 106–14; Dieter Lührmann, *Das Markusevangelium* (HNT 3; Tübingen: Mohr Siebeck, 1987), 38–40. Cf. Joachim Bieneck, *Sohn Gottes als Christusbezeichnung der Synoptiker* (ATANT 21; Zurich: Zwingli-Verlag, 1951). For Bieneck, Jesus's divine sonship is indeed to be understood in terms of his obedience to God (58–69), but it is also indicative of his transcendence (45–57).

[35] Although there is no explicit mention here of Jesus's obedience and suffering, Hay inferred it from Jesus's reference to his resurrection from death ("Son-of-God," 110, n. 17).

[36] Hay, "Son-of-God," 108–10.

[37] Donald Juel, *Messiah and Temple: The Trial of Jesus in the Gospel of Mark* (SBLDS 31; Missoula, MT: Scholars Press, 1977), 79–84, 108–14; Jack Dean Kingsbury, *The Christology of Mark's Gospel* (Philadelphia, PA: Fortress, 1983), 55–156; Adela Yarbro Collins, "Mark and His Readers: The Son of God among Jews," *HTR* 92 (1999): 393–408; Herbert W. Bateman, "Defining the Titles 'Christ' and 'Son of God' in Mark's Narrative Presentation of Jesus," *JETS* 50 (2007): 537–59.

[38] 4Q174 1 I, 10–12; Acts 13:33; Heb 1:5; cf. *1 En.* 105:2; *4 Ezra* 7:28–29; 13:32, 37, 52; 14:9. Although debated, the one who is called "son of God" and "son of the Most High" in 4Q246 may also be a messianic figure; cf. Luke 1:32–35 (see John J. Collins, *The Scepter and the Star: Messianism in Light of the Dead Sea Scrolls* [2nd ed.; Grand Rapids: Eerdmans, 2010], 171–88).

[39] Kingsbury, *Christology*, 65–66, 99–100; Collins, *Mark*, 150, 425–26; Bateman, "Defining," 546–50; France, *Mark*, 80, 355; Stein, *Mark*, 59, 418.

[40] Kingsbury, *Christology*, 55, 161.

[41] See Craig A. Evans, *Mark 8:27–16:20* (WBC 34B; Nashville: Thomas Nelson, 2001), lxxxi–lxxxiv, lxxxix–xci; Adela Yarbro Collins, "Mark and His Readers: The Son of God among Greeks and Romans," *HTR* 93 (2000): 94–96; Michael Peppard, *The Son of God in the Roman World: Divine*

Yet even here, as helpful as these explanations are, they offer only partial answers and do not exhaust the full significance of what it means for Jesus to be the Son of God in Mark. With regard to the view that Jesus's divine sonship primarily concerns his obedience and suffering, there are some Son-of-God passages that do not evoke such connotations, such as (interestingly) those where the demons acknowledge Jesus as the Son of God (3:11; 5:7).[42] These passages give no hint of Jesus's suffering or even of his obedience. Instead, the focus is on his power and authority over the demons, who fall before him at the very sight of him (3:11; 5:6) and beg him not to torment them (5:7). The impression from these texts is that it is in his capacity as Son of God that he has such power and authority over demons, and thus it is this powerful and authoritative (rather than suffering and obedient) Son of God that the demons acknowledge. In other Son-of-God passages, though there may be some connections with suffering and obedience in the contexts, the more direct and obvious associations are with Jesus's transcendence. For instance, in the case of the transfiguration, while Jesus's reference to his resurrection from death (9:9) certainly implies his obedience to God's will to suffer, his divine sonship is more closely tied to his loftiness, since it is as God's Son that he appears to his disciples in radiant splendor (9:2–3), and it is on the basis of his divine sonship that the disciples are instructed to listen to him: "This is my beloved Son; listen to him" (9:7). Jesus is God's Son not only as one who obeys God but also as one who himself is to be obeyed. Similarly, at his hearing before the Jewish authorities, while it is true in a broad sense that Jesus shows himself to be God's obedient Son submitting himself to suffering and death (14:64–65), his claim to divine sonship here is more closely linked to his provocative claim to transcendent status alongside God (14:61–62). Thus, while some passages in Mark may indeed disclose Jesus's divine sonship in terms of suffering and obedience, this is certainly not the only significance attributed to Jesus's identity as the Son of God. Again, in the Gerasene demoniac account, the emphasis is on the demons' recognition of Jesus's *superior*, not lowly, status as the Son of God.

Similarly, while it is agreed that "Son of God" is a messianic designation for Jesus, given that it is only one among others (e.g., "Christ," "Son of David," "King of the Jews/Israel") and is in some sense differentiated from these, these things suggest it discloses unique facets of Jesus's identity. Jack Kingsbury recognizes this and argues that what "Son of God" captures that these other messianic designations do not is Jesus's destiny to be a crucified and resurrected messiah.[43] He does indeed make a strong case that it is in this sense that while the other messianic titles are certainly true of Jesus's messianic identity, they at the same time prove to be insufficient. Thus, although Peter's confession of Jesus as "the Christ" is correct, since it is limited to his understanding of

---

Sonship in Its Social and Political Context (Oxford: Oxford University Press, 2011), 86–131 (esp. pp. 130–31). With regard to the Gerasene demoniac account, Witulski sees an anti-imperial polemic in Jesus's designation as "Son of the Most High God"—whereas the reigning emperor is son of several deified emperors, Jesus is son of the most high and only true God ("Jesus," 123–24).

[42] Hay himself acknowledged this ("Son-of-God," 108), but simply set these passages aside and moved on to discuss the many passages where these themes do appear.
[43] Kingsbury, *Christology*, 89–155.

Jesus in his preaching, teaching and wonder-working ministry and does not embrace his passion and resurrection, it is only partially adequate (8:27–33). Likewise, although Bartimaeus correctly acknowledges Jesus as "Son of David" (10:47–48), Jesus himself later intimates that there is more to his messianic identity than this title conveys (12:35–37). And although Jesus responds affirmatively when Pilate asks if he is "the King of the Jews," his answer ("You say so") suggests this is only adequate in a qualified sense (15:2). Conversely, it is only at the moment of Jesus's death on the cross that a human character (other than Jesus) is portrayed aligning his perception of Jesus with that of God (1:11; 9:7) through his climactic acknowledgment of Jesus's divine sonship (15:39). Therefore, while through a progressive disclosure Jesus is indeed shown to be the royal Davidic Messiah-King, the full picture of Jesus's messianic identity can only be understood aright when it includes the acknowledgment of his death and resurrection, which is integrally tied to his identity as the Son of God.

Yet much like the messianic titles above in Kingsbury's assessment, such significance in Jesus's divine sonship may be correct, but only partially so. In their stress on "Son of God" as a messianic title for Jesus, both Kingsbury and Bateman seem to have overlooked and/or underestimated the way some divine sonship passages show Jesus not only to be much more than a human, earthly messiah but even to be one who is on a par with God.

Beginning with the clearest instance of this, at Jesus's hearing before the Sanhedrin (14:53–65), when the high priest asks Jesus, "Are you the Christ, the Son of the Blessed" (i.e., the Son of God), Jesus's reply ("I am, and you will see the Son of Man seated at the right hand of Power, and coming with the clouds of heaven.") moves the high priest to charge him with blasphemy and to sentence him to death (14:61–64). Due to differing views regarding some of the key details of this pericope, the significance of Jesus's status here is understood differently. For instance, Kingsbury seems to attribute the charge of blasphemy to Jesus's affirmation of being the messiah.[44] Yet while recent studies have shown that the Jewish understanding of blasphemy at the time was indeed fairly broad,[45] there is nevertheless no evidence that a claim to be the messiah was considered blasphemous in Judaism.[46]

Bateman appears to attribute the charge of blasphemy primarily to Jesus's assault on the Jewish authorities as one who will be exalted over them in heaven as their future judge. In his view, since other human figures in Jewish tradition could legitimately be exalted to places of heavenly honor without thereby attaining divine status or compromising monotheism, Jesus's comparable claims here would not have been interpreted as a claim to divinity per se. Thus, Jesus is considered guilty of blasphemy

---

[44] Kingsbury, *Christology*, 120, 124. Similarly, Juel, *Messiah*, 104–6.

[45] See Darrell L. Bock, *Blasphemy and Exaltation in Judaism and the Final Examination of Jesus* (WUNT 2/106; Tübingen: Mohr Siebeck, 1998), 30–112; Adela Yarbro Collins, "The Charge of Blasphemy in Mark 14.64," *JSNT* 26 (2004): 381–95; Evans, *Mark*, 453–55. Blasphemy could include various speeches and actions disrespecting God, his appointed leaders, his people, and his sanctuary.

[46] See Craig A. Evans, "In What Sense 'Blasphemy'? Jesus before Caiaphas in Mark 14:61–64," in *Society of Biblical Literature 1991 Seminar Papers* (SBLSP 30; Atlanta: Scholars Press, 1991), 215; Bock, *Blasphemy*, 230–31; Collins, "Charge," 398.

not for making claims that would imply his divinity, but for making claims that imply his authority over and right to challenge God's appointed leaders.[47] But while the latter point is not problematic, and may indeed be one aspect of the high priest's offense in Jesus's reply, the former almost certainly is. That is, it is doubtful that Jesus's response would only be interpreted as an affront to the Jewish authorities and not as a direct affront to God himself. Bateman's attempt to mitigate Jesus's exalted claims for himself in light of numerous other figures exalted in heaven overlooks important distinctions in the various ways these heavenly exaltations are portrayed in Jewish literature. In most cases, for instance, the texts do not depict a heavenly session beside God as Jesus claims for himself when he speaks of being "seated at the right hand of Power" (i.e., God).[48] Various figures, both human and angelic, may have thrones in heaven, but typically such thrones are spatially distanced from God and his throne, clearly signifying God's unique sovereignty.[49] Other figures may be spatially close to God, but they typically stand rather than sit in his presence, taking the posture of a servant.[50] Nor would the nature of Jesus's cloud riding likely be seen as unexceptional, for while a number of figures may *ascend* from earth to heaven via clouds,[51] Jesus describes himself *descending* from heaven to earth when he speaks first of his right-hand session beside God and then of "coming with the clouds of heaven," which is akin to the common OT motif of God riding the clouds as he descends from heaven to earth.[52] Thus, combining allusions to both Ps 110:1 and Dan 7:13 in his reply to the high priest, Jesus boldly applies the lofty language used to describe the exalted authority figures who appear beside God in these OT texts to himself in such a way that his self-proclaimed grandeur moves well beyond more common descriptions of heavenly exalted humans and approaches the kind of transcendence that is typically characteristic of God.

---

[47] Bateman, "Defining," 556–57.
[48] For much of what follows on this exceptional image of Jesus's enthronement beside God, see Richard Bauckham, "The Throne of God and the Worship of Jesus," in *The Jewish Roots of Christological Monotheism: Papers from the St. Andrews Conference on the Historical Origins of the Worship of Jesus* (ed. Carey C. Newman et al.; Leiden: Brill, 1999), 51–60.
[49] See, for example, *1 En.* 108:12; *2 En.* 20:1–3 (J); *T. Ab.* 11–13 (A); *T. Levi* 3:4–8; 5:1; *L.A.E.* 15:3; 47:3; Rev 4; *Ascen. Isa.* 7:13–10:6; 11:32–33. The few exceptional cases are less remarkable than is sometimes thought. In *2 En.* 24:1 (J), God invites Enoch to sit at his left hand but only temporarily. Ultimately, he is made to *stand* before God forever (*2 En.* 67:2). In *T. Job* 33:3, with regard to Job's heavenly throne, it is best to understand ἡ τούτου δόξα καὶ ἡ εὐπρέπεια ἐκ δεξιῶν τοῦ πατρός as signifying that its glory and majesty *come from* the right hand of God (Bock, *Blasphemy*, 160). And in Ezek. Trag. 74–76, it is clear from the context that Moses's enthronement on God's throne is meant to be understood figuratively (see discussion on pp. 136–37 below). The only two relevant contemporary parallels to Jesus's heavenly session alongside God are those of the Enochic Son of Man and divine Wisdom, who are both depicted sharing a seat with God on the divine "throne of glory" (*1 En.* 45:3; 51:3; 55:4; 61:8; 62:2–5; 69:29; Wis 9:4, 10; *1 En.* 84:2–3[?]).
[50] For example, 1 Kgs 22:19; Dan 7:10; 4 Macc 17:18; *1 En.* 14:22; 39:12–40:1; 47:3; 60:2; *2 En.* 21:1; 4 Ezra 8:21; *2 Bar.* 21:6; 48:10; *T. Ab.* 7:11; 8:1; 9:7 (A); Luke 1:19; Rev 7:11; 8:2.
[51] For example, Enoch (*1 En.* 14:8; *2 En.* 3:1 [J]); Abraham (*T. Ab.* 10:1 [A]; 8:3 [B]); Christians (1 Thess 4:17); the Two Witnesses (Rev 11:12).
[52] For example, Exod 13:21; 24:16; 34:5; Lev 16:2; Num 11:25; 14:14; Deut 1:33; 1 Kgs 8:10–11; Ps 104:3; Isa 19:1; Ezek 1:4 (see also 2 Macc 2:8; *T. Job* 42:1). For this observation, see Daniel Johansson, "Jesus and God in the Gospel of Mark: Unity and Distinction" (PhD diss., University of Edinburgh, 2011), 145–46, esp. n. 29. Significantly, the messianic figure of *4 Ezra* 13 does not descend from heaven to earth in his cloud riding (Johansson, "Jesus," 155, n. 86).

A detailed survey of the various types of blasphemy in the OT and early Jewish literature leads both Adela Yarbro Collins and Darrell Bock to conclude that Jesus's claims approximate Caligula's claims to deity and a governor of Egypt's claims to godlike power, both of which Philo regards as blasphemies against God for likening mere humans to God (*Legat.* 353–57, 367–68; *Somn.* 2.123–32).[53] It is possible that since the Enochic Son of Man in the *Similitudes of Enoch* provides evidence that some Jews at the time contemplated the notion of an exceptionally exalted figure enthroned with God, it is not the notion of having such an exalted position itself that constitutes Jesus's blasphemy but rather his claim as a living human to arrogate such a status to himself.[54] On the other hand, other Jews may have taken strict exception to such a highly exalted position next to God for any figure. According to rabbinic tradition, Rabbi Akiba (early second century C.E.) was sternly rebuked by his contemporary, Rabbi Yose, and charged with profaning the Shekinah for supposing that the plural "thrones" of Dan 7:9 envisage one throne for God and another for David (i.e., the messiah) seated beside God (*b. Sanh.* 38b).[55] Whether the Sanhedrin would have taken qualified exception to Jesus's exalted status as a contemporary living human, or full exception to such a status attributed to any figure, Bock, Evans, and Collins all agree that the offense lies in Jesus's claim to have a share in God's rule, authority, and power, thereby encroaching upon the uniqueness of God.[56] Bock ultimately concludes that Jesus's reply was regarded as blasphemous on two levels: it was, as Bateman would agree, an offense to the Jewish authorities for implying his authority to be their future judge, but it was also, and probably foremost, an offense to God for implying he could do so as one who participates in God's cosmic rule and authority.[57] It is hard to imagine that such claims would not have been understood by the Jewish authorities as a claim to divine status.

So then, when the high priest asks Jesus if he is the Christ, the Son of God, he not only affirms this (ἐγώ εἰμι[58]) but goes on to explain the profound significance of this aspect of his identity. It is as the Son of God that Jesus has this exceptional privilege to participate in God's cosmic rule and authority.[59] So while the juxtaposition of "Son of

---

[53] Collins, "Charge," 387–89, 399–401; Bock, *Blasphemy*, 203.
[54] Bock, *Blasphemy*, 202; Collins, "Charge," 399.
[55] Evans, *Mark*, 456.
[56] Bock, *Blasphemy*, 203–6; Evans, *Mark*, 456–57; Collins, "Charge," 401. Cf. the blasphemy charge in Mark 2:7. On this passage, see Daniel Johansson, "'Who Can Forgive Sins but God Alone?' Human and Angelic Agents, and Divine Forgiveness in Early Judaism," *JSNT* 33 (2011): 351–74.
[57] Bock, *Blasphemy*, 236. So too Evans, *Mark*, 457. Collins, "Charge," 399, disputes the notion that Jesus implicitly claims to return as judge. Thus, in her view, Jesus's blasphemy essentially constitutes a direct affront to God alone.
[58] In light of the use of ἐγώ εἰμι as an allusion to the OT divine self-declaration in Jesus's sea-walking miracle (6:50) as a way of uniquely identifying Jesus with God (see Johansson, "Jesus," 113–16), it is possible that its use here has a similar function so that "Jesus's answer is on a deeper level an affirmation of his divine status!" (Larry W. Hurtado, *Mark* [NIBC; Peabody, MA: Hendrickson, 1989], 254).
[59] Although it is unlikely that the high priest's question of Jesus's identification as "the Christ, the Son of God" was *his* way of specifying whether Jesus considered himself to be a divine messiah—as opposed to a priestly messiah (Messiah, son of Aaron) or a royal "restorative" messiah (Messiah, son of David)—as Joel Marcus argues ("Mark 14:61: 'Are You the Messiah-Son-of-God?," *NovT* 31 [1989]: 125–41), it is nevertheless essentially how Jesus answers the question. It is only unwittingly that the high priest comes to ask precisely the right question to get at the heart of what it means for Jesus to be "the Christ, the Son of God."

God" with "Christ" certainly shows that it is a messianic designation as Kingsbury and Bateman argue, Jesus's provocative statement and the high priest's severe response to it show that Jesus's divine sonship is being defined in exceptionally high terms that go beyond more common messianic expectations. As the Christ, Jesus is indeed "the Son of David" (10:47–48; 11:7–10) and "the King of the Jews/Israel" (15:26, 32, etc.), but he is much more than this (12:35–37; 15:2), not only because he is the obedient Son of God who suffers and dies to atone for sin but also because he is the transcendent Son of God, exalted alongside God to participate in his cosmic sovereignty.

Other divine sonship passages similarly have a highly exalted portrait of Jesus in view. As in 14:61–62, both 8:38 and 13:24–32 closely link Jesus's declaration of himself as the apocalyptic Son of Man, whose end-time return from heaven to earth is described using OT language and imagery associated with the "day of the Lord" and the eschatological coming of God himself,[60] with his identity as God's Son. In 8:38, Jesus warns of the consequences of denying him and his teachings, stating that he, the Son of Man, will also be ashamed of such individuals "when he comes in the glory of *his Father* with the holy angels." In 13:24–32, after again speaking of himself as the heavenly Son of Man and of his cataclysmic, theophanic appearance in which he sends out the angels to gather all his elect, he again refers to his divine sonship when he states that no one knows the exact moment of his appearing, not even the angels in heaven, nor even "the Son," but only the Father. Through this convergence of Son-of-Man language with Son-of-God language, Mark shows that Jesus, the heavenly Son of Man, whose glorious return recalls OT depictions of God's own coming, is none other than Jesus, the Son of God.[61]

An objection might be raised that since such passages clearly depict Jesus in his future glory, it is perhaps not Jesus's identity as Son of God per se that points to his transcendent, godlike status, but rather he attains this exalted status upon his resurrection.[62] If so, this could support Kingsbury's and Bateman's contention that "Son of God" is essentially a non-divine messianic title for Jesus and that the demons'

---

[60] See Edward Adams, "The Coming of the Son of Man in Mark's Gospel," *TynBul* 56 (2005): 39–61; Joshua E. Leim, "In the Glory of His Father: Intertextuality and the Apocalyptic Son of Man in the Gospel of Mark," *JTI* 7 (2013): 213–32; Johansson, "Jesus," 141–53.

[61] Although both Johansson and Leim consider certain features of Mark's depiction of Jesus's godlike eschatological activity here to be exceptional, they seem to have overlooked comparable similarities in the case of the Son of Man in the *Similitudes of Enoch*. Though they claim Jesus uniquely exercises godlike command over the angels (Mark 13:27a), appears in God's glory (8:38), and has godlike claim over the elect as "his elect" (13:28b) (Johansson, "Jesus," 153–38; Leim, "Glory," 226–28), the Enochic Son of Man comparably acts as eschatological judge of the angels (*1 En.* 61:8), occupies the divine throne of glory in his exercise of eschatological judgment (45:3; 51:3; 62:2–5; etc.), and may very well be said to have God's "congregation" (*maḥbar*) (46:8; cf. 38:1; 62:8) also belonging to him (53:6).

[62] Differing perspectives on this issue can be seen in the way scholars disagree over the significance of the transfiguration account (9:2–8). While some argue that the glorious form Jesus manifests is merely a proleptic glimpse of his post-resurrection glory (Howard C. Kee, "The Transfiguration in Mark: Epiphany or Apocalyptic Vision?" in *Understanding the Sacred Text* [ed. John Reumann; Valley Forge: Judson, 1972], 143–44; Kingsbury, *Christology*, 99; Stein, *Mark*, 416–17), others maintain it is a brief disclosure of his present, though hidden, supernatural identity (Simon J. Gathercole, *The Preexistent Son: Recovering the Christologies of Matthew, Mark, and Luke* [Grand Rapids: Eerdmans, 2006], 47–50; Johansson, "Jesus," 130–32; Leim, "Glory," 222, n. 47).

recognition of him as the Son of God, which occurs in his earthly ministry quite removed from any reference to his exalted post-resurrection status, is nothing more than an acknowledgment of his messianic identity.[63]

Yet even in his earthly ministry as the Son of God, Jesus appears to be more than a mere human, earthly messiah. While in the passages above, Jesus does indeed speak of his highly exalted position in future terms ("the Son of Man *will* be ashamed [ἐπαισχυνθήσεται] of him when he comes in the glory of his Father" [8:38]; "they *will* see [ὄψονται] the Son of Man coming in the clouds with great power and glory" [13:26]; "you *will* see [ὄψεσθε] the Son of Man seated at the right hand of Power" [14:62]), he also speaks of himself as one who even in his earthly ministry as God's Son already ranks higher than the angels (13:32).[64] Although here Jesus includes himself among those who are ignorant of his end-time return (no one knows, not even the angels in heaven, nor even the Son—only the Father), he presents this idea in such a way that one would otherwise expect those closest to God, such as the angels in heaven, who were often thought to be privy to such special knowledge as heavenly beings who took part in God's heavenly council,[65] to know such things.[66] Thus, when Jesus speaks of himself as one who already in his earthly ministry shares a closer relationship to God as his Son than God's heavenly council of angels, he places himself in the heavenly hierarchy above the angels second only to God, implying his heavenly status, if not his heavenly identity.

Even the nature of Jesus's battle with the demons who recognize and acknowledge him as the Son of God likewise suggests a deeper significance to his divine sonship. Although Bateman contends that Jesus's triumph over the demonic forces is in keeping with contemporary Jewish messianic expectations,[67] some points of clarification are in order. First, he broadens such expectations to include instances where a messianic figure removes impurity and brings about restoration in general, whether or not there is any mention of spiritual forces involved. In fact, the majority of examples cited for support (*Pss. Sol.* 17:21–27, 30–32; 18:5–9; *2 Bar.* 72:2; 73:1–4; 1Q28b V, 20–25) give no indication that the messianic figure engages spiritual powers as he brings about such purification and restoration, and therefore hardly count as relevant for comparison with Jesus's dealings with the demonic. Second, it is significant that the only example cited that serves as a comparable parallel is that of the *heavenly* eschatological figure Melchizedek in 11Q13.[68] Just as this heavenly figure was expected to deliver God's people from the hand of the demonic Belial and his spiritual forces (11Q13 II, 13), so

---

[63] Bateman, "Defining," 550–54.
[64] Gathercole, *Preexistent*, 50; Johansson, "Jesus," 196–97; cf. Witherington, *Mark*, 349; Leim, "Glory," 228.
[65] 1 Kgs 22:19–22; Job 1:6–12; 15:8; Ps 82:1; Isa 6:8; *Jub.* 17:15–18; Rev 5:1–2.
[66] Gathercole, *Preexistent*, 50.
[67] Bateman, "Defining," 551–52.
[68] For a discussion of the majority view that this Melchizedek is an angelic figure, see Eric F. Mason, *"You Are a Priest Forever": Second Temple Jewish Messianism and the Priestly Christology of the Epistle to the Hebrews* (STDJ 74; Leiden: Brill, 2008), 177–90; Adela Yarbro Collins and John J. Collins, *King and Messiah as Son of God: Divine, Human, and Angelic Messianic Figures in Biblical and Related Literature* (Grand Rapids: Eerdmans, 2008), 79–86. See also p. 72, n. 93 below.

Jesus, as discussed above, understood his exorcism of demons as an assault on Satan himself and the beginning of the overthrow of his kingdom (3:22-27). Third, and building from this second point, it is typically heavenly beings, not humans, who have significant lead roles in eschatological or large-scale warfare against or judgment of evil spiritual powers in early Jewish literature.[69] For example, the archangel Michael takes a lead role in assisting God's people in the war against Belial and his forces (1QM XIII, 10-11; XVII, 5-9; cf. Rev 12:7-9). The heavenly Enochic Son of Man judges the demonic Azazel and his hosts (*1 En.* 55:4). Significantly, much like Jesus's "binding" of Satan (Mark 3:27), it is heavenly beings who are typically responsible for "binding" evil spirits and their leader, such as the angels Raphael (*1 En.* 10:4-6), Michael (*1 En.* 10:11-12), the host of angels in general (*Jub.* 5:6; 10:7-14; 48:15-19; cf. Rev 20:1-3), and God himself (*1 En.* 18:16; cf. Isa 24:21-22).[70] With hardly any clear contemporary evidence of an expectation that a mere human messiah would engage in the kind of cosmic conflict with evil spiritual powers that Mark attributes to Jesus and instead an abundance of evidence that such activity is carried out by heavenly figures, Jesus is characterized much more like a heavenly figure than a human figure in his confrontations with evil spirits. Since even in Jesus's earthly ministry as the Son of God, he is already superior to the angels and second only to God as his Son (13:32), the likelihood increases that when the demons uncannily recognize Jesus as the Son of God—one who is capable of overpowering Satan and his hosts, and bringing about the end of his reign (1:24; 3:23-27), as only heavenly beings are thought to do—they acknowledge one who is not merely a human messiah, but a transcendent supernatural messiah.[71]

It may be, then, that the Gerasene demoniac's προσκύνησις of Jesus as Son of the Most High God not only is a gesture of submission to a mighty ruler and conqueror but also is reflective of the demons' special insight into Jesus's supernatural identity. Jesus, the Son of God is no mere earthly ruler or conqueror battling earthly powers but does

---

[69] For what follows, see Elizabeth E. Shively, *Apocalyptic Imagination in the Gospel of Mark: The Literary and Theological Role of Mark 3:22-30* (BZNW 189; Berlin: de Gruyter, 2012), 113-42.

[70] Although there is some evidence of a human messianic figure waging war with and binding Beliar in the *Testaments of the Twelve Patriarchs* (*T. Levi* 18:12; *T. Zeb.* 9:8; *T. Dan* 5:10-11), since this work in its present form as a second-century C.E. Christian document, it is difficult to be certain of the extent to which this figure is free of Christian reflections on Christ, if at all (cf. *T. Zeb.* 9:8, where the one who frees captives from Beliar is said to be "God in human form." For further discussion of possible Christian influence on these passages, see Graham H. Twelftree, *Jesus the Exorcist: A Contribution to the Study of the Historical Jesus* [WUNT 2/54; Tübingen: Mohr Siebeck, 1993], 185-87).

[71] One could argue that it is simply as a human messiah empowered by the divine Spirit (1:10-11) that Jesus acts as a superhuman figure (Collins, *Mark*, 39-40) and receives the overawed reverence of the demons (Bateman, "Defining," 554). On the other hand, the bestowal of the Spirit does not necessarily preclude Jesus's own transcendent identity (cf. John 1:1-18, 32-33). It is also striking that Mark generally emphasizes the autonomous character of Jesus's miraculous activity (1:23-27, 40-42; 3:1-6; 5:34-43; etc.)—especially remarkable are such instances where he does what only God does (2:1-12; 4:35-41; 6:45-52)—rather than explicitly linking such activity with an empowerment by the Spirit (cf. Judg 13:25; 14:6, 19; 15:14). Even an implicit link to the Spirit in Jesus's supernatural deeds is somewhat complicated by 6:45-52, since here, when Jesus walks on the sea and identifies himself by the OT divine self-declaration, "ἐγώ εἰμι," he appears to correlate his unique ability to do what only God does with his own unique identification with God (Johansson, "Jesus," 103-21).

what only heavenly figures do: waging cosmic war with Satan and the demons while being uniquely recognized as such a transcendent figure by his spiritual opponents. Once again, this makes the contrast with the προσκύνησις of the soldiers in 15:19 even starker, as the one whom they take to be a mere earthly royal pretender in their mock obeisance is in fact the unique, transcendent Son of God, superior to angels, strong enough to overpower the ruler of demons, and who moments before his abasement at the hands of the soldiers declared in 14:61–62 that as the Son of God he has a share with God in his cosmic sovereignty.

D. Conclusion

For Mark's Jesus to be portrayed as a recipient of προσκύνησις is for him to be recognized as a mighty ruler and conqueror. Whereas several individuals bow before Jesus as healer and teacher, Mark reserves the term προσκυνέω for the Roman soldiers' mock reverence of Jesus as the King of the Jews and the Gerasene demoniac's reverence of Jesus as the Son of God, two titles which certainly have royal connotations. Yet, especially in light of the profound significance of the latter title, Mark's Jesus proves to be no ordinary human sovereign. Much more than an earthly King of the Jews, whom most saw as a rival to Caesar at best, Jesus is the unique, transcendent Son of God. As such, he is superior to the angels, poses a unique threat not ultimately to the lordship of Caesar but to that of Satan and is destined to reign in the heavens at God's side. Much more than one worthy of προσκύνησις by humans as an earthly king, Jesus is even worthy of προσκύνησις from those who belong to the spirit world and who truly perceive the significance of his transcendent status as the Son of God. Thus, the προσκύνησις of Jesus in Mark is likely to be understood as worship of an exalted supernatural sovereign who uniquely participates in the heavenly rule of God, a status the Jewish authorities equated with blasphemous claims to equality with God.

3

The Προσκύνησις of Jesus in the Gospel of Matthew

More than any other work among the NT writings, the Gospel of Matthew stands out for its frequent use of προσκυνέω with Jesus as its object (ten times), far exceeding the one or two instances in the other works. Not only does προσκυνέω prove to be a Matthean favorite as a term of reverence for Jesus in view of its many instances from the Gospel's beginning (Matt 2:2, 8, 11) to its end (28:9, 17) and all throughout (8:2; 9:18; 14:33; 15:25; 20:20) but also in view of its appearance in material entirely unique to Matthew (2:2, 8, 11; 28:9) and in view of its appearance as a result of Matthew's redaction of Markan material (8:2 [cf. Mark 1:40]; 9:18 [cf. Mark 5:22]; etc.[1]). Moreover, the other uses of προσκυνέω may also enhance the christological significance of the Matthean Jesus's reception of προσκύνησις, for it is used not only to describe a type of reverence desired by Satan (4:9) yet denied to him, but in response to this, it is also used to signify that which is reserved for God alone (4:10).[2] Is it possible that Matthew uses προσκυνέω, in some sense, to include Jesus as a recipient of what is otherwise typically reserved for God? As we will see, there is quite a diversity of scholarly responses to this and other related questions regarding the significance of the προσκύνησις of Jesus in Matthew, which gives us an opportunity to discuss these matters afresh. We will begin by making some preliminary observations on each passage where Matthew uses προσκυνέω, then proceed to survey scholarly opinions regarding the significance of the προσκύνησις of Jesus in Matthew, which will allow us to consider other relevant material both internal and external to Matthew in offering our own assessment. In the end, I will argue that the primary significance of Matthew's inclusion of Jesus along with God as the only legitimate recipients of προσκύνησις is rooted in Jesus's share in God's lordship over all. It is primarily in this sense that Matthew portrays Jesus as one worthy to be acknowledged as only God otherwise is.

---

[1] See p. 55 below.
[2] Note also the only other προσκυνέω passage (Matt 18:26), where the recipient of προσκύνησις is God, parabolically represented by a royal figure (see discussion below).

A. The Προσκύνησις of God

Although Matthew largely uses προσκυνέω with Jesus as its object, there are two instances where the term has God as its object (the first straightforwardly so, the second symbolically so). In the first instance, the term is used for the exclusive devotion reserved for God, a point stressed in direct response to the devil's/Satan's desire to receive a similar type of reverence from Jesus. In the temptation account (4:1–11), Satan's temptation of Jesus reaches its climax when he takes him to a very high mountain from which he shows him all the kingdoms of the world (4:8), offering to give them to him if he would only prostrate himself in προσκύνησις before Satan (ταῦτά σοι πάντα δώσω, ἐὰν πεσὼν προσκυνήσῃς μοι [4:9]). There is certainly a sense in which the προσκύνησις requested here is politically charged as Satan is depicted as a mighty ruler who claims to have authority to grant Jesus a share in his lordship over the kingdoms of the world. Just as client kings would be expected to pay homage and swear fealty to those sovereigns who grant them positions of rulership,[3] so Jesus is to render homage and allegiance to Satan through προσκύνησις should he agree to exercise his reign on Satan's terms. At the same time, however, such προσκύνησις is clearly far more than a mere display of political obeisance. It is also, and more fundamentally so, interpreted as a type of idolatrous worship since Satan sets himself up in competition with God as one worthy of ultimate allegiance. Jesus's response exposes the idolatrous nature of Satan's request for προσκύνησις as he makes clear that such reverence is to be given to God alone: ὕπαγε, σατανᾶ· γέγραπται γάρ· κύριον τὸν θεόν σου προσκυνήσεις καὶ αὐτῷ μόνῳ λατρεύσεις (4:10). Here, in the slightly modified words of LXX Deut 6:13,[4] whose context calls for Israel's complete devotion to God to the exclusion of all other gods (Deut 6:14–15), Jesus's rebuff of Satan's desire for reverence through προσκύνησις shows that he interprets it as an attempt to arrogate the kind of worship that Israel's Scriptures reserve for God alone.

A second instance is found in the parable of the unforgiving servant (18:23–35). When the unforgiving servant is brought before his king to settle accounts concerning his enormous debt, he falls in προσκύνησις before him (πεσὼν οὖν ὁ δοῦλος προσεκύνει αὐτῷ [18:26]) and begs for leniency, to which the king responds by graciously cancelling the debt. As is often noted, the "king"/"lord" of the parable represents God (cf. 18:35), and thus some argue that Matthew intends for this προσκύνησις to be interpreted allegorically to signify the worship of God.[5] Such a reading may also explain why a different term is used soon after for what is a nearly identical description

---

[3] Theissen, *Gospels*, 214–15.

[4] προσκυνήσεις replaces the LXX's φοβηθήσῃ to match Satan's request, and μόνῳ is added to emphasize the exclusivity of such worship implicit in the original context (see W. D. Davies and Dale C. Allison, Jr., *A Critical and Exegetical Commentary on the Gospel according to Saint Matthew* [3 vols.; ICC; Edinburgh: T&T Clark, 1988–1997], 1:373).

[5] Horst, *Proskynein*, 226–27; Martinus C. De Boer, "Ten Thousand Talents? Matthew's Interpretation and Redaction of the Parable of the Unforgiving Servant (Matt 18:23–35)," *CBQ* 50 (1988): 222–23. Cf. Robert H. Gundry, *Matthew: A Commentary on His Handbook for a Mixed Church under Persecution* (2nd ed.; Grand Rapids, MI: Eerdmans, 1994), 373, who similarly reads προσκυνέω here as conveying divine worship but argues (unconvincingly) that the "king"/"lord" who receives this προσκύνησις primarily represents Jesus.

of a fellow-servant's similar prostration and plea for leniency before the unforgiving servant (cf. πεσὼν οὖν ὁ δοῦλος <u>προσεκύνει</u> αὐτῷ λέγων· μακροθύμησον ἐπ᾽ ἐμοί, καὶ πάντα ἀποδώσω σοι [18:26] with πεσὼν οὖν ὁ σύνδουλος αὐτοῦ <u>παρεκάλει</u> αὐτὸν λέγων·μακροθύμησον ἐπ᾽ ἐμοί, καὶ ἀποδώσω σοι [18:29]). While both the king in the first instance and the unforgiving servant in the second are on the receiving end of another's lowly display of submissiveness, only the former, since he represents God, is considered worthy of προσκύνησις.

Yet, while there is little doubt that the king stands for God in the parable, it is not entirely clear that προσκυνέω is correspondingly intended to reflect the kind of cultic worship that God alone is worthy to receive as some seem to intimate. Johannes Horst, for instance, seems to have taken the προσκύνησις to be reflective of "der anbetende Dank für den Erlass so ungeheurer Schuld" as only God could conceivably receive.[6] Such an interpretation is unlikely, however, since the unforgiving servant renders προσκύνησις to the king *before* he forgives his debt, not *after*, as would be expected were the προσκύνησις an expression of "worshipful gratitude" (cf., e.g., Gen 24:12–27; 2 Kgdms 9:7–8). If anything, the servant's προσκύνησις is more likely motivated by a fearful desire to appease the king in order to avoid punishment (cf. Gen 32:3–8; 33:1–3). With regard to the change in terminology from προσκυνέω in 18:26 to παρακαλέω in 18:29, this may simply be reflective of the servants' social equality as σύνδουλοι, who accordingly would not render προσκύνησις to one another, while they would certainly render προσκύνησις to the king as their social superior.[7] In sum, while this parabolic image of God as a king receiving προσκύνησις from his servant is certainly an apt depiction of God's sovereignty, it is less clear that προσκυνέω is being used to represent the kind of cultic worship reserved for God alone.

B. The Προσκύνησις of Jesus

The rest of Matthew's προσκυνέω uses all have Jesus as their object. We have divided these instances of προσκύνησις of Jesus into four subgroups: (1) the προσκύνησις of Jesus by the magi at his birth; (2) the προσκύνησις of Jesus by various suppliants throughout his earthly ministry; (3) the προσκύνησις of Jesus by the disciples at his theophanic walk upon the sea; and (4) the προσκύνησις of Jesus by the women and the disciples at his resurrection appearances.

1. By the magi at Jesus's birth

As early as his birth in Matt 1–2, Jesus is already depicted as a recipient of προσκύνησις. Magi from the east arrive in Jerusalem in search of the one who has been born King of the Jews, explaining that they had seen his star and so have come to render

---

[6] Horst, *Proskynein*, 227.
[7] Cf. Davies and Allison, *Matthew*, 2:801; Donald A. Hagner, *Matthew* (2 vols.; WBC 33A–B; Dallas, TX: Word Books, 1993–1995), 2:539; R. T. France, *The Gospel of Matthew* (NICNT; Grand Rapids, MI: Eerdmans, 2007), 701, n. 4.

προσκύνησις to him (ἤλθομεν προσκυνῆσαι αὐτῷ [2:2]). Following King Herod's duplicitous response to the magi in which he feigns a mutual eagerness to come and render προσκύνησις to Jesus (κἀγὼ ἐλθὼν προσκυνήσω αὐτῷ [2:8]), the magi set out for Bethlehem where they find the infant Jesus. Upon seeing him, the magi prostrate themselves in προσκύνησις before him (πεσόντες προσεκύνησαν αὐτῷ), and they offer him gifts of gold, frankincense, and myrrh (2:11).

Many details in this pericope lead to a view of the magi's προσκύνησις of Jesus as homage rendered to royalty. First, from the magi's own words, it is clear that they have come to Jerusalem to render προσκύνησις to one whom they take to be a king (2:2). Second, Jesus is portrayed fulfilling OT prophecies that anticipate the rise of a Davidic "ruler" (2:4-6). Third, the appearance of Jesus's "star" (2:2, 7, 9, 10), which guides the magi, is reflective of the widespread ancient belief that such astral phenomena heralded the birth of important figures, especially rulers (cf. Num 24:17).[8] Fourth, most commentators agree that the gifts the magi present to Jesus are "luxury gifts, fit for a king."[9] Fifth, Matthew's depiction of foreign dignitaries coming to reverence Jesus and to present gifts to him recalls OT descriptions of foreigners coming to Jerusalem to pay homage to Israel's king and to offer gifts of gold and spices (1 Kgs 10:1-13; Ps 72:10-11, 15).[10] Sixth, the prominence of "King Herod" serves to underscore the contrast between this illegitimate, Roman-appointed client king and Jesus, the Davidic descendant who has a legitimate claim to Israel's throne, and thus is rightly acknowledged as "the one who has been born King of the Jews."[11]

Of course, the Matthean material that immediately precedes the account of the magi's προσκύνησις of Jesus discloses more profound aspects of Jesus's identity, as he is described as one who was supernaturally conceived, who "will save his people from their sins," and who is to be called Emmanuel, "God with us" (1:18-25). Such a characterization of Jesus suggests he is no ordinary human king, and Matthew may very well be leading his readers to discern a deeper significance in Jesus's reception of the magi's προσκύνησις, one which moves beyond viewing προσκύνησις as a mere customary gesture of homage so commonly shown to human superiors. But before proceeding to further discussion on these matters, we will first consider the other passages where Matthew presents Jesus as a recipient of προσκύνησις.

---

[8] Davies and Allison, *Matthew*, 1:233-34; France, *Matthew*, 68. See examples highlighted in Raymond E. Brown, *The Birth of the Messiah: A Commentary on the Infancy Narratives in the Gospels of Matthew and Luke* (rev. ed.; ABRL; New York: Doubleday, 1993), 170-71; and Warren Carter, *Matthew and the Margins: A Socio-Political and Religious Reading* (JSNTSup 204; Sheffield: Sheffield Academic, 2000), 75-76.

[9] France, *Matthew*, 76. See also Walter Grundmann, *Das Evangelium nach Matthäus* (THKNT; Berlin: Evangelische Verlagsanstalt, 1968), 79; Davies and Allison, *Matthew*, 1:249-51; Hagner, *Matthew*, 1:31; Craig S. Keener, *A Commentary on the Gospel of Matthew* (Grand Rapids, MI: Eerdmans, 1999), 104.

[10] Brown, *Birth*, 187-88; Grundmann, *Matthäus*, 79; Davies and Allison, *Matthew*, 1:250; Hagner, *Matthew*, 1:31; Keener, *Matthew*, 104-5; France, *Matthew*, 61-62.

[11] David R. Bauer, "The Kingship of Jesus in the Matthean Infancy Narrative: A Literary Analysis," *CBQ* 57 (1995): 306-23.

2. By various suppliants throughout Jesus's earthly ministry

On four separate occasions during Jesus's earthly ministry, Matthew describes an individual approaching Jesus and reverencing him with προσκύνησις as he/she presents a request to Jesus. Beginning with the first of many detailed accounts of Jesus's healing ministry, a leper is described approaching Jesus with προσκύνησις (ἰδοὺ λεπρὸς προσελθὼν προσεκύνει αὐτῷ), addressing him as κύριε as he confidently affirms Jesus's ability to cleanse him if only he be so willing (8:2). Jesus responds by touching the leper as he affirms his willingness to cleanse him, which instantly results in the leper's miraculous healing (8:3). Later on, a ruler similarly approaches Jesus with προσκύνησις (ἰδοὺ ἄρχων εἷς ἐλθὼν προσεκύνει αὐτῷ) and likewise expresses a remarkable confidence in Jesus's healing powers—in this case, to bring his dead daughter back to life (9:18), which Jesus accomplishes (9:25). On another occasion, a Canaanite woman pursues Jesus, crying out to him as κύριε υἱὸς Δαυίδ in hopes that he will heal her demon-possessed daughter (15:22). After a period of being ignored, the woman finally approaches Jesus with προσκύνησις (ἡ δὲ ἐλθοῦσα προσεκύνει αὐτῷ) and appeals to him as κύριε to help her (15:25). Eventually, the woman's faithful persistence is rewarded as the simple pronouncement by Jesus that her request be granted is sufficient to bring about her daughter's healing from a distance (15:28). Finally, the mother of the sons of Zebedee also approaches Jesus with προσκύνησις (προσῆλθεν αὐτῷ ἡ μήτηρ τῶν υἱῶν Ζεβεδαίου μετὰ τῶν υἱῶν αὐτῆς προσκυνοῦσα [20:20]) and asks for Jesus to grant her sons positions of highest honor beside him when he enters his kingdom reign (20:21).

The use of προσκυνέω in these supplicatory episodes certainly in part signifies the lowly, reverential posture often assumed by those who approach another with a plea or request. Horst was probably on the right track when he observed that the distinctive use of the imperfect tense of προσκυνέω in most of these cases (8:2; 9:18; 15:25; cf. 18:26) characterizes these acts as "Bittproskynesen."[12] But there is good reason to think that Matthew uses προσκυνέω here to convey more than just a humble, deferential petitionary posture. A comparison of the synoptic parallels to these accounts reveals Matthew's programmatic alterations to his Markan source, both substituting προσκυνέω for the leper's γονυπετῶν (Mark 1:40; cf. Luke 5:12 [πεσὼν ἐπὶ πρόσωπον]), the ruler's/ synagogue official's πίπτει πρὸς τοὺς πόδας (Mark 5:22; cf. Luke 8:41 [πεσὼν παρὰ τοὺς πόδας]) and the Canaanite/Syrophoenician woman's προσέπεσεν πρὸς τοὺς πόδας (Mark 7:25), as well as including προσκυνέω in the account regarding the places of honor for the sons of Zebedee (cf. Mark 10:35). As Larry Hurtado rightly suspects, such Matthean alterations are "not simply a matter of preference of one somewhat synonymous word for others."[13]

Indeed, it appears that in general προσκυνέω is far less commonly associated with supplication compared to other prostration terms. Even in the rare instances where someone is explicitly said to render προσκύνησις as he/she supplicates (LXX Exod 11:8; 1 Kgdms 2:36; 2 Kgdms 14:4; 15:1–6; 3 Kgdms 1:16), it seems the primary import

---

[12] Horst, *Proskynein*, 217–18.
[13] Larry W. Hurtado, "Homage to the Historical Jesus and Early Christian Devotion," *JSHJ* 1 (2003): 143.

of προσκυνέω in such cases is the acknowledgment of another's superiority. In the latter three examples, προσκύνησις and supplication are directed to royalty, to whom one would offer προσκύνησις simply by virtue of their status as authority figures, regardless of whether or not one approached with a petition. By contrast, there is much more evidence for the use of other prostration terminology comparable to Mark's and Luke's usage above in places where individuals prostrate themselves as they supplicate.[14] These observations also best account for the use of different terminology in the parable of the unforgiving servant discussed earlier. While both servants in 18:26 and 18:29 perform the same physical actions (prostration and supplication), Matthew reserves προσκυνέω for the former instance precisely because the recipient is a king and therefore uniquely acknowledged as such with προσκύνησις. In sum, while προσκυνέω is in some respects associated with an individual's humble petitionary approach, what is foregrounded and emphasized by the use of the term is the acknowledgment of a superior figure. Thus, Matthew's use of προσκυνέω in these four supplicatory scenes points beyond the suppliants' humble posture to highlight the superiority of Jesus.

It is also often noted that since Matthew omits προσκυνέω in the two places where Mark has Jesus's opponents rendering προσκύνησις to him (Mark 5:6 [cf. Matt 8:29]; Mark 15:19 [cf. Matt 27:29]), there is a sense in which the term is being reserved for those who express genuine faith in Jesus.[15] This is indeed a likely component guiding Matthew's selective use of the term with respect to Jesus. The four suppliants who render προσκύνησις to Jesus all exhibit an exemplary, unswerving conviction that Jesus can grant their extraordinary requests if he so wills. But it is also essential to note in this regard that their faith is rightly placed in the one who has such power and authority to grant their extraordinary requests.[16] Thus, while προσκυνέω in these instances is indeed reflective of the great faith of those who approach Jesus with such reverence, it is also, and probably more so, reflective of the high rank of Jesus.

3. By the disciples at Jesus's theophanic walk upon the sea

A more overtly striking image of Jesus's transcendence in close connection with his reception of προσκύνησις comes into play in the sea-walking episode (14:22–33). The disciples are out at sea, battered by the winds and waves, when they suddenly encounter a mysterious figure walking toward them on the sea (14:22–25). Their initial fear that the figure is an apparition is quickly dispelled when Jesus identifies himself as

---

[14] For example, LXX Num 16:22; Josh 7:6–9; 4 Kgdms 1:13; 4:27; 1 Chr 21:16–17; Esth 8:3; Ezek 9:8; 2 Macc 10:4, 25–26; 3 Macc 1:16; *Sib. Or.* 3:716–17; *T. Ab.* 9:2–3; 18:10 (A); *T. Jos.* 13:2; *Apoc. Mos.* 36:1; *Apoc. Sedr.* 14:2; Josephus, *Ant.* 10.11; 11.231; 17.94; 19.234.

[15] Heinz J. Held, "Matthew as Interpreter of the Miracle Stories," in *Tradition and Interpretation in Matthew* (ed. Günther Bornkamm et al.; trans. Percy Scott; London: SCM, 1963), 229; Richard Bauckham, "Jesus, Worship of," *ABD* 3:813; Hurtado, "Homage," 143.

[16] Jesus's denial of the mother's request (20:23) may suggest some limits to his authority, or perhaps alternatively, his explanation that such has already been prepared by his Father suggests the emphasis is on the predetermined will of God in these matters rather than on any lack in Jesus's authority (cf. Mark Allan Powell, "A Typology of Worship in the Gospel of Matthew," *JSNT* 57 [1995]: 8).

the mysterious figure and encourages them not to fear (14:26–27). Peter then appeals to Jesus as κύριε, both in seeking to be called by Jesus to come to him on the water and in seeking to be rescued by him when he later starts to sink (14:28–31). After witnessing Jesus's own miraculous walk on the sea, his direction and rescue of Peter as he too trod the waters, and the instant stilling of the winds just as the two climbed into the boat (14:32), the disciples respond by rendering προσκύνησις to Jesus (οἱ δὲ ἐν τῷ πλοίῳ προσεκύνησαν αὐτῷ) and confessing that he is truly the Son of God (14:33).

What is particularly astonishing in this episode, as most interpreters observe, is that Jesus is portrayed acting and speaking in ways characteristic of Yahweh in the OT—in a number of ways, uniquely so:[17] (1) Jesus walks upon the sea (14:25–26) as only God does (Job 9:8; 38:16; Ps 77:19; Hab 3:15);[18] (2) he identifies himself to the disciples with the words "ἐγώ εἰμι" (14:27), which evokes OT language of Yahweh's exclusive claim to divinity (Deut 32:39; Isa 41:4; 43:10);[19] (3) he tells the disciples "μὴ φοβεῖσθε" (14:27), words often spoken to humans by heavenly beings in angelophanic and theophanic appearances (Gen 15:1; 26:24; Judg 6:23; Dan 10:12; Tob 12:17; Luke 1:13; 2:10; *Jos. Asen.* 14:11; etc.);[20] (4) as Peter sinks and cries out to Jesus, "Lord, save me!," Jesus

---

[17] See esp. John Paul Heil, *Jesus Walking on the Sea: Meaning and Gospel Functions of Matt 14:22-33, Mark 6:45-52 and John 6:15b-21* (AnBib 87; Rome: Biblical Institute Press, 1981), 31–67; Catrin H. Williams, *I Am He: The Interpretation of 'Ani Hû' in Jewish and Early Christian Literature* (WUNT 2/113; Tübingen: Mohr Siebeck, 2000), 214–25. See also Davies and Allison, *Matthew*, 2:504–10.

[18] Some scholars draw attention to the sea-walking motif in Greco-Roman literature, where not only the gods but even certain divine men are ascribed the power to walk on water (Adela Yarbro Collins, "Rulers, Divine Men, and Walking on the Water [Mark 6:45–52]," in *Religious Propaganda and Missionary Competition in the New Testament World* [ed. Lukas Bormann et al.; NovTSup 74; Leiden: Brill, 1994], 214–23; Ulrich Luz, *Matthew: A Commentary* [trans. James E. Crouch; 3 vols.; Hermeneia; Minneapolis, MN: Fortress, 2001–2007], 2:319–20). There are, however, some important differences and qualifications that should be taken into account. For instance, divinity is rather loosely ascribed to Xerxes for bridging the Hellespont (Herodotus, *Hist.* 7.56; Dio Chrysostom, *Or.* 3.30–31), a technological achievement rather than a miracle (Johansson, "Jesus," 105, n. 14). Unlike Jesus, Abaris requires the assistance of a magical arrow to travel over waters (Porphyry, *Vit. Pyth.* 29). Besides the gods themselves, the closest parallels are found in references to sons of the gods, who are more straightforwardly described walking on water: Euphemus, son of Poseidon (Apollonius Rhodius, *Argon.* 1.179–84); Orion, son of Poseidon (Hesiod = Ps.-Eratosthenes, frg. 182); and Hercules, son of Zeus (Seneca, *Herc. fur.* 322–24). Yet none of these divine men both walk upon the sea *and* rescue others from the sea's perils as Jesus does in Matthew. While this does liken him more to the gods in Greco-Roman literature in this respect (Homer, *Il.* 13.26–30; Virgil, *Aen.* 5.800–21; Hesiod, *Homeric Hymns* 22; Theocritus, *Id.* 22.1–26; Diodorus Siculus, *Hist.* 4.43.1–2; BGU 423.6–7 = *SelPap* I, 112), a number of OT resonances in Matt 14:22–33 (Heil, *Jesus*, 31–67) make it more likely that Jesus's sea-walking ability is to be interpreted primarily within a Jewish context, which reserves sea-walking for Yahweh alone (cf. Johansson, "Jesus," 106–9).

[19] Although some commentators see ἐγώ εἰμι here as little more than "the most natural form of self-identification" (France, *Matthew*, 569–70, n. 14; similarly John Nolland, *The Gospel of Matthew: A Commentary on the Greek Text* [NIGTC; Grand Rapids, MI: Eerdmans, 2005], 601), most agree that while it certainly has this function at the story level, in light of Jesus's Yahweh-like activity throughout this episode, it is also meant to recall Yahweh's absolute "I am" declarations (Luz, *Matthew*, 2:320; Davies and Allison, *Matthew*, 2:506; Hagner, *Matthew*, 2:423; Carter, *Matthew*, 310; Gundry, *Matthew*, 299; Grundmann, *Matthäus*, 368; Joachim Gnilka, *Das Matthäusevangelium* [2 vols.; HThKNT; Freiburg: Herder, 1986–1988], 2:13), which, on the lips of Jesus, closely links him to God.

[20] It may very well be, as Heil contends, that Isa 43 is a key text standing behind the sea-walking narrative in view of three striking correspondences: (1) the comfort-bringing μὴ φοβεῖσθε

responds by reaching out his hand and rescuing Peter from drowning (14:30–31), which resembles psalmic descriptions of one crying out to God to reach out and save him from overwhelming waters (Pss 18:16; 69:1–3, 14–15; 144:7); and (5) Jesus brings about a calm over the sea (14:32)[21] as only God does (Job 26:11–12; Pss 65:7; 89:8–9; 107:29).

In the OT and early Jewish literature, it is the God of Israel alone who is truly sovereign over the sea as its creator and lord.[22] Accordingly, he is described manifesting such exclusive lordship in a variety of ways, such as setting bounds for the sea, stirring up and calming the sea, rescuing humans from perishing in the sea, and making a way both for himself as well as for others upon/through the sea.[23] Oftentimes, Israel's God is explicitly identified as the one true God over against all other gods on the basis of such sovereignty.[24] By portraying Jesus as one who exercises such uniquely godlike power and authority over the sea, Jesus is likened to God in a manner unparalleled by any other human or angelic figure in Jewish tradition.[25]

It is in view of Jesus's godlike activity that the disciples' climactic response of προσκύνησις and confession of Jesus's divine sonship in 14:33 is undoubtedly to be understood in exceptionally high terms.[26] A prior experience in which the disciples similarly witness Jesus's godlike rebuke and calm of a sea storm (8:23–27) led them climactically to ponder, "What kind of person is this that even the winds and the sea

---

(Matt 14:27; cf. Isa 43:1, 5); (2) the divine self-declaration ἐγώ εἰμι/אני הוא (Matt 14:27; cf. Isa 43:10, 13 [MT]); and (3) the water-crossing motif (Matt 14:25–26, 28–29; cf. Isa 43:2, 16) (*Jesus*, 59). In Isa 43, God encourages his people not to fear, assuring them that he is with them and makes a way for them as they pass through the waters, and he emphatically declares that it is he (ἐγώ εἰμι) who delivers in this way as the only true God and savior. In Matthew, Jesus acts and speaks as Yahweh, encouraging the disciples not to fear, controlling the sea so that he and his disciples pass safely over the waters, and identifying himself by the theologically loaded ἐγώ εἰμι formula as he does so.

[21] Whereas in 8:26, the winds and the sea are stilled at Jesus's command, here in 14:32, they are stilled at Jesus's mere presence (Carter, *Matthew*, 312).

[22] Gen 1:1–10; Exod 20:11; Neh 9:6; Pss 29:3; 33:7; 95:5; 135:6; 146:6; Jonah 1:9; Jdt 9:12; Sir 43:23; 1QH IX, 13–14; *1 En.* 101:6. See also Johansson, "Jesus," 66–74.

[23] Exod 14:1–15:21; Job 9:8; 26:11–12; 38:8–11, 16; Pss 18:16; 65:7; 69:1–3, 14–15; 74:12–15; 77:19; 89:9; 104:7–9; 107:23–30; 144:7; Prov 8:29; Isa 43:2, 16; 50:2; 51:10, 15; Jer 5:22; 31:35; Amos 5:8; Jonah 1:4–16; Nah 1:3–4; Hab 3:15; Wis 14:3–7; *1 En.* 101:4–9; *T. Naph.* 6:1–10.

[24] Exod 15:10–11; Pss 77:13–20; 89:6–9; 135:5–6; Jonah 1:4–16; Wis 14:1–11.

[25] As Johansson rightly observes, Jesus transcends Moses (Exod 14:15–31), Joshua (Josh 3:7–4:18), Elijah (2 Kgs 2:8), and Elisha (2 Kgs 2:13–14) by walking *on* water as only God does, whereas the latter pass *through* the waters ("Jesus," 106, n. 21; similarly Wendy Cotter, *Miracles in Greco-Roman Antiquity: A Sourcebook for the Study of New Testament Miracle Stories* [London: Routledge, 1999], 159–60). Moreover, unlike these others, who perform water miracles either upon God's instruction (Exod 14:16, 26; Josh 3:8–13) and/or by an instrument of some sort (Exod 14:16; 2 Kgs 2:8, 13–14), Jesus exercises control over the sea in a much more autonomous fashion. Although Philo appears to ascribe godlike authority over the elements to Moses (*Mos.* 1.156), this is probably loosely expressed, since elsewhere Philo frequently makes it clear that Moses exercises such power upon God's instruction or by appealing to God (see Eric Eve, *The Jewish Context of Jesus' Miracles* [JSNTSup 231; Sheffield: Sheffield Academic, 2002], 65–72).

Jesus's godlike authority over the sea in Matthew also appears to surpass that of the angels. Although the latter have some measure of power and authority over waters (e.g., *1 En.* 61:10; 66:1-2; *2 En.* 19:4; Rev 16:5), none appear to match Jesus's godlike ability to rebuke the sea on his own authority (Matt 8:26) as only God does (Job 26:11–12; Pss 18:15; 104:7; 106:9; Isa 50:2; Nah 1:4).

[26] This is one of the few instances where France was inclined to view the προσκύνησις of Jesus as worship/acknowledgment of a divine figure (*Matthew*, 303, n. 6, 566, n. 7). Cf. Nolland, *Matthew*, 603. See also Dunn, *First*, 10, n. 9.

obey him?" (8:27). Matthew uniquely underscores the more-than-human character of Jesus here by referring to the disciples as ἄνθρωποι and having them ask more pointedly not merely "who" (τίς) but "what kind" (ποταπός) of person Jesus could be (cf. Mark 4:41; Luke 8:25). The contrast is thus sharpened between the disciples, who are ordinary ἄνθρωποι, and Jesus, whose extraordinary power over the sea leads these mere men to suspect that he must be a different kind of person.[27] As the Gospel narrative progresses, the disciples eventually answer their own question in the sea-walking episode. One who wields such divine power over the winds and the sea as Jesus does must be, as they confess, one who is truly God's Son: ἀληθῶς θεοῦ υἱὸς εἶ. Although a fully adequate understanding of the significance of this designation must take the whole of Matthew's Gospel into account,[28] what is brought to the forefront here is an awareness of Jesus's special relationship to God as his Son by virtue of his exceptional participation in God's lordship over wind and sea.

Just as it is Jesus's manifestation of Yahweh's unique power and authority in his own person that triggers the disciples' profound confession of his divine sonship,[29] it is certainly also that which triggers their προσκύνησις of Jesus as well. The disciples' προσκύνησις here seems to correspond most closely to instances where humans similarly react with reverential προσκύνησις when they encounter supernatural activity and/or when they realize they are in the presence of a supernatural being (Exod 34:5-8; Num 22:31; 2 Chr 7:3; *T. Ab.* 3:5-6 [A]; Josephus, *Ant.* 8.343). There is an instructive similarity between the disciples' response to Jesus and the sons of the prophets' response to Elisha in 4 Kgdms 2:14-15. When Elisha miraculously parts and crosses the Jordan River by striking it with the aid of Elijah's cloak, the sons of the prophets respond by doing προσκύνησις before Elisha and by notably exclaiming that the spirit of Elijah rests on Elisha. This close association of Elisha with Elijah is made because of Elijah's own prior miraculous parting and crossing of the Jordan by striking it with his cloak (4 Kgdms 2:8). In a similar way, Jesus's more-than-human behavior compels the disciples to reverence him with προσκύνησις, but the unique Yahweh-like nature of Jesus's activity and the confession of divine sonship evoked by it make clear that Jesus does not receive this προσκύνησις as a mere miracle worker but as one who is uniquely related to God and thus is perhaps in some sense himself divine.

4. By the women and the disciples at Jesus's resurrection appearances

Matthew's Gospel closes with two final instances of προσκύνησις. In both instances, προσκύνησις is directed toward the risen Jesus. First, when the two Marys leave Jesus's empty tomb after being informed by an angel of the Lord that he has been raised from

---

[27] Cf. Davies and Allison, *Matthew*, 2:75-76; Gundry, *Matthew*, 156; Hagner, *Matthew*, 1:222; France, *Matthew*, 337.
[28] See discussion below.
[29] Up to this point in Matthew, it has only been supernatural beings (God [3:17]; Satan [4:3, 6]; demons [8:29]) and Jesus himself (11:27; cf. 7:21; 10:32-33; 12:50) who have acknowledged Jesus's divine sonship.

the dead, they soon encounter the risen Jesus and respond by taking hold of his feet and rendering him προσκύνησις (ἐκράτησαν αὐτοῦ τοὺς πόδας καὶ προσεκύνησαν αὐτῷ [28:9]). Soon after, Jesus meets the eleven disciples on a mountain in Galilee, and upon seeing him, they too did προσκύνησις (ἰδόντες αὐτὸν προσεκύνησαν [28:17]).[30] This episode—and indeed the entire Gospel—comes to a close with the risen Jesus declaring his cosmic authority, instructing his disciples to carry out the Great Commission and assuring them of his eternal presence with them as they do so (28:18–20).

Once again, the more-than-human character of Jesus in this episode is readily apparent. In a fairly broad sense, the portrayal of Jesus here is comparable to accounts of certain extraordinary individuals, appearing in both Jewish and Greco-Roman literature, who in some spectacular way pass beyond the earthly realm of mortal existence and enter the heavenly realm of immortality.[31] Within Jewish sources, one finds biblical accounts relating mysterious earthly departures of Enoch, whom God "took" (Gen 5:24), Moses, whose burial place was unknown (Deut 34:6), and Elijah, who was taken up to heaven by whirlwind and fiery chariot (2 Kgs 2:1–18), along with later Jewish reflections on such accounts confirming and elaborating on these unique translations.[32] Several diverse examples abound in the Greco-Roman literature. Heracles was thought to have ascended to the gods after mounting his own funeral pyre and leaving no trace of his remains.[33] Empedocles mysteriously goes missing at a gathering, and when someone attests to hearing a loud voice call for the philosopher and to seeing a light in the heavens, it is soon concluded that he is now a god and is to receive sacrifice.[34] Romulus vanishes in the midst of a dark, stormy disturbance but subsequently appears to Julius Proculus in radiant attire as the newly deified Quirinus to encourage him in Rome's ongoing prosperity.[35] Both Julius Caesar and Caesar Augustus experience death, but witnesses to a passing comet in the case of the former and to the emperor's form ascending to heaven in the case of the latter are regarded

---

[30] Even though προσεκύνησαν probably has no stated object (as attested in MSS ℵ B D et al.), it seems clear enough that the one seen and encountered (i.e., Jesus) is the one reverenced (cf. Num 22:31; Acts 10:25–26). Cf. MSS A W Θ et al., which includes a pronoun to signify Jesus is the object of προσεκύνησαν.

[31] See Charles H. Talbert, "The Concept of Immortals in Mediterranean Antiquity," *JBL* 94 (1975): 419–36; John E. Alsup, *The Post-Resurrection Appearance Stories of the Gospel-Tradition* (CThM 5; Stuttgart: Calwer, 1975), 214–39; Adela Yarbro Collins, "Apotheosis and Resurrection," in *The New Testament and Hellenistic Judaism* (ed. Peder Borgen and Søren Giversen; Peabody, MA: Hendrickson, 1997), 88–100; Wendy Cotter, "Greco-Roman Apotheosis Traditions and the Resurrection Appearances in Matthew," in *The Gospel of Matthew in Current Study: Studies in Memory of William G. Thompson, S.J.* (ed. David E. Aune; Grand Rapids, MI: Eerdmans, 2001), 127–53; Daniel A. Smith, *The Post-Mortem Vindication of Jesus in the Sayings Gospel Q* (LNTS 338; London: T&T Clark, 2006), 53–86.

[32] ENOCH (LXX Gen 5:24; Sir 44:16; 49:14; *2 En.* 67:1–3; Philo, *QG* 1.86; Josephus, *Ant.* 1.85; 9.28) / MOSES (Josephus, *Ant.* 4.326; cf. Philo, *Mos.* 2.288–91; *Sacr.* 8–10; *QG* 1.86) / ELIJAH (Sir 48:9; 1 Macc 2:58; Philo, *QG* 1.86; Josephus, *Ant.* 9.28). See Smith, *Post-Mortem*, 68–77.

[33] Diodorus Siculus, *Hist.* 4.38.4–5; cf. Apollodorus, *Bibl.* 2.7.7.

[34] Diogenes Laertius, *Vit. phil.* 8.68. Others are similarly said to have mysteriously vanished and taken residence with the gods, such as Aristaeus (Diodorus Siculus, *Hist.* 4.82.6), Aeneas (Dionysius of Halicarnassus, *Ant. rom.* 1.64.4–5), and Cleomedes of Astypalaea (Pausanias, *Descr.* 6.9.6–9).

[35] Plutarch, *Rom.* 27.6–28.3; cf. Livy, *Hist.* 1.16; Dionysius of Halicarnassus, *Ant. rom.* 2.63.3–4; Ovid, *Fast.* 2.475–512.

as proof of their apotheosis.[36] Apollonius of Tyana is said to have fled to Dictynna's sanctuary where it is implied he has ascended to heaven, and then later he mysteriously appears to one of his followers.[37]

While pagan texts are often explicit about the deification of such heavenly translated figures, Jewish texts, by comparison, are rather silent in this regard.[38] Given the thoroughly Jewish character of the Gospel of Matthew, it could be, then, that the Matthean Jesus who rises from the dead is, like other comparable Jewish heroes, a remarkable figure but not necessarily divine. However, the final words of the risen Jesus set him apart from Enoch, Moses, and Elijah, as he makes quite lofty claims for himself that these others do not:

> All authority in heaven and on earth has been given to me. Therefore, go make disciples of all the nations, baptizing them into the name of the Father and of the Son and of the Holy Spirit, teaching them to keep all that I have commanded you. And behold, I am with you all the days until the end of the age. (Matt 28:18-20)

As remarkable as the accounts are of Elijah's spirit bestowed upon Elisha at his heavenly ascension (2 Kgs 2:9-12; cf. Sir 48:9, 12), or of Moses's prophecy over the tribes of Israel before his mysterious burial (Deut 33:1-34:6; cf. Philo, *Mos.* 2.288-91; Josephus, *Ant.* 4.320-26), or of Enoch's revelation of things past, present, and future before his heavenly ascension to stand eternally in the presence of God (*2 En.* 39:1-67:3), none of these figures are said to possess cosmic authority, nor to assure personal ongoing presence, nor to have a prominent place alongside God (and his Spirit) in identifying those who are to become converts from all over the world, as Jesus does here. Matthew's resurrected Jesus clearly surpasses the Jewish heroes in these ways.[39]

Jesus does indeed appear to be depicted as a godlike figure. It is sometimes noted—although the parallels are far from exact—that there are a number of similarities shared between Jesus and Rome's legendary deified founder, Romulus.[40] Both figures'

---

[36] JULIUS CAESAR (Pliny, *Nat.* 2.94; cf. Ovid, *Metam.* 15.746-51) / CAESAR AUGUSTUS (Suetonius, *Aug.* 99.4; Dio Cassius, *Hist. rom.* 56.46.1-2).

[37] Philostratus, *Vit. Apoll.* 8.30-31.

[38] With regard to the former, the figure receives divine status (e.g., "[Julius] Caesar is god in his own city . . . his glory quickly won, changed to a new heavenly body, a flaming star; but still more his offspring deified him" [Ovid, *Metam.* 15.746-50]), divine worship (e.g., "And after dwelling some time in the neighbourhood of Mount Haemus [Aristaeus] never was seen again of men, and became the recipient of immortal honours" [Diodorus Siculus, *Hist.* 4.82.6]), or both (e.g., "When the body of Aeneas was nowhere to be seen, some concluded that it had been translated to the gods. . . . And the Latins built a hero-shrine to him with this inscription: 'To the father and god of this place'" [Dionysius of Halicarnassus, *Ant. rom.* 1.64.4-5]; cf. Diogenes Laertius, *Vit. phil.* 8.68; Plutarch, *Rom.* 27.7-8). With regard to the latter, such divine ascriptions are lacking. If anything, Jewish texts note the worship of God who brings about such translations (*2 En.* 67:1-3; *T. Job* 39:8-40:4; cf. Rev 11:7-13).

[39] Although to some extent, Philo elsewhere makes somewhat comparable statements concerning the scope of Moses's authority ("[God] gave into [Moses's] hands the whole world as a portion well fitted for His heir" [*Mos.* 1.155]), such authority is limited to his earthly career, whereas Jesus's cosmic authority and presence continues on for all time (Matt 28:20).

[40] M. Eugene Boring, Klaus Berger, and Carsten Colpe, eds., *Hellenistic Commentary to the New Testament* (Nashville: Abingdon, 1995), 162-65; Carter, *Matthew*, 550, 553-54; Cotter, "Greco-Roman," *passim*.

passages are accompanied by unusual natural disturbances (Matt 27:45, 51; Plutarch, *Rom.* 27.6); both mysteriously vanish (Matt 28:5-6; Plutarch, *Rom.* 27.7); both make postmortem appearances to their followers (Matt 28:9-10, 17; Plutarch, *Rom.* 28.1); both issue a charge toward the advancement of their respective kingdoms (Matt 28:19; Plutarch, *Rom.* 28.2; cf. Livy, *Hist.* 1.16.7); both assure their followers of their godlike authority and presence (Matt 28:18, 20; Plutarch, *Rom.* 28.2; Livy, *Hist.* 1.16.7); and both are recipients of προσκύνησις (Matt 28:9, 17; Plutarch, *Rom.* 27.8). Without discounting Jesus's resemblance to this divine figure from the pagan world and its possible implications for Jesus's own divine status, there are also a couple of key OT allusions and echoes to take into consideration.

Most scholars agree that in Jesus's statement regarding all authority in heaven and on earth being given to him (Matt 28:18), there is an allusion to LXX Dan 7:13-14,[41] such that Jesus is identified with Daniel's heavenly figure ("one like a son of man"), who is given authority from God, whom all the nations shall serve (cf. Matt 28:19-20a [cf. also 28:9, 17]), and whose authority and reign are eternal (cf. Matt 28:20b). One could argue that Jesus's transcendence surpasses that of Daniel's heavenly Son of Man since, while the latter is said to have been given authority (ἐδόθη αὐτῷ ἐξουσία), Jesus has been given *all* authority, both on earth *and in heaven* (ἐδόθη μοι πᾶσα ἐξουσία ἐν οὐρανῷ καὶ ἐπὶ [τῆς] γῆς).[42]

It is also often observed that Jesus's commission of the disciples (Matt 28:19-20) resembles several OT commission narratives where God (or his spokesman) calls his servants to a task, charges them to observe his commands, and/or promises to be with them as they do so (Deut 31:1-8, 23; Josh 1:1-9; Judg 6:11-16; 1 Chron 22:7-16; Jer 1:4-10).[43] Jesus acts precisely as God in this way: he commissions his disciples to continue the task of disciple making for all the nations, calls for *his* commandments to be observed, and promises that *he* is with them forever. By contrast, note how Moses makes no claim of his own perpetual presence to follow his earthly departure but rather assures Joshua and Israel of God's presence (Deut 31:6, 8; cf. 1 Chron 22:11, 16).[44] By echoing these OT divine commissions in Jesus's closing words, Jesus appears to be associated with God in such a way that he is somehow—as his final reassurance and its harkening back to his identification as Emmanuel signify—"God with us."

From the risen Jesus's resemblance to divine figures such as the deified Romulus, to the more direct links to the Danielic Son of Man, and even to God himself, it is clear

---

[41] Davies and Allison, *Matthew*, 3:682-83; Hagner, *Matthew*, 2:886; Nolland, *Matthew*, 1264; France, *Matthew*, 1112-13 (cf. Luz, *Matthew*, 3:619-20). See esp. Jane Schaberg, *The Father, the Son and the Holy Spirit: The Triadic Phrase in Matthew 28:19b* (SBLDS 61; Chico, CA: Scholars Press, 1982), 111-41.

[42] Although this difference is one of the reasons David R. Bauer disputes an allusion to Dan 7:13-14 (*The Structure of Matthew's Gospel: A Study in Literary Design* [JSNTSup 31; Sheffield: Almond Press, 1988], 111-12), it is better to conclude with France that Matthew has reshaped the Danielic model so that Jesus transcends it in this way (*Matthew*, 1112-13, n. 22).

[43] Davies and Allison, *Matthew*, 3:679-80; Hagner, *Matthew*, 2:883; Carter, *Matthew*, 549; Nolland, *Matthew*, 1261; France, *Matthew*, 1109 (cf. Luz, *Matthew*, 3:618-20). See esp. Benjamin J. Hubbard, *The Matthean Redaction of a Primitive Apostolic Commissioning: An Exegesis of Matthew 28:16-20* (SBLDS 19; Missoula, MT: Scholars Press, 1974).

[44] Thus, *pace* Davies and Allison, Jesus is not so much presented here as a new Moses (*Matthew*, 3:679-80), but rather he is presented speaking and acting as God does (Luz, *Matthew*, 3:619-20).

that Jesus is presented as a transcendent, godlike figure, even taking a place alongside God the Father and the Holy Spirit, and in this divine association, identifying himself by the highly suggestive designation "Son" (i.e., God's Son).

In view of the foregoing, it is again reasonable to conclude that the προσκύνησις of the risen Jesus is intended to correspond to his superhuman loftiness and thus is to be understood as a proper reverential response to it. Certain details linked to both instances of προσκύνησις seem to further support this. The women's προσκύνησις, for example, is described with the somewhat unique accompanying action of grasping Jesus's feet (28:9). While this may simply further signify the lowly posture of those who reverence another with προσκύνησις (cf. 2:11; 4:9; 18:26),[45] it is probably not a coincidence that whereas in all three of these other instances, Matthew consistently uses πίπτω + προσκυνέω to describe the prostration,[46] here he departs from this pattern and instead combines προσκυνέω with ἐκράτησαν αὐτοῦ τοὺς πόδας. It may be that along with reverencing Jesus with προσκύνησις, the women grasp his feet to be assured of his corporeality,[47] since the appearance of Jesus following his death might have given the women the initial impression that they were encountering a spirit (cf. Luke 24:36-43). Although Matthew gives no description of Jesus's appearance, hints of its epiphanic character are suggested by Jesus's words to the women, "μὴ φοβεῖσθε" (28:10), which, again, are words of comfort typically spoken by heavenly figures in angelophanic and theophanic appearances (cf. 28:5, where the angel who suddenly appears to the women also utters these words).

The eleven disciples' προσκύνησις of Jesus is juxtaposed with the immediately following comment "οἱ δὲ ἐδίστασαν" (28:17). Although difficulties surrounding this terse clause have generated considerable scholarly debate regarding its precise meaning,[48] there appears to be a general consensus that, as Richard France put it, there is a sense in which those confronted by the risen Jesus "did not know how to respond to Jesus in this new situation, where he was familiar and yet now different."[49]

---

[45] Luz, *Matthew*, 3:607.
[46] All other uses of προσκυνέω in Matthew appear without any accompanying prostration terminology.
[47] Grundmann, *Matthäus*, 570; Gnilka, *Matthäusevangelium*, 2:495; Carter, *Matthew*, 547; France, *Matthew*, 1102. See esp. Dale C. Allison Jr., *Studies in Matthew: Interpretation Past and Present* (Grand Rapids, MI: Baker, 2005), 107-16.
[48] The two main difficulties concern the referents implied by οἱ δὲ (does it refer to all eleven disciples, to some of the eleven, or to a separate group of people present with the eleven?), and the nuance of the term ἐδίστασαν–"doubt" (is it to be understood in a strong sense [i.e., disbelieve] or a mild sense [i.e., hesitate]?). For discussions of these difficulties and the various solutions offered, see I. P. Ellis, "But Some Doubted," *NTS* 14 (1968): 574-80; Charles H. Giblin, "A Note on Doubt and Reassurance in Mt 28:16-20," *CBQ* 37 (1975): 68-75; Kenneth Grayston, "The Translation of Matthew 28:17," *JSNT* 21 (1984): 105-9; Kenneth L. McKay, "The Use of *hoi de* in Matthew 28.17: A Response to K. Grayston," *JSNT* 24 (1985): 71-72; P. W. van der Horst, "Once More: The Translation of οἱ δὲ in Matthew 28.17," *JSNT* 27 (1986): 27-30, and Keith H. Reeves, "They Worshipped Him, and They Doubted: Matthew 28.17," *BT* 49 (1998): 344-49.

L. G. Parkhurst argues that the doubt/hesitation concerned the propriety of worshiping Jesus, which Jesus dispels in his closing words, affirming his divinity and thus his proper reception of worship ("Matthew 28:16-20 Reconsidered," *ExpTim* 90 [1979]: 179-80). The problem with this proposal is Jesus has frequently been the recipient of προσκύνησις in Matthew, even in scenes where he appears to stand in the role of Yahweh (14:22-33), and there is no suggestion that its propriety is an issue.

[49] France, *Matthew*, 1112.

Whether the "doubt" or "hesitation" here is due to complications in fully recognizing or accepting a resurrected Jesus himself (cf. Luke 24:16, 36–43; John 20:14, 25; 21:4)[50] or to uncertainties regarding the implications of Jesus truly being raised from the dead,[51] so astonishing is the appearance of a resurrected Jesus that it even generates a certain disorientation among those who knew him best, which undoubtedly heightens the sense of the προσκύνησις he is portrayed receiving.

In both instances, it is immediately upon encountering the resurrected Jesus that his followers reverence him with προσκύνησις. Although, technically, neither of the two instances of προσκύνησις are in response to Jesus's loaded closing statement, a key intratextual link shows Matthew intends for the προσκύνησις of Jesus here to be understood not merely as a spontaneous, startled response to the appearance of the risen Jesus but even more so as the appropriate reverence directed to one who is as Jesus claims to be in his final words. Recalling our discussion of the temptation account, we noted Satan's futile attempt on a mountain to receive προσκύνησις from Jesus as one who claimed he could give Jesus all the kingdoms of the world (4:8–10). Here in the resurrection account, it is the risen Jesus, appearing to his disciples on a mountain, who possesses comprehensive authority, not only over the earthly realm (cf. Satan's earthly offer of the kingdoms of the world) but over the heavenly realm as well, and is therefore truly worthy to receive the kind of reverence through προσκύνησις that Satan attempts to obtain.[52]

A final, related observation and question allows us to segue from our initial findings thus far toward more holistic considerations concerning the significance of Jesus's reception of προσκύνησις in Matthew. This harkening back to the temptation episode not only recalls Satan's attempt to receive the προσκύνησις from Jesus that Jesus comes to receive from his followers but also recalls Jesus's response to Satan that προσκύνησις is to be given to God alone. Does Matthew suggest by such use of προσκυνέω language that Jesus is worthy of the kind of worship typically reserved for God and/or that Jesus shares a status equal to that of God? In light of some of the observations already made in which Jesus is found speaking and acting in ways uniquely characteristic of God himself, and is besides God the only other legitimate recipient of προσκύνησις, we must certainly give further consideration to this possibility.

C. The significance of the Προσκύνησις of Jesus in Matthew

There is no question that the term προσκυνέω is a Matthean favorite in the Gospel's depiction of the reverence of Jesus. Yet scholarly opinions regarding the precise significances and christological implications of the προσκύνησις of Jesus in Matthew

---

[50] Cf. Horst, "Once," 29; Davies and Allison, *Matthew*, 3:682; Nolland, *Matthew*, 1263.
[51] Cf. Hagner, *Matthew*, 2:885; France, *Matthew*, 1112.
[52] On the verbal (ὄρος, πᾶς, δίδωμι, and προσκυνέω) and conceptual links tying 4:8–10 and 28:16–18 together, see Grundmann, *Matthäus*, 103, 576–77; Davies and Allison, *Matthew*, 1:369, 404; Luz, *Matthew*, 1:153; 3:621; France, *Matthew*, 126, 1113.

remain divided. For some, the προσκύνησις of Jesus in Matthew falls short of signifying divine worship or an acknowledgment of Jesus's equality with God. Eugene Lemcio, for example, notes how frequently the contexts point to Jesus's reception of προσκύνησις as a kingly figure, as in the homage he receives from the magi as "King of the Jews" (2:2, 11; cf. 2:8), from the Canaanite woman who cries out to him for help as "Lord, Son of David" (15:22, 25), and from the mother of the sons of Zebedee who petitions him as a king capable of granting positions of honor and authority in his kingdom (20:20–21).[53] Although the προσκύνησις of Jesus by his disciples in the sea-walking and resurrection accounts may suggest something more than mere homage is meant, the mixed reactions of προσκύνησις and doubt (14:31, 33; 28:17), according to Lemcio, just as much suggest something less than worship is probably meant. He concludes accordingly: "The προσκυνεῖν of Jesus may be something more than reverence/obeisance but less than worship *per se*."[54]

Peter Head shares a similar view.[55] While he agrees with those who find Matthew's redactional preference for προσκυνέω noteworthy, he is unconvinced that his preference for this term is best explained by a desire to emphasize worship of Jesus as divine. Rather, Matthew may have simply desired to use a term that more clearly expresses an attitude of reverence. Thus, his substitution of προσκυνέω for Mark's prostration terms is simply "to translate the physical gesture of Mark."[56] Moreover, Head explains, προσκυνέω in Matthew is used so variously for a number of different types of supplication, submission, and reverence—including some negative examples, such as Herod's "insincere worship" (2:8), the mother's "scheming and ill-informed attitude" (20:20), and the disciples' "hesitant or doubting worship" (28:17)—that the term is hardly likely to have been used to connote worship of Jesus as divine.[57]

Although neither Lemcio nor Head brings Matt 4:10 into this discussion, other scholars, who are representative of their overall position, do. David Kupp says this passage makes clear that while Jesus's frequent reception of προσκύνησις elsewhere in Matthew may indeed be highly significant, it is not equivalent to the divine worship God receives since, as Jesus himself states plainly here in 4:10, such worship is reserved for God alone.[58] Jesus is God's Son, "the Emmanuel Messiah," and his frequent reception

---

[53] Eugene E. Lemcio, *The Past of Jesus in the Gospels* (SNTSMS 68; Cambridge: Cambridge University Press, 1991), 67–68.
[54] Lemcio, *Past*, 68.
[55] Peter M. Head, *Christology and the Synoptic Problem: An Argument for Markan Priority* (SNTSMS 94; Cambridge: Cambridge University Press, 1997), 129–30.
[56] Head, *Christology*, 129–30.
[57] Head, *Christology*, 130. He does go on to explain, however, that it probably would not have been long for later Christian readers to have seen such deeper significance in Matthew's προσκυνέω language (*Christology*, 130–31). If so, one wonders if such impressions from Christian readers are more likely a result of importing a significance Matthew himself did not originally intend or of drawing out a significance he did indeed intend!
[58] David D. Kupp, *Matthew's Emmanuel: Divine Presence and God's People in the First Gospel* (SNTSMS 90; Cambridge: Cambridge University Press, 1996), 226.

of προσκύνησις is certainly a recognition and reflection of this aspect of his identity, "but he is not God," and the προσκύνησις he receives is not the worship God receives.[59]

Markus Müller responds similarly in this matter, as he too considers whether there is an inconsistency between 4:10 and Matthew's frequent depiction of Jesus receiving προσκύνησις.[60] He appeals to the leper's encounter with Jesus as one helpful example in resolving this apparent contradiction, since here we see that the leper's προσκύνησις of Jesus is followed by Jesus's charge that he offer the sacrifices prescribed in the Mosaic Law (8:4), thereby ultimately giving worship to God.[61] Thus, while Jesus may rightly receive προσκύνησις because "in der Person Jesu Gott gegenwärtig ist,"[62] this is not quite equivalent to the worship that Jesus himself states in 4:10 and demonstrates in 8:4 is to be given to God alone.

Finally, Horst came to similar conclusions when he differentiated between what he considered to be "unwillkommene und willkommene Proskynesen" extended to Jesus.[63] The former are rebuffed since they border on an idolization of man (e.g., 15:22ff; 19:16–17; 20:20ff),[64] while the latter are approved (or at least tolerated), since those who extend such reverence to Jesus are those "die die Hilfe Gottes durch ihn begehren, und die, die Gott im Sohne Gottes oder im Messias die Ehre geben, wenn eine Machterweisung Gottes die Herzen zum Glauben überwältigt."[65] Ultimately then, the προσκύνησις of Jesus is the recognition of God at work through Jesus and therefore is understood to be worship directed to God through Jesus.[66]

For others, the προσκύνησις of Jesus in Matthew does indeed have implications for his worthiness to receive divine worship and/or his equality with God. Mark Powell considers Jesus to be worthy of divine worship in his reception of προσκύνησις without this contradicting 4:10, since, as he states, "Matthew regards Jesus as one in whom God is uniquely present (1.23)."[67]

Richard Bauckham finds Matthew's redactional preference for προσκυνέω highly significant, especially in view of his observation that while the term could be used in a mild sense for respect or homage paid to a human, over time it came to be associated with a type of reverence which in certain contexts could imply idolatrous worship of humans or angels (e.g., LXX Add Esth C 5–7; *Apoc. Zeph.* 6:14–15; Philo, *Legat.* 116).

---

[59] Kupp, *Emmanuel*, 227. He states elsewhere his view that Matthew's "Emmanuel christology" amounts to "a basic functional or representative equivalence between Jesus and God," yet "it does not require that Jesus is God" (*Emmanuel*, 220–21).

[60] Markus Müller, "Proskynese und Christologie nach Matthäus," in *Kirche und Volk Gottes: Festschrift für Jürgen Roloff zum 70. Geburtstag* (ed. Martin Karrer et al.; Neukirchen-Vluyn: Neukirchener Verlag, 2000), 213.

[61] Müller, "Proskynese," 220–21.

[62] Müller, "Proskynese," 223. By this is meant that "Gottes helfende und heilende Gegenwart—die Gegenwart des Emmanuel—in der Person Jesu erkennbar werden läßt" ("Proskynese," 223).

[63] Horst, *Proskynein*, 236.

[64] This is how Horst viewed Jesus's responses in his encounters with the Canaanite woman (yet only initially in this case is Jesus repulsed by the woman's reverence), the rich man, and the mother of the sons of Zebedee (see *Proskynein*, 223–25, 227–30, 233).

[65] Horst, *Proskynein*, 236.

[66] See further Horst, *Proskynein*, 185–94.

[67] Powell, "Typology," 4–5.

This becomes all the more significant when one observes that "[Matthew's] unparalleled uses tend to be in epiphanic contexts (Matt 2:2, 8, 11; 14:33; 28:9, 17)."[68] He goes on to conclude, "Combined with his emphasis on the presence of the exalted Christ among his people (18:20; 28:20), Matthew's usage must reflect the practice of the worship of Jesus in his church."[69]

Larry Hurtado is in basic agreement with Bauckham on these points.[70] Having argued extensively for the binitarian shape of early Christian devotion in previous publications,[71] and agreeing with Bauckham that Matthew's preference for προσκυνέω is highly significant, which is particularly evident in contexts where Jesus's transcendent, godlike status is most prominent (14:33; 28:9, 17), Hurtado argues that "[Matthew] rather consistently portrays Jesus's disciples and those who approached him for favours as offering him reverence that was almost certainly to be seen by readers as prefiguring their own 'post-Easter' devotional practice."[72]

David Peterson essentially agrees that while most of the characters in the story who reverence Jesus with προσκύνησις do so in a way that would have been appropriate for a human superior, Matthew expects his readers, who have been alerted from the start to more profound aspects of Jesus's identity (1:18–23), to discern the deeper significance: Jesus is truly worthy of worship because he is God's Son and Emmanuel, "God with us."[73]

Finally, Hak Chol Kim also highlights a number of these same points in making the case that the προσκύνησις of Jesus is equivalent to the worship typically reserved for God. From there, he proceeds to discuss the sociopolitical implications that the worship of Jesus had for Matthew's community.[74]

From this brief survey, we get the sense that several questions can be raised that perhaps have not been adequately or thoroughly addressed in making sense of the προσκύνησις of Jesus in Matthew and which may account for such scholarly divide. For instance, what does it mean for Matthew's Jesus to be the Son of God or Emmanuel? Do these hint at his divine identity and therefore his worthiness to receive divine worship (Powell; Peterson), or do they simply point to his divine agency and therefore his worthiness to receive a kind of reverence which may be something more than human obeisance, but still less than divine worship (Kupp; Müller)? If προσκυνέω is to be understood as divine worship, is Jesus truly the ultimate object, or is it to be understood as worship of God through Jesus (Horst)? Can the προσκύνησις of Jesus simply be interpreted straightforwardly as a kind of reverence shown to humans common in the day (Lemcio; Head), or is it also at another level designed to be reflective of the church's worship of Jesus in Matthew's day (Bauckham; Hurtado)? A number of these

---

[68] Bauckham, "Jesus," 3:813.
[69] Bauckham, "Jesus," 3:813. See also Bauckham, "Throne," 67–68.
[70] Larry W. Hurtado, "Pre-70 CE Jewish Opposition to Christ-Devotion," *JTS* 50 (1999): 40–41; Hurtado, *Lord*, 337–38; Hurtado, "Homage," 141–46.
[71] Hurtado, *One*, 99–114; Hurtado, "Binitarian," 187–213; Hurtado, *Lord*, esp. 134–53.
[72] Hurtado, "Homage," 146. Cf. Held, "Matthew," 229–30.
[73] David Peterson, *Engaging with God: A Biblical Theology of Worship* (Grand Rapids, MI: Eerdmans, 1993), 84–87.
[74] Hak Chol Kim, "The Worship of Jesus in the Gospel of Matthew," *Bib* 93 (2012): 227–41.

studies lack the kind of detailed attention to the Gospel of Matthew that is necessary for providing more satisfactory answers to these and other related questions.

The most recent work on this subject by Joshua Leim offers the fullest study to date and attempts to address many of these and other issues related to the significance of the προσκύνησις of Jesus in Matthew.[75] He too notes the various ways these scholars address these issues and raises concerns regarding the problems they encounter in doing so.[76] Essentially, the main problem he finds plaguing every scholarly approach thus far is a failure to pay adequate attention to Matthew's literary artistry at work in two key ways: (1) the use of προσκυνέω in such a way that Matthew does indeed direct the reader to view the προσκύνησις of Jesus as the worship typically reserved for Israel's God; and (2) the rearticulation of the identity of Israel's κύριος ὁ θεός around the Father-Son relation. Leim argues that the reason Jesus can be portrayed receiving through προσκύνησις the worship which Jesus himself says is reserved for Israel's God alone in 4:10 is because he is included in the identity of κύριος ὁ θεός as the filial κύριος alongside the paternal κύριος.

Leim gives detailed attention to a number of important features in the Gospel of Matthew in making his case for Jesus's divinity and his reception of divine worship. Since his is the most thorough treatment of this debated issue in Matthew and expressly aims at a more precise, coherent understanding of the significance of Jesus's reception of προσκύνησις than has been offered by scholars thus far, we will proceed by giving primary attention to Leim's assessment, bringing other scholarly interlocutors into our discussion along the way where appropriate.

Leim argues extensively for an inextricable bond between God and Jesus in Matthew such that the identity of the God of Israel is reformulated to include Jesus, the Son of God, as the filial κύριος alongside his Father, the paternal κύριος. He reexamines several well-known passages in Matthew, which, though already widely recognized among scholars as exhibiting a high Christology, he feels have generally been underappreciated for the way they contribute to Matthew's reformulation of the identity of Israel's God. A key passage launching his analysis is Matt 22:41–46, which he says, "epitomizes one of the most important christological motifs relevant to my argument, namely, the relationship between the Father, the Son, and their identity as κύριος."[77] Here Jesus questions the Pharisees about the Christ's—and thus, by implication, his own—sonship: "What do you think about the Christ? Whose son is he?" (22:42). The brief exchange reveals the Pharisees' simple response that he is David's son to be somewhat problematic since, through Jesus's appeal to Ps 110 (LXX 109):1, he is shown to be David's κύριος, invited to sit at the right hand of God, who is also referred to as κύριος. Although the Pharisees are left stumped by Jesus's final question, "If then David calls him 'lord,' how is he his son?" (22:45), the reader knows very well by this point in the Gospel narrative that the solution to this conundrum

---

[75] Joshua E. Leim, *Matthew's Theological Grammar: The Father and the Son* (WUNT 2/402; Tübingen: Mohr Siebeck, 2015).
[76] Leim, *Grammar*, 5–14.
[77] Leim, *Grammar*, 177.

is found in the more profound sonship attributed to Jesus; the reason the messianic descendant of David is addressed by him as "lord" is because he is the Son of God (cf. 2:15; 3:17; 4:3, 6; 8:29; 11:27; 14:33; 16:16; 17:5; 21:37–38). Leim calls attention here to an "enormity" that becomes increasingly heightened in view of the following: (1) the application of Ps 110 (LXX 109):1 provocatively envisioning one so exalted as to partake in a heavenly session beside God; (2) the use of the LXX text resulting in both God and this exalted figure being identified by the same appellation κύριος; and (3) the whole of Matthew's story of Jesus being told in such a way that one is compelled to see here an identification between the filial and paternal κύριοι.[78]

Continuing on from this latter point, Leim looks back to earlier passages in Matthew that contribute to this close linking of the filial and paternal κύριοι. In 3:1–17, the coming of the κύριος whose way John the Baptist prepares is told in such a way that while one initially expects the referent to be Israel's God all the way through (e.g., Isa 40:3 is cited [3:3] which portends the advent of Israel's κύριος, Yahweh; John's attire [3:4; cf. 2 Kgs 1:8] and speech [3:10–12; cf. Mal 3:19] recall Elijah and Malachi's prediction of Elijah preceding Yahweh's coming [Mal 3:1, 23–24], respectively; John explicitly refers to "God" [ὁ θεὸς] and his involvement in this context [3:9–10]), subtle hints of a figure distinct from God eventually emerge (e.g., John's unworthiness to carry this figure's sandals [3:11] suggests a human being is in mind) with the final appearance of Jesus in 3:13 ultimately leading the reader to identify him as this "coming one" who follows John and the κύριος whose way John prepares. The movement of this passage leaves an impression of Jesus as one who is closely tied to the activity and identity of God as this OT anticipated κύριος, which finds its ultimate expression in the Father-Son relationship (3:17) through which they share their identity as κύριος.[79]

This movement is reinforced in 11:1–12:8, where Jesus himself confirms that he and John the Baptist fulfill Isaiah's and Malachi's prophecies concerning the coming of Israel's κύριος (11:3–5; cf. Isa 26:19; 29:18–19; 35:5–6; [cf. also Isa 61:1 for the activity of the "anointed one"]) and the messenger "Elijah" who is to prepare his way (11:10, 14; cf. Mal 3:1, 23). None of this is invalidated by the rejection they both experience (11:16–24), since it is in the nature of the relationship of the Father and the Son, who share exclusive knowledge of one another and mutual prerogative to reveal one another, thereby to conceal and reveal such things as they so choose (11:25–27).[80] Leim ties this in with the immediately following pericope where Jesus makes the astonishing claim as Son of Man to be κύριος of the Sabbath (12:1–8). This continuation, he argues, further supports his contention that in 11:25–27, the Son Jesus claims to have a share not only in his Father's revelatory authority but also in his lordship over heaven and earth.[81]

The same general pattern is also observed in 14:22–33, where Jesus exercises Yahweh-like lordship over the sea, which leads to a climactic προσκύνησις and

---

[78] Leim, *Grammar*, 184–86.
[79] Leim, *Grammar*, 186–89.
[80] Leim, *Grammar*, 189–97.
[81] Leim, *Grammar*, 197–202. Here, however, there is considerable debate over whether the πάντα that the Father has handed over to the Son goes beyond revelatory authority to include cosmic authority as Leim holds. See n. 108 below.

confession of Jesus as Son of God. In this theophanic context, Jesus's identity as κύριος (cf. 14:28, 30) once again closely ties him to God and again in such a way that it is ultimately expressed in the Father-Son relationship.[82]

Returning to the more immediate context of 22:41–46, Leim discusses the significance of the immediately preceding and following material for the shared identity between the Father and the Son as κύριος.[83] In 22:34–40, Jesus affirms the love of κύριος ὁ θεός (Deut 6:5) as the first and greatest commandment, but then in his questioning of the Pharisees about the Christ's identity which immediately follows, he hints that "κύριος ὁ θεός has a 'Son,' who is also κύριος," and "this filial κύριος shares the divine throne with his Father."[84] This close linkage of 22:41–46 to 22:34–40 "serves to place a messianic and divine-filial 'impress' on the identity of Israel's κύριος," and "to impose retrospectively a certain christological pressure on the command to 'love the Lord your God.'"[85] This is further developed by what closely follows in 23:8–10, where evocations of Israel's Shema constitutes a reshaping of Israel's confession of the "one" God to include both the Father ("there is one [εἷς] who is your Father—the one in heaven" [23:9]) and Jesus, the Christ ("there is one [εἷς] who is your teacher" [23:8]; "there is one [εἷς] who is your instructor—the Christ" [23:10]).[86]

Leim rounds off his argument by discussing the way Matthew ties together Jesus's identity as Son of God with his identity as Emmanuel in 1:21–25; 18:19–20; and 28:19–20.[87] It is as "the Son" (τοῦ υἱοῦ [28:19]; cf. πατρός μου [18:19]; υἱόν [1:21][88]) that Jesus assures the community formed and gathered "in his name" (εἰς τὸ ἐμὸν ὄνομα [18:20]; cf. εἰς τὸ ὄνομα . . . τοῦ υἱοῦ [28:19]; τὸ ὄνομα αὐτοῦ Ἰησοῦν [1:21]; τὸ ὄνομα αὐτοῦ Ἐμμανουήλ [1:23]) that he is "with them" (ἐγὼ μεθ' ὑμῶν εἰμι [28:20]; cf. εἰμι ἐν μέσῳ αὐτῶν [18:20]; καλέσουσιν τὸ ὄνομα αὐτοῦ Ἐμμανουήλ, ὅ ἐστιν μεθερμηνευόμενον μεθ' ἡμῶν ὁ θεός [1:23]). Through this Son-Emmanuel link, the Father's and Son's shared identity as κύριος is further defined: it is precisely because Jesus is the Son of God, who in the Father-Son relation is included in the identity of Israel's κύριος, that he is truly God with us, "the earthly filial presence of the paternal κύριος."[89]

Leim has certainly honed in on a number of key features of Matthew's christological portrait that pose problems for those who perhaps have too hastily concluded that Matthew's high Christology is merely a "functional" Christology, that is, that Jesus is simply God's agent who takes on divine roles and uniquely manifests God's presence without being identified with God.[90] A comparison of the Matthean Jesus with other exalted intermediary figures in early Jewish literature affords greater clarity in this matter.

---

[82] Leim, *Grammar*, 202.
[83] Leim, *Grammar*, 203–18.
[84] Leim, *Grammar*, 205.
[85] Leim, *Grammar*, 206.
[86] Leim, *Grammar*, 210–15.
[87] Leim, *Grammar*, 218–31.
[88] See Leim, *Grammar*, 221–24, where he argues that Jesus's divine sonship is indeed in view in the infancy narrative.
[89] Leim, *Grammar*, 224.
[90] For example, Kupp, *Emmanuel*, 220–21, 225–27; Müller, "Proskynese," 223; Luz, *Matthew*, 1:96, 3:639.

For instance, while the christological application of OT texts originally concerned with Israel's God and his activity (Matt 3:3; 11:3–5, 10; 24:29–30; etc.) appears to be comparable to the same phenomenon at play in the case of the Enochic Son of Man in the *Similitudes of Enoch*, the messianic figure in *4 Ezra*, and the heavenly figure Melchizedek in 11Q13, there is a notable difference in the case of Jesus that could be seen as taking a significant step beyond these analogues. First, with regard to similarities, the eschatological appearances of some of these figures to carry out divine judgment is, much like the Matthean Jesus, described with language and imagery reminiscent of God's own coming for judgment in the OT. Thus, the cosmic upheaval accompanying the Son of Man's (i.e., Jesus's) Yahweh-like eschatological return (Matt 24:29–30; cf. Isa 13:10) is comparable to the imagery of mountains/people melting like wax at the eschatological appearances of the Enochic Son of Man/Chosen One and the "man from the sea" (*1 En.* 52:6; *4 Ezra* 13:4; cf. Mic 1:3–4; Pss 68:2; 97:5). Similarly, the adaptation of OT prophecy such that preparing the way before "me" (i.e., Yahweh) has become preparing the way before "you" (i.e., Jesus) (Matt 11:10; cf. Mal 3:1) is comparable to the way that "the year of Yahweh's favor" has become "the year of Melchizedek's favor" (11Q13 II, 9; cf. Isa 61:2) and the way that "the day of Yahweh" has become "the day of the Chosen One" (*1 En.* 61:5; cf. Isa 13:6; Joel 2:1; etc.). Clearly, such remarkable biblical adaptations are not entirely unique to Jesus and would undoubtedly be considered by many as evidence that Jesus is no more directly identified with God by virtue of such connections than these other highly exalted figures are.

However, what does appear to be unique to Jesus is the application of an OT text such that Jesus is even suggestively *named* as the κύριος originally referring to Yahweh (Matt 3:3; cf. Isa 40:3). As striking as the adaptations are of "the year of Yahweh's favor" and "the day of Yahweh" to become "the year of Melchizedek's favor" and "the day of the Chosen One," Matt 3:3 is even more striking in the way that it retains LXX Isaiah's original κύριος (the substitute for the divine name Yahweh here) in its christological application. Here, "the way of the κύριος (i.e., Yahweh)" is not, like the examples above, reformulated to become "the way of Jesus," but rather it is provocatively employed in Matthew in such a way that, as Leim correctly observes, the reader's initial and most natural impression that the κύριος of Isa 40:3 whose way John the Baptist prepares must be Yahweh eventually gives way to the identification of this κύριος as Jesus.[91]

Although 11Q13's identification of Melchizedek as the אלוהים of two OT passages (11Q13 II, 10; cf. Ps 82:1 / 11Q13 II, 15–16, 23–25;[92] cf. Isa 52:7) may appear to relativize the significance of Jesus's identification as the κύριος of Isa 40:3, the details suggest otherwise. While in their original contexts, the אלוהים of Ps 82:1 (the first occurrence of the term) and Isa 52:7 refer to Israel's God, the author of 11Q13 appears

---

[91] Leim, *Grammar*, 187–88. See also Carl Davis, *The Name and Way of the Lord: Old Testament Themes, New Testament Christology* (JSNTSup 129; Sheffield: Sheffield Academic, 1996), 72–87. Davis's survey of Jewish interpretations of Isa 40:3 reveals that while there may have been broad connections made between Isa 40:3 and the coming of (a) messianic figure(s), nothing comes close to Matthew's direct identification of Jesus as the coming κύριος of Isa 40:3.

[92] In this latter text, the identification of Melchizedek with the אלוהים of Isa 52:7 is somewhat complicated by the fragmentary state of the text. For a discussion on the justification for this identification, see Mason, *Priest*, 180–82.

to have understood the אלוהים of these two passages to be an exalted angelic figure distinct from Yahweh.[93] In light of other evidence from Qumran that angelic beings could be called אלים (1QM I, 10; 4Q400 1 I, 20; etc.; note this use in 11Q13 II, 14) and אלוהים (4Q400 1 II, 7; 4Q403 1 I, 32–33; note this use for the second occurrence of אלוהים in 11Q13, 10),[94] this association is certainly plausible.[95] This understanding of Melchizedek as an angelic אלוהים distinct from Yahweh is particularly evident in the way the author makes a consistent verbal distinction between Melchizedek, whom he refers to as אלוהים, and Yahweh, for whom he reserves the singular אל.[96] This verbal distinction is maintained both in his citations/applications of OT passages (e.g., "'Elohim (אלוהים —i.e., Melchizedek) will [st]and in the assem[bly of God (אל—i.e., Yahweh)]'" [11Q13 II, 10]; "'[Saying to Zi]on: your God (אלוהיך) rules' And 'your God (אלוהיך)' is [... Melchizedek, who will fr]e[e them from the ha]nd of Belial" [11Q13 II, 23–25]), as well as throughout his discussion (e.g., "turn[ing aside] from the commandments of God (אל—i.e., Yahweh)" [11Q13 II, 12]).[97] By comparison, then, while this application of אלוהים texts such that Melchizedek is even identified as אלוהים is certainly striking and speaks to his exalted status, a unique step beyond this is taken in Jesus's case with the application of LXX Isa 40:3's κύριος/Yahweh text such that Jesus is suggestively identified by this term, which here renders the divine name.[98] It is this specific phenomenon of Jesus being explicitly named as the κύριος of OT texts originally referring not simply to "God," but to "Yahweh," found here and elsewhere in the NT (e.g., Mark 1:3 par; Rom 10:13; 1 Cor 1:31; 1 Thess 5:2; Acts 2:21;

---

[93] See Mason, *Priest*, 177–83; Bauckham, *Jesus*, 222–24. Although there is some debate regarding the identity of this Melchizedek, with some scholars taking the figure to be a human messiah (Paul A. Rainbow, "Melchizedek as a Messiah at Qumran," *BBR* 7 [1997]: 179–94), others, a hypostasis of Yahweh (Józef T. Milik, "*Milkî-ṣedeq et Milkî-rešaʿ* dans les anciens écrits juifs et chrétiens," *JJS* 23 [1972]: 125), and again others, Yahweh himself designated by the title "Melchizedek" (Franco Manzi, *Melchisedek e l'angelologia nell'Epistola agli Ebrei e a Qumran* [AnBib 136; Rome: Pontificio Istituto Biblico, 1997], 102), most consider Melchizedek to be an angelic being, often thought to be identified with the archangel Michael (A. S. van der Woude, "Melchisedek als himmlische Erlösergestalt in den neugefundenen eschatologischen Midraschim aus Qumran Höhle XI," *OtSt* 14 [1965]: 367–70; Paul J. Kobelski, *Melchizedek and Melchiresaʿ* [CBQMS 10; Washington DC: Catholic Biblical Association of America, 1981], 71–74; Émile Puech, "Notes sur le manuscrit de XIQMelkîsédeq," *RevQ* 12 [1987]: 510–13; Collins and Collins, *King and Messiah*, 79–86).

[94] See Carol A. Newsom, *Songs of the Sabbath Sacrifice: A Critical Edition* (Atlanta, GA: Scholars Press, 1985), 23–24.

[95] The unique use of אלוהים in this case, however, to designate a *single* angelic figure is striking and speaks to Melchizedek's distinction as a highly exalted angel.

[96] Mason, *Priest*, 177–83; Bauckham, *Jesus*, 222–24.

[97] All translations of texts of the Dead Sea Scrolls are from *The Dead Sea Scrolls: Study Edition* (ed. Florentino García Martínez and Eibert J. C. Tigchelaar; 2 vols.; Leiden: Brill, 2000).

[98] Although later in Matthew, other OT texts relating to Jesus's identity as the coming κύριος presumes his distinction from God the Father ("Behold, ἐγὼ [i.e., God the Father] send my messenger before σου [i.e., Jesus's] face, who will prepare your way before you" [Matt 11:10; cf. Exod 23:20; Mal 3:1]), this does not employ the kind of significant verbal distinctions between Melchizedek and God in 11Q13 II, 10. One might argue for a distinction in Matthew between Jesus who is κύριος and his Father who is θεός and κύριος ὁ θεός, but this is not decisive since, following Leim's argument, Matthew's narrative rearticulation of the identity of Israel's κύριος ὁ θεός to include the filial κύριος alongside the paternal κύριος allows for Jesus's identification as μεθ' ἡμῶν ὁ θεός (1:23) to be understood in strong terms.

etc.), that distinguishes Jesus from these other exalted intermediary figures, and thus is rightly highlighted as a unique, profound feature of early Christian views of Jesus as one uniquely linked to God.[99]

Another significant point of comparison and contrast concerns the association of the various exalted figures with God in their relation to the faithful community. Again, there do appear to be some similarities between the Matthean Jesus and exalted intermediary figures in Judaism in this respect. Just as Matthew can speak perhaps deliberately suggestively of God's people (2:6) as belonging also to Jesus as "his people" (1:21; cf. also references to Jesus's wheat [3:12] and Jesus's elect [24:31]),[100] 11Q13 speaks of both "the men of the lot of Melchizedek" (11Q13 II, 8; cf. "the men of God's lot" [1QM I, 5; 1QS II, 2]) and "the inheritance of Melchizedek" (11Q13 II, 5; cf. "the inheritance of God" [4Q511 2 I, 5; Deut 32:9; 1 Sam 26:19; etc.]). It could also be that in the *Similitudes*, "the house(s) of his congregation" is said to be both God's congregation (*1 En.* 46:8; cf. 38:1; 62:8) as well as the Righteous and Chosen One's congregation (53:6). Yet again, the Matthean Jesus also appears to transcend these figures by taking a special place in the confessional and ritual devotion to Israel's God. The Shema-like acknowledgment of the one Father and the one Christ in Matt 23:8-10 is a case in point.[101] For Jesus to censure the scribes and Pharisees for seeking their own acclaim and honor from others (23:5-7), yet then proceed to link himself to God by saying in the oneness language reminiscent of the Shema that there is but one Father *and* one teacher/instructor, the Christ is quite a strong statement. Paul Rainbow's study brings such a claim into sharper relief as he demonstrates that while exalted intermediary figures in Jewish literature could be spoken of in high, even godlike terms, the kind of oneness language reminiscent of Israel's monotheistic confession of the one God applied to Jesus in Matt 23:8-10 finds no comparable parallel among Jewish intermediary figures (apart from the qualified exception of figures not clearly independent of God, such as God's Spirit, God's Wisdom, and perhaps God's Word).[102] In conjunction with the immediately preceding pericopae (Matt 22:34-40; 22:41-46), which together affirm that Israel's κύριος ὁ θεός, whom one is to love in accordance with the terms of the Shema, has a Son (Jesus) who is also κύριος and is (to be) enthroned beside him,

---

[99] See discussions in Bauckham, *Jesus*, 186-232; Johansson, "Jesus," 25-31; David B. Capes, *Old Testament Yahweh Texts in Paul's Christology* (WUNT 2/47; Tübingen: Mohr Siebeck, 1992); Gordon D. Fee, *Pauline Christology: An Exegetical-Theological Study* (Peabody, MA: Hendrickson, 2007); Hurtado, *Lord*, 112-13.

[100] Cf. Leim, *Grammar*, 58-59, 188, 189, n. 50.

[101] Leim is not alone in his observation that Matt 23:8-10 appropriates oneness language evocative of the Shema when speaking of the one Father and the one Christ. See also Erik Waaler, *The Shema and the First Commandment in First Corinthians: An Intertextual Approach to Paul's Re-reading of Deuteronomy* (WUNT 2/253; Tübingen: Mohr Siebeck, 2008), 222-25; Samuel Byrskog, *Jesus the Only Teacher: Didactic Authority and Transmission in Ancient Israel, Ancient Judaism and the Matthean Community* (ConBNT 24; Stockholm: Almqvist & Wiksell, 1994), 299-302; Paul A. Rainbow, "Jewish Monotheism as the Matrix for New Testament Christology: A Review Article," *NovT* 33 (1991): 83, n. 14. Cf. Hagner, *Matthew*, 2:661; Davies and Allison, *Matthew*, 3:277.

[102] Rainbow, "Monotheism," 66-98. Although there are texts which closely link the one God with the one Law (*2 Bar.* 48:23-24), the one Temple (Josephus, *Ag. Ap.* 2.193), and one people (Josephus, *Ant.* 4.201), Matt 23:8-10 takes on a different force by uniquely applying such oneness language alongside God to an individual, personal figure.

Jesus's call for Shema-like acknowledgment of himself and his Father as the one Christ alongside the one Father must certainly be understood in strong terms.¹⁰³

So too is the place of Jesus with regard to the baptism of converts (28:19) and with regard to believers coming together in prayer to God on a matter (18:19-20) extraordinary. In 28:19, not only does the risen Jesus advance the task of making disciples by extending it to become a worldwide mission, he includes as an essential component of this mission the baptism of new converts, which involves the ritual use of the name of the Father, the Son, and the Holy Spirit. This seems to go beyond fairly general characterizations of the faithful community as in some sense both God's and an exalted agent's people, as here a ritual component is uniquely introduced in marking those who are so identified.¹⁰⁴ In 18:19-20, when Jesus assures his disciples of the alignment of their deliberations with God's will as they come together in prayer, he grounds this assurance on the certainty of his own presence with them. The scenario envisaged here is clearly one in which Jesus is understood to be physically absent, and yet somehow personally present.¹⁰⁵ Although it is not entirely clear whether or not this gathering is for formal worship,¹⁰⁶ nor is it clear whether or not Jesus is thought to be a recipient of worship in some sense,¹⁰⁷ he nonetheless takes a uniquely central place in this gathering of believers essential to their effectiveness in praying to God.

These observations show that Jesus transcends exalted intermediary figures in significant ways, which strengthens the case Leim makes for Jesus's exceptionally close, unique relation to God. Although in some places in Matthew, it is less clear that Jesus is as closely linked to God as Leim suggests,¹⁰⁸ the cumulative weight of the evidence

---

¹⁰³ Leim, *Grammar*, 203-15.
¹⁰⁴ Cf. Hurtado, "Binitarian," 200-1. John Lierman surmises from Jewish texts containing transcendent views of Moses as a unifying, incorporative figure in Judaism that Paul's statement concerning "baptism into Moses" (1 Cor 10:2) is best taken literally as a reference to an actual Jewish practice of baptizing initiates into Moses (*The New Testament Moses: Christian Perceptions of Moses and Israel in the Setting of Jewish Religion* [WUNT 2/173; Tübingen: Mohr Siebeck, 2004], 175-208). However, this suggestion suffers from a complete absence of any clear evidence of Jewish baptism in association with Moses aside from this Pauline reference. It is instead from the vantage point of Christian baptism into Christ that Paul reflects back on the Exodus deliverance and sees in it a type of "baptism," so to speak, illustrating the Christian's deliverance (see Gordon D. Fee, *The First Epistle to the Corinthians* [rev. ed.; NICNT; Grand Rapids, MI: Eerdmans, 2014], 491).
¹⁰⁵ See France, *Matthew*, 697-98. Although Paul can speak of being absent in body, but present in spirit with Christians in a matter of church discipline (1 Cor 5:1-5), he is not "present" in the same sense that Jesus is, since it is "in the name of the Lord Jesus" (1 Cor 5:4; cf. "in my name" in Matt 18:20) and with his power that Paul and other Christians come together in the exercise of church discipline. Whereas Paul is understood to be present as a fellow Christian, the Matthean Jesus is present as the one who is "God with us" (Matt 1:23; 18:20; 28:20).
¹⁰⁶ For a brief discussion of various views, see Kupp, *Emmanuel*, 187-88. Commentators generally agree that αἰτήσωνται here is to be understood as praying to the Father (Davies and Allison, *Matthew*, 2:787-88; Luz, *Matthew*, 2:458, n. 84; France, *Matthew*, 695-96, n. 4; contra J. Duncan M. Derrett, "'Where Two or Three Are Convened in My Name...': A Sad Misunderstanding," *ExpTim* 91 [1979]: 85-86), and thus is probably reflective of some kind of worship gathering.
¹⁰⁷ This gathering of followers "in the name of Jesus" may have also involved the kind of cultic invocation of Jesus's name evidenced elsewhere in the NT (1 Cor 1:2; Acts 9:14, 21; 22:16; 2 Tim 2:22; etc.). See Hurtado, *Lord*, 140-43; cf. Luz, *Matthew*, 2:458-59.
¹⁰⁸ For instance, with regard to 11:25-27, Leim goes beyond a number of scholars who limit the πάντα that the Father has handed over to the Son to signify the whole revelation of God the Father (A. M. Hunter, "Crux Criticorum—Matt. XI. 25-30—A Re-Appraisal," *NTS* 8 [1962]: 246; Celia Deutsch,

certainly bolsters his overall impression of Matthew's christological portrait: Matthew has so closely and uniquely tied "the Son" Jesus to "the Father" God in their mutual identity as κύριος as to rearticulate the identity of Israel's κύριος ὁ θεός around the Father-Son relation.

The foregoing discussion now puts us in a better position to consider afresh the significance of Jesus's reception of προσκύνησις in Matthew. In view of the strong case Leim has made for the Matthean Jesus's close identification with God as Son of God, Emmanuel, and Lord, it would indeed be odd if the προσκύνησις of Jesus were by and large to be understood in the kind of relatively weak terms proposed by Lemcio, Head, and others. Could it be, then, that in accordance with Jesus's identity as Son of God, Emmanuel, and Lord, the προσκύνησις of Jesus is likewise to be understood in much stronger terms?

This leads us to consider Leim's argument in strong favor of an affirmative answer to this question: Matthew moves the reader to see in the προσκύνησις of Jesus the worship that is reserved for Israel's God. As we saw from our own preliminary analysis, there are two abundantly clear instances (namely, the sea-walking account and the resurrection account) where Jesus receives προσκύνησις not only as one who appears to be more than human but even more pointedly as one who speaks and acts in ways characteristic of Yahweh—in a number of ways, uniquely so. In both instances, as Leim points out, this is all closely tied to Jesus's identity as the Son (of God), a key designation in light of Leim's argument concerning the significance of the Father-Son relationship and their shared identity as κύριος. We also saw that in the episodes where a suppliant renders προσκύνησις to Jesus as he/she presents a request, Matthew likely intends to convey more in his preference for προσκυνέω than just a humble posture of

---

Hidden Wisdom and the Easy Yoke: Wisdom, Torah and Discipleship in Matthew 11.25-30 [JSNTSup 18; Sheffield: Sheffield Academic, 1987], 33–34; Davies and Allison, *Matthew*, 2:279; Luz, *Matthew*, 2:166; Carter, *Matthew*, 258) by arguing that it also includes cosmic authority (*Grammar*, 83–87). If it does, then it provides good evidence that Jesus possesses all authority over heaven and earth not only in his post-resurrection state (28:18) but throughout his earthly ministry as well. Yet one clear weakness in Leim's argument concerns his appeal to other passages in Matthew that supposedly show Jesus exercising cosmic authority in his earthly ministry. He cites two passages where an authority over angels could be relevant (4:11; 26:53). But with regard to the former, he seems to overlook a comparable parallel (1 Kgs 19:5–8), which shows angelic sustenance provided for a human does not necessarily indicate the exercise of heavenly authority, and with regard to the latter, he overlooks the fact that Jesus speaks of appealing to God, rather than exercising his own authority in having angels sent to him. The other passages he cites (8:27; 9:6; 11:4–5; 14:33), while certainly indicative of an extraordinary, even Yahweh-like authority and power, are not clear instances of Jesus exercising authority and power over the *heavenly* realm. This is not to say that 11:27 cannot mean Jesus possesses cosmic authority (indeed, some are open to such a comprehensive understanding of πάντα [Nolland, *Matthew*, 471–72; France, *Matthew*, 445]), but the context suggests that it is Jesus's possession of the full revelation of God that is primarily in view.

With regard to 28:19, Leim takes the singular ὄνομα for Father, Son, and Spirit to signify that they share the one divine name (*Grammar*, 220–21 and n. 171). The singular use is certainly striking, and could perhaps, as Leim states, "serve[] as a fitting capstone" to his argument for the narratival binding together of the identity of Father and Son (*Grammar*, 221, n. 171). But as Nolland points out, evidence from Justin Martyr's reference to this passage in *1 Apol.* 61, which shows he "clearly thinks in terms of three names" (*Matthew*, 1269, n. 80), demonstrates that it certainly could be interpreted otherwise by early Christians.

respect, since Jesus in each case is portrayed as one who has an exceptional authority and power to grant these suppliants' extraordinary requests. Leim's insights build on this as he draws attention to other key elements, such as the highly significant address of Jesus as κύριε (8:2; 15:22, 25, 27), the deliverance he effects by his outstretched hand (8:3; 9:18, 25), and so on, which closely relate Jesus to God.[109] On the whole, it does indeed appear that in both subtle ways (8:2; 9:18; 15:25; 20:20) and in much more overt ways (14:33; 28:9, 17), Matthew has narrated these προσκύνησις scenes in such a way that while the characters themselves may not fully realize the significance of their reverence or that of the one whom they reverence, the attentive reader sees in the Son Jesus one who is so closely and uniquely linked to his heavenly Father that he must be in some way worthy to receive through προσκύνησις a kind of worship comparable to the worship of God himself.

Can it be said though that Matthew employs προσκυνέω in such a way that it is even given the kind of cultic charge that most clearly distinguishes the worship typically reserved for God from all other milder forms of reverence? Is the προσκύνησις that Matthew frequently portrays Jesus receiving imbued with cultic overtones, thereby further strengthening the argument that Jesus is worthy to receive the kind of worship that he himself says is reserved for God alone in 4:10? Again, Leim answers affirmatively. In his view, it is as early as the temptation narrative and its intratextual link back to the infancy narrative that the reader is confronted with the "ungrammaticality" of Matthew's προσκυνέω usage, becoming "rightly perplexed" by the apparent grammatical contradiction of Jesus being an object of προσκυνέω in Matt 2 when he himself says that God alone is the only rightful object of προσκυνέω according to 4:10.[110] Ultimately, this ungrammaticality only appears on the surface to be a contradiction in terms; in reality, it is a part of Matthew's literary strategy of suggestively including Jesus in the worship that 4:10 says is for Israel's God alone.

But, as a preliminary question, is there really any "ungrammaticality" here? The use of the unambiguously cultic term λατρεύω in 4:10 suggests otherwise. Thus, while it is true that both Jesus and God are indeed objects of προσκυνέω—and this is certainly significant when the whole of the Gospel is taken into account—only God is explicitly said to be the object of what is clearly understood to be the kind of cultic worship reserved for deity by the combination of προσκυνέω *and* λατρεύω. Far from being perplexed, the reader could very easily be inclined to differentiate the προσκύνησις of Jesus in Matt 2 from the προσκύνησις of God in Matt 4 precisely on the basis of such significant terminological distinctions.[111]

---

[109] See Leim's discussion of these and other key elements in *Grammar*, chapter 4.
[110] See chapter 3 of *Grammar*. For Leim's comment that the reader is "rightly perplexed" at this stage in Matthew's προσκυνέω usage, see *Grammar*, 63–64.
[111] Leim is repeatedly found ignoring this important terminological difference when he reminds his readers of the significance of Jesus frequently receiving προσκύνησις, pointing to the statement in 4:10 that God alone is to receive προσκύνησις (yet stopping short of noting the use of λατρεύω!). For example, he says, "In 4:10, Jesus affirms in the language of Deuteronomy 6:13/10:20 that, κύριον τὸν θεόν σου προσκυνήσεις, but the narrative then goes on to show Jesus as the (only other) recipient of προσκύνησις" (*Grammar*, 207; see also pp. 4, 9, 50–51, 63–64, 98–99, and 125).

Perhaps there is still something to be said of Jesus receiving that which is reserved for God alone as Leim argues for the use of cultic language in the magi's προσκύνησις of Jesus.[112] But the problem here is that every element he highlights is just as easily accounted for in royal terms. The combined ἔρχομαι + προσκυνέω (2:2, 8, 11) which is said to "denote[] a cultic action in the LXX"[113] is also used to describe the approach and reverence of royal figures (LXX Gen 37:10; 42:6; cf. Jdt 10:23).[114] Similarly, the combined προσφέρω + δῶρον (2:11) may often be used in the LXX for cultic offerings to God (particularly throughout Leviticus and Numbers),[115] but it is also often used for tribute paid to royalty (LXX Gen 43:26; Judg 3:17–18; 3 Kgdms 2:46b), most notably in LXX Ps 71:10 which, as already noted, is widely accepted as a key background text for Matt 2.[116] And while λίβανος is certainly used in cultic worship (LXX Lev 2:1–2; Isa 43:23; Jer 6:20; etc.), it too appears to be an item associated with royalty (LXX Song 3:6; 4:6, 14).[117] In view of what is already very clearly presented as a story about the search for Israel's true *king*, it is difficult to suppose that such features, which are all readily intelligible when understood simply in royal terms, are instead to be heard in cultic terms. While Leim does make a good case for the close link between Jesus and God early in the Gospel such that reducing the magi's προσκύνησις to mere homage of an ordinary human king may not suffice,[118] it is not at all clear that this close link has gone all the way to applying to Jesus the language of Israel's cultic worship of God in Matt 2:1–12.

However, other elements further on in Matthew may perhaps offer better evidence of a view of Jesus as one worthy to receive something approximating cultic worship typically reserved for God. Although some features fail to convince in this regard (such as the use of προσέρχομαι[119]), others are not so easily dismissed. For instance, it could

---

[112] Leim, *Grammar*, 59–61.
[113] Leim, *Grammar*, 60 (citing Davies and Allison, *Matthew*, 1:237).
[114] Surprisingly, neither Leim, nor Davies and Allison (whom Leim cites), nor even Johannes Schneider, "ἔρχομαι," *TDNT* 2:667 (whom Davies and Allison cite) give any examples from the LXX of what is alleged to be a common way of describing a cultic action by the combined use of ἔρχομαι + προσκυνέω. While my own investigation did confirm some use of these paired terms in the context of cultic activity (LXX Deut 17:3; Jer 33:2), it is neither frequently nor exclusively used in this way.
[115] Leim, *Grammar*, 60–61.
[116] See p. 54 above.
[117] Leim may be justified in dismissing the significance of Song 3:6; 4:6, 14 for a Jesus/Solomon typology (as proposed by Davies and Allison, *Matthew*, 1:250), but the broader point still stands that these texts provide some evidence that λίβανος/frankincense could be used in non-cultic settings and was perhaps considered a kind of luxury fragrance "fit for a king" (France, *Matthew*, 75–76). See Gus W. Van Beek, "Frankincense and Myrrh," *BA* 23 (1960): 82–83.
[118] Leim, *Grammar*, 56–58.
[119] Leim attempts to build his case for cultic connotations in the combined ἔρχομαι + προσκυνέω used for the reverential approach of Jesus (2:2, 8, 11; 15:25) by noting a very similar use of the cultically loaded προσέρχομαι (*Grammar*, 60, 102, 119–20, 238; see also James R. Edwards, "The Use of προσέρχεσθαι in the Gospel of Matthew," *JBL* 106 [1987]: 65–74). This term is also a Matthean favorite for those who approach Jesus and is occasionally combined with προσκυνέω (8:2; 9:18[?]; 20:20; 28:9). Once again, however, it is not at all clear that προσέρχομαι + προσκυνέω would have been heard in cultic terms (this combination is nowhere attested in the LXX!). Nor is it clear that προσκυνέω takes on cultic significance by virtue of its combination with προσέρχομαι. As Head correctly observes, although προσέρχομαι can be used in the LXX for approaching God in cultic worship, this is only one of a number of ways the term is used (*Christology*, 127). The Gospel of

very well be that in the cries of those who appeal to Jesus, saying, "Lord, have mercy!" (κύριε, ἐλέησόν [17:15; cf. 15:22; 20:30–31]), "Lord, help!" (κύριε, βοήθει [15:25]), and "Lord, save!" (κύριε, σῶσόν [8:25; 14:30]), one is to hear echoes of psalmic prayers to Israel's God.[120] Although similar cries for mercy, help, and deliverance are found in a wide variety of contexts and are addressed to various figures (human, angelic, and divine),[121] which could potentially weaken the argument for a liturgical ring in these cries addressed to Jesus, it nevertheless seems likely that Matthew is particularly indebted to the prayer language of the Psalms. All three cries appear numerous times throughout the Psalms in prayers addressed to God.[122] A number of uniquely Matthean quotations from and likely allusions to the Psalms show his own familiarity and engagement with the Psalms.[123] Although most of the cries to Jesus in Matthew lack any clear connection to a particular psalmic cry to God, there is one exception to this in Peter's cry (ἔκραξεν) to Jesus, "Lord, save me!" (κύριε, σῶσόν με) as he sank (καταποντίζεσθαι) in the sea (Matt 14:30), which echoes the psalmist's cry (κράζων) to God, "Save me!" (σῶσόν με) as he too sank (κατεπόντισέν) in the sea (LXX Ps 68:2–4, 15–16).[124] This clear instance of one psalm's prayer language to God applied to Jesus, along with Matthew's broad engagement with the Psalms as a whole, where many of these prayers to God for mercy, help, and deliverance appear, may very well be an indication that the other cries to Jesus are similarly modeled after these psalmic pleas to God. Moreover, unlike most of the more general instances of these cries noted above,[125] Jesus is almost always addressed each time as κύριε (Matt 8:25; 9:27–28; 14:30; 15:25; 17:15; 20:30–33), which heightens the verbal resonance between the cries to Jesus and those to God in the Psalms, who is often addressed in such instances as κύριε.[126]

Matthew itself attests a broader range of meaning as others besides Jesus are objects of προσέρχομαι, such as Peter (17:24; 26:69, 73), the disciples (17:7; 28:18), the corpse of John the Baptist (14:12), and Pilate (27:58).

[120] Along with Leim (*Grammar*, 85, 119–20, 129), many commentators have noted the way these cries reflect the prayer language of the Psalms (Davies and Allison, *Matthew*, 2:73, 552, 722; 3:107; Grundmann, *Matthäus*, 369, 377; Gnilka, *Matthäusevangelium*, 2:30, 31; Hagner, *Matthew*, 2:503; Gundry, *Matthew*, 300, 314; Carter, *Matthew*, 210, 311, 322, 323; Nolland, *Matthew*, 602, 632, 633; Luz, *Matthew*, 1:44; 2:20–21, 321, 339, 340, 549).

[121] See the following texts where appeals "have mercy!" (ἐλεέω), "help!" (βοηθέω), and "save!" (σῴζω) are addressed to family/friends (Job 19:21; 2 Macc 7:27; *T. Zeb.* 2:2), OT patriarchs (Luke 16:24; *T. Ab.* 10:4 [B]), rulers (Josh 10:4; 2 Kgdms 14:4; 4 Kgdms 6:26; 16:7; *Jos. Asen.* 24:12; 28:2–3; Josephus, *Ant.* 9.64), angels (*T. Ab.* 7:6 [A]; *Apoc. Sedr.* 14:1), and deities (*4 Bar.* 7:29–30).

[122] "Have mercy!" (ἐλεέω): (LXX Pss 6:3; 9:14; 24:16; 25:11; 26:7; 30:10; 40:5, 11; 50:3; 55:2; 56:2; 85:3, 16; 118:29, 58, 132; 122:3. See also Isa 33:2; Jdt 6:19; Sir 36:1, 11; Bar 3:2; 3 Macc 6:12) / "Help!" (βοηθέω): (LXX Pss 43:27; 69:6; 78:9; 108:26; 118:86, 117) / "Save!" (σῴζω): (LXX Pss 3:8; 6:5; 7:2; 11:2; 19:10; 21:22; 27:9; 30:17; 53:3; 58:3; 59:7; 68:2, 15; 70:2; 85:2, 16; 105:47; 107:7; 108:26; 117:25; 118:94, 146. See also 4 Kgdms 19:19; 1 Chr 16:35; Job 33:28; Isa 37:20; Jer 2:27; 17:14; *Apoc. Mos.* 25:3; *Jos. Asen.* 12:11; Josephus, *Ant.* 1.273; 4.50).

[123] Quotations: Ps 78:2 (Matt 13:35), Ps 8:3 (Matt 21:16); likely allusions: Ps 130:8 (Matt 1:21), Ps 72:10–11, 15 (Matt 2:11), Ps 37:11 (Matt 5:5), Ps 24:3–4 (Matt 5:8), Ps 119:176 (Matt 18:12), Ps 1:3 (Matt 21:41), and Ps 22:8 (Matt 27:43). See also Maarten J. J. Menken, "The Psalms in Matthew's Gospel," in *The Psalms in the New Testament* (ed. Steve Moyise and Maarten J. J. Menken; New York: T&T Clark, 2004), 61–82.

[124] Davies and Allison, *Matthew*, 2:508.

[125] See n. 121.

[126] Cf. LXX Pss 6:3; 9:14; 11:2; 19:10; 30:10; 40:5, 11; 43:27; 55:2; 85:3; 105:47; 108:26; 117:25; 122:3.

In these cries to Jesus, then, where petitions are made not for generally mundane favors but for restoration of sight (9:27–31; 20:30–34), exorcism of demons (15:21–28; 17:14–18), and perhaps even more profoundly, rescue from the sea's perils (8:23–27; 14:22–33), by couching these pleas in the prayer language of the Psalms, Matthew may be hinting that Jesus's close link to God extends to include him as a recipient of prayerful cries typically directed to God.[127]

Another intriguing passage to consider, which Leim discusses, is Jesus's quotation of LXX Ps 8:3 in Matt 21:16.[128] Following his triumphal entry into Jerusalem (21:1–11), as Jesus is in the Temple healing the blind and the lame and receiving praises from children ("Hosanna to the Son of David!" [cf. 21:9]), the chief priests and scribes become angry (21:14–15). When they ask Jesus, "Do you hear what these [children] are saying?," he responds affirmatively and proceeds to justify their praise by quoting LXX Ps 8:3: "From the mouth of infants and nursing babies you have prepared for yourself praise" (21:16). For a number of commentators, the purpose of the psalm citation is essentially to affirm the children's praise as that directed by God.[129] Thus, just as in Ps 8:3 God moves through children to utter appropriate praise, so the children's acclamation of Jesus as Son of David is not at all misguided but rather is also that which God himself has prepared and thus is appropriate. Leim and others, however, hone in on the significance of the psalm's application with respect to the recipient of praise.[130] That is, by taking a psalm that originally speaks of little ones praising *God* and applying it to himself, Jesus likens the children's praise of him to the children's praise of God in Ps 8:3.

It could be supposed that since it is as "Son of David" that the children (and the crowd earlier) acclaim Jesus, the Jewish authorities are understood to be taking exception to Jesus's acceptance of messianic acclamation rather than a kind of worship on par with the worship of God, which is how the Pharisees' complaint in the Lukan parallel reads (Luke 19:35–40). Yet Leim points out key features unique to Matthew's account, such as the emphasis on the Temple setting (Matt 21:12 [2x], 14, 15) and the note that Jesus was doing wonderful things (τὰ θαυμάσια ἃ ἐποίησεν [21:15]), language especially evocative of Yahweh's activity in the OT, which may suggest there is more at play.[131] Thus, Matthew suggestively portrays Jesus receiving the praises of the children while doing God's deeds in God's Temple.

While it is possible that Ps 8:3 is cited simply to defend the children's praise as God-inspired, the striking christological appropriation of such a text which also shows such praise is given to God, and particularly in the context of Jesus being praised in the Temple as he does Yahweh-like wonders may very well hint at a deeper significance in

---

[127] It may even be that such language is reflective of the liturgical language of Matthew's church and their own prayerful invocations of Jesus as Lord (Held, "Matthew," 265; cf. Hagner, *Matthew*, 1:222).
[128] Leim, *Grammar*, 166–73.
[129] Davies and Allison, *Matthew*, 3:141; Carter, *Matthew*, 421; Keener, *Matthew*, 502–03; Hagner, *Matthew*, 2:602; cf. Nolland, *Matthew*, 848.
[130] Leim, *Grammar*, 170–73; Andrew E. Nelson, "'Who Is This?' Narration of the Divine Identity of Jesus in Matthew 21:10-17," *JTI* 7 (2013): 208–10; Menken, "Psalms," 72; France, *Matthew*, 789–90.
[131] Leim, *Grammar*, 171–72.

the worship Jesus is considered to be worthy to receive. Along with the many instances we have seen of the transferal of OT texts relating God's speech and action to Jesus, and of OT prayer language to God applied to Jesus, it may not be much of a stretch to find this portrayal of Jesus suggestively appropriating God's praise for himself through this psalm citation.

Taking all relevant evidence into account (the Shema-like confession of the One Father and the One Christ [23:8–10], the ritual use of the name(s) of Father, Son, and Spirit in baptism [28:19], the believing community gathered in Jesus's name [18:20], the cries to Jesus evocative of psalmic prayers to God [8:25; 14:30; 15:22, 25; 17:15; cf. 9:27; 20:30–31], and Jesus's provocative application of Ps 8:3's praise of God by children to himself [21:16]), there do appear to be both subtle hints as well as strong indications that Jesus's close association with God even includes his worthiness to receive the kind of cultic worship reserved for God. Although a number of these are not directly related to Matthew's προσκυνέω language and Jesus's reception of such, some are (15:22–25; 14:30–33; 28:17–20), which may perhaps gradually signal the reader to see even in the προσκύνησις of Jesus a kind of worship comparable to the cultic worship of God. Even if it is unlikely, then, that the reader is perplexed as early in the narrative as Leim suggests by Jesus's reception of προσκύνησις in Matt 2 once he/she comes to the dictum of 4:10, as the narrative progresses, the reader is gradually given more and more clues to Jesus's worthiness to receive that which approximates the cultic worship of God.

That being said, however, the primary overarching significance of Matthew's use of προσκυνέω seems not necessarily to be to link Jesus with God specifically as a co-recipient of cultic worship but to link them as co-sovereigns over God's kingdom. We see evidence of this even in the two instances of the προσκύνησις of God (4:10; 18:26). While only the first of these passages uses προσκυνέω to denote the kind of exclusive cultic worship that is for God alone, both passages can be said to use προσκυνέω to signify acknowledgment of God's unique sovereignty. In the first passage, when Satan attempts to offer lordship to Jesus in exchange for Jesus's acknowledgment of him through προσκύνησις, Jesus's response reveals he interprets this as a direct challenge to the ultimate allegiance due to God as he states in the strongest, clearest possible terms that such allegiance, expressed most concretely in Israel's exclusivistic cultic worship practice (signified here by the combined προσκυνέω and λατρεύω), is to be given to God alone. Undoubtedly, the rationale for such exclusive devotion to God concerns his unique sovereignty as the true Lord of all (cf. 11:25).[132] This is why Satan, whose limited claim to lordship does not compare to God's (cf. 12:25–29), is legitimately rebuffed for any hint of such a claim to be worthy to receive an allegiance comparable to and alternative to allegiance to God. In the second passage, on the other hand, while the parabolic king/lord certainly represents God, this does not mean that the προσκύνησις he receives is to be interpreted as the kind of worship reserved for God *in a cultic sense*. This seems to be the way Leim interprets the προσκύνησις of God here when he says, "it represents the 'worship' reserved for Israel's *compassionate* God,"[133] implying

---

[132] So rightly Leim, *Grammar*, 74–75.
[133] Leim, *Grammar*, 65 (italics mine).

something akin to Horst's suggestion that it represents the worshipful thanks to God for his lavish forgiveness of the sinner's debt as only God could conceivably receive.[134] But as discussed earlier, the προσκύνησις is rendered *before* the king forgives the debt, not *after*, and thus does not likely represent worshipful gratitude given to God. Rather, the king/lord receives προσκύνησις simply because he is the ultimate sovereign in the world of the parable and is worthy of being appropriately acknowledged as such, which is an apt representation of God, his unique sovereignty as King and Lord over everything, and his worthiness to be acknowledged as such. Certainly, he who exercises such unique sovereignty is worthy of the highest worship, but that does not necessarily mean that every instance of reverence expressed with προσκύνησις, even when God is the recipient, represents the kind of *cultic* worship reserved for God.

The same can also be said for the προσκύνησις of Jesus. From the beginning of the Gospel (2:1–12) to the end (28:9, 17–20) and throughout (14:22–33), Jesus is presented as a ruler with authority and power, and thus is worthy of honor befitting a ruler. But the whole of the Gospel makes clear that Jesus is no ordinary ruler, and the προσκύνησις he frequently receives must retrospectively be seen to be something more than the ordinary προσκύνησις extended to mere human rulers. The end of the Gospel makes abundantly clear what is hinted at throughout Matthew with varying degrees of intensity: Jesus is the unique messianic Son of God who has a share in his Father's cosmic lordship (profound aspects of which he can even be seen exercising in his earthly ministry [e.g., 14:22–33]), and thus, just as his Father is truly worthy of προσκύνησις as Lord of all, so too is his Son Jesus. It is not surprising also to find hints of Jesus's worthiness to receive reverence comparable to the cultic worship of God, and in *some* cases in close association with his reception of προσκύνησις, but it is not at all clear that every use of προσκυνέω for Jesus is to be heard as worship given to God in the *cultic* sense (e.g., 20:20).[135] Rather, it is as one who rules as κύριος along with his Father over all things that Jesus is considered like God to be worthy of acknowledgment as supreme Lord over all through προσκύνησις.

D. Conclusion

Any attempt to make fairly comprehensive sense of the ten instances in Matthew where Jesus is the recipient of προσκύνησις, and how this relates to the only other instances where Israel's God is the rightful (even exclusive) recipient of προσκύνησις, must take a number of factors into account. Most discussions of this christological theme in Matthew are simply too brief to address such matters and as a result often fall short of providing adequate treatment of it. Leim's recent study is a welcome exception, as

---

[134] See p. 53 above.
[135] Leim does not give much attention to this passage (*Grammar*, 124, n. 126) where the προσκύνησις of Jesus is quite clearly honor paid to royalty with no hint of cultic overtones whatsoever. Yet his brief comments accord with our observation that προσκυνέω is primarily used in Matthew to link Jesus with God as co-sovereigns over all.

he not only gives detailed attention to Matthew's usages of προσκυνέω, situating them in their immediate as well as their wider narrative contexts, but also discusses their connection to other closely related and vital christological themes in Matthew, such as Jesus's identity as Son of God, Lord, and Emmanuel. Our own observations are in basic agreement with his that Matthew has so closely and uniquely linked Jesus to God that even the προσκύνησις that he is frequently depicted rightly receiving is in some way understood to be comparable to the προσκύνησις that is otherwise to be rendered to God.

But one may still ask more pointedly, in what precise sense is the Matthean Jesus included as a recipient of the προσκύνησις reserved for God? Although there do seem to be a number of hints and indications that Jesus is considered worthy to receive the kind of cultic worship reserved for God and occasionally in close connection with his reception of προσκύνησις, this does not appear to be the primary significance in Matthew's portrayal of Jesus as a recipient of προσκύνησις (as Leim at points seems to suggest). Rather, just as God is the rightful recipient of προσκύνησις *par excellence* as the King and Lord of all (4:10; cf. 18:26), so too, the reader gradually comes to see, is the Messiah Jesus.

In the first instances (2:2, 8, 11), it is clearly as a ruler/king that Jesus is acknowledged with προσκύνησις. And while there are indeed already hints of his close association with God (e.g., 1:23), there are no clear cultic overtones here to signal such a nuance is already present in this προσκύνησις of Jesus. Instead there are hints that this messianic ruler so closely linked to God is not only Israel's king but also the Gentiles' king. The scope of his kingdom, and with it the significance of the προσκύνησις with which he is acknowledged, is already portrayed expanding. As the reader comes to the temptation account, although he/she is not at this point puzzled or astounded by Jesus's reception of προσκύνησις in light of God's reception of προσκύνησις (since only in the latter case does προσκυνέω [+ λατρεύω] clearly represent the cultic, exclusive worship reserved for God), it is nevertheless clear that only legitimate rulers are considered worthy of προσκύνησις. As the narrative progresses, it becomes more and more clear that Jesus is no ordinary ruler wielding a mere human authority and power, but rather he is one who removes leprosy, exorcises demons, raises the dead, and even exercises what is clearly a Yahweh-like lordship over the sea. Once again, as the domains over which he is shown exercising his authority and power expand, so too does the significance in his worthiness to receive προσκύνησις (8:2; 9:18; 14:33; 15:25; 20:20). This motif reaches its climactic conclusion in the resurrection account where the risen Jesus receives προσκύνησις (28:9, 17) as one who possesses all earthly and heavenly authority. Whether Jesus is fully in possession of such cosmic lordship in his earthly ministry (11:27?) or only partially so (e.g., 14:22–33) is not entirely clear. But it is undoubtedly as one who is at least destined to exercise fully such divine lordship that Matthew considers Jesus to be worthy of the kind of acknowledgment through προσκύνησις that is otherwise rendered to Israel's God.

4

The Προσκύνησις of Jesus in the Gospel of Luke and the Book of Acts

In the two-volume work of Luke-Acts, προσκυνέω is used seven times. While in the majority of these instances, the objects are figures other than Jesus, it is precisely in view of one's initial impression from this usage elsewhere in Luke-Acts that one senses that the sole instance of προσκυνέω with Jesus as its object is likely to be seen as a high form of reverence. The use of the term for cultic worship of God (Luke 4:8; Acts 8:27; 24:11), idolatrous worship of false gods (Luke 4:7; Acts 7:43), and some form of reverence for God's human servant, which is quickly rejected for being excessive (Acts 10:25–26), strongly suggests that Luke conceives of προσκύνησις as reverence or worship in rather strong terms. Indeed, the one instance of Jesus as the object of προσκυνέω seems to fit this pattern as the disciples are portrayed rendering προσκύνησις to the risen Jesus as he ascends into heaven (Luke 24:52). Yet does Luke intend for such προσκύνησις of the risen Jesus to be seen as comparable to the kind of divine worship legitimately given to God and illegitimately given to false gods? Could a mere human's rejection of προσκύνησις in Acts 10:25–26 perhaps suggest that while such reverence is at least indicative of the recipient's perceived more-than-human status, it might yet stop short of signifying the kind of strong worship given to deities? These questions call for a closer examination of Luke's προσκυνέω passages, as well as of other relevant material in Luke-Acts, in order to get a better sense of the significance of the προσκύνησις of the risen Jesus in Luke 24:52. I will argue that the evidence points in the direction of Luke's conception of Jesus as a legitimate recipient of the kind of worship otherwise reserved for God when he depicts the risen Lord Jesus receiving προσκύνησις from his followers.

A. The Προσκύνησις of God

The first instance of προσκυνέω with God as its object occurs in Luke's version of the temptation account (Luke 4:1–13). Despite some differences between Matthew's and Luke's versions of the temptation concerning the offer of the kingdoms of the world, both are in general accord regarding the substance of the episode: the devil's/Satan's attempt to offer to Jesus worldwide dominion in exchange for προσκύνησις (σὺ οὖν ἐὰν προσκυνήσῃς ἐνώπιον ἐμοῦ, ἔσται σοῦ πᾶσα [4:7]) is firmly rejected since, as Jesus states, γέγραπται·κύριον τὸν θεόν σου προσκυνήσεις καὶ αὐτῷ μόνῳ λατρεύσεις (4:8). Luke uniquely brings out in an explicit way what is perhaps implicit in Matthew that Satan claims to have been given authority over all the earthly kingdoms and can grant such authority to whomever he chooses (4:6). Although, as in Matthew, Satan does possess some power and authority on earth in Luke-Acts (Luke 11:18; 13:16; Acts 26:18; cf. Matt 12:26), it is just as clear in Luke-Acts as it is in Matthew that his claim to lordship does not match the absolute sovereignty of God, who alone is Lord of heaven and earth (Luke 10:21; Acts 4:24; 7:49; 17:24; cf. Matt 11:25). Luke agrees with Matthew that it is because of God's unique sovereignty over everything that no contender to it, such as Satan here, is in any way worthy of a reverence which compromises one's ultimate allegiance to God, which is emphatically articulated by Jesus in some of the clearest words of Israel's Scriptures regarding the exclusive cultic devotion reserved for God.

The remaining two instances both appear in the context of a pilgrimage made to Jerusalem for the purpose of worshiping Israel's God at the Temple. In the first instance, an Ethiopian eunuch who is a court official of the Queen of the Ethiopians is said to have come to Jerusalem to render προσκύνησις (ἐληλύθει προσκυνήσων εἰς Ἰερουσαλήμ [Acts 8:27]). Similarly, in the second instance, Paul mentions having recently gone up to Jerusalem to render προσκύνησις (ἀνέβην προσκυνήσων εἰς Ἰερουσαλήμ [Acts 24:11]). Although no object of προσκυνέω is stated, the reference to Jerusalem where God's Temple resides indicates that both men have come to Jerusalem to render προσκύνησις to God (cf. 4 Kgdms 18:22; Tob 5:14). Most likely, προσκυνέω is being used abstractly in these instances to convey cultic worship of God in his Temple in a general sense. Prostration itself may certainly be a part of Paul's and the Ethiopian eunuch's worship of God, but the use of προσκυνέω here is not necessarily meant to suggest that only prostration is in mind.[1] Just as we saw that in cultic contexts προσκυνέω was often associated with other cultic worship terms such as λατρεύω, θύω, αἰνέω, and so on, and as a result could even appear by itself as a general term for cultic worship of God,[2] so too in these instances is προσκυνέω used to convey cultic worship of God in general.

B. The Προσκύνησις of false gods

Along with the instance mentioned above where Satan desires a form of idolatrous worship through προσκύνησις in Luke 4:7, there is another instance of idolatrous

---

[1] In Paul's case, he goes on to mention more specifically in Acts 24:17 that he had come to Jerusalem both to bring alms for the poor and to make sacrificial offerings (προσφοράς), the details of which are given in 21:17–26. This suggests that at least one aspect of Paul's statement, "ἀνέβην προσκυνήσων εἰς Ἰερουσαλήμ" includes taking part in sacrificial offerings. In the Ethiopian's case, his status as a eunuch suggests he is incapable of becoming a full proselyte (Deut 23:1) and so would have been restricted to worshiping God from the Court of the Gentiles (cf. Josephus, J.W. 2.341). While this may mean that he was limited to worshiping in the form of prayer and prostration, Daniel R. Schwartz argues that even in the case of Gentiles, certain provisions were made to allow them to partake in sacrificial worship, albeit in a much more restricted fashion ("On Sacrifice by Gentiles in the Temple of Jerusalem," in *Studies in the Jewish Background of Christianity* [WUNT 60; Tübingen: Mohr Siebeck, 1992], 102–16).

[2] See pp. 21–22 above.

worship through προσκύνησις in Acts 7:43. In Stephen's speech before the Sanhedrin, he makes reference to Israel's idolatrous worship of the golden calf in the wilderness (7:41–43). In his elaboration on this incident as the inception of a long history of Israel's idolatrous rebellion, he makes use of the prophetic words of Amos 5:25–27, charging the wilderness generation with making sacrifices that were offered not to God but to false gods and taking along with them the tent of Moloch and the star of Raiphan, which they made for themselves. What is added to the Amos reference as a natural inference to having made such idols is the note that they reverenced them with προσκύνησις (τοὺς τύπους οὓς ἐποιήσατε προσκυνεῖν αὐτοῖς [7:43]). As the context indicates, this προσκύνησις of Moloch and Raiphan is cited as a more specific example of the cultic worship of the host of heaven (λατρεύειν τῇ στρατιᾷ τοῦ οὐρανοῦ) to which God ultimately gave the Israelites over (7:42).

C. The Προσκύνησις of Peter

Thus far we have seen that every use of προσκυνέω in Luke-Acts has the strong sense of worship, whether positively for cultic worship of God or negatively for idolatrous worship of false gods. This instance in Acts 10:25 of a human rendering προσκύνησις to another human may, in one sense, show the broader range of application of the term, but matters become more complicated here when such προσκύνησις is immediately rejected in 10:26. A man named Cornelius has a vision of an angel who tells him to send for Peter (10:1–6). Cornelius is obedient and sends men to seek out Peter, who agrees to accompany them being so directed himself by the Spirit (10:7–23). It is immediately upon Peter's arrival that Cornelius falls at Peter's feet in προσκύνησις (ὁ Κορνήλιος πεσὼν ἐπὶ τοὺς πόδας προσεκύνησεν [10:25]). Yet Peter responds by raising Cornelius up and exclaiming, "Stand up! I myself am also just a human" (10:26). What might someone like Cornelius have intended in reverencing someone like Peter with προσκύνησις? What might someone like Peter have thought someone like Cornelius intended by such reverential προσκύνησις? How might Luke have intended the reader to view this act of προσκύνησις rendered to a human?

Since Cornelius is the one doing προσκύνησις, it makes sense to consider the intent behind the act from the perspective of the actor. Although, unfortunately Cornelius does not say or do anything else as he falls in προσκύνησις that might fill out what he means by such reverence, Luke does provide relevant details regarding the person of Cornelius that may offer some help in filling in the gaps. For instance, we are told that Cornelius is a devout man who fears God, gives alms to the Jewish people, and regularly prays to God (10:2). These prove to be important aspects of his character as they reappear and are reaffirmed by the angel who appears to him (10:4, 31) and by the men sent by Cornelius who commend him to Peter (10:22). Such testimony to Cornelius's piety toward the God of Israel seems to speak against a view of his προσκύνησις of Peter as a type of blatant idolatrous worship. Indeed, compared to those among the clearly pagan who praise Herod Agrippa I exclaiming, "The voice of a god and not of a human!" (12:22), or who are ready to sacrifice to Paul and Barnabas as Hermes and Zeus (14:11–13), or who regard Paul as a god after surviving a viper's venomous bite (28:3–6), Cornelius's προσκύνησις of Peter appears rather mild. When it is recalled that both Jews and non-Jews could speak of προσκύνησις being rendered to ordinary (though not necessarily unimportant) humans,[3] it could very well be that Cornelius intends nothing more in his προσκύνησις of Peter than to extend a respectful welcome to a fellow human.

There are, however, other factors to take into consideration. It is clear that Cornelius is a Gentile, which could potentially muddy the waters with respect to his piety toward Israel's God. Although many commentators recognize that as a Gentile "God-fearer," Cornelius's level of interest in and commitment to Judaism could be expressed in a number of various ways, some of which Luke himself highlights (i.e., almsgiving and prayer), rarely is the standard of devotion to Israel's God discussed as an aspect of such variation. For example, when F. F. Bruce stated that "[Cornelius] had every qualification, short of circumcision, which could satisfy Jewish requirements,"[4] it is clear from his discussion that he assumed Cornelius's exclusive devotion to the God of Israel. Other scholars, however, argue that part of the variation in a God-fearer's adherence to Judaism includes the possibility of being either monotheistic or polytheistic in one's worship of God.[5] A key detail closely related to this issue concerns Cornelius's identity as a centurion (10:1). Evidence of Roman soldiers' involvement both in the worship of the gods and in the imperial cult as part of their loyalty to Rome, the gods, and the emperor whom they serve may very well suggest that Cornelius would have been inclined, if not obligated, to demonstrate his own loyalty accordingly.[6] It is not impossible, then, that Cornelius is the type of God-fearer who does indeed worship the God of Israel but in such a way that he has simply incorporated him into his worship of the gods and of the emperor.[7] In turn, it is not impossible that Cornelius's προσκύνησις of Peter could be reflective of the kind of pagan worship of divine men more clearly seen in the cases of Paul, Barnabas, and Herod mentioned above.

Soon after Peter's refusal of Cornelius's show of reverence, Cornelius recounts his vision to Peter, and in this he makes clear that he understood the heavenly call to summon Peter to mean that Peter has a message from God to deliver to him (10:33). This undoubtedly relates to Cornelius's προσκύνησις of Peter. It is his high regard

---

[3] See pp. 15–16 and 24–26 above.
[4] F. F. Bruce, *The Book of the Acts* (rev. ed.; NICNT; Grand Rapids, MI: Eerdmans, 1988), 203.
[5] See Shaye J. D. Cohen, "Crossing the Boundary and Becoming a Jew," *HTR* 82 (1989): 14–15, who notes the following seven ways in which a Gentile can express interest in Judaism: "(1) admiring some aspect of Judaism; (2) acknowledging the power of the god of the Jews or incorporating him into the pagan pantheon; (3) benefiting the Jews or being conspicuously friendly to Jews; (4) practicing some or many of the rituals of the Jews; (5) venerating the god of the Jews and denying or ignoring the pagan gods; (6) joining the Jewish community; (7) converting to Judaism and 'becoming a Jew.'" Cohen later explains that while converting to Judaism (category 7) entails categories 4 to 6 (and thus, exclusive devotion to Israel's God [category 5]), those regarded as God-fearers could express their worship of God in terms of either category 2 or category 5 ("Crossing," 26, 31–32).
[6] For details, see Justin R. Howell, "The Imperial Authority and Benefaction of Centurions and Acts 10.34–43: A Response to C. Kavin Rowe," *JSNT* 31 (2008): 33–36; Bonnie J. Flessen, *An Exemplary Man: Cornelius and Characterization in Acts 10* (Eugene, OR: Pickwick, 2011), 88–91; Craig S. Keener, *Acts: An Exegetical Commentary* (4 vols.; Grand Rapids, MI: Baker, 2012–2015), 2:1753–54.
[7] Irina Levinskaya, *The Book of Acts in Its Diaspora Setting*, vol. 5 of *The Book of Acts in Its First Century Setting* (Grand Rapids, MI: Eerdmans, 1996), 78–79, 121. Cf. Flessen, *Exemplary*, 97.

for this eagerly expected messenger from God which moves Cornelius to welcome and honor Peter with the reverence that he considers appropriate for God's special representative. But the question remains, does this Gentile God-fearing centurion reverence God's representative in accordance with Jewish sentiments (cf. 4 Kgdms 2:14–15) or Gentile sentiments (cf. Dan 2:46–47)?[8]

In the end, the challenges in determining Cornelius's overall religious position make it difficult to say whether he reverences Peter with προσκύνησις simply as a man sent by God, as a god taking the form of a man, or something in between these extremes. And yet it is perhaps precisely in light of these complications that we are in a better position to make sense of Peter's reaction to a Gentile God-fearing centurion reverencing him with προσκύνησις. Notice that in 10:22 Peter is told the very things about Cornelius that could leave him with a sense of uncertainty and ambivalence regarding Cornelius's religious stance. Cornelius is said to be "a righteous man who fears God," but Peter might wonder if he fears and worships God alone. He is said to be "a centurion," so Peter might wonder if his affiliation with the Roman army requires him to engage in worship of the gods and of the emperor. If these concerns make it reasonable to assume that Peter might have doubts about the exclusivity of Cornelius's devotion to God, then he also could not safely suppose that Cornelius's προσκύνησις is an innocent gesture of respect paid from one ordinary man to another. It could be then that Peter refuses Cornelius's προσκύνησις not because Cornelius *does* in fact view Peter as more than human, as a number of interpreters seem to conclude, but because someone like Cornelius *might* view him accordingly. In sum, it is likely that because Peter cannot be entirely sure of the religious views of Cornelius, and thus cannot be sure of whether he reverences him with προσκύνησις simply as an ordinary human or as one who is in some sense more than human, he makes clear either way that Cornelius understands he is also just a human (καὶ ἐγὼ αὐτὸς ἄνθρωπός εἰμι).[9]

That Peter's claim to be but an ἄνθρωπός is to be taken as a rejection of being considered some sort of more-than-human figure and not merely as a rejection of being an important human is not only the best way to make sense of his reaction as a

---

[8] Many interpreters speak more confidently about how Cornelius regarded and reverenced Peter than the details permit. Some more reservedly take Cornelius to be reverencing Peter as a man esteemed "for the heavenly authority attached to Peter's visit and mission" (Joseph A. Fitzmyer, *The Acts of the Apostles: A New Translation with Introduction and Commentary* [AB 31; New Haven, CT: Yale University Press, 1998], 461). Most take Cornelius to be reverencing Peter as "more than man" (C. K. Barrett, *A Critical and Exegetical Commentary on the Acts of the Apostles* [2 vols.; ICC; Edinburgh: T&T Clark, 1994–1998], 1:513), as "an angelic messenger" (David G. Peterson, *The Acts of the Apostles* [PNTC; Grand Rapids, MI: Eerdmans, 2009], 333; cf. Darrell L. Bock, *Acts* [BECNT; Grand Rapids, MI: Baker Academic, 2007], 393), or in accordance with "pagan categories" (Christoph W. Stenschke, *Luke's Portrait of Gentiles Prior to Their Coming to Faith* [WUNT 2/108; Tübingen: Mohr Siebeck, 1999], 151–52; cf. Horst, *Proskynein*, 246–47). Although Peter certainly reacts strongly to Cornelius's reverence, this may or may not correspond to how Cornelius himself regarded Peter.

[9] Peter's own experience during Jesus's earthly ministry of falling before Jesus in whom he sensed something of the numinous (Luke 5:4–8) may have also influenced his sense of caution. He most certainly would not have wanted to be thought worthy of a kind of reverence that might in any way be considered comparable to his reverence of Jesus. (Still, even here Luke refrains from using προσκυνέω for Peter's reverential prostration before the earthly Jesus. See discussion below for Luke's use of προσκυνέω with Jesus as the object.)

character in light of the points discussed above, but it is also undoubtedly how Luke intends it to be understood in light of his use of ἄνθρωπος. Particularly in Acts, Luke frequently draws contrasts between ἄνθρωπος and θεός: "You have not lied to humans (ἀνθρώποις) but to God (τῷ θεῷ)" (5:4); "We must obey God (θεῷ) rather than humans (ἀνθρώποις)" (5:29); "If this plan or this work is of humans (ἐξ ἀνθρώπων), it will be overthrown, but if it is of God (ἐκ θεοῦ), you will not be able to overthrow them" (5:38–39). Most notable are those instances, which have already been mentioned above, where humans are likened to or are directly identified as gods by pagans. Herod is struck down by an angel for accepting the blasphemous praise of those who said of him, "The voice of a god (θεοῦ) and not of a human (ἀνθρώπου)!" (12:22–23). The people of Lystra regard Paul and Barnabas as gods in human form (οἱ θεοὶ ὁμοιωθέντες ἀνθρώποις) and worthy of sacrifice, but Paul and Barnabas tear their garments in rejection of such blasphemy and explain that they are in fact merely humans of the same nature as them (καὶ ἡμεῖς ὁμοιοπαθεῖς ἐσμεν ὑμῖν ἄνθρωποι) (14:11–15). And when Paul survives a viper's attack, the people of Malta no longer thought of him as a murderous human (φονεύς ἐστιν ὁ ἄνθρωπος οὗτος) who got what he deserved but said instead that he was a god (ἔλεγον αὐτὸν εἶναι θεόν) (28:3–6). In light of Luke's numerous ἄνθρωπος/θεός contrasts, particularly these last three examples where mere humans are treated as or mistaken for divine beings, Peter's insistence that he is an ἄνθρωπος is certainly intended by Luke to be seen as a correction of a (potentially) mistaken view and misplaced reverence of Peter as a more-than-human, godlike figure.

Luke's preference for προσκυνέω in this complicated scene of reverence proves to be an apt and quite telling lexical choice. On the one hand, up until Peter's reaction to Cornelius's reverence, the reader is probably not quite sure what such reverence represented by the potentially ambiguous προσκυνέω performed by a Gentile God-fearing centurion might signify. On the other hand, Peter's resolve to err on the side of caution by making clear either way that he is merely a mortal human ultimately leads the reader to interpret προσκυνέω here in the kind of stronger terms of worship that Luke clearly regards as inappropriate for mere humans as the passages above show.[10]

Yet while Peter as a mere ἄνθρωπος will accept no hint of reverence that may elevate him beyond his mortal rank, he tells Cornelius about one whom God has raised from the dead, whom he has appointed to be the judge of the living and the dead, and through whose name forgiveness of sins is made available for those who believe in him (10:40–43). "This one," Peter proclaims, "is Lord of all" (οὗτός ἐστιν πάντων κύριος)—Jesus Christ (10:36). It is the risen Jesus who, unlike other humans, is no mere ἄνθρωπος,[11] and it is instead the risen Jesus, as we will now see, whom Peter and Jesus's other followers considered worthy to be reverenced with προσκύνησις.

---

[10] The lack of censure of the Maltese who regard Paul as a god (28:3–6) is not an exception, as Luke has already made clear his view of such treatment of mere ἄνθρωποι (10:25–26; 12:22–23; 14:11–15). Presumably, Paul is unaware of the Maltese's opinion of him (cf. "they were saying to one another" [28:4]). There is no question of how he would have responded were he privy to their view of him as a god (cf. 14:11–15). Cf. Ben Witherington, *The Acts of the Apostles: A Socio-Rhetorical Commentary* (Grand Rapids, MI: Eerdmans, 1998), 778–79.

[11] Significantly, Luke never refers to the risen Jesus as ἄνθρωπος. He is occasionally referred to as such in his earthly ministry, mostly by those opposed to him (Luke 7:34; 23:4, 6, 14, 47; cf. 7:8), and

D. The Προσκύνησις of Jesus by the disciples at his ascension

Much like Mark, Luke more commonly uses less loaded terminology to describe the lowly postures of those who humbly and reverentially approach Jesus throughout his earthly ministry (προσέπεσεν τοῖς γόνασιν [Luke 5:8]; πεσὼν ἐπὶ πρόσωπον [5:12]; προσέπεσεν αὐτῷ [8:28]; πεσὼν παρὰ τοὺς πόδας [8:41]; προσπεσοῦσα αὐτῷ [8:47]; ἔπεσεν ἐπὶ πρόσωπον παρὰ τοὺς πόδας [17:16]; cf. 7:38; 10:39). So when the sole instance of προσκυνέω with Jesus as the object is uniquely used to portray the disciples' reverence of the risen and ascended Jesus in Luke 24:52, it is likely to be a deliberate and significant lexical choice on Luke's part.[12] Following Jesus's resurrection and his appearances to his disciples, Luke's Gospel comes to a close with the risen Jesus blessing the disciples, ascending into heaven, being reverenced with προσκύνησις from his disciples (αὐτοὶ προσκυνήσαντες αὐτὸν [24:52]), and the disciples returning to Jerusalem where they were continually in the Temple blessing God (24:50–53).

Before moving forward, we must first note that there are complex text-critical issues involved here. Although the phrases describing Jesus's heavenly ascension (καὶ ἀνεφέρετο εἰς τὸν οὐρανόν) and his reception of προσκύνησις (προσκυνήσαντες αὐτὸν) are well attested and present in a number of weighty manuscripts (𝔓⁷⁵ ℵ [ℵ* for the latter phrase, ℵᶜ for the former phrase] A B C W et al.), they are yet missing in other important witnesses (ℵ* [but only with respect to the former phrase] D it syˢ geo), leading to ongoing scholarly debate over their authenticity. While admittedly the issue is not entirely settled and a few scholars continue to advance arguments against the authenticity of these phrases,[13] in view of the scholarly majority in favor of their authenticity,[14] we will consider the significance of the text from this latter perspective. Since then, as most scholars agree, the προσκύνησις of Jesus following his ascension is very likely a part of the original conclusion to Luke's Gospel, what might its significance be?

---

only once following his death and resurrection by the antagonistic high priest who clearly regarded him as a mere mortal (Acts 5:28). This restrictive use of ἄνθρωπος for Jesus by no means calls into question his humanity but rather is one aspect of Luke's portrayal of Jesus as one who is ultimately shown to be more than human.

[12] Cf. Hurtado, "Homage," 139.
[13] Mikeal C. Parsons, "A Christological Tendency in 𝔓⁷⁵," *JBL* 105 (1986): 463–79; Bart D. Ehrman, *The Orthodox Corruption of Scripture: The Effect of Early Christological Controversies on the Text of the New Testament* (Oxford: Oxford University Press, 1993), 227–32; Michael W. Martin, "Defending the 'Western Non-Interpolations': The Case for an Anti-Separationist *Tendenz* in the Longer Alexandrian Readings," *JBL* 124 (2005): 269–94.
[14] So most recent commentaries. See also Bruce M. Metzger, *A Textual Commentary on the Greek New Testament: A Companion Volume to the United Bible Societies' Greek New Testament* (2nd ed.; Stuttgart: Deutsche Bibelgesellschaft, 1994), 162–66; Daniel A. Smith, *Revisiting the Empty Tomb: The Early History of Easter* (Minneapolis, MN: Fortress, 2010), 115–18; Stanley E. Porter, "The Unity of Luke-Acts and the Ascension Narratives," in *Ascent into Heaven in Luke-Acts: New Explorations of Luke's Narrative Hinge* (ed. David K. Bryan and David W. Pao; Minneapolis, MN: Fortress, 2016), 114–17. See esp. Arie W. Zwiep, "The Text of the Ascension Narratives (Luke 24.50-3; Acts 1.1-2, 9-11)," *NTS* 42 (1996): 219–44 (see also p. 219, nn. 1–4, where he cites numerous studies, Greek text editions, and translations that affirm the authenticity of the disputed phrases).

As in Matthew's account of the risen Jesus, the more-than-human character of the risen Jesus in Luke 24 is also readily apparent. Following the angelic figures' announcement of Jesus's resurrection to the women who discover his empty tomb (24:1–12), Luke tells of two disciples on the road to Emmaus conversing with and offering hospitality to a traveling companion whom they eventually recognize as Jesus just before he mysteriously vanishes from their sight (24:13–35). A number of scholars draw attention to the similarities this episode shares with ancient Jewish and Greco-Roman stories of humans conversing with and offering hospitality to incognito heavenly beings (e.g., Gen 18–19; Judg 6; 13; Tob 5–12; Homer, *Od.* 1.96–324; and Ovid, *Metam.* 8.611–724).[15] Like the heavenly figures of these stories, the risen Jesus both mysteriously appears (conveyed by the intensively expressed καὶ αὐτὸς Ἰησοῦς ἐγγίσας [24:15]) and also mysteriously disappears (αὐτὸς ἄφαντος[16] ἐγένετο ἀπ' αὐτῶν [24:31]), all the while remaining unrecognized by his hosts until the climactic moment of disclosure is reached.

The next scene carries forward Luke's portrayal of the risen Jesus as a supernatural figure in his appearance to a larger gathering of disciples in Jerusalem (24:36–43). The initial appearance is cast in angelophanic terms[17] as Jesus is said suddenly to stand (ἔστη) in their midst (24:36; cf. 1 Chr 21:16; Dan 8:15; Tob 5:4 [S]; etc.), which induces the kind of fearful reaction (πτοηθέντες δὲ καὶ ἔμφοβοι γενόμενοι [24:37]) common to angelophanies (cf. Dan 8:17; Tob 12:16; Luke 1:12; 2:9; etc.; cf. esp. Luke 24:5, where the same terms are used for the women's fearful reaction to the angelic figures' appearance [ἐμφόβων δὲ γενομένων]).[18] So disorienting is the disciples' encounter with the risen Jesus that they take him for an apparition of some sort. Although Jesus will go on to counter this impression of him by demonstrating his corporality (24:38–43), this only intensifies the aura of mystery surrounding the person of the risen Jesus since it is somehow as a physical being that Jesus nevertheless appears as one belonging to the supernatural realm.

In what follows next in Jesus's final words and instructions (24:44–49), it becomes even clearer that the risen Jesus is not just a remarkable, more-than-human figure but

---

[15] See Adelbert Denaux, "The Theme of Divine Visits and Human (In)Hospitality in Luke-Acts: Its Old Testament and Graeco-Roman Antecedents," in *The Unity of Luke-Acts* (ed. Jozef Verheyden; BETL 142; Leuven: Leuven University Press, 1999), 263–75; Alsup, *Post-Resurrection*, 214–65; Arnold Ehrhardt, "The Disciples of Emmaus," *NTS* 10 (1964): 185, 193–95. See also Joseph A. Fitzmyer, *The Gospel according to Luke X–XXIV: A New Translation with Introduction and Commentary* (AB 28A; New York: Doubleday, 1985), 1556; John Nolland, *Luke 18:35–24:53* (WBC 35C; Dallas, TX: Word Books, 1993), 1208.

[16] It is often noted that ἄφαντος is occasionally used to describe the disappearance of gods and other heavenly beings (see Euripides, *Hel.* 605–06; Apollonius Rhodius, *Argon.* 4.1330; cf. 2 Macc 3:34) (I. Howard Marshall, *The Gospel of Luke: A Commentary on the Greek Text* [NIGTC; Exeter: Paternoster, 1978], 898; Fitzmyer, *Luke*, 1568; Darrell L. Bock, *Luke 9:51–24:53* [BECNT; Grand Rapids, MI: Baker Academic, 1996], 1920). Significantly, by comparison, note how Philip's mysterious departure in Acts 8:39–40 is described not in terms analogous to the disappearance of a heavenly being but in terms analogous to the transport of a mere human by the Spirit of the Lord to another earthly locale (see 1 Kgs 18:12; 2 Kgs 2:16; Ezek 11:24; cf. Bel 36) (see Keener, *Acts*, 2:1594; Bock, *Acts*, 346).

[17] Joel B. Green, *The Gospel of Luke* (NICNT; Grand Rapids, MI: Eerdmans, 1997), 852.

[18] Nolland, *Luke*, 1212.

is one closely and uniquely related to God. Similar to the Matthean Jesus who places himself alongside God and prior to the Spirit when he speaks of people of all nations coming to faith by being baptized in the name of the Father, the Son, and the Holy Spirit (Matt 28:19), the Lukan Jesus also gives himself an integral and highly exalted place in these respects as he calls for repentance for forgiveness of sins to be proclaimed in his name to all the nations (24:47) and, in an unprecedented way in Judaism, ascribes to himself the divine prerogative of bestowing the Spirit of God: "*I am sending the promise of my Father* (i.e., the Holy Spirit [cf. Acts 1:4–5, 8]) *upon you*" (24:49; cf. Isa 44:3; Ezek 36:27; Joel 2:29).[19]

It is immediately following this increasingly elevated portrayal of the risen Jesus that a climax is reached in the disciples' προσκύνησις of Jesus as he ascends into heaven (24:51–52). The various features of Luke's two ascension accounts (Luke 24:50–53; Acts 1:1–11) have generated different scholarly assessments regarding the degree to which Jesus's ascension is illuminated by Jewish and/or Greco-Roman parallels and thus the likely context(s) in which it is to be understood. Arie Zwiep, for instance, stresses the primacy of the former by highlighting numerous points of correspondence with Jewish rapture stories, especially those concerning Elijah (e.g., the use of ἀναλαμβάνω for Jesus's/Elijah's heavenly assumption [Acts 1:2, 11; cf. 4 Kgdms 2:9–11]; a forty-day period of final instruction prior to Jesus's/Ezra's/Baruch's assumption [Acts 1:3; cf. *4 Ezra* 14; *2 Bar.* 76]; anticipation of spirit empowerment for successor(s) [Acts 1:4–5, 8; cf. 4 Kgdms 2:9–10]; and assurance of Jesus's/Elijah's eschatological return [Acts 1:11; cf. Mal 3:23; Sir 48:9–10]), which, in line with such models, signifies that Jesus's ascension is to be understood not in terms of an exaltation but in terms of a preservation in heaven until his eschatological return.[20] Yet not only are these key connections largely confined to the ascension account in Acts—which could suggest that Zwiep's insights are relevant for drawing out some of Luke's particular emphases in the second (Acts 1:1–11), but not necessarily the first (Luke 24:50–53), of the ascension accounts—but certain features unique to the Gospel account, as Gerhard Lohfink notes, seem to resonate more with Greco-Roman ascension parlance and motifs, such as the use of ἀναφέρω for both Jesus's and Romulus's ascension to heaven (Luke 24:51; cf. Plutarch, *Num.* 2.3; see also Hesiod, frg. 148; Antoninus Liberalis, *Metam.* 25.4) and, most notably, reverence through προσκύνησις directed to both Jesus and Romulus following their ascensions (Luke 24:52; cf. Plutarch, *Rom.* 27.7–8;

---

[19] Despite some attempts to make a case for the contrary (e.g., James D. G. Dunn, "Spirit-and-Fire Baptism," *NovT* 14 [1972]: 88–91), there is no clear evidence in early Judaism of any figure other than God bestowing his Spirit (see Max Turner, "The Spirit of Christ and Christology," in *Christ the Lord: Studies in Christology Presented to Donald Guthrie* [ed. Harold H. Rowdon; Leicester: Inter-Varsity Press, 1982], 181–84; Johansson, "Jesus," 32–34), making Jesus's claim to do so here in Luke 24:49 (cf. Acts 2:33; 16:7) another astounding piece of evidence of Christian views of a highly exalted (indeed, arguably divine) Jesus (see also Max Turner, "The Spirit of Christ and 'Divine' Christology," in *Jesus of Nazareth, Lord and Christ: Essays on the Historical Jesus and New Testament Christology* [ed. Joel B. Green and Max Turner; Grand Rapids, MI: Eerdmans, 1994], 413–24).

[20] Arie W. Zwiep, *The Ascension of the Messiah in Lukan Christology* (NovTSup 87; Leiden: Brill, 1997). See chapters 2 and 3, and the summaries on pp. 115–16 and 194 in Zwiep, *Ascension*.

see also Lucian, *Peregr.* 39).[21] Just as Romulus and other figures like him in the Greco-Roman world are acknowledged as godlike beings in close relation to their ascension to the heavenly realm, there is undoubtedly a similar sense in which Jesus's heavenly ascension is meant to be seen as a powerful image and proof of his exalted status, which leads the disciples who recognize this in the risen and ascended Jesus to reverence him with προσκύνησις.

But this does not necessarily mean that Jesus's godlike status is ultimately to be understood along the lines of pagan conceptions of divinity. Jesus is not regarded as one among the many "divine-man" figures of the pagan world who receive divine honors characteristic of pagan polytheistic religion but rather is one whose exalted status is grounded in his close, unique relationship to the God of Israel, and who therefore is to be reverenced as such. We have already noted one key detail pointing in this direction as Jesus speaks of himself taking on the exceptional divine prerogative of sending the Holy Spirit promised by God, his Father. We now turn to consider another significant feature of the Gospel's ascension account that seems to suggest that Luke regards the προσκύνησις of the risen and ascended Jesus as his worthiness to have a share in the kind of worship typically reserved for Israel's God.

It is widely acknowledged among commentators and other interpreters of Luke 24:50–53 that the language and imagery of this passage evince the influence of Sir 50:20–22.[22] Just as in Sir 50:20–22, the high priest Simon II lifts his hands to bless (ἐπῆρεν χεῖρας αὐτοῦ . . . δοῦναι εὐλογίαν [50:20]) the congregation of Israel gathered in worship at the Temple, the people respond with προσκύνησις (προσκυνήσει [50:21]), then comes a call to bless God (εὐλογήσατε τὸν θεὸν [50:22]), so in Luke 24:50–53, Jesus lifts his hands to bless the disciples (ἐπάρας τὰς χεῖρας αὐτοῦ εὐλόγησεν αὐτούς [24:50]), the disciples respond with προσκύνησις (προσκυνήσαντες [24:52]) and then bless God (εὐλογοῦντες τὸν θεόν [24:53]) in his Temple. Such close correspondences very likely suggest a thematic and not merely formal connection is intended,[23] though there are slight differences of opinion over Luke's purpose(s) in making such a connection. While some propose a priestly significance, arguing that the connection lies in Jesus's capacity to offer priestly blessing over God's people as the high priest Simon does,[24] others argue that Luke's Jesus is like (and even greater than) Ben Sirach's

---

[21] Gerhard Lohfink, *Die Himmelfahrt Jesu: Untersuchungen zu den Himmelfahrts-und Erhöhungstexten bei Lukas* (SANT 26; Munich: Kösel, 1971), 42, 48–49, 171, 173. See also p. 61, n. 38 above where we noted the general contrast between divine worship/status commonly ascribed to heavenly translated humans in Greco-Roman tradition and the lack of such in the case of heavenly translated humans in Jewish tradition.

[22] P. A. van Stempvoort, "Interpretation of the Ascension in Luke and Acts," *NTS* 5 (1958): 34–37; Dennis Hamm, "The Tamid Service in Luke-Acts: The Cultic Background behind Luke's Theology of Worship (Luke 1:5–25; 18:9–14; 24:50–53; Acts 3:1; 10:3, 30)," *CBQ* 65 (2003): 217–20; Richard J. Dillon, *From Eye-Witnesses to Ministers of the Word* (AnBib 82; Rome: Biblical Institute Press, 1978), 179–80, 220–24; Lohfink, *Himmelfahrt*, 167–69; Zwiep, *Ascension*, 87–88; Marshall, *Luke*, 908–9; Fitzmyer, *Luke*, 1590; Nolland, *Luke*, 1227–29; Green, *Luke*, 860–61; François Bovon, *Luke 3: A Commentary on the Gospel of Luke 19:28–24:53* (trans. James E. Crouch; Hermeneia; Minneapolis, MN: Fortress, 2012), 409, 411–12.

[23] Dillon, *Eye-Witnesses*, 179.

[24] Stempvoort, "Interpretation," 34–37.

Simon who stands at the climactic end of a long line of Israel's biblical heroes (Sir 44–50).[25] Still others find merit in both of these interpretive options; just as for Ben Sirach, Israel's sacred history reaches a climax in the life of his contemporary, the high priest Simon II, whose greatness is captured in the key role he fulfills as priest in mediating the blessings and worship of God, so Jesus is Israel's chief mediator *par excellence* and therefore most fully mediates the blessings and worship of God for his people.[26]

Since such proposals clearly speak against a merely superficial link between Luke 24:50–53 and Sir 50:20–22, then undoubtedly the προσκύνησις element could hardly have been incidentally and unreflectively carried over. Yet significantly, whereas in Sir 50:21 the people direct their cultic worship through προσκύνησις to God[27] just as they had done earlier (Sir 50:17), Luke has the disciples rendering προσκύνησις to the risen and ascended Jesus rather than to God.[28] This προσκύνησις of Jesus does not replace or compete with the worship of God, as Luke notes in the final words of the Gospel that the disciples were continually in the Temple blessing God (24:53). But just as Luke regards Jesus as having an exceptional share in divine prerogatives (24:49), so too might this interesting literary adaptation of a passage involving Israel's cultic worship of God be a hint that Luke regards Jesus as having a share in the reception of divine worship. By reworking the language and imagery of Sir 50 so that the cultic προσκύνησις (Sir 50:17, 21) and cultic εὐλογία (Sir 50:22) directed entirely to God in Sirach has two recipients (προσκύνησις of Jesus [Luke 24:52], εὐλογία of God [Luke 24:53]), Luke may very well suggest by this that the risen and ascended Jesus is included with God as a rightful recipient of the kind of worship typically reserved for God.

E. The significance of the Προσκύνησις of Jesus in Luke-Acts

In view of all of Luke's other uses of προσκυνέω, from the more frequent instances where the term is clearly used in its strongest sense for either cultic worship of Israel's God (Luke 4:8; Acts 8:27; 24:11) or idolatrous worship of false gods (Luke 4:7; Acts

---

[25] Dillon, *Eye-Witnesses*, 220–23.
[26] Hamm, "Tamid," 220.
[27] It is unlikely that the lack of a stated recipient of προσκυνήσει in Sir 50:21 and the preceding statement in 50:20 that Simon "ἐν ὀνόματι αὐτοῦ [i.e., the divine name] καυχήσασθαι" can be taken to mean that the high priest is included with God as a mutual recipient of προσκύνησις (*pace* Fletcher-Louis, "Worship," 118). While the Hebrew התאר of manuscript B *could* perhaps be taken to mean that Simon "is himself glorified" in the utterance of the divine name, that the LXX typically renders the MT occurrences of ראתה with a passive form of δοξάζω (e.g., Isa 10:15; 44:23; 49:3) suggests a different nuance is in mind when LXX Sir 50:20 uses καυχήσασθαι. Indeed, Simon's καυχήσασθαι in the name of the Lord is probably analogous to other instances where God's people καυχάομαι in him without the implication of being glorified in a strong sense (LXX Ps 5:12; Jer 9:22–23; *Pss. Sol.* 17:1; Rom 2:17; 1 Cor 1:31). Since the people are ultimately said to do προσκύνησις to receive *God's* blessing (καὶ ἐδευτέρωσαν ἐν προσκυνήσει ἐπιδέξασθαι τὴν εὐλογίαν παρὰ ὑψίστου), it makes more sense to take this second act of προσκύνησις as worship directed to God just as the first act of προσκύνησις was in Sir 50:17.
[28] Cf. Nolland, *Luke*, 1228; Bovon, *Luke*, 412.

7:43), to one complex instance where the term is ultimately to be interpreted as representing a kind of reverence inappropriate for mere humans (Acts 10:25), it comes as little surprise that the use of προσκυνέω for the climactic expression of reverence of the risen and ascended Jesus at the conclusion of the Gospel is also found to be consistent with Luke's pattern of usage and is meant to be interpreted in rather high terms. But one may perhaps question whether Luke has in fact gone all the way to presenting Jesus as a recipient of the kind of cultic worship given to deities so clearly represented in Luke 4:7-8; Acts 7:43; 8:27; 24:11. We have argued that Luke's suggestive adaptation of the language and imagery of Sir 50:20-22 could be taken as hinting in this direction. But could it be that Luke ultimately makes a distinction between the reverence of Jesus and that of God since only the latter is portrayed taking place in a cultic setting (Luke 24:53)? It is undoubtedly significant that Luke makes terminological distinctions between the reverence shown to the earthly Jesus[29] and the reverence through προσκύνησις shown to the risen and ascended Jesus, but can it be said that Luke conceives of the προσκύνησις of Jesus as being comparable to the προσκύνησις and λατρεία reserved for God alone (Luke 4:8)? In order to address these concerns adequately, we must consider other relevant material in Luke-Acts.

With the exaltation of Jesus through his resurrection and ascension in Luke 24, it becomes abundantly clear in what follows in Acts that Jesus's followers now see him in a new light and accordingly relate to him in new ways. They have come to the conviction, as the many speeches in Acts show, that the risen and ascended Jesus is now at the right hand of God in heaven (Acts 2:33; 5:31; 7:55-56), acknowledged as both Lord and Christ (2:36), indeed, even "Lord of all" (10:36), that through him both healing (3:16; 4:10) as well as forgiveness of sins (10:43; 13:38-39) are available to all, and that God has appointed him as eschatological judge (10:42; 17:31). Such views of Jesus as a highly exalted, transcendent figure are shown to have quite an impact on the ways they now relate to him in their ministerial and devotional activities.

One way this is seen is in the healings, exorcisms, signs and wonders that his followers successfully perform by declaring they be done "in the name of Jesus" (3:6-7; 16:18; cf. 4:30). To some extent, these occurrences resemble practices in magic common in the ancient world in which one invokes the names of deities, angels, and other supernatural beings as a means of tapping into their power in order to achieve some end. On the other hand, as is often noted, certain "anti-magical passages" in Acts suggest that Luke seeks to differentiate Jesus's followers' use of his name from the use of names in magic.[30] For instance, in 19:13-20, not only does the unsuccessful exorcism in Jesus's name attempted by those who are not true followers of Jesus show Luke's repudiation of the kind of manipulative and merely formulaic use of Jesus's name characteristic of magical invocations, but the resultant positive response of many renouncing their magical practices by divulging magical spells and burning magical

---

[29] See p. 89 above.
[30] Barrett, *Acts*, 1:176-77, 182-83; Witherington, *Acts*, 175, 577-79; Keener, *Acts*, 2:1066. See esp. Susan R. Garrett, *The Demise of the Devil: Magic and the Demonic in Luke's Writings* (Minneapolis, MN: Fortress, 1989).

books, which undoubtedly contained various supernatural figures' names, points to the exceptional regard that one is to have for Jesus and his name (cf. 4:12).[31]

Other uses of Jesus's name in Acts also reveal a broadening and deepening of the scope of its significance beyond associations with magic. Jesus's followers speak, teach, and preach (in) his name (4:17–18; 5:28, 40; 8:12; 9:27–28; cf. 9:15), suffer for his name (5:41; 9:16; 15:26; 21:13), proclaim forgiveness of sins is received through his name (10:43), and baptize in his name (2:38; 8:16; 10:48; 19:5). Far from being merely added to a long list of supernatural powers that one may invoke, in Acts 3–4 Jesus is not only singled out as the one responsible for healing (3:16; 4:9–10) but even more importantly, as Peter goes on to stress, it is in his name alone that salvation for all mankind is found (4:12).

Since the significance of "the name of Jesus" in Acts cannot be fully accounted for against the background of ancient magical practices, it is not surprising to find that scholars appeal to other possible backgrounds. In particular, many find that Luke's use of "name" with reference to Jesus is mostly reminiscent of the way the OT frequently uses "name" with reference to Yahweh.[32] Although in most cases, it appears that any such connections can only be shown to be echoes of OT language at a more general level, there is yet one demonstrable and highly significant OT connection, which arguably both impacts the way other "name of Jesus" passages in Acts are ultimately to be understood and presents Jesus as one worthy of receiving the kind of cultic and devotional worship that Israel reserved for God. It is the use of LXX Joel 3:5 (ἔσται πᾶς ὃς ἂν ἐπικαλέσηται τὸ ὄνομα κυρίου σωθήσεται) in Acts 2:21 such that Jesus is understood to be the κύριος whose name people must call upon for salvation.[33]

When soon after Jesus's mission instructions (Acts 1:2–3, 8; cf. Luke 24:44–48), his promise of the coming of the Holy Spirit (Acts 1:4–5, 8; cf. Luke 24:49), and his heavenly ascension (Acts 1:9; cf. Luke 24:51) the disciples are all filled with the Spirit at Pentecost (Acts 2:1–4), it becomes clear through Peter's explanatory sermon which follows how all of this relates to the significance of the person of Jesus and accordingly how one is now to relate to him. What is being witnessed, Peter says in 2:14–21, is the fulfillment of Joel's prophecy (LXX Joel 3:1–5), which anticipated the eschatological outpouring of God's Spirit on all his people, the approach of the day of the Lord for final judgment, and an assurance in this that "all who call upon the name of the Lord will be saved." Yet much like the use of Isa 40:3 in the Gospels, it soon becomes clear that it is Jesus who is identified as the κύριος, which originally referred to Yahweh in Joel, who is called upon for salvation. This is because it is Jesus who, as other Scriptures foresaw

---

[31] Cf. Hurtado, *Lord*, 204.

[32] See Robert F. O'Toole, "Activity of the Risen Jesus in Luke-Acts," *Bib* 62 (1981): 487–91; H. Douglas Buckwalter, "The Divine Saviour," in *Witness to the Gospel: The Theology of Acts* (ed. I. Howard Marshall and David Peterson; Grand Rapids, MI: Eerdmans, 1998), 114–15, 118–19; Adelheid Ruck-Schröder, *Der Name Gottes und der Name Jesu: Eine neutestamentliche Studie* (WMANT 80; Neukirchen-Vluyn: Neukirchener Verlag, 1999), 160–202. For other possible backgrounds, see John A. Ziesler "The Name of Jesus in the Acts of the Apostles," *JSNT* 4 (1979): 28–41.

[33] For much of what follows, see Darrell L. Bock, *Proclamation from Prophecy and Pattern: Lucan Old Testament Christology* (JSNTSup 12; Sheffield: Sheffield Academic, 1987), 156–87; Davis, *Name*, 103–29; Hurtado, *Lord*, 179–82, 197–206; Turner, "Christology," 174–84.

(Ps 16:8–11 and Ps 110:1), is both the χριστός and the κύριος whom God would raise from the dead (2:22–32) and enthrone in heaven at his right hand (2:33–36), the highly exalted place from which Jesus himself has poured out the promised Holy Spirit which he received from the Father (2:33). Just as Jesus had explained to his disciples that he himself would send the Spirit of his Father (Luke 24:49) and undoubtedly also that he would do so as the one seated in heaven at God's right hand (Luke 20:41–44), so Peter explains how the Spirit's outpouring has come about as a result of Jesus's heavenly exaltation. When Peter concludes by stating that the proper response to all of this is to repent, be baptized in the "name" of Jesus Christ for the forgiveness of sins, and thereby receive the gift of the Spirit (2:38), this harkens back to the "name" of the κύριος who is to be called upon for salvation and points to the identification of Jesus with this κύριος.[34]

With such an equivalent status with God ascribed to Jesus by virtue of both his exceptionally close position alongside ὁ κύριος (God) as one who is also κύριος, as well as his unique share with God in bestowing the Spirit, the implications are carried forward as this equivalence even extends to Jesus being called upon for salvation in terms reminiscent of Israel's cultic and devotional worship of God. The phrase "call upon the name of the Lord" (קרא בשׁם יהוה/ἐπικαλεῖσθαι τὸ ὄνομα κυρίου)—along with slight variations of it—appears frequently in the OT and early Jewish literature[35] and has unmistakable evocations not only of specific acts of prayerful worship of Yahweh but also of an overall devotional commitment to him to the exclusion of other gods.[36] Indeed, in Joel those who call upon the name of the Lord are envisioned not just praying to God but (re-)turning to a true lifelong exclusive commitment to the worship of God.[37] For Luke and other Christians (Rom 10:13; cf. 1 Cor 1:2) to make the move of identifying Jesus as LXX Joel 3:5's κύριος so worshipfully invoked in the OT language of Israel's worship of Yahweh is astounding and highly suggestive of Jesus's worthiness to receive such worship otherwise reserved for God.[38]

---

[34] Fitzmyer, *Acts*, 253–54; Peterson, *Acts*, 144; Bock, *Acts*, 118.

[35] See esp. Gen 4:26; 12:8; 13:4; 26:25; 1 Kgs 18:24; 2 Kgs 5:11; Ps 116:13; Joel 3:5; Zeph 3:9; *Pss. Sol.*6:1; 15:1. Note also "call upon his/my/your (i.e., God's) name" (1 Chron 16:8; Ps 79:6; Isa 64:6; Zech 13:9; Jdt 16:2; etc.); "call upon him/me/you (i.e., God)" (1 Kgs 8:43; Pss 31:18; 91:15; 145:18; Hos 7:7; *Pss. Sol.* 2:36, etc.); "call upon the Lord/God/the Most High," and so on (1 Sam 12:17–18; 2 Sam 22:4; Ps 14:4; Sir 46:5; 51:10; 2 Macc 3:31; 8:2; 12:15; *Let. Aris.* 193; Josephus, *J.W.* 2.394; etc.).

[36] Thus, along with the numerous instances of prayer-like invocations of (the name of) the Lord/God (1 Sam 12:17–18; 2 Sam 22:7; 1 Kgs 17:21; 18:24; 2 Kgs 5:11; LXX Esth 4:8; 5:1; Pss 18:7; 99:6; 116:4; Lam 3:55–57; Jonah 1:6; Jdt 8:17; Sir 46:5; 2 Macc 3:15; etc.), note also the use of the phrase as a way of characterizing those who (come to) know/worship God (Isa 55:5–6 [LXX]; Zeph 3:9; Zech 13:9; *Pss. Sol.* 9:6). The overtones of religious worship are further reinforced by negative examples of "calling upon" false gods (1 Kgs 18:24–28; Jdt 3:8; Wis 13:17; *4 Bar.* 7:30), and the characterization of those who do not know/worship God as those who do not call upon (the name of) the Lord/God (Pss 14:4; 53:5; 79:6; Jer 10:25; cf. Isa 64:6). Furthermore, the relatively rare use of קרא/ἐπικαλεῖσθαι for appeals made to non-divine figures (Isa 44:5 [MT]; Hos 7:11; Jdt 7:26) is indicative of its strong associations with cultic invocations of God/gods rather than with appeals of a more general sort (there are also figurative instances of "calling upon" wisdom/understanding [Prov 1:28; 2:3; 8:12; Wis 11:4] and death [Job 17:14 [LXX]; Prov 18:6 [LXX]], perhaps as if to a god).

[37] Cf. Douglas K. Stuart, *Hosea-Jonah* (WBC 31; Nashville, TN: Thomas Nelson, 1987), 261.

[38] The only moderately close, roughly contemporary parallel to this particular phenomenon is in *T. Levi* 5:5, where Levi addresses an angel as κύριε, and, in the words of LXX Ps 49:15, asks for

Lest it be thought that there is perhaps a substantial attenuation of the worship overtones when this OT passage is christologically applied here in Acts 2,³⁹ other material in Acts speak against this. In Acts 7:55–60, for instance, as Stephen is being stoned for what his opponents clearly take to be a blasphemous claim of seeing an exalted Jesus alongside God in heaven, Luke portrays him praying to Jesus using language and imagery that recall both the exalted Lord Jesus to be called upon in Acts 2 as well as Jesus's prayers to God in Luke 23.⁴⁰ Kneeling in prayer,⁴¹ Stephen "calls upon" (ἐπικαλούμενον [7:59; cf. 2:21]) Jesus, whom he sees exalted in heaven at the right hand of God (7:55–56; cf. 2:33), addressing him twice as κύριε (7:59, 60; cf. 2:21, 34, 36), and prays to him, just as Jesus had prayed to God on the cross, that he would receive his spirit (7:59; cf. Luke 23:46) and that he would not hold his persecutors' sin against them (7:60; cf. Luke 23:34).⁴² These connections are an indication that the christological application of Joel's "call upon the name of the Lord for salvation" does indeed involve calling upon the exalted Lord Jesus in prayer and petitioning him as one would normally petition God to receive one's spirit and to forgive sins.

Also, just as there is a sense in which those who call upon the name of the Lord (Yahweh) in the OT are presumed to be those who truly (come to) know, worship, and devote themselves to God, so does something similar appear to be the case for those who call upon the name of the Lord Jesus in Acts. It begins at conversion where those who repent and have their sins forgiven are shown to be those who are baptized in the name of Jesus (2:38). As 22:16 attests, this includes calling upon the name of the Lord Jesus (βάπτισαι καὶ ἀπόλουσαι τὰς ἁμαρτίας σου ἐπικαλεσάμενος τὸ ὄνομα αὐτοῦ), which probably means the baptizand utters a prayerful confession and invocation of Jesus as the Lord who saves him/her. From the moment of conversion on, Jesus proves

---

the angel's name that he may call upon him in a day of tribulation (ἐπικαλέσωμαί σε ἐν ἡμέρᾳ θλίψεως; cf. LXX Ps 49:15, where God says, ἐπικάλεσαί με ἐν ἡμέρᾳ θλίψεως). Yet the overall inferior portrayal of this angel invoked in *T. Levi* 5 when compared to the Jesus invoked in Acts may indeed correspond to this slightly looser psalmic application on the one hand and the more direct identification of Jesus with the κύριος called upon for salvation on the other. Thus, whereas the angel has a much more limited role as one invoked in a (general? eschatological?) day of tribulation, Jesus is not only invoked for many things (healings, exorcisms, signs and wonders, etc.) but most significantly, he is necessarily invoked for salvation and for incorporation into the faithful community (Acts 4:12; 22:16). Also noteworthy are the differences in their domains of influence/ authority (the angel is an intercessor for Israel [*T. Levi* 5:6]; Jesus is Lord of all [Acts 10:36]), and in their designation as κύριος (the angel is only addressed as such once; Jesus is not only frequently addressed and designated as such along with God, but there are a number of passages in Luke-Acts [especially in Acts] where it is often difficult to determine whether κύριος refers to Jesus or God [see n. 46 below]).

³⁹ Cf. P. Maurice Casey, "Monotheism, Worship and Christological Developments in the Pauline Churches," in *The Jewish Roots of Christological Monotheism: Papers from the St. Andrews Conference on the Historical Origins of the Worship of Jesus* (ed. Carey C. Newman et al.; Leiden: Brill, 1999), 225.

⁴⁰ See Bruce, *Acts*, 160; Barrett, *Acts*, 1:387–88; Witherington, *Acts*, 276; Bock, *Acts*, 315; Peterson, *Acts*, 269; Keener, *Acts*, 2:1458, 1460, 1462.

⁴¹ Luke uses the phrase θεὶς τὰ γόνατα (7:60), which he often and only uses elsewhere to depict people kneeling in prayer (Luke 22:41; Acts 9:40; 20:36; 21:5; cf. Mark 15:19, where there is a different connotation in this phrase).

⁴² On the textual authenticity of Jesus's prayer in Luke 23:34, see David M. Crump, *Jesus the Intercessor: Prayer and Christology in Luke-Acts* (WUNT 2/49; Tübingen: Mohr Siebeck, 1992), 79–85.

to have a central place in the life and ministry of believers as is clearly seen (as we saw earlier) in the many things done in and for the name of Jesus. Indeed, so conspicuous and extensive is the believer's devotion to Jesus that they are even identified as those who call upon his name, and so controversial is such devotion that they are intensely persecuted because of it (9:14, 21; cf. 7:55–60).[43]

The exceptional character of this positive portrayal of Christians calling upon the name of the Lord Jesus in prayer and in overall allegiance to him as Israel did with respect to God stands out all the more when we recall the negative portrayals of any hint of godlike reverence of humans (10:25–26; 12:22–23; 14:11–15; 28:6).[44] This speaks against Luke having uninhibitedly opened the floodgates of divine-man worship with Jesus merely being added to an ever-expanding list of deified humans. Rather, it is Jesus alone who is uniquely included with God as a legitimate recipient of the worship otherwise reserved for God.[45]

The Jesus whom Luke suggestively presents to his readers throughout his two-volume work as κύριος,[46] even from the womb (Luke 1:43; 2:11), is most fully recognized and acknowledged as such by his followers in his resurrection and exaltation to God's right hand (Luke 24:34; Acts 1:21; 2:36; 7:59–60; 9:17; 10:36; etc.). In line with the disciples' recognition that it is from this exceptionally exalted position beside God in heaven that he has a share in divine dignity (he too is κύριος along with God [Acts 2:33–36]) and in (uniquely) divine activity (he sends God's Spirit [Acts 2:33]; he judges the world [Acts

---

[43] Cf. Hurtado, "Pre-70," 42–44.

[44] See Ilze Kezbere, *Umstrittener Monotheismus: Wahre und falsche Apotheose im lukanischen Doppelwerk* (NTOA 60; Göttingen: Vandenhoeck & Ruprecht, 2007), 140–203. Kezbere also discusses the prostration of the jailer before Paul and Silas (16:29). It could be that this pagan jailer, sensing that the supernatural activity that occurs is connected with Paul and Silas, regarded and reverenced them as divine men (*Umstrittener*, 182–85; cf. Barrett, *Acts*, 2:796). On the other hand, the use of προσπίπτω instead of the more suggestive προσκυνέω and the lack of rebuke of this show of reverence (cf. 10:25–26) may indicate that Luke intends for the jailer's prostration to be seen as a relatively milder form of reverence (cf. Bock, *Acts*, 541). In any case, their answer to the jailer's question concerning salvation makes clear who is to be reverenced: "Believe in the Lord Jesus, and you will be saved" (16:31). (The choice of πίπτω and καταπίπτω rather than προσκυνέω for Paul's prostration in his encounter with the heavenly Jesus [9:4; 22:7; 26:14], by contrast, is not due to its mild character but due to its involuntary character. Jesus's appearance to Paul is so overwhelming that it floors him!)

[45] There are two passages where it is not entirely clear if the "Lord" addressed in prayer (1:24–25) or cultically served (13:2) is Jesus or God. Some favor God in the former (Fitzmyer, *Acts*, 227; Bock, *Acts*, 89; Keener, *Acts*, 1:773) and the latter passage (Dunn, *First*, 14; Fitzmyer, *Acts*, 497), while others make a plausible case for Jesus in the former (Bruce, *Acts*, 47; Barrett, *Acts*, 1:103; Peterson, *Acts*, 127–28) as well as the latter passage (Larry W. Hurtado, "Christology in Acts: Jesus in Early Christian Belief and Practice," in *Issues in Luke-Acts: Selected Essays* [ed. Sean A. Adams and Michael Pahl; Gorgias Handbooks 26; Piscataway, NJ: Gorgias, 2012], 236; see also Witherington, *Acts*, 150).

[46] It is well known that the use of κύριος for Jesus in both Luke's Gospel and in Acts is a Lukan favorite. Significantly, not only does Luke use the word frequently and almost entirely to refer to either Jesus or God but he also does so in such a way that he establishes a *Verbindungsidentität* between Jesus and God (C. Kavin Rowe, *Early Narrative Christology: The Lord in the Gospel of Luke* [BZNW 139; Berlin: de Gruyter, 2006]). Thus, in deliberately ambiguous ways, Luke often employs κύριος such that either it ultimately refers to both God and Jesus (particularly so in Luke's Gospel [e.g., Luke 1:17, 76; 3:4; 4:19; 10:2]), or it is unclear whether it refers to God or Jesus (particularly so in Acts [e.g., Acts 2:47; 5:14; 8:25; 9:31, 35; 11:21; 13:10, 11, 44; 16:14; 21:14]).

10:42; 17:31]; he offers salvation [Acts 2:21; 4:12; 16:31])[47] comes the recognition that he is also worthy of the worship, devotion, and allegiance characteristically reserved for God. While this is most clearly seen in Acts where Jesus is already the risen and exalted Lord, the first sign of a new recognition and a new way of relating to Jesus as one relates to God comes at the end of Luke's Gospel where the risen and ascended Lord Jesus is portrayed receiving προσκύνησις from his disciples in language drawn from Sir 50's cultic προσκύνησις offered to God.

F. Conclusion

In contrast with Johannes Horst, who disappointingly had little to say concerning the προσκύνησις of Jesus in Luke-Acts,[48] we have given much more attention to it in order to discern its significance. What becomes much clearer in Acts already begins to surface in the disciples' προσκύνησις of the risen and ascended Jesus at the end of Luke's Gospel: he who is ultimately recognized and acknowledged as the risen Lord seated beside God in heaven (Acts 2:33–36; cf. Luke 22:69; 24:34), participating in divine rule (Acts 10:36) and other significant divine activity (Acts 2:33; cf. Luke 24:49), is accordingly to receive the kind of cultic and devotional worship otherwise reserved for God (Acts 2:21; 7:59–60; 9:14; 22:16 [perhaps also 1:24; 13:2]). That Luke's characterization of the disciples' προσκύνησις of the risen Jesus is also to be seen as an indication of Jesus's worthiness to receive the kind of worship reserved for God is likely for the following reasons. One, his use of προσκυνέω elsewhere always signifies reverence/worship in strong terms (cultic worship of God [Luke 4:8; Acts 8:27; 24:11]; idolatrous worship of false gods [Luke 4:7; Acts 7:43]; excessive reverence of mere men [Acts 10:25–26]). Two, Luke's adaptation of language and imagery from Sir 50:20–22 in Luke 24:50–53 suggests Luke considers the προσκύνησις of the risen Jesus to be comparable to the cultic προσκύνησις of God in Sir 50. Finally, just as in Acts, the risen Lord Jesus who is enthroned beside God in heaven and who bestows God's Spirit is thereby acknowledged by the disciples as one worthy of being worshipfully called upon (Acts 2), so does Luke already begin to suggest at the end of the Gospel that the risen Jesus, whom the disciples now fully recognize as "Lord" (Luke 24:34), and who speaks of taking on the uniquely divine prerogative of sending God's Spirit (Luke 24:49), is a legitimate recipient of προσκύνησις and thus of the kind of worship reserved for God.

---

[47] For more on these and other ways in which Luke presents Jesus in ways characteristic of God in the OT, see chapters 8 and 9 in H. Douglas Buckwalter, *The Character and Purpose of Luke's Christology* (SNTSMS 89; Cambridge: Cambridge University Press, 1996), and chapter 9 in Robert F. O'Toole, *Luke's Presentation of Jesus: A Christology* (SubBi 25; Rome: Pontificio Istituto Biblico, 2004).

[48] Horst, *Proskynein*, 244. His brief treatment here is limited to expressing doubts about the textual authenticity of προσκυνήσαντες αὐτὸν in Luke 24:52 (however, see p. 89 in this book) and to giving the overall passage the same general significance as that in Matthew of rendering προσκύνησις to the risen Jesus in obedience to his missionary instructions.

5

The Προσκύνησις of Jesus in the Gospel of John

In the Gospel of John, προσκυνέω is used frequently (eleven times, along with one instance of the substantive προσκυνητής in John 4:23). The majority of the instances of the term appear in the episode of Jesus's discussion with the Samaritan woman over the proper worship of the God of Israel (4:20–24). In another instance, there is mention of Greeks who are among those who go up to Jerusalem to worship God at the Passover festival (12:20). In all ten of these instances of προσκυνέω, the term is clearly used for the worship that is reserved for Israel's God, most concretely expressed in cultic worship. In light of this usage in John, it is striking to find that the only other use of προσκυνέω occurs with Jesus as the object, as a man born blind who is healed by Jesus eventually professes his faith in him and renders προσκύνησις to him (9:38). On the one hand, the choice of προσκυνέω to characterize this act of reverence may indeed be highly significant and indicative of Jesus's worthiness to receive that which is otherwise reserved for God. On the other hand, this would be the only instance of the earthly Jesus allegedly receiving the kind of worship reserved for God, which may suggest that such προσκύνησις of the earthly Jesus should be regarded as something less than the worship given to God. While some interpreters ultimately come to the conclusion that Jesus is indeed portrayed receiving divine worship, others conclude that such reverence of Jesus with προσκύνησις is to be understood not as worship of Jesus himself, but as worship of God in Jesus. I will argue that a careful assessment of the relevant evidence in John's Gospel best supports the view that by depicting Jesus as a recipient of προσκύνησις, he is indeed intended to be seen as a legitimate recipient himself of the kind of worship that John elsewhere reserves for God.

A. The Προσκύνησις of God

As noted above, προσκυνέω appears numerous times in Jesus's discussion with the Samaritan woman over the proper worship of Israel's God in John 4:20–24. When the woman suggests to Jesus that it is the Samaritan site of worship on Mount Gerizim, where their ancestors rendered προσκύνησις (οἱ πατέρες ἡμῶν ἐν τῷ ὄρει τούτῳ προσεκύνησαν), rather than that in Jerusalem, where Jews say one must render προσκύνησις (ὑμεῖς λέγετε ὅτι ἐν Ἱεροσολύμοις ἐστὶν ὁ τόπος ὅπου προσκυνεῖν δεῖ), that is the proper place for the worship of God (4:20), she invites a response from Jesus. He says to her:

> Believe me, woman, the hour is coming when neither on this mountain nor in Jerusalem will you give προσκύνησις (προσκυνήσετε) to the Father. You give προσκύνησις (προσκυνεῖτε) to what you do not know; we give προσκύνησις (προσκυνοῦμεν) to what we know, for salvation is from the Jews. But the hour is coming, and is now here, when the true worshipers (προσκυνηταί) will give προσκύνησις (προσκυνήσουσιν) to the Father in Spirit and truth, for the Father seeks such people to give προσκύνησις (προσκυνοῦντας) to him. God is Spirit, and it is necessary for those who give προσκύνησις (προσκυνοῦντας) to him to render προσκύνησις (προσκυνεῖν) in Spirit and truth. (John 4:21–24)[1]

As is clearly indicated by the Samaritan woman's reference to the dispute between Samaritans and Jews over the legitimate center for the cultic worship of God, προσκυνέω here represents the kind of worship reserved for God alone, most concretely expressed through cultic worship at his sanctuary. Although in Jesus's response, both sites of cultic worship are ultimately rendered obsolete in view of the new way in which the worship of God is to be characterized, this is not necessarily a repudiation of ritual or cultic worship of God as such. As we will see, the significance of both Gerizim and Jerusalem being set aside lies not in a replacement of external worship of God with an interiorization of worship but rather lies in the replacement of these two sites with a new "place" where such worship of God will truly be carried out.[2] Much like what we argued in the previous chapter regarding Paul's and the Ethiopian eunuch's προσκύνησις of God at his Temple, προσκυνέω here also represents cultic worship in general without necessarily specifically signifying worship through prostration.[3] The difference here is in the emphasis that such προσκύνησις of God, which the Samaritan woman assumes has its center in one of two earthly locales, now has an entirely new center.

While on the one hand, Jesus does indeed affirm a precedence of Jewish worship over against Samaritan worship up to the present point in view of the alignment of the former with God's revelation of salvation ("You [i.e., Samaritans] give προσκύνησις to what you do not know; we [i.e., Jews] give προσκύνησις to what we know, for salvation is from the Jews" [4:22]), on the other hand, Jesus ultimately points ahead to an intimate worship of God as Father, which transcends Jewish-Samaritan worship controversies.[4] Concerning such worship, Jesus says that the hour is coming, and

---

[1] Despite the curious variation here between προσκυνέω with the dative (4:21, 23) and with the accusative (4:22 [2x], 23, 24) (absolute uses appear in 4:20 [2x], 24), there does not appear to be any discernible difference in meaning (contra Edwin A. Abbott, *Johannine Vocabulary: A Comparison of the Words of the Fourth Gospel with Those of the Three* [London: A&C Black, 1905], 138–42). See discussion in Horst, *Proskynein*, 33–39. Cf. *Let. Aris.* 135–38.

[2] Cf. Marianne Meye Thompson, *John: A Commentary* (NTL; Louisville, KY: Westminster John Knox, 2015), 104–5.

[3] See p. 84 above.

[4] The peculiar use of the neuter relative pronoun ὅ for both the Samaritans' present ignorant worship ("you give προσκύνησις to what [ὅ] you do not know") and the Jews' present informed worship

indeed is already here, when the true worshipers will give προσκύνησις to the Father "ἐν πνεύματι καὶ ἀληθείᾳ" (4:23). This is immediately reiterated as Jesus goes on to explain that "πνεῦμα ὁ θεός" and so those who give προσκύνησις to him must do so "ἐν πνεύματι καὶ ἀληθείᾳ" (4:24).

What exactly is meant by the doubly emphasized statement regarding worshiping God "ἐν πνεύματι καὶ ἀληθείᾳ" and by the statement that "πνεῦμα ὁ θεός," which seems to give the basis for such worship? There is some variation of interpretation among commentators regarding these phrases. Concerning the second, some understand it as a description of God's nature or character. So for instance, πνεῦμα ὁ θεός is understood to mean that God is "a spiritual rather than material being,"[5] that "he is invisible and unknowable,"[6] that he is "other than flesh, mortal, and confined in space and time,"[7] and/or that he is "different from all that is earthly and human."[8] Others take it to be a way of describing God's activity in the world, as for example in the explanations that "the πνεῦμα is God's miraculous dealing with men which takes place in the revelation"[9] or that "God is Spirit toward men because he gives the Spirit (xiv 16) which begets them anew."[10] Despite such slight variation, what is common to most of these interpretations is that the understanding of πνεῦμα ὁ θεός is typically informed by what is said elsewhere in John about the (Holy) Spirit. Thus, God is πνεῦμα—invisible, unconfined, life-giving, different from that which is earthly, and so on—just as the Spirit is invisible, unconfined ("the wind/Spirit[11] blows where it desires, and you hear its sound, but you do not know where it comes from or where it goes" [3:8]),[12] life-giving ("unless one is born of water and Spirit, he cannot enter the kingdom of God" [3:5; cf. 4:10, 14; 7:38–39]),[13] and different from that which is earthly ("What is born of the flesh is flesh, and what is born of the Spirit is spirit" [3:6]).[14] In saying πνεῦμα ὁ θεός, the sense is not merely that God is spirit-like but more specifically that he is Spirit-like.

("we give προσκύνησις to what [ὅ] we know") may suggest the relative incompleteness of both types of worship compared to the true worship of the new era in which God will be worshiped as Father (cf. Ignace de la Potterie, "'Nous adorons, nous, ce que nous connaissons, car le salut vient des Juifs': Histoire de l'exégèse et interprétation de Jn 4,22," *Bib* 64 [1983]: 97–98).

5   Andreas J. Köstenberger, *John* (BECNT; Grand Rapids: Baker Academic, 2004), 156.
6   C. K. Barrett, *The Gospel according to St. John: An Introduction with Commentary and Notes on the Greek Text* (2nd ed.; Philadelphia. PA: Westminster, 1978), 238.
7   Thompson, *John*, 105.
8   Rudolf Schnackenburg, *The Gospel according to St. John* (trans. Kevin Smyth et al.; 3 vols.; New York: Herder and Herder, 1968–1982), 1:439. See also D. A. Carson, *The Gospel according to John* (PNTC; Grand Rapids, MI: Eerdmans, 1991), 225; Craig S. Keener, *The Gospel of John: A Commentary* (2 vols.; Peabody, MA: Hendrickson, 2003), 1:618–19; J. Ramsey Michaels, *The Gospel of John* (NICNT; Grand Rapids, MI: Eerdmans, 2010), 253.
9   Rudolf Bultmann, *The Gospel of John: A Commentary* (trans. George R. Beasley-Murray et al.; Philadelphia, PA: Westminster, 1971), 190. See also George R. Beasley-Murray, *John* (WBC 36; Nashville, TN: Thomas Nelson, 1999), 62.
10 Raymond E. Brown, *The Gospel according to John: Introduction, Translation, and Notes* (2 vols.; AB 29–29A; Garden City, NY: Doubleday, 1966–1970), 1:172.
11 On the double meaning of the first instance of πνεῦμα in 3:8 as both "wind" and "Spirit," see Barrett, *John*, 210–11.
12 Barrett, *John*, 238; Carson, *John*, 225; Thompson, *John*, 105.
13 Brown, *John*, 1:172, 180.
14 Keener, *John*, 1:618–19; Carson, *John*, 225; cf. Schnackenburg, *John*, 1:439.

Thus, worship ἐν πνεύματι καὶ ἀληθείᾳ is worship that is consonant with this πνεῦμα (i.e., Spirit) ὁ θεός reality. Yet it is unlikely, as some commentators have suggested, that immateriality is the key here, positing that πνεύματι refers to the human spirit so that one truly worships the immaterial God when he/she does so within his/her own immaterial self.[15] Rather, the focus is on the life-giving qualities of the Spirit, the "living water" (4:10, 14; cf. 7:38–39), who effects new-life change in humans so that they are no longer those who belong to the mortal human realm (ἐκ τῆς σαρκὸς [3:6]) but become those who belong to the eternal life realm of the Spirit (ἐκ τοῦ πνεύματος [3:6]). The true worshiper, then, is not being characterized here as one who worships God in his/her inner spirit but as one who worships God "in Spirit," that is, out of the new life made possible by the Holy Spirit.[16] Later in John, this Spirit is referred to as "the Spirit of truth" (14:17; 15:26; 16:13), which is likely equivalent to and more clearly expresses the hendiadic "ἐν πνεύματι καὶ ἀληθείᾳ."[17] The new life through the Spirit brings the believer into true fellowship with God the Father. Yet it is also clear in John's Gospel that both Spirit and truth are closely tied to Jesus himself. Indeed, he who is the truth (14:6; cf. 1:14, 17) and who gives the Spirit of truth (15:26; 16:7; cf. 20:22) proves to be the new center for worship of God the Father in Spirit and truth.[18] John 4:20–24, as many observe, continues the development of the Johannine theme of Jesus as the new temple (cf. 1:14, 51; 2:13–22).[19] He is the new tabernacle that dwelt/"tabernacled" (ἐσκήνωσεν) among people (1:14), he is the new Bethel where the angels of God ascend and descend (1:51),[20] and he is the new temple that replaces the Jerusalem Temple (2:13–22). It is in the person and work of Jesus, who himself gives eternal life through the Spirit (4:10, 14; 7:37–39; cf. 3:5), that the eschatological new age is inaugurated, which is why Jesus can say that while, in its fullest sense, the hour of

---

[15] Leon Morris, *The Gospel according to John* (rev. ed.; NICNT; Grand Rapids, MI: Eerdmans, 1995), 239–40; C. John Collins, "John 4:23-24, 'In Spirit and Truth': An Idiomatic Proposal," *Presb* 21 (1995): 120–21.

[16] Schnackenburg, *John*, 1:437–40; Brown, *John*, 1:180; Beasley-Murray, *John*, 62; Michaels, *John*, 254; Thompson, *John*, 104–5; cf. Keener, *John*, 1:615–19. Other commentators offer interpretations that are not far from this understanding (Barrett, *John*, 238–39; Carson, *John*, 225–26; Köstenberger, *John*, 156–57).

[17] Brown, *John*, 1:180; Keener, *John*, 1:618; Michaels, *John*, 253; Thompson, *John*, 104. Cf. Barrett, *John*, 238–39; Carson, *John*, 225–26; Köstenberger, *John*, 157.

[18] Cf. Andrew T. Lincoln, *The Gospel according to Saint John* (BNTC 4; Peabody, MA: Hendrickson, 2005), 177–78: "Since Jesus is the giver of the Spirit and the embodiment of the truth, worship in Spirit and in truth is also worship centered in and mediated by Jesus."

[19] Along with most commentaries, see also Mary L. Coloe, *God Dwells with Us: Temple Symbolism in the Fourth Gospel* (Collegeville, MN: Liturgical Press, 2001) (for John 4, see chapter 5); Alan R. Kerr, *The Temple of Jesus' Body: The Temple Theme in the Gospel of John* (JSNTSup 220; London: Sheffield Academic, 2002) (for John 4, see chapter 6); Paul M. Hoskins, *Jesus as the Fulfillment of the Temple in the Gospel of John* (PBM; Milton Keynes: Paternoster, 2006) (for John 4, see chapter 3); Stephen T. Um, *The Theme of Temple Christology in John's Gospel* (LNTS 312; London: T&T Clark, 2006); Benny Thettayil, *In Spirit and Truth: An Exegetical Study of John 4:19-26 and a Theological Investigation of the Replacement Theme in the Fourth Gospel* (CBET 46; Leuven: Peeters, 2007).

[20] In this case, there is less agreement that the allusion here to Gen 28:12 in John 1:51 is intended to present Jesus as a new Bethel (cf. Gen 28:17, 19); see, for example, Kerr, *Temple*, 136–66. Still, Brown observes that Jesus is nevertheless understood to be "the locus of divine glory" by this allusion, even if the specific idea of Jesus as the new Bethel is less clear (*John*, 1:91).

worshiping God the Father in Spirit and truth is a future reality ("the hour is coming"), it is also, in a sense, proleptically present ("and is now here").[21] Worship of the Father in Spirit and truth, which is most fully realized following Jesus's death and resurrection and the bestowal of the Spirit to all who believe in him, is already dawning with the arrival of him who is endowed with the life-giving Spirit without measure (3:34), and who is the true temple of God (2:19–22).

Προσκυνέω is also similarly used for cultic worship of God in 12:20. Here it is said that there were some Greeks among those who went up to render προσκύνησις at the festival (Ἦσαν δὲ Ἕλληνές τινες ἐκ τῶν ἀναβαινόντων ἵνα προσκυνήσωσιν ἐν τῇ ἑορτῇ). From the larger context, it is clear that the festival in view is Passover (11:55; 12:1; 13:1) and thus those "going up" (ἀναβαινόντων) to render προσκύνησις are making a pilgrimage to Jerusalem to worship God (cf. Zech 14:16–17; Acts 24:11; Josephus, *Ant.* 20.164), in this case at one of Israel's most important religious festivals (for similar instances in John of "going up" to Jerusalem for Jewish festival observance, see 2:13; 5:1; 7:8, 10; 11:55). The "Greeks" (Ἕλληνές) who are a part of this larger group of worshipers are almost certainly non-Jews rather than Greek-speaking Jews, both in view of the immediately preceding hyperbolic remark of the Pharisees that the whole world has gone after Jesus (12:19; cf. also 12:32) and since Ἑλληνισταί is more likely to have been used if Greek-speaking Jews were in mind (cf. Acts 6:1; 9:29; 11:20).[22] In what follows, it is said that these Greeks approached Jesus's disciple Philip expressing a desire to see Jesus (12:21). When this request is reported to Jesus, it prompts him to announce the arrival of the hour of his glorification, which will result in Jesus drawing all people to himself (12:23–32).

It appears that here too John once again closely relates Jesus to Israel's worship in significant ways. Just as we noted above that John presents Jesus as the new temple with one of its significant ramifications being that he is the new locus for true worship of God the Father in the new age, so does John similarly and frequently relate Jesus to Israel's religious festivals by suggesting that their significance and fulfillment are found in him (e.g., 2:13–22; 6:1–71; 7:1–8:59; 10:22–39).[23] At the Festival of Tabernacles (7:1–8:59), which featured water-pouring and torch-lighting ceremonies, Jesus declares himself to be the source of living water for all (7:37–38) and the light of the world (8:12). At the Festival of Dedication (10:22–39), which commemorated the reconsecration of the Temple following its desecration at the hands of Antiochus IV Epiphanes, Jesus declares that he has been consecrated by the

---

[21] Cf. Brown, *John*, 1:172; Schnackenburg, *John*, 1:435, 436; Barrett, *John*, 237; Carson, *John*, 224; Beasley-Murray, *John*, 65–66; Thompson, *John*, 104.

[22] See Hendrik B. Kossen, "Who Were the Greeks of John XII 20?" in *Studies in John: Presented to Professor Dr. J. N. Sevenster on the Occasion of His Seventieth Birthday* (NovTSup 24; Leiden: Brill, 1970), 97–110; Johannes Beutler, "Greeks Come to See Jesus (John 12,20f)," *Bib* 71 (1990): 342–43. See also Bultmann, *John*, 423; Brown, *John*, 1:466; Schnackenburg, *John*, 2:381; Barrett, *John*, 421–22; Carson, *John*, 435–36; Morris, *John*, 525; Keener, *John*, 2:871–72; Köstenberger, *John*, 377; Lincoln, *John*, 348; Michaels, *John*, 685–86. Contra Thompson, *John*, 268.

[23] Again, along with most commentaries, see Coloe, *God*, 115–56; Kerr, *Temple*, 205–67; Hoskins, *Jesus*, 160–81; Gerry Wheaton, *The Role of Jewish Feasts in John's Gospel* (SNTSMS 162; Cambridge: Cambridge University Press, 2015).

Father (10:36).²⁴ Here, in the coming of Gentiles to Jesus at the time of the Passover celebration, we find a continuation of the theme of Jesus as the fulfillment of Passover (1:29–36; 2:13–25; 6:1–14, 22–71; 11:47–12:8; 13:1–17:26; 19:13–42).²⁵ Just as Passover associated Israel's exodus deliverance with the slaughter of the paschal lamb, so Jesus is understood to be the true paschal victim whose death brings about deliverance for all who turn to him.

When toward the end of Jesus's public ministry and as Passover approaches (11:55) the Jewish authorities resolve to put Jesus to death in order to prevent his growing popularity from inciting Roman action against their temple²⁶ and their nation (11:47–50), they are unaware of the profound sense in which their plan to put Jesus to death would indeed be for the benefit of not only Jews but Gentiles as well. By his death, John explains, Jesus will gather into one all the children of God, both Jew and Gentile (11:51–52).²⁷ It is with this understanding in mind that the significance of the appearance of Gentiles desiring to "see"²⁸ Jesus during Passover is found. It anticipates, as expected in 11:51–52 and as Jesus himself goes on to explain in 12:23–32, the universal scope of his salvific death, which "bears much fruit" (12:24) and results in Jesus drawing all people to himself (12:32). From the initial appearance of Jesus as "the Lamb of God who takes away the sin of the world" (1:29)²⁹ to the moment of his death on the cross at the time when the Passover lamb is slaughtered (19:14, 31, 42),³⁰ Jesus is presented fulfilling Passover as the true Passover lamb whose sacrificial death is not only for the deliverance of Israel but for the whole world.

B. The Προσκύνησις of Jesus by the formerly blind man

The only other use of προσκυνέω appears in the dramatic conclusion to the story of the healing of the man born blind, who confesses his belief in Jesus and renders

---

[24] Some, however, deny any particularly significant connection between Jesus and the Festival of Dedication (Schnackenburg, *John*, 2:305; Barrett, *John*, 379).

[25] For a discussion of the Johannine theme of Jesus as the perfect Passover lamb developed in these passages, see Stanley E. Porter, "Can Traditional Exegesis Enlighten Literary Analysis of the Fourth Gospel? An Examination of the Old Testament Fulfillment Motif and the Passover Theme," in *The Gospels and the Scriptures of Israel* (ed. Craig A. Evans and W. Richard Stegner; JSNTSup 104; Sheffield: Sheffield Academic, 1994), 401–21.

[26] Most commentators agree that τὸν τόπον (11:48) refers to the Jerusalem Temple (cf. 4:20).

[27] In John, the true "children of God" are all who believe in Jesus (1:12–13), Jew and Gentile alike (Keener, *John*, 2:857; Lincoln, *John*, 330; Thompson, *John*, 255).

[28] Often in John, seeing is associated with and/or takes on the sense of believing (e.g., 1:50; 4:48; 6:30; 9:35–41; 11:45; 12:44–45; 20:25–29). It is likely that while at the story level, the Greeks' desire to "see" Jesus simply signifies a desire to "meet" Jesus, there is a more profound sense in which this "seeing" connotes "believing," since these Greeks prefigure those from the larger Gentile world who would turn to Jesus (see Sherri Brown, "The Greeks: Jesus' Hour and the Weight of the World," in *Character Studies in the Fourth Gospel: Narrative Approaches to Seventy Figures in John* [ed. Steven A. Hunt et al.; Grand Rapids, MI: Eerdmans, 2016], 397, 400–1).

[29] This is likely a conflated image of Jesus as the Passover lamb and Isaiah's Suffering Servant. See Porter, "Traditional," 407–11.

[30] Note also other likely allusions to the Passover slaughter such as the hyssop (John 19:29; cf. Exod 12:22) and the unbroken bones (John 19:33, 36; cf. Exod 12:46). For these and other possible Passover allusions, see Porter, "Traditional," 418–21.

προσκύνησις to him (ὁ δὲ ἔφη· πιστεύω, κύριε· καὶ προσεκύνησεν αὐτῷ [9:38]).[31] When Jesus heals the man born blind (9:1–7), it not only piques the interest of those who knew the formerly blind man (9:8–12) but also gets the attention of the Pharisees (9:13–34), some of whom take offense to Jesus's healing since it was done on the Sabbath (9:14, 16). They interrogate the formerly blind man (9:13–17, 24–34) as well as his parents (9:18–23). While the latter are reluctant to give any information as to how their blind-born son now sees, the former is much more bold. Also by contrast, as is often noted, while the Pharisees are progressively shown to be ignorant and "blind" in their estimation of Jesus, the formerly blind man progressively "sees" more clearly as he offers his own evaluation of Jesus.[32] Thus, the Pharisees move downward from being divided over Jesus (9:16), to doubting that the blind man was ever blind at all (9:18), to being more united in their conviction that Jesus is a sinner (9:24), to questioning, and thereby showing themselves ignorant of, Jesus's origin (9:29). The formerly blind man, on the other hand, moves upward from acknowledging Jesus as his healer (9:11, 15, 30), to acknowledging him as a prophet (9:17), to being a disciple of Jesus (9:27–28), to acknowledging that Jesus is from God (9:33). When the exchange between the Pharisees and the formerly blind man over the person of Jesus and his act of healing comes to a close, with the healed man emerging as one who has "schooled" the religious teachers,[33] the Pharisees resort to casting out the formerly blind man (9:34).[34]

Jesus will soon vindicate him from the judgments of the Pharisees as he now returns to the scene, having been entirely absent during the lengthy interrogation, and pronounces his own judgment that he has come "that those who do not see may see" (e.g., the formerly blind man) "and those who see may become blind" (e.g., these Pharisees) (9:39). It is not the formerly blind man but these Pharisees who are "blind" and whose sin remains (9:40–41; cf. 9:34). But before this happens, when Jesus finds the formerly blind man, having heard of his expulsion, he asks him, "Do you believe in the Son of Man?" (9:35).[35] It is not entirely clear at first what is meant in this call to

---

[31] Although this entire phrase is missing from some key textual witnesses ($\mathfrak{P}^{75}$ ℵ* W it^b et al.), leading some to consider it a later addition (Brown, *John*, 1:375; Barnabas Lindars, *The Gospel of John* [NCB; London: Oliphants, 1972], 351; Calvin L. Porter, "John IX. 38, 39a: A Liturgical Addition to the Text," *NTS* 13 [1967]: 387–94), its otherwise strong textual attestation leads most to support its originality (Metzger, *Textual Commentary*, 195; Schnackenburg, *John*, 2:499; Carson, *John*, 379; Beasley-Murray, *John*, 151; Köstenberger, *John*, 296; Michaels, *John*, 567–68; Thompson, *John*, 217).

[32] See James L. Resseguie, "John 9: A Literary-Critical Analysis," in *Literary Interpretations of Biblical Narratives* (ed. Kenneth R. R. Gros Louis; vol. 2; Nashville, TN: Abingdon, 1982), 302; Paul D. Duke, *Irony in the Fourth Gospel* (Atlanta: John Knox, 1985), 125–26.

[33] Andy M. Reimer, "The Man Born Blind: True Disciple of Jesus," in *Character Studies in the Fourth Gospel: Narrative Approaches to Seventy Figures in John* (ed. Steven A. Hunt et al.; Grand Rapids, MI: Eerdmans, 2016), 435; Duke, *Irony*, 122–23.

[34] In view of the threat of expulsion from the synagogue for confessing Jesus (9:22), this is the likely sense in which the Pharisees' "casting out" of the formerly blind man is to be understood here in 9:34 (Lindars, *John*, 349; Barrett, *John*, 364; Carson, *John*, 375; Keener, *John*, 1:794; Köstenberger, *John*, 293–94; Lincoln, *John*, 286; Michaels, *John*, 564; cf. Schnackenburg, *John*, 2:252).

[35] The reading τὸν υἱὸν τοῦ ἀνθρώπου ($\mathfrak{P}^{66}$ $\mathfrak{P}^{75}$ ℵ B D W et al.) is certainly to be preferred over the variant reading τὸν υἱὸν τοῦ θεοῦ (A L Δ Θ 070 $f^{1.13}$ et al.) as the former is the more difficult reading. "Son of God" as an object of belief is well attested in the Gospel of John (John 1:34, 49; 3:18; 11:27; 20:31) and in other NT writings (Matt 14:33; 16:16; 27:54; Mark 3:11; 15:39; Luke 1:35; Acts 9:20;

believe in Jesus as "the Son of Man." The designation appears thirteen times in John and is linked with Jesus's descent and ascent (3:13; 6:62), his being "lifted up" (ὑψόω) in the dual sense of crucifixion and exaltation (3:14; 8:28; 12:34 [2x]), his glorification (12:23; 13:31), and his roles in judgment (5:27) and salvation (6:27, 53).[36] The reference to coming for judgment in 9:39 is noteworthy, but it makes more sense to see this as the consequence of belief and unbelief in the Son of Man rather than the basis of belief.[37] Most likely, the key is to be found in the first Son-of-Man passage (1:51), which is arguably programmatic for all subsequent Son-of-Man passages and for Jesus's life and ministry as a whole.[38] As the Son of Man for whom heaven is opened and upon whom angels ascend and descend, Jesus is the point of contact between earth and heaven. It is in this Son of Man that the disciples are assured of seeing the very revelation of God. Thus, when the formerly blind man asks who the Son of Man is that he might believe in him (9:36), Jesus's response is significant for his revelatory role as Son of Man. By telling the man that he has "seen" him and the one "speaking" with him is that one (9:37), he not only identifies himself as the Son of Man but does so in such a way that it highlights his uniqueness as one who alone has true knowledge of and thus is the true revealer of God (cf. 3:11–13, 32).[39] To truly see and hear the one who has seen and heard the things of heaven is to recognize him in whom God's revelation is uniquely manifested.

The formerly blind man's response is indicative of such recognition as he makes a climactic profession of faith in Jesus: "I believe, Lord" (πιστεύω, κύριε), and reverences him with προσκύνησις (καὶ προσεκύνησεν αὐτῷ [9:38]). But how should this προσκύνησις of Jesus by the formerly blind man be interpreted?

---

2 Cor 1:19; Gal 2:20; 1 John 4:15; 5:5; etc.), whereas "Son of Man" as an object of belief is otherwise nonexistent in the NT (although cf. John 3:14–15). Later copyists appear to have replaced τὸν υἱὸν τοῦ ἀνθρώπου with τὸν υἱὸν τοῦ θεοῦ to fit this pattern (Carson, *John*, 376; Beasley-Murray, *John*, 151).

[36] See Benjamin E. Reynolds, "The Use of the Son of Man Idiom in the Gospel of John," in *"Who Is This Son of Man?" The Latest Scholarship on a Puzzling Expression of the Historical Jesus* (ed. Larry W. Hurtado and Paul L. Owen; LNTS 390; London: Bloomsbury T&T Clark, 2011), 106–19.

[37] Cf. Schnackenburg, *John*, 2:253, who similarly notes the judgment theme but concludes that with regard to the exchange between Jesus and the formerly blind man, judgment "is not the main idea." For similar remarks, see Beasley-Murray, *John*, 159.

[38] Cf. Francis J. Moloney, *The Johannine Son of Man* (2nd ed.; BSRel 14; Rome: LAS, 1978), 35; Beasley-Murray, *John*, 28.

[39] See Moloney, *Johannine*, 154–55; cf. Carson, *John*, 376. "Jesus's identification of himself, in v. 37, as the Son of Man who is seen and who is heard must mean that in Jesus, the Son of Man, the man born blind can see and hear the revelation of God among men. Jesus asks him to put all his faith in this revelation of God which he has come to bring" (Moloney, *Johannine*, 155). With regard to 3:11, whatever the explanation for the "we" who are included with Jesus in his special knowledge (for an overview of suggestions, see Michaels, *John*, 190–91), these others clearly have such knowledge in a derivative sense, since Jesus goes on to explain that he alone, the Son of Man, is uniquely qualified to reveal heavenly things as the one who has descended from his heavenly dwelling (3:12–13; cf. 3:31–32).

C. The significance of the Προσκύνησις of Jesus in John

While the formerly blind man's insight into the person of Jesus certainly increases rapidly as the narrative progresses, the question remains as to whether such increasing insight culminates in the acknowledgment of Jesus as divine in his reception of προσκύνησις. Significantly, most interpreters are indeed largely inclined to interpret προσεκύνησεν in 9:38 along the lines of the strong sense of divine worship. It is often noted, as already discussed above, that all other instances of προσκυνέω in John are clearly used in the strong sense of cultic worship given to God (4:20–24; 12:20). There is, however, some disagreement over the place Jesus holds in this act of worship in 9:38. For some interpreters, it is Jesus himself who in his reception of προσκύνησις from the formerly blind man is considered worthy of the kind of worship otherwise reserved for God.[40] For others, it is God, not Jesus, who is truly worshiped, since the προσκύνησις that Jesus receives is ultimately to be understood as worship of God in Jesus.[41]

Although the majority of the scholarly discussions on this issue are fairly brief, a recent article by Martijn Steegen gives greater attention to the matter.[42] As the title of his article suggests, Steegen argues that John 9:38's portrayal of the worship of Jesus as the Son of Man is to be refocused on God the Father, meaning, in agreement with the second group of interpreters above, that the προσκύνησις of Jesus is not to be understood as worship of Jesus himself as divine but rather as worship of God in Jesus. According to Steegen, it is clear in John's Gospel that true worship is always and only to be given to God the Father (4:20–24).[43] Although the προσκύνησις of Jesus by the formerly blind man may at first appear to be a peculiar exception, since at no other point in John is Jesus worshiped,[44] such is not in fact the case. Jesus is the true temple (2:21) where worship of God in Spirit and truth takes place (4:23).[45] Jesus is also, as the Son of Man, the one who makes God known (1:51; 3:13–14; 5:27; 6:27, 53, 62; etc.).[46]

---

[40] While some in this group speak rather straightforwardly about the formerly blind man's worship of Jesus as divine (Morris, *John*, 440; Michaels, *John*, 568–69), others consider it more likely that while on the story level, the formerly blind man reverences Jesus simply as redeemer and revealer of God, the author expects his readers to perceive the more profound sense in which such προσκύνησις hints that "the healed man is 'worshipping' better than he knew" (Carson, *John*, 377; cf. Barrett, *John*, 365; Keener, *John*, 1:795; Köstenberger, *John*, 295, n. 82; Lincoln, *John*, 287).

[41] Horst, *Proskynein*, 292–93; Schnackenburg, *John*, 2:254; Beasley-Murray, *John*, 159–60; Hartwig Thyen, *Das Johannesevangelium* (HNT 6; Tübingen: Mohr Siebeck, 2005), 471. There are, of course, many more studies on John 9 (e.g., Resseguie, "John," 295–303; Duke, *Irony*, 117–26; Reimer, "Man," 428–37; John Painter, "John 9 and the Interpretation of the Fourth Gospel," *JSNT* 28 [1986]: 31–61; Jeffrey L. Staley, "Stumbling in the Dark, Reaching for the Light: Reading Character in John 5 and 9," *Semeia* 53 [1991]: 55–80; J. Warren Holleran, "Seeing the Light: A Narrative Reading of John 9," *ETL* 69 [1993]: 5–26, 354–82), but many of them do not discuss the sense in which Jesus's reception of προσκύνησις is to be understood. For a recent study which discusses worship in John in broader terms, see John Paul Heil, *The Gospel of John: Worship for Divine Life Eternal* (Eugene, OR: Cascade, 2015).

[42] Martijn Steegen, "To Worship the Johannine 'Son of Man': John 9,38 as Refocusing on the Father," *Bib* 91 (2010): 534–54.

[43] Steegen, "Worship," 540, 547–48.

[44] Steegen, "Worship," 540–41.

[45] Steegen, "Worship," 547–48.

[46] Steegen, "Worship," 548–49.

Thus, in Steegen's view, "the worship of Jesus can hardly be seen as a goal in itself," but rather "worship of the Son of Man opens access to the Father."[47] In agreement with Rudolf Schnackenburg, he contends, "The healed man's worship in 9,38 has to be understood as honour due to the God-sent messenger, which in itself gives honour and adoration to God."[48] So then, "the προσεκύνησεν of the man can be seen neither as ordinary homage to a human being nor as the adoration of Jesus as God."[49]

Despite this more focused effort to make sense of Jesus's reception of προσκύνησις, there are nevertheless problems with the contention that there are no implications for the worship of Jesus as divine in his reception of προσκύνησις. Steegen develops his position in response to those, such as Craig Keener, taking issue with Keener's appeal to John's larger christological portrait of Jesus's divinity (e.g., 1:1, 18; 20:28) to support the worship of Jesus as divine in 9:38.[50] The focus, Steegen maintains, should instead be on determining the significance of the προσκύνησις of Jesus as the Son of Man, which indeed, as he rightly observes, puts an emphasis on reverence of the one in whose person the revelation of God is manifested to others. But an important element in this that Steegen does not adequately take into account is the basis for Jesus's qualification to so reveal God. The Son of Man's ability truly to make God known to others is directly related to his highly significant heavenly origin and unique preexistent relation to God the Father. As noted above, a significant motif associated with the Son-of-Man designation is descent from heaven to earth. It is Jesus, the Son of Man, who truly reveals heavenly things because he alone has descended from his heavenly dwelling and reveals what he has seen and heard (3:11–13; cf. 3:31–32). Similarly, it is Jesus, the Son of Man, who is the true bread that comes down from heaven to be consumed that one may have eternal life (6:50–62).[51] His heavenly descent harks back to the prologue,[52] where he is first introduced not only as the Word who became flesh (1:14), as Steegen notes[53] but also as the Word who was in the beginning, who was with God, and who was God (1:1). Indeed, at the end of the prologue, he is said to be the only Son, (himself) God (μονογενὴς θεός),[54] at the Father's side, who has made God

---

[47] Steegen, "Worship," 549–50.
[48] Steegen, "Worship," 550. Cf. Schnackenburg, *John*, 2:254.
[49] Steegen, "Worship," 553.
[50] Steegen, "Worship," 544–45. Cf. Keener, *John*, 1:795.
[51] Cf. Reynolds, "Use," 106–08.
[52] See Elizabeth Harris, *Prologue and Gospel: The Theology of the Fourth Evangelist* (JSNTSup 107; Sheffield: Sheffield Academic, 1994), 119–20, 126; Warren Carter, "The Prologue and John's Gospel: Function, Symbol and the Definitive Word," *JSNT* 39 (1990): 41.
[53] Steegen, "Worship," 548, 549.
[54] Although there is some preference for the reading ὁ μονογενὴς υἱός (A C³ W K Δ Θ $f^{1.13}$ et al.) (Bultmann, *John*, 81–82; Schnackenburg, *John*, 1:279–80; Thompson, *John*, 27), the reading [ὁ] μονογενὴς θεός ($\mathfrak{P}^{66}$ $\mathfrak{P}^{75}$ ℵ B C* L et al.) is more widely supported as the original since it is the better attested and more difficult reading (Brown, *John*, 1:17, 36; Lindars, *John*, 98–99; Carson, *John*, 139; Morris, *John*, 100–01; Beasley-Murray, *John*, 2–3; Keener, *John*, 1:425–26; Köstenberger, *John*, 50; Lincoln, *John*, 108; Michaels, *John*, 92; Metzger, *Textual Commentary*, 169–70; Harris, *Prologue*, 101–09; B. A. Mastin, "A Neglected Feature of the Christology of the Fourth Gospel," *NTS* 22 [1975]: 37–41; David A. Fennema, "John 1.18: 'God the Only Son,'" *NTS* 31 [1985]: 124–35; Otfried Hofius, "'Der in des Vaters Schoß ist' Joh 1,18," *ZNW* 80 [1989]: 163–64; Murray J. Harris, *Jesus as God: The New Testament Use of Theos in Reference to Jesus* [Grand Rapids, MI: Baker, 1992], 73–103).

known (1:18). As Brian Mastin aptly puts it, "By using the phrase μονογενὴς θεός, [the evangelist] is able to insist that only God can reveal God."[55] Thus, the reason the Son of Man, Jesus, alone can make God known, in contrast to all others who have never even seen God (1:18), is precisely because he is the eternally preexistent Word and only Son who has a share in his Father's identity as θεός.[56]

Does this mean then that the formerly blind man is portrayed fully recognizing this profound aspect of Jesus's identity by worshiping him with προσκύνησις? Would not Steegen's assertion that Jesus is nowhere else worshiped in the Gospel of John make such a suggestion far less likely? First, with regard to the latter point, this claim is not entirely accurate. Steegen attempts to bolster his case by drawing attention to 20:17, which he interprets as a refusal of the risen Jesus to be worshiped by Mary.[57] But if Jesus's statement here, "Do not touch/cling to me" (μή μου ἅπτου), is to be interpreted as a refusal to be worshiped (which is not how most commentators interpret Jesus's words[58]), how does one explain what soon follows in Thomas's climactic confession of the risen Jesus as "my Lord and my God!" in 20:28, which most would agree constitutes worship of Jesus?[59] In Steegen's view, Jesus redirects Mary away from worship of himself and focuses her attention on God instead in 20:17,[60] but it is undoubtedly not without significance that Jesus's words to Mary that he is ascending to "my God and your God" (θεόν μου καὶ θεὸν ὑμῶν) is echoed in Thomas's own confession of Jesus as "my God" (ὁ θεός μου) in 20:28.[61] Certainly 20:17 shows that God the Father retains the primacy

---

For the translation "the only Son, (himself) God," taking μονογενὴς as a substantive (cf. 1:14) with θεός in apposition, see Fennema, "John 1.18," 128, 131; Hofius, "Vaters," 164; Harris, *Jesus*, 88–92; Brown, *John*, 1:17; Carson, *John*, 134; Beasley-Murray, *John*, 15; Köstenberger, *John*, 49.

[55] Mastin, "Neglected," 41; cf. Lincoln, *John*, 108.
[56] As Catrin Williams observes, in 1:18, Jesus is not so much contrasted with those who have never seen God as one who has seen God, and therefore can make him known, but more profoundly as one who is uniquely identified as μονογενὴς θεός. She too echoes Mastin in stating that John's insistence here is that "only God can reveal God" ("(Not) Seeing God in the Prologue and Body of John's Gospel," in *The Prologue of the Gospel of John: Its Literary, Theological, and Philosophical Contexts* [ed. Jan G. van der Watt et al.; WUNT 359; Tübingen: Mohr Siebeck, 2016], 84–87).
[57] Steegen, "Worship," 540. In support of this interpretation, Steegen cites Reimund Bieringer, "'I am ascending to my Father and your Father, to my God and your God' (John 20:17): Resurrection and Ascension in the Gospel of John," in *The Resurrection of Jesus in the Gospel of John* (ed. Craig R. Koester and Reimund Bieringer; WUNT 222; Tübingen: Mohr Siebeck, 2008), 209–35.
[58] Most agree that Jesus's refusal to be touched (or better clung to) is to be understood as a refusal for Jesus's followers to continue to "hold on to him" in the same fleshly way they knew him before his crucifixion (Brown, *John*, 2:1012; Barrett, *John*, 565–66; Lindars, *John*, 607; Morris, *John*, 742–43; Köstenberger, *John*, 569–70; Lincoln, *John*, 493–94; Thompson, *John*, 416–17). See also Christopher Tuckett, "Seeing and Believing in John 20," in *Paul, John, and Apocalyptic Eschatology: Studies in Honour of Martinus C. de Boer* (ed. Jan Krans et al.; NovTSup 149; Leiden: Brill, 2013), 180–82.
[59] Bultmann, *John*, 694–95; Brown, *John*, 2:1046–48; Barrett, *John*, 572–73; Carson, *John*, 659; Morris, *John*, 753; Beasley-Murray, *John*, 385–86; Thompson, *John*, 425–26. See also Harris, *Jesus*, 121–29; Marianne Meye Thompson, *The God of the Gospel of John* (Grand Rapids, MI: Eerdmans, 2001), 223–26. Building on the common observation that the combination of κύριος and θεός has biblical language for the God of Israel as its primary source (see Brown, *John*, 2:1047), Thompson further notes, "'My God,' both with and without LORD, is especially prominent in the Psalms, in petition, lament, and praise" (*John*, 426), which is suggestive of the liturgical character of Thomas's confession of Jesus as "my Lord and my God."
[60] Steegen, "Worship," 540; cf. Bieringer, "ascending," 232.
[61] Cf. Michaels, *John*, 1018.

in the Father-Son relationship (thus, Jesus's full response to Mary is "I am ascending to my Father and your Father, and to my God and your God"), but 20:28 shows that Jesus is legitimately included with his Father as one to be acknowledged and worshiped as "my God."

Still, while this provides reasonable evidence for concluding that the risen Jesus is worshiped as a divine figure in John's Gospel, perhaps it is otherwise with regard to Jesus in his earthly ministry. After all, as keen as the formerly blind man's growing insight into the person of Jesus is, he does not confess Jesus as "my Lord and my God" as Thomas does the risen Jesus. However, while it is probably right to insist that on the story level, the formerly blind man does not himself fully recognize and render προσκύνησις to Jesus as divine, the reader of John's Gospel perceives the deeper significance of key narrative details and motifs, and accordingly is meant to see that the formerly blind man is portrayed worshiping Jesus better than he knew.

Particularly significant here is the continuation of the Johannine motif of Jesus's heavenly origin. In the debate between the Pharisees and the formerly blind man over the person of Jesus, there is disagreement over whether or not Jesus is "from God" (9:16, 33; cf. 9:29, 30). For the characters of the story themselves, this is more simply a debate over whether Jesus is one whom God has authorized as his messenger in much the same way that any other human teacher, prophet, wonder-worker, and so on in Israel's history would be understood to be God's authorized messenger. Thus, while the Pharisees conclude that Jesus is a sinner for having broken the Sabbath and so cannot be one sent from God (9:16, 24), the formerly blind man reasons from his own experience of being healed by Jesus that he is a prophet, that is, one indeed sent from God (9:17, 25). Later on, while the Pharisees attempt to discredit Jesus as one sent from God by pointing out that his origin/authorization is unestablished (9:29), the formerly blind man calls attention to their ignorance in this matter (9:30), and becomes all the more convinced that Jesus's unique healing of one born blind must mean not only that he is not a sinner (9:31–32) but that he is indeed one "from God" (9:33). The reader, however, is much more cognizant than the characters in the narrative of the more profound and unique sense in which Jesus is indeed "from God." From the prologue's introduction of the preexistent divine Word (1:1), the μονογενὴς θεός who alone truly makes God known (1:18), who came into the world (1:9) taking on human flesh (1:14), the reader has privileged insight into the true sense in which the earthly Jesus is/comes/descends from above/heaven (3:13, 31; 6:33, 38, 50, 51, 58; 8:23; cf. 6:62; 17:5), comes/is sent into the world (3:17, 19; 6:14; 9:39; 10:36; 11:27; 12:46; 16:28; 17:18; 18:37), and is/comes from God (3:2; 6:46; 7:29; 8:14, 42; 13:3; 16:27–28, 30; 17:8). Again, while there is certainly a more mundane sense in which any of God's human servants may be somewhat analogously said to be, for example, "sent from God," as in the case of John the Baptist (1:6, 33; 3:28), or "sent into the world," as in the case of Jesus's disciples (17:18), only Jesus, as the prologue makes abundantly clear, is said to have a heavenly origin, and only he is said more suggestively to be/come/descend from above/heaven. Hence, the reader is well equipped to discern the significant way in which Jesus is distinguished from all others as one "from God." So while the formerly blind man rightly concludes that he who is able uniquely to heal one born blind and do so on the

Sabbath is one "from God" (i.e., acting as God's authorized agent), the reader knows the fuller picture of this divine figure who is "from God" and so finds that the formerly blind man speaks of Jesus better than he knew.

So too then, as discussed above, when the formerly blind man professes his faith in Jesus, the Son of Man, the one in whose person the revelation of God is uniquely manifested, the reader knows the fuller picture: the man has put his faith in one who has descended from his heavenly abode (3:13; 6:62)[62] and is thereby uniquely qualified to make God known in his own person, not merely, however, as *a* heavenly being but as the only one who has a share in God the Father's identity as θεός (1:1, 18). In believing in this one who makes God known, the formerly blind man once again responds better than he realized.

In light of the foregoing discussion, it is our contention that when the formerly blind man makes a climactic profession of faith in Jesus, declaring, "I believe, Lord (κύριε[63])," and renders προσκύνησις to him (9:38), the language is once again intended to signal the profound sense in which the man is portrayed appropriately responding to Jesus better than he knew, now by worshiping him with προσκύνησις.[64] Just as the attentive reader knows the deeper significance of Jesus as one "from God" (9:33) who has "come into the world" (9:39), so does he/she perceive the more profound sense in which Jesus, like his Father (4:20–24), is himself worthy of προσκύνησις.

Although it may seem peculiar that the formerly blind man is the only character suggestively portrayed worshiping Jesus before his resurrection, he is arguably a prime character best suited for such a portrayal. It is often rightly noted that the formerly blind man stands out as one of the most attractive, exemplary figures in the entire Gospel.[65] When he is healed of his blindness, it becomes increasingly clear that his ability to "see" transcends mere physical seeing as he proves more significantly to be capable of the kind of spiritual seeing that leads to deeper insight into the person of Jesus. Again, the great irony in this episode is that the religious leaders who think they see clearly regarding the person of Jesus prove themselves to be blind instead, while he who was once blind proves by his increasing insight into the person of Jesus that he now truly sees. The formerly blind man is the only character in John's Gospel besides Jesus himself who stands up to Jesus's opponents, disputes their negative evaluation of

---

[62] Note here too in the immediate context Jesus's suggestive statement, "I came into this world" (9:39).

[63] Jesus is often addressed as κύριε throughout his earthly ministry where it may simply be a respectful address equivalent to "sir" (4:11, 49; 5:7; 6:34), though it is also more frequently used in the somewhat stronger sense of "lord"/"master" by Jesus's disciples (6:68; 11:3, 21; 13:6; 37; 14:5, 8, 22; etc.; cf. 13:13–14), and in its even stronger sense of "the Lord," that is, the risen Lord (20:18, 20, 25, 28. Cf. 4:1[?]; 6:23; 11:2, for John's reference to Jesus as "the Lord," clearly reflecting the post-Easter perspective). While the formerly blind man's first address of Jesus as κύριε in 9:36 has the weaker sense of "sir," as the man does not yet realize with whom he is speaking, the second address of Jesus as κύριε in 9:38 certainly means much more than "sir" as the man now realizes Jesus is this Son of Man and makes a climactic profession of faith in him ("I believe, Lord [κύριε]"). Given the confessional nature of this κύριε address, it may very well be intended to be a partial reflection and anticipation of the full and climactic confession of the risen Jesus as "my Lord and my God" (20:28) (cf. esp. Lincoln, *John*, 287; Thompson, *John*, 219).

[64] Cf. esp. Carson, *John*, 377.

[65] Brown, *John*, 1:377; Keener, *John*, 1:775; Lincoln, *John*, 280; Holleran, "Seeing," 20.

Jesus, and boldly affirms Jesus as one "from God" even though doing so will inevitably lead to his expulsion. As one commentator puts it, "His character undergoes greater development than that of any other figure in the Gospel."[66] Thus, it is not all that surprising to find that such a model character as this is very suggestively portrayed in the end rendering προσκύνησις to Jesus and thereby worshiping him even better than he realized. While others are said to fall prostrate before Jesus—such as Mary who falls at Jesus's feet (ἔπεσεν αὐτοῦ πρὸς τοὺς πόδας), weeping and grieving over Lazarus's death (11:32–33), and the arresting mob who come looking for Jesus but then fall to the ground (ἔπεσαν χαμαί) when Jesus identifies himself by the suggestive ἐγώ εἰμι (18:6)[67]—John significantly reserves προσκυνέω for the reverence Jesus receives from one who once was blind, but now truly sees.

Finally, then, it is also our contention that the προσκύνησις of Jesus in John's Gospel is not to be understood merely as worship through Jesus that is ultimately directed to God the Father (as if to bypass Jesus himself as a proper recipient of worship) but is better understood as worship of Jesus himself as a proper recipient, and that this, far from conflicting with the worship of God the Father, redounds to his glory. Certainly, the focus of 4:20–24 is on worship of God the Father, and Jesus is the true temple, the true "place" in which the new era worship of the Father in Spirit and truth takes place, but this does not preclude the possibility of Jesus himself being included in such worship, as Steegen seems to suppose. Indeed, there is more to the theme of Jesus as the new temple than his being the new locus of worship of God. In the first intimation of the motif, the focus is on Jesus as the new locus of God's presence (1:14), the Word that became flesh and "tabernacled" among people, just as in the OT the God of Israel manifested his presence among his people in the tabernacle.[68] Again, then, we have another key theme tied to the prologue and its clear articulation of Jesus's divinity. As the true temple, Jesus is the place of both the worship of God and the presence of God, bringing people to God as well as God to people in his person. Indeed, one could make a case for a close connection between Jesus making possible true fellowship with and worship of God as Father, and such a one being recognized himself as God. The Johannine Jesus who gives new life in the Spirit through his death and resurrection, enabling his followers to become children of God and to have the intimate fellowship and worship of God as Father characteristic of the new age ("I am ascending to my Father *and your Father*, and to my God *and your God*" [20:17]), is himself climactically recognized, acknowledged and worshiped as Lord and God (20:28). Just as discussed

---

[66] Lincoln, *John*, 280.
[67] In light of the significance of the "I Am" sayings in the Gospel of John (see, for example, Richard Bauckham, "Monotheism and Christology in the Gospel of John," in *Contours of Christology in the New Testament* [ed. Richard N. Longenecker; Grand Rapids, MI: Eerdmans, 2005], 150–63), the reaction of the soldiers and officers who fall down when Jesus utters ἐγώ εἰμι, evocative of Yahweh's "I am" declarations in the OT, is theophanic in character. Yet while this is certainly to be interpreted as a response to an encounter with a divine figure, John undoubtedly refrains from using προσκυνέω since the reverential response is from Jesus's opponents.
[68] Along with the commentaries, see also Hoskins, *Jesus*, 116–25; Kerr, *Temple*, 121–23; Um, *Theme*, 153–54.

above that only God can reveal God, so too in the Gospel of John, only God can make such worship of God as Father possible.

In 5:23, Jesus speaks of the inextricable bond between the honor due to him and the honor due to God the Father. Just as Jesus the Son does whatever God the Father does (5:19), including working on the Sabbath (5:17), granting life (5:21), and executing judgment (5:22), so is he to be honored as his Father is honored. Failure to honor the Son is failure to honor the Father.[69] The idea is similar to what Paul writes in Phil 2:9–11 that it is God who has highly exalted Jesus and given him the divine name so that all will confess, "Jesus Christ is Lord," and all of this is to God's own glory.[70] Ironically, when the Pharisees charge the formerly blind man to "Give glory to God" (9:24), he does precisely that, but not as they would have it by acknowledging Jesus as a sinner but by acknowledging him as one "from God," confessing his faith in him as "Lord," and rendering προσκύνησις to him.

D. Conclusion

The Gospel of John closely relates Jesus to Israel's worship in various ways. He is the true source of living water and the true light of the world (Festival of Tabernacles), he is the one truly consecrated by God (Festival of Dedication), and he is the true paschal lamb whose death brings about eschatological deliverance for many peoples (Festival of Passover). He is also the true temple of God, the place where both true worship of God as Father takes place, as well as where the presence of God is truly manifested. These two aspects of Jesus as temple are closely related not only to one another but to other aspects of Jesus's identity as well. The divine Word (1:1) who took on human flesh and manifested the presence of God as he "tabernacled" among people (1:14) is the Son of Man who descended from his heavenly home (3:13; 6:62). Because he alone truly makes God known as μονογενὴς θεὸς (1:18), the heavenly descended Son of Man is the point of contact between earth and heaven, the one in whose very person the revelation of God is manifested to humans (1:51). While the characters in the Gospel narrative have limited insight in their recognition (or denial) of Jesus as one who makes God known and who brings his followers into true fellowship with and worship of God, the reader is aware of how the transcendent aspects of Jesus's identity give deeper meaning to these ideas.

It is precisely in view of John's larger christological portrait, in which these key aspects of Jesus's identity are uniquely made available to the reader, that the reader perceives the deeper significance in the portrayal of Jesus, the heavenly descended

---

[69] The Jewish charge here that Jesus was "making himself equal to God" (5:18; cf. 10:33; 19:7) is certainly false, not because he is not equal to God but because he does not *make himself* such. Again, as the reader knows well from the prologue, "Jesus was not wrong to claim divine status, and he did not attempt to appropriate it for himself; it was his by rights from the beginning" (Hurtado, *Lord*, 369). See also Jerome H. Neyrey, *The Gospel of John in Cultural and Rhetorical Perspective* (Grand Rapids, MI: Eerdmans, 2009), 178–80.

[70] Carson, *John*, 255; Hurtado, *Lord*, 52.

Son of Man who makes God known in his person, receiving προσκύνησις from one who "sees" in 9:38. Although it is not until the conclusion of the Gospel that Jesus's followers clearly recognize and acknowledge him in the divine terms of the prologue (20:28; cf. 1:1, 18), the formerly blind man is presented as a significant precursor to such recognition as he suggestively sees Jesus more clearly than he realizes through his speech and action. In line with the prologue (1:1–18), he acknowledges Jesus as one "from God" (9:33), and in anticipation of the fuller confession of the risen Jesus (20:28), he professes his faith in Jesus as he addresses him as κύριε (9:38a). And by rendering προσκύνησις to Jesus (9:38b), he is portrayed reverencing him in the same terms used elsewhere for the worship reserved for God the Father (4:20–24; 12:20).

Although some interpreters reduce the significance of Jesus's reception of προσκύνησις to worship of God in or through Jesus, this does not do justice to the fuller christological picture. Jesus is indeed the temple where true worship of God as Father takes place, but he is also the temple where God himself dwells and manifests his presence. Just as the Johannine Jesus has a share with his Father in his identity as θεός, so too does he have a share with his Father in his reception of προσκύνησις.

6

The Προσκύνησις of Jesus in the Epistle to the Hebrews

In the midst of one of the highest christological units in the entire NT corpus, Hebrews 1 describes Jesus, "the Son," receiving προσκύνησις from all the angels at God's command (Heb 1:6). So extraordinary is this particular instance of the προσκύνησις of Jesus that even James Dunn is compelled to acknowledge it as "very striking" and that it "seem[s] to move well beyond the sense of someone acknowledging the authority of someone of higher status."[1] But just how striking and how far beyond the norm of acknowledgment of a superior remains a matter of contention. This is due in part to a number of complexities confronting the interpreter, such as the passage's brevity and its almost exclusive use of scriptural citations here and in the surrounding context to make its argument (among other difficulties). As a result, opinions vary regarding some of the most crucial aspects related to this προσκύνησις of Jesus, such as the scenario envisaged, the setting in which this act of reverence takes place, and the extent to which it is equivalent to the worship normally reserved for God. After a careful consideration of these and other closely related issues in Heb 1, I will argue that despite some details that may continue to pose interpretive challenges, Hebrews portrays Jesus enthroned with God in heaven as he receives the προσκύνησις of the angels and that such a portrayal most closely corresponds to the ideal celestial worship of God enthroned in heaven. In this regard, such a depiction, along with other contextual evidence pointing to Jesus's divinity, signifies that Jesus receives the kind of worship typically reserved for God.[2]

A. The Προσκύνησις of Jesus by the angels

The προσκύνησις of the Son by angels appears in Heb 1 as one element in an extensive, scripturally grounded defense of the Son's superiority over the angels. Following an elaborate prologue highlighting several aspects of the Son's grandeur, which ends

---

[1] Dunn, *First*, 11.
[2] Although in one other place, the author uses προσκυνέω for the faithful, worshipful posture of the patriarch Jacob toward God (Heb 11:21), since this is the only other use of this term, it is best not to give too much weight to any authorial use of this term.

with the assertion of his superiority to the angels (1:1-4), the author launches into a catena of seven OT citations presented as the direct speech of God himself, affirming by comparison with the angels that the Son indeed proves to be vastly superior to them (1:5-14).

The argument begins with a rhetorical question, asking which angel had God ever declared to be his son or established between them an intimate father-son relationship (1:5). Although the OT may occasionally refer to angelic beings collectively as "sons of God" (Gen 6:2, 4; Ps 29:1; 89:7),[3] no individual angel has ever been singled out by God as having the kind of unique filial relationship with him that Hebrews attributes to the Son.[4] The two OT texts cited here in defense of the Son's superiority via divine sonship (Ps 2:7 and 2 Sam 7:14) share significant commonalities. In both texts, God himself speaks to/about Israel's king whom he declares to be his own son. Both passages envision an idealistic reign for Israel and the king decreed by God (e.g., a promise of the nations as the king's inheritance [Ps 2:8] and of an eternally established throne and kingdom [2 Sam 7:12-13, 16]), which many in antiquity regarded as having yet to be fulfilled, thereby opening these biblical texts to messianic interpretations.[5] It appears that the author of Hebrews was drawn to such features of the texts in his defense of the Son's supremacy. That both OT passages use the term "son" is certainly one key factor for their inclusion in the catena, as the author occasionally follows a conventional Jewish interpretive practice of associating passages containing relevant catchwords.[6] Yet this does not mean that his selection of passages is carried out atomistically or arbitrarily, for he also shows an awareness of the contexts of these passages and of common themes shared between them.[7] Thus, along with a number of his contemporaries, the author of Hebrews considers these texts to have messianic import, which he regards as finding their fulfillment in the Son. The divine promises of the nations as the Israelite king's inheritance (Ps 2:8) and of an eternal throne and kingdom (2 Sam 7:12-13, 16) have been fulfilled in the Son, who has inherited all things (Heb 1:2) and has an eternal throne (1:8) where he is presently seated at the right hand of God (1:3, 13), all of which authenticates his unique relationship to God as his Son.

---

[3] In a few instances where the MT has "sons of God," the LXX has "angels of God" (Job 1:6; 2:1; 38:7).

[4] Luke T. Johnson, *Hebrews: A Commentary* (NTL; Louisville, KY: Westminster John Knox, 2006), 76-77. The angelic figure in the Theodotion version of Dan 3:92 whom Nebuchadnezzar describes as "like a son of god" (ὁμοία υἱῷ θεοῦ) is not an exception since this is not a divine declaration (Paul Ellingworth, *The Epistle to the Hebrews: A Commentary on the Greek Text* [NIGTC; Grand Rapids, MI: Eerdmans, 1993], 111).

[5] For example, *Pss. Sol.* 17:4, 21-24; 4Q174 1 I, 10-12; Mark 1:11 par.; 9:7 par.; Luke 1:32-35; Acts 13:33.

[6] This Jewish interpretive principle (*gezera shawa*) can also be seen in Heb 4:1-11 where Gen 2:2 and Ps 95:11 are linked in the author's discussion based on the catchword "rest"/"rested" (see, for example, William L. Lane, *Hebrews* [2 vols.; WBC 47A-B; Dallas, TX: Word Books, 1991], 1:cxxi).

[7] For a growing consensus on this perspective of Hebrews's use of the OT, see Susan E. Docherty, *The Use of the Old Testament in Hebrews: A Case Study in Early Jewish Bible Interpretation* (WUNT 2/260; Tübingen: Mohr Siebeck, 2009), 150-52; Radu Gheorghita, *The Role of the Septuagint in Hebrews: An Investigation of Its Influence with Special Consideration to the Use of Hab 2:3-4 in Heb 10:37-38* (WUNT 2/160; Tübingen: Mohr Siebeck, 2003), 57.

Just as in 1:5 the unique divine sonship predicated of the Son to the exclusion of the angels implies the Son's superiority to the angels, so in 1:6 the προσκύνησις that the Son receives from the angels likewise implies his superiority to them. The occasion of the angels' reverence of the Son, however, is debated among scholars. Certain ambiguities in the temporal phrase introducing the event (ὅταν δὲ πάλιν εἰσαγάγῃ τὸν πρωτότοκον εἰς τὴν οἰκουμένην) have been interpreted in various ways, generating three main views concerning the scenario envisaged: (1) the incarnation;[8] (2) the parousia;[9] and (3) the exaltation.[10] The following representative translations of the Greek of 1:6a illustrate the interpretive similarities and differences between the three views:

Incarnation- "Again, when [God] brings the Firstborn into the earthly world"
Parousia- "When [God] brings the Firstborn into the earthly world again"
Exaltation- "Again, when [God] brings the Firstborn into the heavenly world."

Proponents of the incarnation view argue that since outside of Hebrews the term οἰκουμένη most commonly refers to the habitable realms of earth, it probably has the same meaning here in 1:6.[11] Thus, it is when the Son enters the human world that God calls the angels to render him προσκύνησις. Moreover, they argue that since πάλιν is best understood as a connective used to link scriptural texts, consistent with the author's pattern both in the immediate context (1:5) and elsewhere in Hebrews (2:12–13; 4:4–5; 10:30), it signifies not another coming to earth but another biblical citation

---

[8] Proponents include Ceslas Spicq, *L'Épître aux Hébreux* (2 vols.; EBib; Paris: Gabalda, 1952–1953), 2:17; Harold W. Attridge, *The Epistle to the Hebrews: A Commentary on the Epistle to the Hebrews* (Hermeneia; Philadelphia, PA: Fortress, 1989), 55–56; Hugh Montefiore, *A Commentary on the Epistle to the Hebrews* (BNTC; London: A&C Black, 1964), 45–46. See also North, "Jesus," 189.

[9] Proponents include Horst, *Proskynein*, 249–50; Brooke F. Westcott, *The Epistle to the Hebrews: The Greek Text* (London: Macmillan, 1903), 21–23; Otto Michel, *Der Brief an die Hebräer* (14th ed.; KEK 13; Göttingen: Vandenhoeck & Ruprecht, 1984), 112–13; Herbert Braun, *An die Hebräer* (HNT 14; Tübingen: Mohr Siebeck, 1984), 36–37; Jean Héring, *L'Épître aux Hébreux* (Neuchâtel: Delachaux & Niestlé, 1954), 25; William R. G. Loader, *Sohn und Hoherpriester: Eine traditionsgeschichtliche Untersuchung zur Christologie des Hebräerbriefes* (WMANT 53; Neukirchen-Vluyn: Neukirchener Verlag, 1981), 23–25; Lukas Stolz, "Das Einführen des Erstgeborenen in die οἰκουμένη (Hebr 1,6a)," *Bib* 95 (2014): 405–23.

[10] Proponents include Albert Vanhoye, "L'οἰκουμένη dans l'Épître aux Hébreux," *Bib* 45 (1964): 248–53; P. C. B. Andriessen, "La teneur judéo-chrétienne de He I 6 et II 14B–III 2," *NovT* 18 (1976): 293–95; F. F. Bruce, *The Epistle to the Hebrews* (rev. ed.; NICNT; Grand Rapids, MI: Eerdmans, 1990), 56–58; James W. Thompson, "The Structure and Purpose of the Catena in Heb 1:5-13," *CBQ* 38 (1976): 356; Lane, *Hebrews*, 1:26–28; Ellingworth, *Hebrews*, 117–18; Craig R. Koester, *Hebrews: A New Translation with Introduction and Commentary* (AB 36; New York: Doubleday, 2001), 192–93; Johnson, *Hebrews*, 79; Gareth L. Cockerill, *The Epistle to the Hebrews* (NICNT; Grand Rapids, MI: Eerdmans, 2012), 104–5; Ardel B. Caneday, "The Eschatological World Already Subjected to the Son: The Οἰκουμένη of Hebrews 1.6 and the Son's Enthronement," in *A Cloud of Witnesses: The Theology of Hebrews in Its Ancient Contexts* (ed. Richard Bauckham et al.; LNTS 387; London: T&T Clark, 2008), 30–36; David M. Allen, *Deuteronomy and Exhortation in Hebrews* (WUNT 2/238; Tübingen: Mohr Siebeck, 2008), 52–58; Joshua W. Jipp, "The Son's Entrance into the Heavenly World: The Soteriological Necessity of the Scriptural Catena in Hebrews 1.5-14," *NTS* 56 (2010): 562–63; and David M. Moffitt, *Atonement and the Logic of the Resurrection in the Epistle to the Hebrews* (NovTSup 141; Leiden: Brill, 2011), 53–69.

[11] Spicq, *Hébreux*, 2:17; Attridge, *Hebrews*, 56.

in defense of the Son's supremacy.¹² Incarnation advocates also note that "εἰσάγειν εἰς τὴν οἰκουμένην" may very well be an idiomatic expression for giving birth.¹³ Yet, a serious problem with this view, as many critics point out, is that elsewhere in Hebrews the Son is said to be lower than the angels in his earthly life (2:9), making it very unlikely that the angels would render him προσκύνησις in his lowly incarnate state.¹⁴ Similarly, outside of Hebrews, Christ's condescension results in angelic praise of God rather than Christ (Luke 2:13)¹⁵ and even explicit withholding of angelic praise of Christ (*Ascen. Isa.* 10:20–29).

Proponents of the parousia view agree with the position above that the lexical evidence strongly suggests οἰκουμένη refers to the habitable earthly realms in 1:6.¹⁶ They disagree, however, over the significance of πάλιν, arguing instead that it modifies εἰσαγάγῃ, thereby signifying that the angels' προσκύνησις of the Son occurs when he enters again into the earthly world (i.e., at his second coming or parousia).¹⁷ They also argue that since ὅταν with an aorist subjunctive typically signifies a future event, ὅταν δὲ πάλιν εἰσαγάγῃ must point ahead to a time when God will bring the Son into the οἰκουμένη, which leaves the parousia as the only plausible option of the three views.¹⁸ These points, however, are not decisive. Although the placement of πάλιν within the ὅταν clause close to εἰσαγάγῃ may very well support the sense of a "second coming," the consistent use of πάλιν to string together OT citations certainly cannot be overlooked.¹⁹ The seemingly odd position of πάλιν may actually be due to its link with δὲ as a connective, following the conjunction in taking a postpositive position.²⁰ With regard to the ὅταν + aorist subjunctive construction, it may often point to a future event, but this is not necessitated by the construction (cf. 1 Cor 15:27; Philo, *Somn.* 1.5). Rather, the construction is best understood as indicating "time coordinate with that of the main verb,"²¹ which in this case is the present tense λέγει. Since here, however, "λέγει has a rather general temporal reference,"²² the time element remains ambiguous and therefore "cannot be resolved solely on grammatical and syntactical grounds."²³ Finally, outside of Hebrews, the angels are not said to

---

[12] Spicq, *Hébreux*, 2:17; Attridge, *Hebrews*, 55.
[13] Spicq, *Hébreux*, 2:17; Attridge, *Hebrews*, 56, n. 67.
[14] Andriessen, "Teneur," 294; Loader, *Sohn*, 23; Lane, *Hebrews*, 1:27; Koester, *Hebrews*, 192; Caneday, "Eschatological," 31; Moffitt, *Atonement*, 55–56.
[15] Contra Montefiore, *Hebrews*, 46.
[16] Loader, *Sohn*, 24; Stolz, "Einführen," 418.
[17] Westcott, *Hebrews*, 22; Michel, *Hebräer*, 112–13; Héring, *Hébreux*, 25.
[18] Westcott, *Hebrews*, 22; Stolz, "Einführen," 414–16.
[19] Lane, *Hebrews*, 1:26; Koester, *Hebrews*, 192; Cockerill, *Hebrews*, 104, n. 22; Caneday, "Eschatological," 32–33; Jipp, "Entrance," 563. Even if πάλιν modifies εἰσαγάγῃ, this would not preclude an exaltation interpretation, since the sense could be that the preexistent Son (cf. 1:2) is led back into the heavenly arena following his earthly life (see Bruce, *Hebrews*, 58, n. 78; Allen, *Deuteronomy*, 54–55; Moffitt, *Atonement*, 57).
[20] Moffitt, *Atonement*, 57. Bruce and others point to Wis 14:1 as a relevant parallel for an analogous construction using πάλιν (*Hebrews*, 56, n. 71; Caneday, "Eschatological," 32, n. 25).
[21] Cockerill, *Hebrews*, 104, n. 23. Cf. Nigel Turner, *A Grammar of New Testament Greek: Volume III: Syntax* (Edinburgh: T&T Clark, 1963), 112.
[22] Ellingworth, *Hebrews*, 117.
[23] Lane, *Hebrews*, 1:26.

reverence Christ at his parousia but rather are said to form his entourage (Matt 16:27; Rev 19:14[?]).[24] Ultimately, the wider context of Hebrews must be considered in settling this matter, which is where, similar to the incarnation view, the parousia view falls short, and where the exaltation view by contrast offers the best explanation for the scenario in mind in 1:6.

The Son's exaltation to the right hand of God proves to be the central motif in the author's detailed Son-angel comparison.[25] It is the claim that the Son "sat down at the right hand of the Majesty on high" (1:3) that leads into the comparison with the angels and the question of whether any angel was ever invited to "sit at [God's] right hand" (1:13) that brings the catena to a close.[26] There are also other indications throughout the comparison that the Son's heavenly exaltation and enthronement remain in view, such as the use of royal imagery (throne, scepter, kingdom [1:8]), royal psalms (Ps 2 [1:5]; Ps 45 [1:8-9]; Ps 110 [1:13]), and other OT texts concerning royalty (2 Sam 7 [1:5]). The designation of the Son here in 1:6 as "firstborn" (πρωτότοκος) is often regarded as an allusion to Ps 89(LXX 88) where not only is King David called God's firstborn whom God will make higher than the kings of earth (Ps 89:28) but he calls God his father (Ps 89:27; cf. Heb 1:5) and is assured an enduring throne (Ps 89:30; cf. Heb 1:8).[27] The scenario presented in 1:6 immediately follows the two divine speeches discussed above which associated the Son's divine sonship with his fulfillment of messianic hopes (1:5), thereby qualifying him to sit at God's right hand (1:3). It is more likely that 1:6 continues this focus on the Son's exaltation and its implications for the Son-angel distinction than that a different occasion, such as the incarnation or the parousia, is suddenly introduced. Thus, having asserted the Son's heavenly exaltation to the right hand of God in 1:3, Hebrews associates this occasion with the affirmation of his divine sonship and supremacy on the one hand (1:5) and with the angels' προσκύνησις of the enthroned Son and their inferiority on the other (1:6).

The main charge raised against the exaltation view is that it takes οἰκουμένη as a reference to the heavenly world, which goes against the more widely attested use of the term as a reference to the earthly world. But other evidence within Hebrews strongly suggests the term is indeed being used in a unique way by the author. The only other occurrence of the term in Hebrews (2:5) is qualified eschatologically as τὴν οἰκουμένην τὴν μέλλουσαν, which clearly goes against taking οἰκουμένη here in its typical, mundane "this-worldly" sense. Although Lukas Stolz may be correct in pointing out that μέλλων only characterizes this οἰκουμένη as a "future world" and says nothing of its alleged heavenly nature,[28] he overlooks passages in Hebrews which

---

[24] Andriessen, "Teneur," 294; Cockerill, *Hebrews*, 104, n. 24.
[25] See esp. Kenneth L. Schenck, "A Celebration of the Enthroned Son: The Catena of Hebrews 1," *JBL* 120 (2001): 472–79 (although it is debatable that the catena is *only* concerned with the Son's superiority to the angels vis-à-vis his exaltation, as Schenck argues. See discussion below).
[26] Thompson, "Structure," 353.
[27] Attridge, *Hebrews*, 56; Michel, *Hebräer*, 113; Schenck, "Celebration," 479, n. 40; Caneday, "Eschatological," 33, n. 26; Docherty, *Use*, 158; Jipp, "Entrance," 563. For the possibility that the Son is presented as the true firstborn whom God leads into the true heavenly promised land (cf. Deut 6:10; 11:29), see Andriessen, "Teneur," 295–300.
[28] Stolz, "Einführen," 419.

speak of the same eschatological reality standing behind this designation as a heavenly entity. Thus, "the world to come" is certainly described elsewhere in similar terms as "the age to come" (6:5) and "the city to come" (13:14), but it is also described as the better "heavenly country" (11:16) and "the heavenly Jerusalem" (12:22).[29] Returning to the οἰκουμένη in 1:6, although its unqualified form may imply it is not to be identified with the eschatological οἰκουμένη to come in 2:5,[30] it is more likely that when the author mentions it is this world to come "of which we are speaking" (περὶ ἧς λαλοῦμεν), he points back to the οἰκουμένη in 1:6.[31] It is this heavenly world which the Son has already entered at his exaltation and where he received προσκύνησις from the angels (1:6) that is also the world to come for believers (2:5) and the great salvation they are about to inherit (1:14; 2:3). As David deSilva aptly puts it, this οἰκουμένη about which the author speaks is "'coming' from the perspective of the author and his audience, but already present for God, his Son, and his angels."[32]

The heavenly exaltation of the Son to the right hand of God leads to the divine command: καὶ προσκυνησάτωσαν αὐτῷ πάντες ἄγγελοι θεοῦ (1:6). Although the phrase is similar to LXX Ps 96:7, the OT citation behind this divine command is almost certainly from an Old Greek version of Deut 32:43 (or perhaps from Odes 2:43).[33] Here, the angels are called to worship God because he will vindicate his people, judge his enemies, and cleanse his people's land. It is likely that the author of Hebrews understood the eschatological tone of this text christologically as it is through the Son that salvation comes to God's people (2:9–10), judgment comes to his enemies (10:28–30),[34] and cleansing/purification is made (1:3; 9:13–14).[35] This last point in particular is explicitly linked with the Son's exaltation in 1:3 ("After making purification for sins, he sat down at the right hand of the Majesty on high"), providing further support for the exaltation view as the occasion of the angels' προσκύνησις of the Son. Thus, in light of his fulfillment of Deut 32:43, the Son is invited to sit at God's right hand (1:3) and to receive the προσκύνησις of the angels (1:6).

The defense of the Son's superiority to angels moves forward with another set of contrasting statements. Beginning this time with the angels, Hebrews cites Ps 104(LXX 103):4 to relate what God says concerning them: "He makes his angels winds, and his ministers a flame of fire" (1:7). It is not entirely clear from this passage alone how the angels are shown to be inferior to the Son here. Some scholars seem to limit the

---

[29] Cf. Andrew T. Lincoln, *Hebrews: A Guide* (London: T&T Clark, 2006), 95, who also draws attention to such passages and similarly concludes that what is to come in Hebrews is also heavenly.
[30] So Attridge, *Hebrews*, 56.
[31] Andriessen, "Teneur," 294; Caneday, "Eschatological," 34–35; Moffitt, *Atonement*, 62–63; Allen, *Deuteronomy*, 55; Cockerill, *Hebrews*, 126–27; Koester, *Hebrews*, 213; Ellingworth, *Hebrews*, 117–18; Lane, *Hebrews*, 1:27; Bruce, *Hebrews*, 58, n. 78.
[32] David A. deSilva, *Perseverance in Gratitude: A Socio-Rhetorical Commentary on the Epistle "to the Hebrews"* (Grand Rapids, MI: Eerdmans, 2000), 97.
[33] See discussions in Gareth L. Cockerill, "Hebrews 1:6: Source and Significance," *BBR* 9 (1999): 51–60; Allen, *Deuteronomy*, 44–52; Docherty, *Use*, 133–34; Ellingworth, *Hebrews*, 118–19.
[34] The author's citation of Deut 32:35, 36 in Heb 10:30 suggests his familiarity with the wider context of Deut 32.
[35] Cockerill, "Hebrews," 60–63.

significance of the inferior rank of the angels in 1:7 to their servant status.³⁶ They appeal to 1:14, which uses language reminiscent of 1:7 in its clear description of the angels as "ministering spirits" (λειτουργικὰ πνεύματα [cf. πνεύματα and λειτουργοὺς in 1:7]) sent out for "service" (διακονίαν), as evidence that 1:7 likewise signifies the servant status of the angels. This certainly fits with the image of the angels being entirely subject to the will of God to be used as wind and fire. It is also an apt contrast to the image of the Son as a royal figure immediately following in 1:8-9. But this explanation alone does not exhaust the significance of the angels' inferiority. The quotation in 1:7 comes from a psalm that praises God in his initial and ongoing activity in creation. Like the other OT passages quoted thus far, evidence suggests the author of Hebrews was aware of the broader context of Ps 104 and thus of its creator-creation theme.³⁷ In line with the psalm's overall theme and the earthy terms used to describe the angels (wind³⁸ and fire), it is likely that the author includes this text as part of his argument for the angels' inferiority because of their explicit association in this passage with the created order, which underscores their finite nature.³⁹ Of course, it certainly follows that since the angels belong to the created order, they are subject to the will of their creator as servants to be made into wind and fire. They are thus characterized as inferior beings because of their servant status as well as their creaturely status.

This is confirmed by the two citations that follow relating what God says by contrast concerning the Son in 1:8-12. First, in the words of the royal psalm, Ps 45(LXX 44):7-8, God affirms the eternal and righteous reign of the Son, here addressed as ὁ θεὸς,⁴⁰ whom he anoints and exalts beyond his companions.⁴¹ Whereas the angels are cast as servants who obey their superior's desire to be used as he sees fit, the Son is cast as a king in possession of a throne, scepter, and kingdom. Next, in the words of Ps 102(LXX 101):26-28, God affirms the Son's role in both the foundation and dissolution of the world,⁴² which substantiates and underscores the contrast between creation's transience and the Son's eternity. Here then, whereas the angels belong to the created

---

36   Schenck, "Celebration," 474-75; Ellingworth, *Hebrews*, 120-21. So too Moffitt, *Atonement*, 51-52, although in the lowly description of angels as "ministering spirits," places greater emphasis on the latter term.
37   Most notable in this regard are two striking similarities that the immediate context of this quoted psalm shares with Ps 102(LXX 101):26-28, which is quoted in Heb 1:10-12 and which likewise concerns the relationship between the creator and his creation. Both speak of the creative act of God in "laying the foundation of the earth" (ἐθεμελίωσεν τὴν γῆν [LXX Ps 103:5] / τὴν γῆν ἐθεμελίωσας [LXX Ps 101:26]) and of the creation either cloaking God or wearing out "as a garment" (ὡς ἱμάτιον [103:2; 101:27]). Both Ellingworth (*Hebrews*, 121) and Docherty (*Use*, 163) note the latter connection but surprisingly overlook the former.
38   Since πνεύματα is here parallel to πυρὸς φλόγα, it should be rendered as "winds" rather than "spirits" (*pace* Koester, *Hebrews*, 193-94; Moffitt, *Atonement*, 51-52), although, as already noted, the author will later exploit the language of 1:7 to describe angels as "ministering spirits" in 1:14. For similar associations of angels with wind and fire, cf. *Jub.* 2:2; *4 Ezra* 8:21-22; *2 Bar.* 21:6.
39   Cockerill, *Hebrews*, 108; Lane, *Hebrews*, 1:29.
40   See Murray J. Harris, "The Translation and Significance of ὁ θεός in Hebrews 1:8-9," *TynBul* 36 (1985): 138-49.
41   Whether "companions" (μέτοχοι) here refers to angels (Attridge, *Hebrews*, 60; Lane, *Hebrews*, 1:30; Braun, *Hebräer*, 40-41) or believers (Bruce, *Hebrews*, 61; Koester, *Hebrews*, 195; Cockerill, *Hebrews*, 111), the Son's heavenly exaltation signifies his superiority over both groups.
42   Lane, *Hebrews*, 1:30.

order and so are pejoratively associated with its temporal, perishable nature, the Son stands above the created order as one responsible for its beginning and end. In short, there is a dual contrast in 1:7–12 between the angels, who are portrayed as servants and creatures, and the Son, who is portrayed as king and creator.[43]

The last set of contrasting statements consists of a final climactic citation of Ps 110(LXX 109):1 concerning the exalted status of the Son, and a final comment regarding the subordinate status of the angels. The assertion of the Son's heavenly enthronement at the right hand of God (1:3), a key aspect of the Son's superior status which both launches the detailed Son-angel comparison and remains in view throughout the comparison, is finally given explicit scriptural support in 1:13. Much like 1:5, the rhetorical question ("To which of the angels has God ever said . . . ?") prefacing this key text here underscores the unique privilege of the Son to sit at God's right hand, since this was never granted to any angel. Rather, in contrast to the Son who is depicted as God's exalted vice-regent, the angels are ministering spirits sent out to serve (1:14). Thus, the conclusion to the Son-angel comparison reinforces the distinction between the subordinate servant status of the angels and the superior royal status of the Son.

Hebrews goes to great lengths here in 1:5–14 to demonstrate the various ways in which the Son is superior to the angels.[44] Whereas the angels are submissive servants, the Son is enthroned on high beside God as a kingly figure. Whereas the angels belong to the created order, the Son stands above the created order. Only the latter enjoys the privilege of being God's Son, and thus it is fitting that such a transcendent figure should also receive προσκύνησις from the clearly subordinate angels.

B. The significance of the Προσκύνησις of Jesus in Hebrews

The depiction in Heb 1:6 of Jesus, the Son, receiving προσκύνησις from the angels at God's command when he is exalted and enthroned in the heavenly realm is no doubt indicative of a high Christology. The question is, how high? Although much of the detailed scholarly discussion on 1:6 tends to be concerned with determining its temporal setting (incarnation, parousia, or exaltation), there has been more focused attention in recent times on the significance of the Son's reception of the angels' προσκύνησις, particularly in the works of Richard Bauckham,[45] Kenneth Schenck,[46]

---

[43] Cf. Kiwoong Son, *Zion Symbolism in Hebrews: Hebrews 12:18-24 as a Hermeneutical Key to the Epistle* (PBM; Milton Keynes: Paternoster, 2005), 117–23.

[44] Although some scholars consider the author to be combating some form of angel worship or angel Christology (see esp. Stuckenbruck, *Angel*, 124–25, nn. 197 and 198, for a list of scholars who take such views), this is very unlikely since there is no clear evidence of such threats anywhere in Hebrews (Attridge, *Hebrews*, 51–52; Lane, *Hebrews*, 1:9; Koester, *Hebrews*, 200; Jipp, "Entrance," 558).

[45] Richard Bauckham, "Monotheism and Christology in Hebrews 1," in *Early Jewish and Christian Monotheism*, (ed. L. T. Stuckenbruck and W. E. S. North; JSNTSup 263; London: T&T Clark, 2004), 167–85; Richard Bauckham, "The Divinity of Jesus Christ in the Epistle to the Hebrews," in *The Epistle to the Hebrews and Christian Theology* (ed. Richard Bauckham et al.; Grand Rapids, MI: Eerdmans, 2009), 15–36.

[46] Kenneth L. Schenck, "The Worship of Jesus among Early Christians: The Evidence of Hebrews," in *Jesus and Paul: Global Perspectives in Honor of James D. G. Dunn for His 70th Birthday* (ed. B. J. Oropeza et al.; LNTS 414; London: T&T Clark, 2009), 114–24.

Jody Barnard,[47] and David Allen.[48] All four scholars agree on the exaltation as the occasion of the angels' reverence of the Son,[49] but they differ over the character of the reverence. Whereas Schenck considers it to fall short of the kind of divine worship typically reserved for God,[50] Bauckham and Barnard consider it to be equivalent to the worship of God.[51] In the most recent discussion on this issue, Allen considers the strengths and weaknesses of these other three scholars and seems to come to a more intermediate position, stating on the one hand that though "the text may not bear the full weight of cultic devotion,"[52] yet on the other hand "there is something significant and distinctive about this act of angelic worship, something that is related to the status and character of the Son himself, and which approximates to the Christ devotion found elsewhere in the NT."[53] What accounts for these different views?

Since it seems that to a certain extent, one's view of the angels' προσκύνησις of the Son tends to correspond to his/her impression of other material in this context that may or may not point to the Son's divinity, we begin with a consideration of such material.

At the end of the exordium, it is said that one aspect of the Son's superiority to the angels has to do with his inheritance of a more excellent name (1:4). Since this "name" is unspecified in 1:4, there are different views as to what it could be. The majority of interpreters take the name to be "Son,"[54] particularly in view of what immediately follows in 1:5. That is, when the author rhetorically asks to which angel God has ever said, "You are my Son" (1:5), the most natural inference is that it is this distinctive designation of the Son as God's "Son" that the author has in mind as the more excellent name distinguishing the Son from the angels (1:4). Others contend that the more excellent name inherited is the divine name.[55] According to Jarl Ulrichsen, in order to discern the name in question, one must not stop at 1:5 but follow Hebrews's progression in identifying the Son first as υἱός (1:5), then as θεός (1:8–9), and finally, reaching the highpoint of the christological designations, as κύριος (1:10), the conventional

---

[47] Jody A. Barnard, *The Mysticism of Hebrews: Exploring the Role of Jewish Apocalyptic Mysticism in the Epistle to the Hebrews* (WUNT 2/331; Tübingen: Mohr Siebeck, 2012), 247–52.
[48] David M. Allen, "Who, What, and Why? The Worship of the Firstborn in Hebrews 1:6," in *Mark, Manuscripts, and Monotheism: Essays in Honor of Larry W. Hurtado* (ed. Chris Keith and Dieter T. Roth; LNTS 528; London: Bloomsbury T&T Clark, 2015), 159–75.
[49] Bauckham, "Hebrews," 169–70; Schenck, "Celebration," 477–79; Barnard, *Mysticism*, 237–41; Allen, *Deuteronomy*, 52–58 (although Allen seems to have slightly modified his position here in "Who," 168; see n. 105 below).
[50] Schenck, "Worship," 121–23.
[51] Bauckham, "Hebrews," 179–80; Bauckham, "Divinity," 25; Barnard, *Mysticism*, 249–52.
[52] Allen, "Who," 175.
[53] Allen, "Who," 174.
[54] Bruce, *Hebrews*, 50; Thompson, "Structure," 355; Loader, *Sohn*, 21; Attridge, *Hebrews*, 47; Lane, *Hebrews*, 1:17; deSilva, *Perseverance*, 92; Koester, *Hebrews*, 181–82; Schenck, "Celebration," 472; Cockerill, *Hebrews*, 98.
[55] Jarl H. Ulrichsen, "Διαφορώτερον ὄνομα in Hebr. 1,4: Christus als Träger des Gottesnamens," *ST* 38 (1984): 65–75; Charles A. Gieschen, *Angelomorphic Christology: Antecedents and Early Evidence* (AGJU 42; Leiden: Brill, 1998), 296–97; Bauckham, "Hebrews," 175; Johnson, *Hebrews*, 73; Barnard, *Mysticism*, 162–64; Amy L. B. Peeler, *You Are My Son: The Family of God in the Epistle to the Hebrews* (LNTS 486; London: Bloomsbury T&T Clark, 2014), 59–61.

Greek substitute for the divine name, which is the more excellent name meant in 1:4.[56] Against the majority view, both Ulrichsen and Bauckham raise a cogent point that it makes better sense to regard "Son" as "*the one* who inherits from his Father, not *what* he inherits"[57] and, continuing the logic, to regard what is inherited as that which belongs to the Father, which in this case would be his name.[58] They also both draw attention to Phil 2:9–11, which similarly attests Christ's reception of the divine name at his exaltation.[59] While these are certainly notable observations that should not be too lightly dismissed, they might not be enough to overturn the weighty contextual evidence in favor of the majority view. Not only is "Son" dually emphasized ("You are my *Son* . . . he shall be to me a *Son*") immediately following the mention of the more excellent name, but it also continues as a significant designation distinguishing Christ from the angels ("Of the angels he says . . . . But of the *Son* he says . . ." [1:7–8]) and is the designation for Christ that introduces this unit, and indeed the whole work ("[I]n these last days, He has spoken to us by a *Son*" [1:2]). This interpretation may also better account for the author's use of the comparative form of διάφορος to describe the name (διαφορώτερον: "more excellent") rather than the superlative (διαφορώτατον: "most excellent"), which would certainly be the more appropriate descriptor if the divine name were in mind.

A number of interpreters consider the ascription of ὁ θεός to the Son in 1:8 (and perhaps 1:9 as well[60]) to be an affirmation of his divinity. Some even go so far as to suggest that it is this divine address in Ps 45:7–8 applied to the Son that "is probably the chief factor in the pastor's choice of this psalm."[61] Others are not so inclined to derive such significance from the ascription, and their reservations are worth considering. Lincoln Hurst, for example, argued that just as the original royal psalm could address the Israelite king as אלהים without thereby implying any literal divinization of the king, the application of this psalm with its divine ascriptions to the Son is likewise simply intended to point to him as an "ideal king" who "represents God to the people."[62] Even beyond Ps 45, Dunn notes how the terms אלהים and θεός could at times be used for

---

[56] Ulrichsen, "Διαφορώτερον," 66. It is also in view of the whole of what follows in 1:5–14 that some scholars take ὄνομα as a reference not to any one designation but to the series of designations within this unit (i.e., υἱός, πρωτότοκος, θεός, and κύριος); see Lala K. K. Dey, *The Intermediary World and Patterns of Perfection in Philo and Hebrews* (SBLDS 25; Missoula, MT: Scholars Press, 1975), 147; Mathias Rissi, *Die Theologie des Hebräerbriefs: Ihre Verankerung in der Situation des Verfassers und seiner Leser* (WUNT 41; Tübingen: Mohr Siebeck, 1987), 52.
[57] Bauckham, "Hebrews," 175 (italics his).
[58] Ulrichsen, "Διαφορώτερον," 67.
[59] Bauckham, "Hebrews," 175; Ulrichsen, "Διαφορώτερον," 67.
[60] Those who also take the first ὁ θεός in 1:9 as an address to the Son include Bruce, *Hebrews*, 60; Spicq, *Hébreux*, 2:19–20; Braun, *Hebräer*, 40; Attridge, *Hebrews*, 59; Ellingworth, *Hebrews*, 124; deSilva, *Perseverance*, 99, n. 31; Koester, *Hebrews*, 195; Johnson, *Hebrews*, 80; Cockerill, *Hebrews*, 110. For the alternative view that both instances of ὁ θεός in 1:9 refer to the Father, see Harris, "Translation," 149–51; Bauckham, "Hebrews," 182, n. 33.
[61] Cockerill, *Hebrews*, 109. Similarly, Oscar Cullmann, *The Christology of the New Testament* (trans. Shirley C. Guthrie and Charles A. M. Hall; rev. ed.; Philadelphia, PA: Westminster, 1963), 310.
[62] Lincoln D. Hurst, "The Christology of Hebrews 1 and 2," in *The Glory of Christ in the New Testament: Studies in Christology in Memory of George Bradford Caird* (ed. Lincoln D. Hurst and N. T. Wright; Oxford: Clarendon, 1987), 159–60. See also Schenck, "Celebration," 474; Dunn, *First*, 136.

figures other than deities, such as angels and humans, both in biblical literature and early Jewish literature, and again, no real divinization of these figures is intended.[63] Bauckham voices similar concerns regarding the limits of θεός/אלהים language, drawing particular attention to the heavenly figure Melchizedek in 11Q13 II, 10. Like the Son in Hebrews, Melchizedek is discerned from an OT psalm (Ps 82:1) to be an "אלהים" distinguished from Yahweh (אל). Bauckham reasons that just as Melchizedek can have such terminology applied to him from a biblical text without the implication of his divinity, similarly in the case of the Son "it is not the mere application of a scriptural use of the word 'god' to Jesus Christ which makes Heb. 1.8 more significant."[64]

Still, in light of these observations, it may in fact be all the more significant that the NT writings by contrast generally reserve the term θεός for deities (especially the one true God of Israel,[65] though also false/supposed gods[66]) with the notable exception of a few rare cases where the term is applied to Christ.[67] Although in the case of Heb 1:8–9, the application of a royal psalm that figuratively hails the human king as "god" may likewise suggest that a figurative sense of the Son as θεός is implied, the way certain elements of this psalm when applied to the heavenly exalted Son take on cosmic significance may speak against a merely figurative rendering of the θεός ascription. Whereas the Israelite king's throne and kingdom were established in the earthly realm, the Son's throne and kingdom are in the heavenly realm (cf. 1:3, 13; 8:1; 10:12; 12:2). Whereas the duration of the Israelite king's reign is "forever and ever" in a figurative sense (or at least speaks more to the king's dynastic line than to the king himself), the Son's reign is truly eternal (cf. 1:10–12; 7:24; 13:8).[68] Thus, just as the Son transcends the human king of Ps 45:7 by more fittingly fulfilling such things attributed to him, the θεός ascription may very well fall in line with this movement, going beyond its original figurative application in the psalm to take on a more proper sense of the term befitting one whom Hebrews regards as truly reigning eternally in heaven.[69] Although difficult to argue that the divine ascription is "the chief factor" in the selection of Ps 45:7–8 in light of other more defensible connections (e.g., possession of "throne" and "kingdom" [cf. 2 Sam 7:13, 16]; an "eternal" session [cf. 2 Sam 7:13, 16; Ps 110:4]), it may be just as

---

[63] James D. G. Dunn, *Christology in the Making: A New Testament Inquiry into the Origins of the Doctrine of the Incarnation* (2nd ed.; Grand Rapids, MI: Eerdmans, 1996), 16–17. See, for example, Exod 7:1; Ps 82:1, 6; 4Q400 1 II, 7; 4Q403 1 I, 32–33; 11Q13 II, 10; Philo, *Sacr.* 9; *Mut.* 125–29; *Mos.* 1.158. Cf. Exod 21:6; 22:8; Pss 8:6; 97:7; 138:1.

[64] Bauckham, "Hebrews," 182.

[65] Matt 15:31; Mark 10:18; Luke 1:68; John 17:3; Acts 24:14; 1 Cor 8:6; Gal 3:6; Eph 4:6; 1 Thess 1:9; 1 Tim 2:5; Heb 1:1; and so on.

[66] Acts 7:43; 17:23; 19:26, 37; 1 Cor 8:4–5; 2 Cor 4:4; Gal 4:8; Phil 3:19 (figurative use); 2 Thess 2:4. In Acts, certain exceptional men are hailed as θεοί by pagans (Acts 12:22; 14:11; 28:6), but this is regarded as blasphemous (cf. 12:23; 14:14–15).

[67] The clearest examples are from John 1:1 and 20:28, though there are a number of other passages with varying degrees of probability that might also be included (John 1:18; Acts 20:28; Rom 9:5; Titus 2:13; 2 Pet 1:1; 1 John 5:20). See discussions in Raymond E. Brown, "Does the New Testament Call Jesus God?" *TS* 26 (1965): 551–65; Vincent Taylor, "Does the New Testament Call Jesus God?" *ExpTim* 73 (1962): 116–18; Harris, *Jesus*.

[68] Herbert W. Bateman, "Psalm 45:6-7 and Its Christological Contributions to Hebrews," *TJ* 22 (2001): 5–9.

[69] Spicq, *Hébreux*, 2:19.

problematic to downplay the significance of this aspect of the psalm applied to the Son on the grounds that it is merely "carried over with the rest of the quotation."[70]

Perhaps the clearest indication of the Son's divinity in this unit is in the affirmation of his role in the uniquely divine act of creation. It is widely attested in the OT and early Jewish literature that the God of Israel alone is the creator of all things and is thereby distinguished from all other reality as the one true God.[71] In light of this, it is highly significant when in 1:10–12, the Son is said to be the "Lord" who founded creation and will bring it to its end. Although some scholars either deny that any real role in creation is being ascribed to the Son or minimize the significance of the Son's role in creation, such views are not convincing.

Schenck, for example, states that the emphasis in the application of Ps 102:26–28 to the Son here is on "the permanence of Christ's lordship over the creation in contrast to its passing existence and the passing function of the angels in it."[72] He opines that the point of the citation "is not that Christ was the agent of creation," cautioning that "one cannot assume that all the salient points of a quotation are meant to be extracted from another author's use of it."[73] Yet, one cannot help but wonder why the author of Hebrews cites the portion of the psalm that ascribes creation to the Son (Ps 102:26 in Heb 1:10) if his only concern is to affirm the permanence of the Son's lordship over creation (Ps 102:27–28 in Heb 1:11–12). It is clear elsewhere in Hebrews that the author is not averse to omitting portions of biblical citations that are not directly relevant to his purposes.[74] One might protest as Bauckham does in response to Schenck, that "if the author's quotation from Ps. 102 was not meant to present Christ as the personal agent of creation, he chose his text very badly."[75]

According to Hurst, a better understanding of the sense of this creative role ascribed to the Son is facilitated by the Wisdom of Solomon. Here, Pseudo-Solomon desires to possess the Wisdom by whom God created all things (Wis 9:1–4), who enters into holy souls (7:27), and who grants eternal reign for rulers who honor her (6:21). In view of this background text, Hurst posited that Hebrews's portrayal of God addressing the Son as creator is better understood as God "addressing his own wisdom in its earthly receptacle, the Messiah-king" who as an "ideal human (royal) figure . . . possesses and enshrines in this world the divine, creative wisdom."[76] Barnard highlights the problems with this suggestion.[77] First, as discussed above with regard to Heb 1:8–9, it

---

[70] Taylor, "New Testament," 117.
[71] 2 Kgs 19:15; Neh 9:6; Ps 96:5; Isa 40:28; 44:24; 45:18; Jer 10:10–12; LXX Hos 13:4; 4Q403 1 I, 30–36; Bel 5; 2 Macc 1:24; Sir 18:1; 43:33; *Jub.* 12:3–5; *Sib. Or.* 3:20–35; *Sib. Or.* frg. 3; *1 En.* 9:4–5; 81:3; *2 En.* 24:2–3; 33:3–8; 47:3–4; *4 Ezra* 3:4; 6:1–6; *2 Bar.* 21:4–7; *Apoc. Ab.* 7:10; *Jos. Asen.* 12:1–2; Josephus, *Ag. Ap.* 2.192. See Bauckham, *Jesus*, 8–11; Barnard, *Mysticism*, 267–68.
[72] Schenck, "Celebration," 475.
[73] Schenck, "Celebration," 476.
[74] Ellingworth, *Hebrews*, 40, draws attention to this in the author's use of Ps 8:4–6 in Heb 2:6–8 and Deut 32:35–36 in Heb 10:30.
[75] Bauckham, "Divinity," 22, n. 13.
[76] Hurst, "Christology," 161–62. Hurst followed the lead of George B. Caird, "Son by Appointment," in *The New Testament Age: Essays in Honor of Bo Reicke* (ed. William C. Weinrich; 2 vols.; Macon, GA: Mercer University Press, 1984), 76: "[Christ] is the man in whom the divine Wisdom has been appointed to dwell, so as to make him the bearer of the whole purpose of creation."
[77] For what follows, see Barnard, *Mysticism*, 265–66.

is not necessarily the case that exalted language applied figuratively to royalty in the background text is also intended to be interpreted figuratively in Hebrews's application of such texts to the Son. For example, although both the Wisdom of Solomon and Hebrews ascribe eternity to their respective royal figures, they mean very different things by it. Whereas in the Wisdom of Solomon, the "eternity" of the king who acquires Wisdom is clearly meant to be taken figuratively, since he describes his "immortality" as leaving a legacy following his death (Wis 8:13), in Hebrews, no such qualification is mentioned with respect to the Son. On the contrary, it is precisely in view of the true permanence of the Son in his heavenly reign that believers are encouraged to place their confidence in him (Heb 7:11–28). If "eternity" language applied to the Son ("you remain . . . you are the same, and your years will have no end" [Heb 1:11–12]) is not meant to be reduced to the kind of extravagant, hyperbolic flattery characteristic of ancient Near Eastern court protocol, perhaps it is a mistake to assume the creator ascription should likewise be qualified in some figurative sense. Second, although Hebrews may have been influenced by such Wisdom speculations as are found in the Wisdom of Solomon, it is not in the end said that God speaks to Wisdom embodied in the Son but that he speaks directly to the Son himself ("to the *Son* [God says], 'Your throne, O God . . .' and 'You, in the beginning, O Lord'" [Heb 1:8–12]).

Jared Compton argues that the biblical texts cited in Heb 1:5–14 are employed to establish the Son's superiority to the angels as a messianic figure, not as a divine figure, and that even the ascription of a role in creation to the Son is not inconsistent with this since there is messianic precedent for such an idea.[78] Here too, however, there are problems. To begin with, the latter claim is simply untenable. Compton states, "The idea that the messiah preceded—if not also facilitated—creation was itself not unprecedented," citing LXX Ps 109:3; LXX Mic 5:2; Dan 7:13; *1 En.* 48:2; 69:27; *Pesiq. Rab.* 36 (161a) as evidence.[79] But while all of these texts may speak of the messianic figure's preexistence, none of them speak of him as an agent in creation. Thus, one cannot downplay the significance of the Son's role in creation on the basis of messianic precedent.

There are also complications with the former claim. First, although a number of the OT citations applied to the Son may indeed be readily explicable as messianic texts (2 Sam 7:14; Pss 2:7; 45:7–8; 110:1), the christological applications of Deut 32:43 in Heb 1:6 and Ps 102:26–28 in Heb 1:10–12 are potentially unique in this respect, since these texts appear to be addressed not to a messianic figure, but to God. It could be, as Compton and others have argued, that the author of Hebrews discerned within these texts a second exalted figure distinguishable from God.[80] In the case of Deut 32:43, this could be due to the lack of a clear grammatical antecedent for the αὐτῷ called to receive

---

[78] Jared Compton, *Psalm 110 and the Logic of Hebrews* (LNTS 537; London: Bloomsbury T&T Clark, 2015), 20–37.

[79] Compton, *Psalm*, 33.

[80] Compton, *Psalm*, 31–36; B. W. Bacon, "Heb 1, 10-12 and the Septuagint Rendering of Ps 102, 23," *ZNW* 3 (1902): 282–85; T. F. Glasson, "'Plurality of Divine Persons' and the Quotations in Hebrews 1:6ff," *NTS* 12 (1966): 270–72; Stephen Motyer, "The Psalm Quotations of Hebrews 1: A Hermeneutic-Free Zone?" *TynBul* 50 [1999]: 18–21; Bauckham, "Hebrews," 179; Ellingworth, *Hebrews*, 120, 126.

προσκύνησις from the angels of God.⁸¹ Others suggest it is due to a merging of Deut 32:43 with LXX Ps 96:7, whose superscription (τῷ Δαυιδ ὅτε ἡ γῆ αὐτοῦ καθίσταται) lends itself to a messianic interpretation, allowing for the κύριος who receives προσκύνησις from the angels to be viewed as a messianic figure.⁸² In the case of Ps 102:26–28, some scholars note how the distinctive wording of the Greek text (ἀπεκρίθη αὐτῷ ἐν ὁδῷ ἰσχύος αὐτοῦ [LXX Ps 101:24; cf. MT Ps 102:24]) opens up the possibility for an addressee distinguished from God to emerge, though there is some disagreement over whether the phrase signifies a change of speaker from the "poor man" (101:1–23) to God (101:24–29)⁸³ or a return to the poor man's speech (101:1–16, 24–29) following an answer to his prayer (101:17–23).⁸⁴ In any case, LXX Ps 101:24–29 is understood to be directed to another κύριος (101:26; cf. 101:23) distinguished from God.

Yet certain difficulties with each of these suggestions allow for the plausibility of the alternative view that the author of Hebrews may very well have applied to the Son texts which he considered to be addressed to God.⁸⁵ The αὐτῷ in Deut 32:43 may indeed have no clear grammatical antecedent, but the context seems to point to God alone as his people's deliverer and thus as the likely referent of the αὐτῷ who is to receive προσκύνησις. Although Bauckham maintains that God is the speaker from Deut 32:39 onwards and so must be distinguished from the αὐτῷ whom he commands to receive προσκύνησις,⁸⁶ the numerous abrupt, unannounced shifts of speaker throughout Deut 32 could certainly have led the author of Hebrews to discern another abrupt shift at Deut 32:43 from God back to the human author who calls for praise of God. A supposed merging of Deut 32:43 with LXX Ps 96:7 is questionable, since the formal features of the citation are most likely from an Old Greek version of Deut 32:43. Compton acknowledges this difficulty but maintains the likelihood of an inclusion of LXX Ps 96 as a source text in light of the features of the text that facilitate the discernment of a messianic figure. This, however, assumes the very point needing to be proved! Finally, Barnard offers reasons for doubting that the particular wording of the Greek in Ps 101:24a would have given the impression that an exalted figure distinguished from God was being addressed in Ps 101:24b–29.⁸⁷ To suggest, as one interpretation does, that God addresses this figure results in attributing an unlikely statement to God: "Tell me the paucity of my days. Do not take me away at the mid-point of my days" (101:24b–25a). To suggest, as another interpretation does, that the poor man addresses this figure avoids this problem but may perhaps be no more likely a reading than one which views this figure as the speaker who addresses God.⁸⁸ There are also

---

⁸¹ Glasson, "Plurality," 271; Bauckham, "Hebrews," 179; Ellingworth, *Hebrews*, 120.
⁸² Motyer, "Psalm," 18–19; Compton, *Psalm*, 33–36.
⁸³ Bacon, "Heb," 282. Cf. Glasson, "Plurality," 271–72; Compton, *Psalm*, 31–32.
⁸⁴ Motyer, "Psalm," 20, n. 54.
⁸⁵ See Attridge, *Hebrews*, 57, 60; Johnson, *Hebrews*, 78, 81; Bateman, "Psalm," 11–12; Barnard, *Mysticism*, 229–33, 247.
⁸⁶ Bauckham, "Hebrews," 179, n. 28.
⁸⁷ For what follows, see Barnard, *Mysticism*, 231–32.
⁸⁸ Perhaps even more probable, rather than the poor man resuming his speech and replying to the exalted figure following the answer to his prayer (LXX Ps 101:17–23) as Motyer proposes ("Psalm," 20, n. 54), he simply replies to God, since he is the one who answered his prayer.

other ways of interpreting the phrasing of Ps 101:24a without introducing additional participants, such as rendering ἀπεκρίθη αὐτῷ as the resumption of the poor man's petition to God[89] or as a concluding affirmation that God responded to the poor man's pleas, which is followed by the poor man's closing words to God in Ps 101:24b-29. In the end, the nature of the evidence suggests that while it is certainly possible that the author of Hebrews discerned a second exalted figure distinguishable from God in Deut 32:43 and Ps 101:26-28, it is far from clear that this interpretation of these texts is more preferable than one which holds that the author applied to the Son texts that he understood to be addressed solely to God.

Second, and more importantly, even if it is granted that all of the citations were interpreted messianically, it still leaves open the question of what kind of messiah the Son is understood to be. To suggest, as Compton seems to, that any or all of the citations are interpreted and applied to the Son *either* as a messianic figure *or* as a divine figure is to impose a false dichotomy. Bauckham, for example, agrees that the citations are concerned with the messianic rule of the Son, yet he rightly observes that in their application to the Son he is shown to transcend more traditional expectations of the earthly ruling Davidic messiah through the affirmation of his eternal, cosmic rule in the heavens at the right hand of God above all creation, which he not only brings to its end but had a hand in in its beginning as creator.[90] Although there is certainly much in LXX Ps 101 that is eschatological and introduces ambiguities that allow for the discernment of a messianic figure, it is remarkable that the author of Hebrews applies to the Son that portion of the psalm which contains elements never ascribed elsewhere to a messianic figure but rather are characteristic of the unique activity of God. By ascribing a role in creation to the Son, the author uniquely links him to God in such a way that he effectively affirms the Son's divinity.

Lest it still be thought that it is questionable to derive such a view of the Son from a mere biblical quote which seems to receive no immediate comment from Hebrews on the nature and limits of its significance, one finds the same affirmation of the Son's involvement in creation in the prologue where the author very straightforwardly states that God made the world through the Son (1:2). In fact, by highlighting the close correspondences between the prologue (1:1–4) and the catena of OT citations (1:5–14), John Meier demonstrates that the citations are intended to provide biblical grounding for the prologue's christological claims.[91]

Even here, however, some argue against taking the direct assertion of the Son's agency in creation literally. Dunn observes that much of what is said about the Son in the exordium echoes language used of God's Wisdom and Word in Jewish tradition: (1) agent in creation (Son [Heb 1:2]; cf. Wisdom [Wis 7:22; 9:2; Philo, *Det.* 54; *Her.* 199];

---

[89] Though ἀποκρίνομαι typically introduces a reply and thus a change in speaker, it could also indicate continuation of discourse (cf. Matt 11:25; 22:1).

[90] Bauckham, "Hebrews," 178.

[91] John P. Meier, "Structure and Theology in Heb 1,1-14," *Bib* 66 (1985): 168–89; John P. Meier, "Symmetry and Theology in the Old Testament Citations of Heb 1,5-14," *Bib* 66 (1985): 504–33; cf. Lane, *Hebrews*, 1:22; Koester, *Hebrews*, 197–98. Thus, the Son is the heir of all things (1:2b; 1:5), creator and sustainer of creation (1:2c, 3b; 1:10-12), radiance and representation of God (1:3a; 1:8-9), and is seated at the right hand of God (1:3d; 1:13).

Word [Wis 9:1; Philo, *Sacr.* 8; *Deus.* 57; *Migr.* 6, etc.]); (2) ἀπαύγασμα of God's glory (Son [Heb 1:3]; cf. Wisdom [Wis 7:26]); (3) χαρακτὴρ of God's nature (Son [Heb 1:3]; cf. Word [Philo, *Plant.* 18]); (4) sustainer of creation (Son [Heb 1:3]; cf. Word [Philo, *Plant.* 8]), which suggests an influence of such traditions on Hebrews's characterization of the Son.[92] By associating the Son through such language with these two figures, who were most likely simply personified aspects of God (i.e., they were not real, personal beings separate from God but rather represented ways of speaking about God and his activity),[93] it is argued that the significance of the statement regarding the Son's role in creation is likewise to be understood in more figurative terms. That is, just as ascribing a role in creation to Wisdom or Word was in reality a way of describing the creative activity of God himself, so the Son's "role in creation" is in reality a way of pointing to the creative power of God, which is embodied and revealed in the human Jesus. Thus, it is not the Son himself who personally preexists and participates in creation, but rather it is the creative power of God that preexists.[94]

Although it is indeed likely that Wisdom/Word traditions were conceptual sources for Hebrews's christological portrait, one must still consider the nature and extent of such appropriations. For instance, as Dunn himself acknowledges, the evidence suggests that in their own conceptions of Wisdom, ancient Jewish writers were capable of drawing upon pagan religious expressions about various female deities (e.g., Ishtar-Astarte and Isis) without thereby regarding Wisdom similarly as a distinct deity. The adoption of similar language did not necessarily lead to an equivalence between Wisdom and these pagan goddesses in every respect.[95] So, too, Hebrews's use of Wisdom/Word language does not necessarily imply the transferal of these figures' impersonal character to the Son as is rightly noted by Dunn's critics.[96] As William Lane and others observe, reflections on such traditions "provided [the author of Hebrews] with categories and vocabulary with which to interpret the person and work of Christ," yet they have been "thoroughly assimilated and refashioned by a distinctively Christian thinker" and brought "into the service of Christian confession."[97] It is, again, perhaps not an inconsequential detail that it is not as Wisdom or as Word that Christ is identified and addressed throughout but as Son, which seems to move away from impersonal

---

[92] Dunn, *Christology*, 166, 206–09. See also Kenneth L. Schenck, "Keeping His Appointment: Creation and Enthronement in Hebrews," *JSNT* 66 (1997): 106–12; Compton, *Psalm*, 28; Lane, *Hebrews*, 1:12–14.

[93] There is considerable debate over the nature of God's Wisdom and Word (see, for example, discussion in Aquila H. I. Lee, *From Messiah to Preexistent Son: Jesus' Self-Consciousness and Early Christian Exegesis of Messianic Psalms* [WUNT 2/192; Tübingen: Mohr Siebeck, 2005], 37–77), and although some maintain that there is a real sense in which these figures are independent entities distinguished from God (Gieschen, *Angelomorphic*, 89–114; Chester, *Messiah*, 45–51), it is more likely that they are literary personifications and thus represent vivid ways of speaking about God and his activities (Dunn, *Christology*, 168–76, 215–30; Hurtado, *One*, 36–37, 41–50; Lee, *Messiah*, 84; Schenck, "Keeping," 107–10; Barnard, *Mysticism*, 122–23, 154; Peeler, *You*, 23).

[94] Dunn, *Christology*, 209. Cf. Schenck, "Keeping," 113.

[95] Dunn, *Christology*, 168–71.

[96] Peeler, *You*, 26; Cockerill, *Hebrews*, 99, n. 64. Cf. Barnard, *Mysticism*, 153.

[97] Lane, *Hebrews*, 1:12, 13. Cf. Koester, *Hebrews*, 188: Hebrews both appropriates and "transforms" wisdom traditions; deSilva, *Perseverance*, 88: Wisdom traditions provided "the raw material" for Christology. See also Ellingworth, *Hebrews*, 99; Cockerill, *Hebrews*, 99; Barnard, *Mysticism*, 153–54, who similarly emphasize the limits of such traditions on Hebrews's christological portrait.

connotations associated with the former terms. In short, despite attempts to get around the plain sense of Hebrews's statement concerning the Son's role in creation, it is best to agree with the vast majority of scholars who take Heb 1:2 (and 1:10) as clear evidence of an affirmation of Christ's personal agency in creation.[98]

Finally, those who maintain that Heb 1 is not asserting such a view of the Son's divinity often point to 1:4 where the author states that the Son *became* (γενόμενος) superior to the angels.[99] This seems to directly conflict with the arguments above for the Son's divinity. Yet this conflict is not as stark as some suppose. For one thing, it does not follow, as Compton seems to suppose, that such a statement in 1:4 is determinative for the purpose behind all the biblical citations in 1:5–13, namely that they are *all* intended to show the ways the Son *became* superior to the angels. Although it is agreed that Hebrews has the Son's heavenly exaltation in view as the moment of his "becoming" superior to the angels ("After making purification for sins, he sat down at the right hand of the Majesty on high, having become as much superior to the angels" [1:3–4]), and that most of the citations affirm his superiority in this respect, 1:10 does not fit easily into this pattern but instead demonstrates that the author has both eschatological as well as protological aspects of the Son's supremacy in mind.[100] Hebrews understands the one who was exalted to the right hand of God to be the same one who was involved in the creation of the world, which includes the creation of the angels since they belong to the created order (1:7). This indicates the author is just as concerned with highlighting ways the Son has always been superior to the angels as he is with demonstrating how he became superior to them. Although there is admittedly a measure of tension in this idea that he is both the eternal Son of God and yet is said to become superior to the angels at his exaltation where he inherits the name "Son" (1:4–5), this complication is not insurmountable.[101] Otfried Hofius observes a comparable tension in the way the OT can speak of God as both already reigning as king over all (Ps 47:8) and yet becoming king over all at the eschaton (Zech 14:9).[102] With regard to the Son in Hebrews, it is because of his achievement of human salvation and the inauguration of God's eschatological rule over all through his incarnation, sacrificial death, and heavenly exaltation, that he who was always Son "entered into a new dimension in the experience of sonship,"[103] and thus "he who was superior to [the angels] as the eternal Son became superior to them in a new way at the exaltation."[104]

In view of the Son's involvement in creation, along with other possible hints of his divine status, it would be surprising if the angels' προσκύνησις of the Son were not in some sense in accordance with his divinity. To be sure, it is when the Son is led

---

[98] Along with most commentaries, see Bauckham, "Hebrews," 173–85; Barnard, *Mysticism*, 219, 263–69; Peeler, *You*, 26–29, 56–57; Son, *Zion*, 118–20; Meier, "Structure," 178–79; Meier, "Symmetry," 517–18, 531–33; Hurtado, *Lord*, 118–26; Sean M. McDonough, *Christ as Creator: Origins of a New Testament Doctrine* (Oxford: Oxford University Press, 2009), 200–8.
[99] Compton, *Psalm*, 24; Caird, "Son," 76–77; Hurst, "Christology," 156; Dunn, *Christology*, 52.
[100] Meier, "Symmetry," 532.
[101] See discussions in Attridge, *Hebrews*, 54–55; and Schenck, "Keeping," 91–104.
[102] Otfried Hofius, *Der Christushymnus Philipper 2,6-11: Untersuchungen zu Gestalt und Aussage eines urchristlichen Psalms* (2nd ed.; WUNT 17; Tübingen: Mohr Siebeck, 1991), 93–94.
[103] Lane, *Hebrews*, 1:26.
[104] Cockerill, *Hebrews*, 98.

into the heavenly realm at his exaltation and enthronement with God that he receives the angels' προσκύνησις,[105] and thus it is not necessarily *as* creator that he receives such reverence. To what extent then, if at all, does this particular scenario of angelic reverence of the Son as he is enthroned beside God in heaven approximate the worship typically reserved for God? Although it is not explicitly mentioned in Heb 1, it is possible, as Barnard argues, that the author has God's heavenly sanctuary in mind as the setting for the Son's heavenly enthronement.[106] In 8:1–2, it is said concerning the Son that "we have such a high priest, who sat down at the right hand of the throne of the Majesty in the heavens, a minister 'τῶν ἁγίων' and of the true tabernacle." This statement clearly looks back to 1:3, showing that the high priestly Son who made purification for sins and then sat down at the right hand of God does so in what is agreed to be the heavenly equivalent to the earthly tabernacle's inner sanctum, the Most Holy Place, designated here as τῶν ἁγίων (8:2).[107] In what follows in Heb 9, Christ as the high priest *par excellence* is contrasted with the Levitical high priest, who entered the earthly Most Holy Place annually to offer atonement for sins (9:7, 25) whereas Christ passed through the greater and more perfect tabernacle, which is not of this creation, and entered into the heavenly Most Holy Place to make atonement for sins once for all (9:11–12, 24). Hebrews also makes reference to heavenly counterparts to the earthly sanctuary, such as the curtain separating the Holy Place from the Most Holy Place, which Christ passed through as high priest (6:19–20; 10:20; cf. 9:3), and the ark with its mercy seat within the Most Holy Place, of which the heavenly throne of God is undoubtedly its equivalent (8:1–2; cf. 9:3–5; 4:16).[108] It may be that these are representative of a more complete correspondence between the earthly sanctuary and a heavenly archetype, as Hebrews cites Exod 25:40 where God instructs Moses concerning the earthly tabernacle to make everything according to the pattern shown to him (8:5). Some in antiquity considered Moses to have been shown some form of a heavenly sanctuary here (*2 Bar.* 4:5; *Liv. Pro.* 3:15; cf. Wis 9:8). More elaborate developments of this idea appear in *1 Enoch*, the *Songs of the Sabbath Sacrifice*, the *Testament of Levi*, and Revelation, which describe an actual sanctuary in heaven along with a celestial cultus (*1 En.* 14:9–23; 4Q400 1 I, 1–20; 4Q403 1 I, 41–46; *T. Levi* 3:4–8; 5:1;

---

[105] Allen seems hesitant to relate the angels' προσκύνησις to the Son's enthronement. As he sees it, "the divine call unto angelic worship is not ... justified or given a formal basis. Jesus is worshipped *as firstborn Son*, but that is all one can really draw from 1:6" ("Who," 173; see also 168). Yet this overlooks the way Hebrews's christological appropriation of Deut 32:43 in 1:6 signifies that the Son is the fulfillment of God's vindication and purification for his people, which encouraged angelic praise. Since Hebrews relates this to the Son's priestly achievements and subsequent enthronement (1:3), it is reasonable to conclude that the exaltation warrants the angels' προσκύνησις. See p. 122 in this book.
[106] Barnard, *Mysticism*, 88–118.
[107] For this understanding of τῶν ἁγίων here, see Attridge, *Hebrews*, 217–18; Cockerill, *Hebrews*, 354–55; Barnard, *Mysticism*, 93; Kenneth L. Schenck, *Cosmology and Eschatology in Hebrews: The Settings of the Sacrifice* (SNTSMS 143; Cambridge: Cambridge University Press, 2007), 145–47.
[108] The OT often speaks of the ark with its mercy seat, which is overshadowed by the cherubim of glory, as God's throne (1 Sam 4:4; 2 Sam 6:2; 2 Kgs 19:15; Pss 80:1; 99:1; cf. Jer 3:16–17; see Timo Eskola, *Messiah and the Throne: Jewish Merkabah Mysticism and Early Christian Exaltation Discourse* [WUNT 2/142; Tübingen: Mohr Siebeck, 2001], 50–55).

Rev 4:1–5:14; 11:15–19; 14:15–16:17; etc.).[109] Thus, many scholars would agree with Barnard that Hebrews shares a similar perspective regarding an actual sanctuary in the heavenly realms.[110]

For others, Hebrews's heavenly sanctuary language is largely metaphorical.[111] Schenck, for example, argues that the comparison of the earthly two-part tabernacle with the "heavenly sanctuary" ultimately serves the author's primary purpose of demonstrating how the Levitical cultus was merely an imperfect shadow and anticipation of Christ's superior high priestly atonement which resulted in true access to God. While similar key terms, σκηνή and ἅγιος, are used for both the earthly and the heavenly sanctuary, Schenck maintains that they are not used in quite the same way. Rather, whereas the two-part earthly sanctuary is described as a tabernacle (σκηνή) which contains the Most Holy Place (τὰ ἅγια) as its inner chamber, with respect to the heavenly sanctuary, the "tabernacle" (σκηνή) and "Most Holy Place" (τὰ ἅγια) are one and the same. Ultimately, this "heavenly sanctuary," this heavenly Most Holy Place where one enters the very presence of God, is no cultic structure *in* heaven but rather simply *is* heaven itself.

Deciding between which of these two views most accurately represents Hebrews's understanding of the heavenly sanctuary is complicated by numerous interpretive difficulties which continue to divide scholars.[112] As Schenck himself remarks, "The nature of the heavenly tabernacle has long been a matter of debate, and we cannot at present speak of any consensus on its precise character or background."[113] Thus, although it can certainly be deduced that the Son's session at the right hand of God in some meaningful type of heavenly equivalent to the earthly tabernacle's Most Holy Place is at the very least indicative of a sacred setting, the long-standing disagreement over whether Hebrews affirms an actual sanctuary in heaven makes it difficult to be certain that the setting is specifically cultic in nature.[114]

---

[109] Barnard, *Mysticism*, 56–60.
[110] Lincoln D. Hurst, *The Epistle to the Hebrews: Its Background of Thought* (SNTSMS 65; Cambridge: Cambridge University Press, 1990), 24–42; Scott D. Mackie, *Eschatology and Exhortation in the Epistle to the Hebrews* (WUNT 2/223; Tübingen: Mohr Siebeck, 2007), 157–68; Eric F. Mason, "'Sit at My Right Hand': Enthronement and the Heavenly Sanctuary in Hebrews," in *A Teacher for All Generations: Essays in Honor of James C. VanderKam* (JSJSup 153; Leiden: Brill, 2012), 901–16.
[111] Schenck, *Cosmology*, 144–81; Norman H. Young, "The Gospel according to Hebrews 9," *NTS* 27 (1981): 198–210; Jon Laansma, "The Cosmology of Hebrews," in *Cosmology and New Testament Theology* (ed. Jonathan T. Pennington and Sean M. McDonough; LNTS 355; New York: T&T Clark, 2008), 139–43.
[112] For example, with respect to the heavenly sanctuary, do τὰ ἅγια and σκηνή signify a part-whole relationship, or a synonymous relationship (8:2; 9:11–12)? Does 9:24 signify that the heavenly τὰ ἅγια is identified with heaven as a whole, with the highest heaven, or is the wording meant to signify τὰ ἅγια's association with the heavenly realm as opposed to the earthly realm? Do 8:5 and 9:23 imply an actual heavenly sanctuary upon which the earthly sanctuary is modeled, or is such correspondence intended to be understood more generally or loosely? For the various positions on these and other complexities related to this issue, see Hurst, *Epistle*, 24–42; Schenck, *Cosmology*, 144–81; Barnard, *Mysticism*, 88–118.
[113] Schenck, *Cosmology*, 144.
[114] The characterization of the angels in Heb 1 as λειτουργοὺς (1:7) and λειτουργικὰ (1:14), terms with cultic connotations, may lend some support to the view that a heavenly sanctuary is implied (Bauckham, "Hebrews," 179–80; Barnard, *Mysticism*, 255–56), but since the emphasis of their

Perhaps, then, the προσκύνησις of the Son should be understood not in cultic terms but in political terms, especially in light of the heavy emphasis on the Son as a royal figure, as discussed above. Schenck takes this view and argues that the elevated, even godlike portrayal of the Son in this respect is not unusual as there are comparable contemporary parallels in Jewish literature of other transcendent royal figures who similarly mediate God's sovereignty. In particular, Schenck draws attention to Adam in the *Life of Adam and Eve*, Moses in the *Exagogue* of Ezekiel the Tragedian, and the Son of Man in the *Similitudes of Enoch*.[115] To an extent, there are indeed notable similarities. Like the Son, Adam, who is the image of God (*L.A.E.* 13:3; cf. Heb 1:3), is reverenced by angels at God's command (*L.A.E.* 13–15). Also like the Son, both Moses (Ezek. Trag. 68–82) and the Son of Man (*1 En.* 62:3–9) are reverenced while seated on God's heavenly throne.[116]

Yet there are also in each case significant differences that probably should be taken into consideration as well. For instance, although some suggest that, like the Son, Adam is in heaven when he receives the angels' reverence,[117] the terminology suggests otherwise. Whereas Satan is said to be expelled from the "presence" (*facies*) of God (*L.A.E.* 13:2), which certainly implies a heavenly locale (cf. 12:1), Adam on the other hand is said to be in the "sight" (*conspectus*) of God (13:3) when the angels reverence him. The use of *facies* and *conspectus* elsewhere in the work[118] suggests that Adam is in the earthly realm when the angels reverence him. Although Adam is later assured a throne in the eschatological future, it is the throne that formerly belonged to Satan (47:3). This heavenly throne does not appear to be situated next to God, since Satan in his rebellion vows to set his throne above the stars of heaven and be like God (15:3), implying his throne is located in a lower level of heaven. Thus, Hebrews places the Son in a more prominent position than Adam when he receives the προσκύνησις of the angels since this takes place when the Son is enthroned alongside God in heaven.

Moses comes much closer to paralleling the Son in this regard since he is portrayed seated on God's heavenly throne as the stars in heaven fall to their knees before him in reverence (Ezek. Trag. 74–80). Here too, however, an important detail in the *Exagogue* sets the Son apart from Moses. Since the *Exagogue* describes the heavenly exaltation of Moses as occurring in a dream, which Raguel interprets symbolically to signify Moses's earthly role as ruler and prophet for Israel (83–89), Moses's heavenly exaltation is

---

"ministry" is on their being sent out to assist God's people (1:14) rather than sacerdotal service (cf. 8:2, 6; 9:21; 10:11), it is difficult to be certain that the author has cultic aspects of the angels as λειτουργοί in mind.

[115] Schenck, "Worship," 121–24.

[116] Again, depending on the extent to which the earthly tabernacle is representative of a real heavenly counterpart in Hebrews, the Son may be envisaged taking his seat at the right-hand side of the very throne of God, since there was only one "throne" in the Most Holy Place (8:1–2; 9:3–5). Those who take the Son to be seated on God's throne include Hengel, *Studies*, 148–49; Darrell D. Hannah, "The Throne of His Glory: The Divine Throne and Heavenly Mediators in Revelation and the Similitudes of Enoch," *ZNW* 94 (2003): 78; Bauckham, "Divinity," 32–33; Barnard, *Mysticism*, 144–47.

[117] Moffitt, *Atonement*, 136–37; Fletcher-Louis, "Worship," 114.

[118] See, for example, Adam's and Eve's earthly lamentation in the sight (*conspectus*) of God (4:3) with Adam's request while in heaven (25:3) to not be cast away from the presence (*facies*) of God (27:2). For this key terminological distinction, see Barnard, *Mysticism*, 250, n. 30.

ultimately to be understood figuratively, as Bauckham correctly observes.[119] Conversely, Hebrews offers no such symbolic, mundane interpretation of the Son's heavenly enthronement alongside God as he receives προσκύνησις from the angels. Quite the contrary, the author's exhortation to his audience to maintain their confession of the Son is dependent on his conviction that the Son is truly enthroned with God in heaven (e.g., Heb 10:11-23) and is truly superior to the angels who reverence him (e.g., Heb 2:1-18). Again, then, we see a significant way in which the Son surpasses an alleged parallel: while Moses's heavenly exaltation to the divine throne accompanied by celestial reverence is taken figuratively, the Son's heavenly exaltation and angelic reverence is understood literally.

Finally, the Enochic Son of Man also comes quite close to paralleling the Son in Hebrews. This heavenly figure sits on God's own "throne of glory" (*1 En.* 45:3; 55:4; 61:8; 62:2-5; 69:29),[120] he is an object of reverence (48:5; 62:6, 9; cf. 46:5), and there is no indication that such depictions of this exalted view of the Enochic Son of Man are mere figurative representations of a more modest reality. Only in one clear instance, however, is this figure an object of reverence while enthroned in heaven as the Son is in Hebrews. In 48:5, since the text envisages the ultimate eschatological deliverance of all the righteous, including the repentant, among the nations,[121] this Son of Man is likely on earth dwelling among them (cf. 45:4-5; 62:14-16)[122] when it is said that "all those who dwell upon the earth shall fall and worship before him." The allusion here to Isa 49:7 where the Servant of the Lord receives the obeisance of the nations[123] suggests this reverence of the Son of Man similarly signifies political homage.[124] It is only at the climactic eschatological judgment that this figure is reverenced while seated on the divine throne in heaven (62:6, 9).[125] Here, however, it is only the wicked—the kings and the mighty who persecuted the righteous—who "bless, glorify, and extol him" (62:6) and who "fall down before him on their faces, and worship" (62:9), while the righteous by contrast are said to "stand before him" (62:8). The context emphasizes the terror of the wicked and their pleas for mercy, suggesting their "reverence" is largely obsequious in nature, a desperate attempt to avoid punishment by flattering this judge.[126] Thus, while this figure may, like the Son, be depicted as an object of reverence

---

[119] Bauckham, "Throne," 55-57. See also Pierluigi Lanfranchi, "Moses' Vision of the Divine Throne in the *Exagogue* of Ezekiel the Tragedian," in *The Book of Ezekiel and Its Influence* (ed. Henk J. de Jonge and Johannes Tromp; Aldershot: Ashgate, 2007), 55-58.

[120] Despite some debate, it is likely that the Enochic Son of Man's "throne of glory" and God's heavenly "throne of glory" (*1 En.* 47:3; 60:2) are one and the same (see Hannah, "Throne," 82-87).

[121] George W. E. Nickelsburg and James C. VanderKam, *1 Enoch 2: A Commentary on the Book of 1 Enoch, Chapters 37-82* (Hermeneia; Minneapolis, MN: Fortress, 2012), 171-72.

[122] Nickelsburg and VanderKam, *1 Enoch*, 51-52, 151, 266-68.

[123] Nickelsburg and VanderKam, *1 Enoch*, 171.

[124] Hurtado, *Lord*, 38-39.

[125] A heavenly setting for this judgment scene is likely since it immediately follows the initial enthronement of the Son of Man to execute judgment in heaven (*1 En.* 61:8-9), and there is no indication of a change of location or movement of the throne (Nickelsburg and VanderKam, *1 Enoch*, 259).

[126] It should be noted that some of this reverence language ("bless, glorify, and extol"; "fall down and worship") is also applied to God (*1 En.* 39:12; 48:5; 57:3; 63:1-7; etc.), leaving some impression that the Enochic Son of Man is worshiped as God is. On the other hand, the lack of any clear instance

while enthroned in heaven, this portrayal does not quite match that of the Son who is reverenced by all the angels.[127]

Each depiction of the reverence of these figures (Adam, Moses, and the Son of Man) resembles that of the Son but each only does so partially; none is fully comparable. Instead, the closest parallel is that of God himself who is often depicted in Jewish and Christian literature enthroned in heaven being worshiped by his heavenly entourage.[128] Hebrews portrays the Son joining God, enthroned at his right hand, perhaps sharing the very throne of God himself,[129] to receive angelic reverence. Although there may be rare instances where someone other than Christ is said to be seated or enthroned at God's side in heaven,[130] none are portrayed as recipients of worship,[131] as God so often is in such heavenly scenes, and as the Son appears to be in Heb 1:6.

While Schenck appropriately draws attention to Adam, Moses, and the Enochic Son of Man, showing that the ascription of certain godlike qualities to such figures is not entirely out of the ordinary, at a certain point, one must consider the possibility that the nature and proliferation of such ascriptions moves toward an acknowledgment of the figure's divinity. This appears to be the case with the Son in Hebrews. Not only is he said to be enthroned in the heavenly realm at God's side receiving angelic praise, but he also inherits all things, sustains all things, is the radiance of God's glory and the exact representation of God's very being, is ascribed divine titles such as "θεός" and "κύριος," and has a role in both the dissolution as well as the foundation of creation.[132] Perhaps Schenck is correct that the angels' προσκύνησις of the enthroned Son is political rather than cultic in character. But in view of the fact that the Son receives such reverence as one more fully and more closely aligned with God than any of these other alleged parallels, it becomes more difficult to maintain that such reverence is ultimately something less than an acknowledgment of the Son's divinity.

---

of the Son of Man receiving such reverence in a liturgical context, as is frequently the case with God (*1 En.* 39:9–13; 40:3, 6; 47:2; 61:10–13; 69:25; 71:9–12) suggests some distinction is being made between the reverence of the Son of Man and the cultic worship of God. For more detailed discussion on this, see pp. 162–63 below.

[127] Barnard, *Mysticism*, 250–51; Allen, "Who," 171.
[128] 1 Kgs 22:19; Neh 9:6; Pss 11:4; 103:19–21; 4Q405 20 II–21–22; *1 En.* 14:18–20; 39:9–13; 61:10–13; 71:9–12; *2 En.* 17; 20:1–21:1; *4 Ezra* 8:20–21; *2 Bar* 21:6; *Apoc. Ab.* 17; 18:3; *T. Ab.* 20:12–13 (A); 4:4–6 (B); *T. Levi* 3:4–8; 5:1; *T. Isaac* 6:4–5; Rev 4:8–11; 11:16–18; etc.; *Ascen. Isa.* 6:8; 9:37–10:6. See Bauckham, "Throne," 51–53; Barnard, *Mysticism*, 72, 76–78.
[129] See n. 116 above.
[130] See p. 45, n. 49 above.
[131] With the notable exception of the Holy Spirit in the *Ascension of Isaiah*, who, along with Christ, is seated beside God (*Ascen. Isa.* 11:32–33) receiving heavenly worship (*Ascen. Isa.* 9:27–36). Angels encountered in heaven by visionaries often refuse worship that they perceive to be reserved for God (*Apoc. Zeph.* 6:11–15; Rev 19:10; 22:8–9; *Ascen. Isa.* 7:21). Although the archangel Michael receives προσκύνησις in heaven in *3 Bar.* 11:6, the relatively mild nature of this gesture of reverence is apparent in the fact that it is only performed by Baruch's angelic guide who greets Michael as his commander. Baruch is not compelled to render προσκύνησις to Michael.
[132] Especially on this last point, compare the Son with Adam, who is a created being (*L.A.E.* 14:3; 27:2; 46:3; etc.), with Moses, who is a mortal man (Ezek. Trag. 101), and with the Enochic Son of Man, who may be a preexistent being (*1 En.* 48:6; 62:7), but who, along with Adam and Moses, is not said to be an agent in creation as the Son is in Hebrews.

C. Conclusion

With such a terse and somewhat obscure passage such as Heb 1:6 in its depiction of the προσκύνησις of the Son, Jesus by angels, it is little wonder that opinions vary regarding the precise character of this reverence of Jesus. Yet despite some interpretive challenges associated with this text, certain points can be reasonably concluded after careful deliberation, which begin to move the interpreter closer to a clearer sense of this angelic reverence of Jesus. For instance, he receives such reverence as he is exalted and enthroned in heaven at God's side, rather than at the incarnation or the parousia as some suppose. For him to receive such angelic reverence in the heavenly realm while enthroned with God is certainly a profound image. Moreover, despite some debate over certain details that hint at his divine status, Hebrews's assertion of the Son's role in the uniquely divine act of creation is one of the strongest points in favor of his divinity and one which is not so easily dismissed or minimized. The emphasis in the catena of OT citations applied to Jesus may fall on his superiority as a royal messiainic figure, but this does not preclude his divine status. This messianic Son sustains and ultimately brings an end to the very creation he had a role in founding. Even if it is not specifically *as* creator that the angels offer προσκύνησις to the Son, it is nevertheless directed to one who *is* creator, and thus to one uniquely linked with God.

Other important details, however, remain somewhat shrouded. Although certainly possible, it is in the end not entirely clear that the angels' προσκύνησις of Jesus takes place in a cultic setting, nor is their προσκύνησις accompanied by any overtly cultic activity that might point to the cultic character of the προσκύνησις. Moreover, there is a lack of clear evidence elsewhere in Hebrews for cultic worship directed to Jesus, but no lack in such worship directed to God (9:14; 12:28; 13:15-16; etc.).[133] On the other hand, that the angelic reverence of the heavenly enthroned Jesus most closely approximates the many depictions in Jewish and Christian literature of heavenly worship directed to God on his throne strongly suggests that it cannot be so easily ruled out as a depiction of the kind of worship typically reserved for God. Although God certainly retains the primacy in his relation to Jesus (e.g., God is Father, Jesus is Son; God is centrally enthroned with the Son at his right; God creates through the Son; the Son is θεός, and God is his θεός), the emphasis on Jesus's distinction from and superiority to the angels, and his close link to God in a number of profound and even unprecedented ways, strongly suggest that the προσκύνησις he receives from the angels is equivalent to the worship typically reserved for God.

---

[133] Allen, "Who," 164–65. One possible exception to this is the doxology in 13:21, but scholars differ over whether the doxology is directed to Jesus (Spicq, *Hébreux*, 2:437; Attridge, *Hebrews*, 407–8), to God (Lane, *Hebrews*, 2:565; Ellingworth, *Hebrews*, 731), or to both (Johnson, *Hebrews*, 356; Cockerill, *Hebrews*, 718–19), with some undecided on the matter (Michel, *Hebräer*, 541; Koester, *Hebrews*, 574). For discussion of broader worship themes throughout Hebrews, see John Paul Heil, *Worship in the Letter to the Hebrews* (Eugene, OR: Cascade, 2011).

7

The Προσκύνησις of Jesus in the Book of Revelation

The book of Revelation is unmatched among the NT writings in its frequent use of the term προσκυνέω. It appears twenty-four times and proves to be a key term in what is arguably one of the most important themes in the entire work: the theme of worship. Of the twenty-four occurrences of προσκυνέω, only one passage may possibly have Jesus as its object (Rev 5:14). The term is otherwise applied to numerous different figures, including God, Satan, demons, idols, "the beast," the image of the beast, angels, and Christians. Such a variegated spread of recipients of this honor, who certainly vary in rank and status, is bound to manifest different senses of reverence and/or worship given to them. Before considering the sole passage that may possibly have Jesus as a recipient of προσκύνησις, we will first consider the προσκύνησις of these various other figures and the character of the reverence or worship they receive. I will argue that John generally uses the term προσκυνέω to highlight the contrast between true and false worship, a distinction which at its core is determined by a proper acknowledgment of the one(s) to whom ultimate allegiance is due. I will then argue that Jesus is indeed included as a rightful recipient of προσκύνησις in Rev 5:14 and that it clearly constitutes the kind of worship that is typically reserved for God.

A. The Προσκύνησις of God

The προσκύνησις of God is frequent and widespread in Revelation, and proves to be a key motif in this book. It often appears as a recurring feature of the numerous scenes depicting heavenly worship of God (Rev 4:10; 5:14; 7:11; 11:16; 19:4). In these passages, God is enthroned in heaven surrounded by his heavenly entourage who worship him with hymns, shouts of praise and with προσκύνησις. The first heavenly worship scene is reported as follows:

> Day and night [the four living creatures] never cease to say, "Holy, holy, holy, is the Lord God Almighty, who was and is and is to come!" And whenever the living creatures give glory and honor and thanks to him who is seated on the throne, who lives forever and ever, the twenty-four elders fall down before him who is seated on the throne and render προσκύνησις (προσκυνήσουσιν) to him who lives forever

and ever. They cast their crowns before the throne, saying, "Worthy are you, our Lord and God, to receive glory and honor and power, for you created all things, and by your will they existed and were created." (Rev 4:8–11)

A number of other heavenly worship scenes follow a similar pattern in describing worship offered to God:

> [A great multitude] cry out with a loud voice, saying, "Salvation belongs to our God who is seated on the throne, and to the Lamb!" And all the angels were standing around the throne and around the elders and the four living creatures, and they fell on their faces before the throne and rendered προσκύνησις (προσεκύνησαν) to God, saying, "Amen! Blessing and glory and wisdom and thanksgiving and honor and power and might be to our God forever and ever! Amen." (Rev 7:10-12)

> There were loud voices in heaven, saying, "The kingdom of the world has become the kingdom of our Lord and of his Christ, and he will reign forever and ever!" And the twenty-four elders who are seated on their thrones before God fell on their faces and rendered προσκύνησις (προσεκύνησαν) to God, saying, "We give thanks to you, Lord God Almighty, who is and who was, because you have taken your great power and begun to reign." (Rev 11:15–17)

> After these things, I heard what seemed to be the loud voice of a great multitude in heaven, saying, "Hallelujah! Salvation and glory and power belong to our God! . . ." And the twenty-four elders and the four living creatures fell down and rendered προσκύνησις (προσεκύνησαν) to God who is seated on the throne, saying, "Amen. Hallelujah!" (Rev 19:1–4)

Just as in 4:8–11, the verbal praise of the four living creatures moves the twenty-four elders to render προσκύνησις to God, so the praise of God elsewhere often moves other heavenly figures to respond with προσκύνησις to God (7:10–11; 11:15–16; 19:1-4). Similarly, just as the twenty-four elders' worship of God involves both προσκύνησις and hymnic praises of their own, so do other heavenly beings worship God by combining προσκύνησις with hymnic praise (7:11–12; 11:16–18; 19:4). Thus, in these worship scenes, προσκύνησις very often links antiphonal hymnic praises,[1] serving as both an affirmation of the content of preceding praises offered to God and an accompaniment to further praises given to him.

---

[1] Klaus-Peter Jörns, *Das hymnische Evangelium: Untersuchungen zu Aufbau, Funktion und Herkunft der hymnischen Stücke in der Johannesoffenbarung* (Gütersloh: Mohn, 1971), 97. The hymnic material in Revelation's heavenly worship scenes appears in the following passages: 4:8–11; 5:9–14; 7:10–12; 11:15–18; 12:10–12; 15:3–4; 16:5–7; 19:1–8. Independent hymns (12:10–12; 15:3–4) have no accompanying acts of προσκύνησις as part of the heavenly worship. One antiphonal hymnic unit lacks προσκύνησις (16:5–7), perhaps because the twenty-four elders, who are typical performers of προσκύνησις in such scenes, are not involved in this hymnic response. For a study on the role the hymns play in Revelation's cosmic conflict themes, see Steven Grabiner, *Revelation's Hymns: Commentary on the Cosmic Conflict* (LNTS 511; London: Bloomsbury T&T Clark, 2015).

Other passages similarly emphasize the προσκύνησις of God. The command given to John in 11:1 to measure the temple of God and the altar and those who render προσκύνησις there (μέτρησον τὸν ναὸν τοῦ θεοῦ καὶ τὸ θυσιαστήριον καὶ τοὺς προσκυνοῦντας ἐν αὐτῷ) symbolizes divine protection over the Christian community, who are the true worshipers of God. Twice it is reported that John attempted to do προσκύνησις before a guiding angel only to be rebuked by the angel and exhorted both times to give προσκύνησις to God (τῷ θεῷ προσκύνησον [19:10; 22:8–9]).

While most passages describe the προσκύνησις of God by his followers, two passages relate the προσκύνησις of God by those who do not belong to him or perhaps do not yet belong to him. In 14:7, an angel calls for unredeemed humanity to fear God, give him glory, and render προσκύνησις to him (φοβήθητε τὸν θεὸν καὶ δότε αὐτῷ δόξαν . . . καὶ προσκυνήσατε τῷ ποιήσαντι τὸν οὐρανὸν καὶ τὴν γῆν καὶ θάλασσαν καὶ πηγὰς ὑδάτων). In 15:4, a song of praise to God looks ahead to the time when all nations will come and offer προσκύνησις before him (πάντα τὰ ἔθνη ἥξουσιν καὶ προσκυνήσουσιν ἐνώπιόν σου). While some commentators consider the reverence of God in these passages to be compulsory expressions of obeisance,[2] most see it as genuine worship and turning to God in faith.[3] Indeed, the latter view is more likely. Both passages employ the same key terms that fall within the semantic domain of worship, such as φοβέω, δοξάζω/δόξα, and προσκυνέω. Although such terms need not imply "worship" in the strong sense, even in relation to God in some cases,[4] in Revelation when these terms are applied to God elsewhere, they typically have God's true worshipers as the subject.[5] Conversely, it is those who refuse to repent who neither give glory to God (16:9) nor cease from rendering προσκύνησις to false gods (9:20). Yet even if compulsory obeisance is in mind in 14:7 and/or 15:4, it would nevertheless convey the idea that God is considered the rightful recipient of such reverence and of one's ultimate allegiance to the exclusion of his rivals.

---

[2] G. K. Beale, *The Book of Revelation: A Commentary on the Greek Text* (NIGTC; Grand Rapids, MI: Eerdmans, 1999), 751–53, 799 (although in 15:4, Beale views the reverence as involving both willing and unwilling participants); Martin Kiddle, *The Revelation of St. John* (MNTC; London: Hodder & Stoughton, 1940), 278, 309.

[3] David E. Aune, *Revelation* (3 vols.; WBC 52A–C; Dallas, TX: Word Books; Nashville, TN: Thomas Nelson, 1997–1998), 2:827, 876; Brian K. Blount, *Revelation: A Commentary* (NTL; Louisville, KY: Westminster John Knox, 2009), 288–89; Ian Boxall, *The Revelation of Saint John* (BNTC 19; London: A&C Black, 2006), 207, 220; Pierre Prigent, *Commentary on the Apocalypse of St. John* (trans. Wendy Pradels; Tübingen: Mohr Siebeck, 2004), 439–40, 461; Grant R. Osborne, *Revelation* (BECNT; Grand Rapids, MI: Baker Academic, 2002), 535–36, 567–68; George R. Beasley-Murray, *The Book of Revelation* (NCB; London: Oliphants, 1974), 225, 236–37; George B. Caird, *A Commentary on the Revelation of St. John the Divine* (BNTC; London: A&C Black, 1966), 198–99. See esp. Richard Bauckham, *The Climax of Prophecy: Studies on the Book of Revelation* (Edinburgh: T&T Clark, 1993), 286–89, 301–7.

[4] Beale, *Revelation*, 751, rightly notes, for example, the phrase, "Give glory to God." In some cases, this expression is simply a call for a person to tell the truth (e.g., Josh 7:19; John 9:24).

[5] Bauckham, *Climax*, 278–79. It is God's true worshipers who fear him (11:18; 19:5), give him glory (4:9, 11; 5:13; 7:12; 19:1, 7), and give him προσκύνησις (4:10; 5:14; 7:11; 11:1, 16; 19:4, 10; 22:9). Although 11:13, which mentions unbelievers who "were terrified and gave glory to the God of heaven," might be an exception, there is wide support for the view that these individuals are here described repenting and converting (Bauckham, *Climax*, 278; Aune, *Revelation*, 2:628–29. See Osborne, *Revelation*, 433, who mentions many more proponents).

B. The Προσκύνησις of evil figures

Just as frequent and widespread are instances of προσκύνησις rendered to evil entities, such as the dragon/Satan, demons/idols, and especially the satanically empowered figure "the beast," along with its image. The προσκύνησις of Satan (καὶ προσεκύνησαν τῷ δράκοντι [13:4]) and the προσκύνησις of demons/idols (Καὶ οἱ λοιποὶ τῶν ἀνθρώπων . . . οὐδὲ μετενόησαν ἐκ τῶν ἔργων τῶν χειρῶν αὐτῶν, ἵνα μὴ προσκυνήσουσιν τὰ δαιμόνια καὶ τὰ εἴδωλα [9:20]) certainly constitute idolatrous worship of godlike figures, but what of the many references to the προσκύνησις of the beast and its image (13:4, 8, 12, 15; 14:9, 11; 16:2; 19:20; 20:4)?

This motif is introduced in Rev 13:1–18 where John gives a detailed description of Satan's two chief allies, the beast from the sea and the beast from the land. The former receives Satan's authority, leading to worldwide προσκύνησις of both Satan and the beast (καὶ προσεκύνησαν τῷ δράκοντι, ὅτι ἔδωκεν τὴν ἐξουσίαν τῷ θηρίῳ, καὶ προσεκύνησαν τῷ θηρίῳ λέγοντες·τίς ὅμοιος τῷ θηρίῳ καὶ τίς δύναται πολεμῆσαι μετ᾽ αὐτοῦ; [13:4]; καὶ προσκυνήσουσιν αὐτὸν πάντες οἱ κατοικοῦντες ἐπὶ τῆς γῆς [13:8]).[6] The latter compels people to make an image of the first beast (13:14) so that both the beast and its image receive προσκύνησις (καὶ ποιεῖ τὴν γῆν καὶ τοὺς ἐν αὐτῇ κατοικοῦντας ἵνα προσκυνήσουσιν τὸ θηρίον τὸ πρῶτον [13:12]; ὅσοι ἐὰν μὴ προσκυνήσωσιν τῇ εἰκόνι τοῦ θηρίου ἀποκτανθῶσιν [13:15]; cf. 19:20). It is said elsewhere in Revelation that those who render προσκύνησις to the beast and its image incur God's wrath (εἴ τις προσκυνεῖ τὸ θηρίον καὶ τὴν εἰκόνα αὐτοῦ . . . καὶ αὐτὸς πίεται ἐκ τοῦ οἴνου τοῦ θυμοῦ τοῦ θεοῦ . . . καὶ οὐκ ἔχουσιν ἀνάπαυσιν ἡμέρας καὶ νυκτὸς οἱ προσκυνοῦντες τὸ θηρίον καὶ τὴν εἰκόνα αὐτοῦ [14:9–11; cf. 16:2], while those who resist are ultimately vindicated by God (οἵτινες οὐ προσεκύνησαν τὸ θηρίον οὐδὲ τὴν εἰκόνα αὐτοῦ . . . καὶ ἔζησαν καὶ ἐβασίλευσαν μετὰ τοῦ Χριστοῦ χίλια ἔτη [20:4]).

It is clear that the two beasts as literary characters are evil figures who oppose God and his people, and lead many others to devote themselves to the first beast and its image. But who or what are these figures meant to represent and how might this shed some light on the nature of the προσκύνησις offered to the first beast and its image? Since Rev 13, in part, has the Roman Empire and the political-religious phenomenon of the Roman imperial cult as its background and incorporates features from eschatological-antagonist traditions which anticipate the rise of an evil tyrant claiming divinity, the προσκύνησις of the beast and its image is to be understood as both political and religious in character.

---

[6] Although τό θηρίον usually appears in the accusative when it is the object of προσκυνέω (13:8, 12; 14:9, 11; 20:4), in 13:4, it appears in the dative. Ben Witherington regards the former usage as signifying homage while the latter signifies worship (*Revelation* [NCBC; Cambridge: Cambridge University Press, 2003], 2–3), but this is not correct. Rather, as Aune observes, the case is typically determined by gender—dative for masculine and feminine objects, accusative for neuter (*Revelation*, 1:273). The exception appears to be that when two terms are linked as objects of προσκυνέω, the subordinate object takes the case of the dominant object (cf. 14:9, 11; 20:4). Something similar probably explains why 13:4 uncharacteristically has τό θηρίον in the dative, namely, because of its close link with the dominant masculine object ὁ δράκων, which also receives προσκύνησις.

It is widely agreed that "Rev 13 deals with Roman imperial power and with the worship of the Roman emperors."[7] The first beast is typically understood to represent the Roman Empire and/or the emperor, while the second beast represents those individuals or institutions that promoted the imperial cult.[8] Despite some debate over Revelation's precise social setting[9], there is general agreement on the formative influence of the Roman imperial cult for John's characterization of the beasts and the events surrounding them.

The imperial cult was particularly prominent in the province of Asia where the seven churches addressed in Rev 2–3 are located. By the time Revelation was written, three provincial imperial temples were established in the province of Asia: one dedicated to Augustus and the goddess Roma at Pergamum (ca. 29 B.C.E.), another to Tiberius, his mother Livia, and the Senate at Smyrna (ca. 27 C.E.), and the more recent temple dedicated to the *Sebastoi*, which probably included Domitian, Titus, and Vespasian, at Ephesus (89/90 C.E.).[10] At the municipal level were more widespread and diverse forms of imperial cult that permeated community life, and were characteristically more liberal in their reverence by ascribing divine language to living emperors, incorporating imperial worship into an existing cult of a deity and assimilating the emperors and their families to specific deities.[11] Imperial cults varied from region to region, but would have included (1) temples, sanctuaries, altars, and other structures dedicated both to a deity and to the emperor, as well as solely to the emperor; (2) statues and images of the emperor, sometimes in the guise of a god, placed in various locations, both sacred and secular, private and public; (3) sacrifices typically *on behalf of* the emperor but in some cases, *to* the living emperor; and (4) various city-wide public festivals honoring the gods and the emperor with games, feasts, hymns, processions

---

[7] Steven J. Friesen, "Myth and Symbolic Resistance in Revelation 13," *JBL* 123 (2004): 303 (see n. 62, where Friesen lists such proponents).

[8] Steven J. Friesen, "The Beast from the Land: Revelation 13:11-18 and Social Setting," in *Reading the Book of Revelation: A Resource for Students* (ed. David L. Barr; RBS 44; Atlanta, GA: Society of Biblical Literature, 2003), 59–63.

[9] Most scholars support a Domitianic date for Revelation, ca. 95 C.E. (see Aune, *Revelation*, 1:lvi–lxx; Beale, *Revelation*, 4–27; Osborne, *Revelation*, 6–9), but the conditions of this period and their significance for understanding Revelation are debated. Some scholars argue for a generally positive view of Domitian and his reign, and that tensions in Revelation are due to ideological rather than real conflicts between Christians and Rome (Leonard L. Thompson, *The Book of Revelation: Apocalypse and Empire* [Oxford: Oxford University Press, 1990], 95–115, 171–201; Adela Yarbro Collins, *Crisis and Catharsis: The Power of the Apocalypse* [Philadelphia, PA: Westminster, 1984], 69–110). Others maintain that while Domitian may not have enforced emperor worship nor any widespread, official persecution of Christians, it is nevertheless likely that there was sporadic, local oppression (and perhaps persecution) of Christians for their non-participation in the imperial cult, and that John considered such mistreatment to be a prelude to more intense persecution as reflected in Revelation (Thomas B. Slater, "On the Social Setting of the Revelation to John," *NTS* 44 [1998]: 242–56; Elisabeth Schüssler Fiorenza, *Revelation: Vision of a Just World* [Edinburgh: T&T Clark, 1993], 54, 126–28; Osborne, *Revelation*, 7–12; Beale, *Revelation*, 6–15).

[10] Steven J. Friesen, *Imperial Cults and the Apocalypse of John: Reading Revelation in the Ruins* (Oxford: Oxford University Press, 2001), 25–32, 36–38, 43–55.

[11] Friesen, *Imperial*, 56–76.

of their images, and sacrifices at their temples as well as at secular civic centers.[12] As Giancarlo Biguzzi notes, the cult of the emperor "was practised in all seven cities of the Apocalypse: with the exception of Philadelphia and Laodicea, records of priests and altars have survived; and for all but Thyatira, records of temples have survived."[13] Through the imperial cult, the worshipers represented to themselves the godlike power of their earthly rulers whom they considered to be responsible for establishing worldwide peace and prosperity.[14]

For John, however, this devotion to the Roman Empire/emperors through cultic worship is portrayed negatively as two beasts aligned with Satan who are responsible for leading the masses away from God and into idolatrous worship of human rulers. Various details point to the Roman Empire/emperor and the imperial cult as John's models for the beasts, such as the blasphemous names the first beast bears (13:1), which reflect the divine titles attributed to Roman emperors, and the role of the second beast in setting up an image of the first beast and encouraging the worship of the beast and its image (13:12, 14–15), which reflects the activities of the institutions responsible for promoting the imperial cult.[15] Other details show that John incorporates features from eschatological-antagonist traditions, which often portray God's adversary as an evil, tyrannical figure who exalts himself above God.[16] Chief among these sources for John is Dan 7. The first beast takes up features from Daniel's four beastlike kingdoms (Rev 13:1–2; cf. Dan 7:2–7) and from the prominent eschatological adversary, the "little horn" of the fourth beast, making war with the saints and overcoming them (Rev 13:7; cf. Dan 7:21), exercising authority for forty-two months (Rev 13:5; cf. Dan 7:25), and speaking arrogant and blasphemous things against God (Rev 13:5–6; cf. Dan 7:8, 25; 11:36).[17] John may also be indebted to a common eschatological-antagonist tradition shared with *Ascen. Isa.* 4. Parallels include adversarial performance of miracles (Rev 13:13–14; *Ascen. Isa.* 4:10), setting up images of the adversary (Rev 13:14–15; *Ascen. Isa.* 4:11), and universal worship of the adversary (Rev 13:4, 8; *Ascen. Isa.* 4:7–8).[18] Common to all these works is the emergence of a sinister royal figure (Rev 13:1–2; Dan 7:8, 24; *Ascen. Isa.* 4:2–4) who blasphemes and exalts himself above God (Rev 13:5–6; Dan 7:8, 25; 11:36–37; *Ascen. Isa.* 4:6).

---

[12] Pieter J. Botha, "God, Emperor Worship and Society: Contemporary Experiences and the Book of Revelation," *Neot* 22 (1988): 91–97; Price, *Rituals*, 101–233.

[13] Giancarlo Biguzzi, "Ephesus, Its Artemision, Its Temple to the Flavian Emperors, and Idolatry in Revelation," *NovT* 40 (1998): 280.

[14] Price, *Rituals*, 29–30, 233.

[15] Blount, *Revelation*, 246, 257; Boxall, *Revelation*, 187, 194; Osborne, *Revelation*, 491, 513; Beale, *Revelation*, 684, 710; Aune, *Revelation*, 2:734, 756. For other links to Rome, including the *Nero redivivus* legend (13:3) and "666" as a reference to "Nero Caesar" (13:18), see Bauckham, *Climax*, 384–452.

[16] See, for example, Dan 11:36–37 (cf. 7:8, 25); 2 Thess 2:3–4; *Sib. Or.* 5.33–34; *Ascen. Isa.* 4:6; *Did.* 16:4.

[17] These and other possible allusions to Dan 7 are discussed in G. K. Beale, *The Use of Daniel in Jewish Apocalyptic Literature and in the Revelation of St. John* (Lanham, MD: University Press of America, 1984), 229–39.

[18] Bauckham, *Climax*, 425–27.

The portrayal of the beast as a Rome-like power known to have been honored with cult and as the ultimate eschatological godless tyrant who exalts himself above God suggests the προσκύνησις the beast receives is both political and religious in character. Both aspects can be seen in Rev 13:4, where the beast receives προσκύνησις from the masses as one with power, authority, and a throne (cf. 13:2), and as one with godlike incomparability as the people exclaim, "Who is like the beast?," parodying OT praises of God.[19]

It is possible that the use of προσκυνέω for the reverence of the beast and its image is intended to reflect the reverence paid to Roman emperors and their images through prostration, as there is some precedent for both.[20] Yet the complete absence of accompanying terminology to definitively signal prostration often used elsewhere in Revelation[21] suggests the author is not primarily concerned with the particular form of reverence displayed. Rather, the use of προσκυνέω is part of John's pervasive effort to differentiate between true worship (4:10; 5:14; 7:11; 11:1, 16; 14:7; 15:4; 19:4, 10; 20:4; 22:9) and false worship (9:20; 13:4, 8, 12, 15; 14:9, 11; 16:2; 19:20). Showing honor to the Rome-like beast and its image is no harmless matter, for one who does so inevitably worships Satan as well since he empowers the beast (13:4). That the προσκύνησις of the beast and its image is directly opposed to the προσκύνησις of God is clearly seen in 14:6–11. Here, it is presumed that those who respond appropriately to the angelic herald's call to render προσκύνησις to God will be saved, while those who render προσκύνησις to the beast and its image will suffer eternal punishment (cf. 16:2; 20:4). Just as the beast's alliance with Satan indicates the προσκύνησις it receives is no harmless act of deference to a superior, so is the severity of punishment for those who offer προσκύνησις to the beast and its image an indication of its idolatrous nature.[22]

C. The Προσκύνησις of angels

In two separate but parallel passages, when John begins to offer προσκύνησις to a guiding angel, the angel warns him not to do so and commands him instead to direct such reverence to God (19:10; 22:8–9). Both instances of this angelic refusal of προσκύνησις form parallel conclusions to John's visions of the judgment of Babylon (17:1–19:10) and the establishment of the New Jerusalem (21:9–22:9), each of which

---

[19] Exod 15:11; Pss 35:10; 71:19; 89:6–8; Isa 44:7; 46:5; Mic 7:18.
[20] For προσκύνησις of Roman emperors, see Dio Cassius, *Hist. rom.* 59.27.1, 5; 63.2.4; 63.4.3; 63.5.2; 65.5.2; 67.13.4; 68.8.6. For προσκύνησις of imperial images, see Dio Cassius, *Hist. rom.* 62.23.3. According to Duncan Fishwick, although the lack of evidence for prostration before imperial images makes it difficult to determine whether it was a regular component of cultic worship, comparative evidence suggests it probably was (*The Imperial Cult in the Latin West: Studies in the Ruler Cult of the Western Provinces of the Roman Empire, Volume II, 1* [Leiden: Brill, 1991], 527–28, 534).
[21] Cf. Rev 3:9; 4:10; 5:14; 7:11; 11:16; 19:4, 10; 22:8.
[22] Horst, *Proskynein*, 263, 266.

is revealed to him by one of the seven bowl-judgment angels introduced in 15:1.²³ The two texts depicting John's προσκύνησις of the guiding angel are strikingly similar:

> I fell down at his feet to render προσκύνησις (προσκυνῆσαι) to him. But he said to me, "You must not do that! I am a fellow-servant with you and your brothers who hold to the testimony of Jesus. Render προσκύνησις (προσκύνησον) to God." (Rev 19:10)

> I fell down to render προσκύνησις (προσκυνῆσαι) at the feet of the angel who showed these things to me. But he said to me, "You must not do that! I am a fellow-servant with you and your brothers the prophets and those who keep the words of this book. Render προσκύνησις (προσκύνησον) to God." (Rev 22:8–9)

In both passages, John prostrates himself to offer προσκύνησις to the angel, the angel immediately refuses this show of reverence, he identifies himself as a fellow-servant with John and with a larger group of John's brethren, and he exhorts him to render προσκύνησις to God. As parallel conclusions to two visions, these two episodes are obviously employed in part for structural purposes, but this certainly does not preclude the possibility that the repetition is also employed for emphasis. Moreover, as shown above, the passages are similar but not identical, and thus certain distinctive features may introduce new points or underscore common points. For example, whereas in 19:10, the angel states he is a fellow-servant with John and his brethren who hold to the testimony of Jesus (i.e., Christians), in 22:9, he is a fellow-servant with John, his brethren the prophets, and those who keep the words of this book (i.e., Christians). The inclusion of "the prophets" as part of the group of John's brethren is unique to 22:9 and emphasizes the author's prophetic status.²⁴ Thus, 22:9 both reaffirms the equal status between angels and the righteous in general (19:10) and betrays a concern "to legitimate John's activity as a prophet and to link this activity to the status of those who recognize its authority."²⁵

Undoubtedly, the repetition of the angel's refusal of John's προσκύνησις with the express command to direct such reverence to God is not without its own significance. Prostration before an angelic figure is common in the OT and early Jewish literature,²⁶ and while on many occasions the act is not censured or taken to be in conflict with the worship of God, there are a few texts, such as Rev 19:10 and 22:8–9, where the heavenly figure appears to regard such reverence for himself as inappropriate and only to be

---

²³ On the parallel structure of these texts, see Charles H. Giblin, "Structural and Thematic Correlations in the Theology of Revelation 16–22," *Bib* 55 (1974): 487–504.
²⁴ Stuckenbruck, *Angel*, 254–55.
²⁵ Stuckenbruck, *Angel*, 93.
²⁶ Num 22:31; Josh 5:14; Judg 13:20; 1 Chr 21:16; Dan 8:17–18; 10:9–10; Tob 12:16; 4 Macc 4:10–11; *2 En.* 1:7; *T. Ab.* 3:6, 9:1 (A); *Jos. Asen.* 14:3, 10. As Bauckham notes, such prostration may be either voluntary, and thus express awe and reverence (e.g., Josh 5:14), or involuntary, and thus express terror or even fainting (e.g., Dan 8:18) ("Worship," 323–24). John's prostration before the heavenly Jesus in Rev 1:17 (ἔπεσα πρὸς τοὺς πόδας αὐτοῦ ὡς νεκρός) is clearly an example of the latter, which explains the absence of the reverentially charged term προσκυνέω.

given to God. Although some scholars take 19:10 and 22:8–9 as evidence for an angel cult being polemically opposed here by the author,[27] such a position is tenuous in view of the general lack of evidence for a cult of angels in early Judaism. Yet we noted earlier the likelihood that certain reverential attitudes and behaviors toward angels may have been perceived by some as potential or real compromises of monotheistic worship needing to be curbed.[28] With an increasing interest in angels and angelic activity during this period, there may have been more focused efforts to keep such angel speculations in check, as is likely reflected in texts similar to Rev 19:10 and 22:8–9 which depict angels refusing to be reverenced (e.g., *Apoc. Zeph.* 6:11–15; *Ascen. Isa.* 7:21; 8:4–5). It may very well be, as Richard Bauckham and Loren Stuckenbruck argue, that in Rev 19:10 and 22:8–9, the author has employed a traditional motif attested in early Jewish and Christian writings of angels refusing to be worshiped, developed primarily to safeguard monotheism from the danger of inappropriate reverence for angels.[29]

As mentioned above, the two scenes depicting John's προσκύνησις before an angel appear as parallel conclusions to two climactic visions in which a prominent angelic figure (one of the seven bowl-judgment angels) offers to show John both the judgment of Babylon (17:1–19:10) and the establishment of the New Jerusalem (21:9–22:9). It is after each of these revelations comes to a close that John offers προσκύνησις to the angel. Although only 22:8 is explicit in relating John's προσκύνησις of the angel to the latter's role in showing John the things he had heard and seen, this is undoubtedly the same basis for his προσκύνησις of the angel in 19:10. In both cases then, as Bauckham states, "it is as the giver of prophetic revelation that John is tempted to worship the angel."[30] Stuckenbruck observes that whereas it is typically an angelophany that triggers an individual's reverential posture, this is not a feature of 19:10 or 22:8–9. Although the splendor of the bowl-judgment angels is affirmed in 15:6, "an angelophany proper has not prompted John's *proskunesis*"; thus, in agreement with Bauckham, "this would appear to bring the *function* of the angel as mediator and interpreter of the visions into sharper relief."[31] The significance of this revelatory function is underscored and intensified by the key role the angel(s) play(s) in this regard not only in these final climactic visions of the judgment of Babylon and the arrival of the New Jerusalem but also in the vision of the whole book, a feature uniquely highlighted in 22:8. Unlike 19:9–10, which concludes the Babylon vision, 22:6–9 serves not only as the conclusion to the New Jerusalem vision but also as the beginning of the book's epilogue.[32] John's self-identification as witness to the things revealed signals a widening of the scope of such revelations beyond the things heard and seen in the New Jerusalem vision

---

[27] Bousset, *Religion*, 330; R. H. Charles, *A Critical and Exegetical Commentary on the Revelation of St. John* (2 vols.; ICC; Edinburgh: T&T Clark, 1920), 2:224–25; cf. Kiddle, *Revelation*, 382, 449.
[28] See pp. 23–24 above.
[29] Bauckham, "Worship," 322–31; Stuckenbruck, *Angel*, 75–103, 245–56. Along with Rev 19:10 and 22:8–9, Bauckham and Stuckenbruck agree on the following texts as evidence of this tradition: Tob 12:16–22; *Apoc. Zeph.* 6:11–15; *Ascen. Isa.* 7:18–23; 8:1–5; *3 En.* 16:1–5; *Ps.-Mt.* 3:3; Cairo Genizah Hekhalot A/2, 13–18 (for other possible texts, see Stuckenbruck, *Angel*, 76–77).
[30] Bauckham, "Worship," 328.
[31] Stuckenbruck, *Angel*, 246.
[32] Aune, *Revelation*, 3:1148–49.

to include "the entire visionary portion of Revelation (1:9–22:9)."³³ Whereas in 19:10, John does προσκύνησις before the angel who showed him the Babylon vision, in 22:8, he is depicted doing προσκύνησις before the angel who showed him the whole of his prophetic vision (cf. 22:6).³⁴

Ultimately, this prominent role attributed to the angel is built up only to be downplayed through the angel's response to John. The angel considers himself unworthy of John's προσκύνησις, whether for his limited role in one vision (19:10) or for his more comprehensive role in the whole series of visions (22:8–9).³⁵ By rejecting John's προσκύνησις and directing him to the προσκύνησις of God, the angel conveys that "he is not the transcendent giver of prophetic revelation, but a creaturely instrument through whom the revelation is given" and that it is instead God who is to be worshiped "as the true transcendent source of revelation."³⁶

In these two passages, the author more clearly delineates the relationships between the human, the angelic, and the divine, and the implications for worship. Despite John's inclinations to view his angelic guide as his superior for his revelatory role, the angel is instead John's equal since they are both transmitters of divine revelation, and therefore fellow-servants of God, the true source of revelation and thus the rightful recipient of προσκύνησις. Although a response to blatant cultic worship of angels practiced among the author's intended readers is highly doubtful, there may have been certain questionable views held concerning angelic intermediaries that the author implicitly critiques.³⁷ In any case, the dually emphasized rejection of the προσκύνησις of angels, juxtaposed with a firm command to give προσκύνησις to God, clearly disqualifies angels as legitimate objects of worship.

D. The Προσκύνησις of the Philadelphian Christians

Quite possibly the sole unambiguously clear instance of προσκύνησις directed toward mere humans in the entire NT is found in Rev 3:9. Here, the glorified Jesus assures the Philadelphian Christians that certain Jews in their city with whom they appear to have been in conflict will one day come and do προσκύνησις before their feet (προσκυνήσουσιν ἐνώπιον τῶν ποδῶν σου). As many commentators note, John is likely drawing upon those passages in Isaiah where it is predicted that the Gentiles would pay homage to a restored and vindicated Israel at the eschaton (Isa 45:14; 49:23; 60:14).³⁸ Yet in a reversal of expectations, these Philadelphian Jewish agitators will

---

[33] Aune, *Revelation*, 3:1185–86; cf. Stuckenbruck, *Angel*, 253.
[34] It may be that the bowl-judgment angel is here fused with the angel in the introduction to the book sent to reveal "the things that must soon take place" (1:1; 22:6) (Aune, *Revelation*, 3:1182; cf. Bauckham, "Worship," 328).
[35] Cf. Giblin, "Structural," 496–97.
[36] Bauckham, "Worship," 328. Cf. Stuckenbruck, *Angel*, 255–56.
[37] Stuckenbruck, *Angel*, 237–38, 270–72.
[38] Charles, *Revelation*, 1:89; Aune, *Revelation*, 1:237–38; Beale, *Revelation*, 287; Osborne, *Revelation*, 191.

not be receiving but rendering this obeisance to the Philadelphian Christians. While some see in this a picture of Jewish conversion,[39] the primary significance is that of vindication of Christians as the true people of God.[40] Although these Jewish opponents saw themselves as God's true people, in reality they belonged to "the synagogue of Satan" (3:9). Conversely, although the Philadelphian Christians had "little power," which probably suggests they were socially and economically disadvantaged,[41] and so would have been easy targets for oppression and slander by the Jews, they remained faithful to Christ (3:8). Despite present circumstances, Jesus assures these Christians of a reversal of fortunes as their Jewish persecutors would one day humbly acknowledge them as the true people of God.

E. The Προσκύνησις of Jesus by heavenly beings

Thus far we have seen that apart from one clear instance of προσκύνησις offered to mere humans as an act of submission (3:9), John has otherwise made use of προσκυνέω to differentiate between true worship which is rightly given to God and false worship which, when rendered to other figures, conflicts with the worship of God. Neither the blatant idolatrous worship of Satan, the beast, idols, and so on nor even the misdirected reverence of God's angelic intermediaries is tolerated in Revelation.

This brings us to Rev 5:14, the conclusion to the first of many heavenly worship scenes in Revelation, where in response to the immediately preceding worship, the four living creatures utter their "amen" and the twenty-four elders fall down in προσκύνησις (καὶ τὰ τέσσαρα ζῷα ἔλεγον ἀμήν. καὶ οἱ πρεσβύτεροι ἔπεσαν καὶ προσεκύνησαν). With the exception of 11:1, this is the only other passage in Revelation where προσκυνέω appears without a stated object. Yet even in such cases, a recipient of προσκύνησις is always implied and can fairly easily be discerned from the context.[42] It is clear in 11:1, for instance, that God is the implied recipient of προσκύνησις since "those who worship" (τοὺς προσκυνοῦντας) do so in God's Temple. In the case of 5:14, however, many commentators simply note the elders' προσκύνησις without specifying the recipient(s) of such reverence.[43] To whom, then, is προσκύνησις given in 5:14 and what is the character of this προσκύνησις?

---

[39] Beale, *Revelation*, 287–88.
[40] Aune, *Revelation*, 1:238; Osborne, *Revelation*, 190–91.
[41] Aune, *Revelation*, 1:236; Osborne, *Revelation*, 189.
[42] See, for example, Gen 22:5 (Abraham to God); Gen 33:3–7 (Jacob and his family to Esau); Exod 33:10 (Israelites to God); Num 22:31 (Balaam to the angel of the Lord); 2 Kgdms 9:8 (Mephibosheth to David); Tob 5:14 (Jews to God); Josephus, *J.W.* 1.73 (Antigonus to God); Polybius 10.40.3 (Edeco to Scipio); Diodorus Siculus, *Hist.* 3.5.1 (Ethiopians to their king); Plutarch, *Art.* 11.3 (Persians to Cyrus); Plutarch, *Rom.* 27.8 (Romans to Romulus); Plutarch, *Quaest. rom.* 270D (Romans to their gods). Recall also, for example, our discussions of Matt 28:17; Acts 8:27; 24:11.
[43] See, for example, Aune, *Revelation*, 1:367; Beale, *Revelation*, 366; Kiddle, *Revelation*, 105. Some commentators make no mention at all of the elders' προσκύνησις in Rev 5:14 (e.g., Beasley-Murray, *Revelation*, 129; Caird, *Revelation*, 77; Jürgen Roloff, *The Revelation of John: A Continental Commentary* [trans. John E. Alsup; Minneapolis, MN: Fortress, 1993], 82).

We begin with a consideration of the broader literary context in which this passage is situated. As Russell Morton points out, "Most commentators agree that Rev 4–5 constitute a structural unity."[44] Indeed, there are a number of verbal, thematic, and structural parallels connecting these two chapters,[45] especially with respect to worship. Most notably, it is evident that similar worshipers (the twenty-four elders and four living creatures, among others) perform similar acts of worship (hymns and prostration) involving similar elements (e.g., worthiness of a figure to receive glory, and honor) all presented in a highly structured fashion (e.g., two hymns in praise of one figure, followed by two hymns in praise of a second figure, followed by a final hymn in praise of both figures). Without a doubt, Rev 4 and 5 are "integrally related" to one another and constitute "two closely related scenes in one unified vision of God's throne."[46] Together, the two chapters introduce the first, most elaborate, and most foundational scenes of heavenly worship in Revelation, centering first on the praise of God in Rev 4, then on the praise of Jesus ("the Lamb") in Rev 5, and concluding with the joint praise of God and Jesus in Rev 5:13–14.

Revelation 4 begins a new section in which John is ushered into the heavenly realms where he sees God on his throne surrounded by heavenly beings who worship him with hymns and προσκύνησις. Heavenly worship commences with the four living creatures and their unceasing thrice-holy praise of the Lord God Almighty, who was and is and is to come (4:8). The text goes on to explain that when the four living creatures give glory, honor, and thanks to God, the twenty-four elders follow by falling down in προσκύνησις before God, casting their golden crowns before the throne and acclaiming his worthiness to receive glory, honor, and power as the creator of all things (4:9–11). As the vision narrative continues in Rev 5, a number of key features from Rev 4 reappear, confirming the close connection between the two chapters. The theme of worthiness continues on beginning with the introduction of a mighty angel who asks who is worthy to open the sealed scroll which God holds in his right hand (5:1–2). When the slain Lamb appears as the only one worthy and he takes the scroll, the living creatures and the elders worship him in a manner parallel to their worship of God in 4:8–11 by prostrating[47] themselves before him and singing hymns in praise of him (5:8–10). Similar verbal patterns of hymnic praise are also discernible. Just as in the hymn to God in 4:11, the elders proclaim, "Worthy are you" (ἄξιος εἶ) to receive glory, honor, and power "because" (ὅτι) God is the creator, so too in the hymn to Jesus in 5:9–10, the living creatures and elders proclaim, "Worthy are you" (ἄξιος εἶ) to open the scroll "because" (ὅτι) he is the redeemer. In the next hymn to Jesus (5:11–12), the choir of worshipers expands beyond the living creatures and elders to include a countless

---

[44] Russell S. Morton, *One upon the Throne and the Lamb: A Tradition Historical/Theological Analysis of Revelation 4–5* (New York: Lang, 2007), 68 (commentators noted on p. 80, n. 149).

[45] See Ekkehardt Müller, *Microstructural Analysis of Revelation 4–11* (AUSDDS 21; Berrien Springs, MI: Andrews University, 1996), 228–33.

[46] Larry W. Hurtado, "Revelation 4–5 in the Light of Jewish Apocalyptic Analogies," *JSNT* 25 (1985): 110.

[47] Whereas prostration before God in heavenly worship scenes typically includes use of the terms πίπτω and προσκυνέω (4:10; 7:11; 11:16; 19:4), here only πίπτω is used to portray prostration before Jesus. We discuss this below (pp. 166–67).

number of angels whose praise again mirrors the praise of God in 4:11. Just as God is declared "worthy to receive glory, honor, and power" (ἄξιος . . . λαβεῖν τὴν δόξαν καὶ τὴν τιμὴν καὶ τὴν δύναμιν), so too is Jesus declared "worthy to receive power, honor, and glory" among other prerogatives (ἄξιος . . . λαβεῖν τὴν δύναμιν καὶ πλοῦτον καὶ σοφίαν καὶ ἰσχὺν καὶ τιμὴν καὶ δόξαν καὶ εὐλογίαν). Finally, the heavenly worship of Rev 4–5 reaches a dramatic climax in 5:13 as the choir of worshipers once again expands to include the entire created world[48] in a doxological praise of both God and Jesus: "To him who is seated on the throne and to the Lamb be blessing and honor and glory and might forever and ever!" It was mentioned above that since προσκύνησις to God in Revelation characteristically follows hymns of praise to him, it is in part an expression of affirmation of the hymns' contents. Accordingly, here too, the doxology of 5:13 is immediately followed by affirmative expressions of worship with the "amen" of the living creatures and the προσκύνησις of the elders (5:14).

In accordance with the overall structure of the heavenly worship scenes in Rev 4–5, in which hymns featuring common elements are directed first to God, then to Jesus, and finally jointly to God and Jesus, the acts of prostration accompanying these hymns follow the same pattern so that they too are first directed to God (4:10), then to Jesus (5:8), and finally jointly to God and Jesus (5:14). Thus, the context certainly suggests what Robert H. Charles stated directly concerning the προσκύνησις of the elders in 5:14: "Here the Elders prostrate themselves before God and the Lamb."[49]

---

[48] Although the universal worship described here may imply forced homage by God's opponents, as Osborne rightly notes, "[that] is not the emphasis here" (*Revelation*, 265, n. 20).

[49] Charles, *Revelation*, 1:152; cf. Boxall, *Revelation*, 102; Dunn, *First*, 12. According to Gerard Mussies, Rev 4:9–11 anticipates a unique event, which occurs in 5:13–14. That is, there is a specific event in which when the four living creatures give glory, honor, and thanks to God, the twenty-four elders will render προσκύνησις to *God* and sing the ἄξιος-song, namely, the worship scene in 5:13–14 (*The Morphology of Koine Greek as Used in the Apocalypse of St. John: A Study in Bilingualism* [NovTSup 27; Leiden: Brill, 1971], 345). If this is so, would it mean that the elders' προσκύνησις in 5:14 is restricted to God since it is the fulfillment of the elders' προσκύνησις of God in 4:10? Not necessarily. Those who concede Mussies' general point disagree in some respects over which passage(s) fulfill the worship described and anticipated in 4:9–11. This seems to be due in part to differences of opinion regarding how strictly or flexibly one connects the details of 4:9–11 to other passages. For instance, David L. Mathewson proves to be far more flexible by including passages (7:11; 11:16; 19:4) that very generally correspond to 4:9–11 (*Verbal Aspect in the Book of Revelation: The Function of Greek Verb Tenses in John's Apocalypse* [LBS 4; Leiden: Brill, 2010], 113–15). Beale, on the other hand, is even more strict than Mussies, extending the passage to include 5:8–12, no doubt because the ἄξιος-song appears here, not in 5:13–14 (*Revelation*, 334). However, the ἄξιος song is only sung to Jesus in Rev 5, not to God, as is anticipated in 4:11 (Mussies recognizes this and attempts unconvincingly to get around this problem). If, however, 4:9–11 does point to 5:13–14, there is not only a certain measure of flexibility in the details but also an expansion in the details: (1) those who ascribe glory, honor, and thanks have expanded beyond the living creatures to include all creation; (2) the prerogatives ascribed have expanded beyond glory, honor, and thanks/blessing to include might; and it seems (3) the recipient of praise and προσκύνησις has expanded beyond God to include Jesus. It may also be that 4:9–11 does not anticipate any unique event at all but describes in vivid terms the kind of ongoing worship characteristic of these heavenly beings and therefore has no strict, exclusive connection to 5:13–14 (Prigent, *Commentary*, 234–35; Osborne, *Revelation*, 238; Charles, *Revelation*, 1:127; cf. Blount, *Revelation*, 94). In sum, whether or not 5:13–14 is the direct fulfillment of 4:9–11, there is no reason to think that the elders' προσκύνησις in 5:14 is strictly given to God to the exclusion of Jesus.

With regard to the character of the acts of προσκύνησις in Rev 4–5, despite the challenges of certain details of the text and their significance, these two chapters clearly and pervasively employ cultic and political imagery, which are thoroughly interwoven and set the tone for the entire section. Accordingly, the acts of προσκύνησις themselves fit into this overall pattern so that they are neither purely political nor purely religious gestures, but a blend of the two.

There are clues from the furnishings, utensils, and other items described in Rev 4–5 that the setting of this heavenly vision is a combination of royal court and temple.[50] One of the first things John reports seeing in his heavenly vision is a throne (4:2), a key symbol in these two chapters and indeed in all of Revelation. The term θρόνος appears forty-seven times in Revelation with nineteen of these instances appearing here in Rev 4–5. It is most often used with reference to God whom John describes here and elsewhere in Revelation as "One seated on the throne."[51] John also reports seeing thrones encircling God's throne where the twenty-four elders are seated and wearing golden crowns (4:4). With the elders joined by the living creatures as heavenly beings who appear before God on his throne, the image is that of the divine council assembled in a heavenly court setting where God is seated on his throne as king surrounded by his heavenly courtiers.[52] There are also clear indications of a temple setting. Although the term ναός does not appear in Rev 4–5, this same heavenly throne room is revisited several times later in Revelation where it is clear that God's throne is set in his ναός (7:15; 11:19; 14:15–17; 15:5–8; 16:1, 17). The furnishings and utensils associated with the Temple (ark, altar, and censer) are also present in the throne room (8:3; 9:13; 11:19; 14:18; 16:7). Within Rev 4–5 itself, the same significance is likely to be found in some of the objects described here. Both the harps (κιθάρα) and the bowls (φιάλη) filled with incense which the elders hold as they sing hymns (5:8) are items connected to the worship of God in his Temple. The κιθάρα frequently appears in the OT and early Jewish literature as an instrument used to accompany psalm-singing to God in the context of temple worship.[53] The φιάλη is one of many cultic utensils found in Israel's Temple and tabernacle which here in 5:8 appears to correspond most closely to the incense Pan kept on the table for the bread of the presence (Josephus, *Ant.* 3.143; cf. *Let. Aris.* 42; *Ant.* 12.53).[54] It may also be that the seven torches of fire burning before God's throne (4:5) are modeled after the menorah(s) of the temple/tabernacle.[55]

---

[50] Cf. Richard Bauckham, *The Theology of the Book of Revelation* (Cambridge: Cambridge University Press, 1993), 33–34.
[51] Rev 4:2, 9, 10; 5:1, 7, 13; 6:16; 7:10, 15; 19:4; 20:11; 21:5.
[52] Cf. 1 Kgs 22:19–22; Ps. 82:1; Isa 6:1–13; Dan 7:9–10; *1 En.* 14:18–23; 47:3; 71:5–10; *2 En.* 20:1–3; *2 Bar.* 48:10.
[53] LXX Pss 32:2; 42:4; 56:8–9; 70:22; 80:1–3; 91:1–4; 97:5; 107:1–3; 146:7; 150:3; 1 Macc 4:54; *T. Job* 14:1–3.
[54] Aune, *Revelation*, 1:356–58. The term is also used to describe a vessel associated with the altar of burnt offering (LXX Exod 27:3; 38:23; Num 4:14; Josephus, *Ant.* 3.150).
[55] See Craig R. Koester, *Revelation: A New Translation with Introduction and Commentary* (AB 38A; New Haven, CT: Yale University Press, 2014), 363; Beale, *Revelation*, 316; Aune, *Revelation*, 1:295; Thompson, *Revelation*, 70.

These, and perhaps other elements,[56] contribute to the cultic atmosphere of John's heavenly vision.

In this dual throne room/temple setting of Rev 4–5, there are three instances of προσκύνησις/prostration. In the first instance, the twenty-four elders vacate their thrones, fall in προσκύνησις before God on his throne, and cast their crowns before him (4:10). The political imagery in this depiction of the elders' reverence of God is readily apparent as these heavenly figures play the parts of vassals, relinquishing their own symbols of authority in recognition of a greater sovereign to whom they are subject. Yet in light of other considerations, it seems that their offering of προσκύνησις is also invested with religious connotations.

First, many have observed that these and other details have significant parallels with the language, images, and practices associated with the political-religious adoration of the Roman emperor, suggesting that the worship of God here is in part presented as a counterimage to that of the emperor. David Aune notes, for instance, that the portrayal of the elders casting their crowns before the throne "has no parallel in Israelite-Jewish literature, and becomes comprehensible only in light of the ceremonial traditions of Hellenistic and Roman ruler worship."[57] Some have understood the elders' acclamation of God as "worthy" and their ascriptions of glory, honor, power, and so on (4:11) with reference to imperial praise[58] (though it should be noted that these are not exclusively imperial terms and concepts).[59] Widely recognized as a clear link to Roman imperial reverence in this scene is the elders' address of God as "our Lord and God," a divine title strikingly similar to that reputedly claimed by the Emperor Domitian for himself: *dominus et deus noster* (cf. Suetonius, *Dom*. 13.2).[60] If, as seems likely, the elders' reverence of God here is in part modeled after, and is a polemical response to, the adoration of the Roman emperor, then like the adoration of the emperor, the full picture of their reverence of God is inextricably political and religious in character, including the gesture of προσκύνησις. Although it may be that the image of the elders' προσκύνησις is drawn from more general conceptions of bowing in obeisance before a ruler, there is also evidence of similar demonstrations before the emperor.

---

[56] For other possible cultic items in Rev 4–5, see R. Dean Davis, *The Heavenly Court Judgment of Revelation 4–5* (Lanham, MD: University Press of America, 1992), 118–34; and Jon Paulien, "The Role of the Hebrew Cultus, Sanctuary and Temple in the Plot and Structure of the Book of Revelation," *AUSS* 33 (1995): 250.

[57] David E. Aune, "The Influence of Roman Imperial Court Ceremonial on the Apocalypse of John," *BR* 28 (1983): 13. For instances of crowns presented to Greek and Roman rulers, see Tacitus, *Ann*. 15.29; Arrian, *Anab*. 7.23.2; Cicero, *Sest*. 27; Josephus, *Ant*. 14.304, 313.

[58] David Seal, "Shouting in the Apocalypse: The Influence of First-Century Acclamations on the Praise Utterances in Revelation 4:8 and 11," *JETS* 51 (2008): 349–50; J. Daryl Charles, "Imperial Pretensions and the Throne-Vision of the Lamb: Observations on the Function of Revelation 5," *CTR* 7 (1993): 96; Schüssler Fiorenza, *Revelation*, 59.

[59] See David R. Carnegie, "Worthy Is the Lamb: The Hymns in Revelation," in *Christ the Lord: Studies in Christology Presented to Donald Guthrie* (ed. H. H. Rowdon; Leicester: Inter-Varsity Press, 1982), 255–56.

[60] Carnegie, "Worthy," 255; Aune, *Revelation*, 1:310–12; Beale, *Revelation*, 334–35; Osborne, *Revelation*, 240. Whether or not Domitian himself demanded to be addressed in this way, it is likely that such titles attributed to the emperor circulated among his flatterers at a popular level (Yarbro Collins, *Crisis*, 72; Thompson, *Revelation*, 106; Prigent, *Commentary*, 236).

Interestingly, the recorded examples are mostly of those emperors who were known to have entertained divine pretensions. Caligula appears to have made προσκύνησις a regular part of his court ceremonial and greeting from the public (Philo, *Legat.* 116). It is said that the senators rendered προσκύνησις both to Caligula himself (Dio Cassius, *Hist. rom.* 59.27.1) and to his empty throne, which was situated in a temple (Dio Cassius, *Hist. rom.* 59.24.4). Lucius Vitellius received mercy from Caligula when he did προσκύνησις before him, "all the while calling him many divine names" and vowing to sacrifice to Caligula if his life would be spared (Dio Cassius, *Hist. rom.* 59.27.5). The Armenian king Tiridates I rendered προσκύνησις to Nero, stating, "I have come to thee, my god, to worship (προσκυνήσων) thee as I do Mithras" (Dio Cassius, *Hist. rom.* 63.4.3; 63.5.2). It is also reported that he offered προσκύνησις and sacrifice to Nero's images before taking the diadem from his head and placing it upon the images (Dio Cassius, *Hist. rom.* 62.23.3). Similar to Vitellius, Juventius Celsus eluded execution at the hands of Domitian by doing προσκύνησις before him and "repeatedly calling him 'master' and 'god' (terms that were already being applied to him by others)" (Dio Cassius, *Hist. rom.* 67.13.4).[61] Just as others prostrated themselves before the emperor and his throne, placed their own crowns before him, and lauded him with divine ascriptions, so do the elders fall before God on his throne, cast their golden crowns before him, and laud him as the true divine lord. Thus, just as political homage and religious worship overlap in these reverential acts directed to the emperor, the same is true of the elders' worship of God in 4:10–11.

Second, as was mentioned previously, acts of προσκύνησις in heavenly worship scenes are closely linked to hymnic praises. Hymn singing was a regular feature of early Christian worship (1 Cor 14:26; Col 3:16; Eph 5:19; cf. Acts 16:25; Jas 5:13), and a number of NT passages are often thought to preserve hymnic material that may very well have their origin in early Christian liturgy (e.g., Phil 2:6–11; Col 1:15–20; Luke 1:46–55, 68–79; John 1:1–18).[62] Although some scholars have similarly argued that Revelation's hymns have largely been taken over (with perhaps some modifications) from preexisting hymns used in Jewish and/or Christian worship,[63] it is more likely that these hymns are by and large the work of John himself.[64] Yet such proponents also note that Revelation's hymns undoubtedly reflect the character of Christian worship, pointing to the use of traditional Jewish and Christian liturgical elements, such as the amen, the hallelujah, and the doxology as evidence of the affinities of these hymns

---

[61] By contrast to these, it is said that Claudius "forbade any one to worship (προσκυνεῖν) him or to offer him any sacrifice" (Dio Cassius, *Hist. rom.* 50.5.4).

[62] See Hurtado, *One*, 101–04; Hurtado, *Lord*, 146–49; David E. Aune, "Worship, Early Christian," *ABD* 6:982; Ralph P. Martin, *Worship in the Early Church* (London: Marshall, Morgan & Scott, 1964), 39–52.

[63] John J. O'Rourke, "The Hymns of the Apocalypse," *CBQ* 30 (1968): 399–409; Lucetta Mowry, "Revelation 4–5 and Early Christian Liturgical Usage," *JBL* 71 (1952): 75–84.

[64] Reinhard Deichgräber, *Gotteshymnus und Christushymnus in der frühen Christenheit: Untersuchungen zu Form, Sprache und Stil der frühchristlichen Hymnen* (SUNT 5; Göttingen: Vandenhoeck & Ruprecht, 1967), 58–59; Jörns, *Hymnische Evangelium*, 178–79; Carnegie, "Worthy," 243–47; Aune, *Revelation*, 1:315–16; cf. Beale, *Revelation*, 312–13; Osborne, *Revelation*, 220.

with common Jewish and Christian expressions of praise.⁶⁵ The opening hymn in Rev 4:8 recalls Isa 6:3 where seraphim direct their liturgical thrice-holy praise to God enthroned in his temple,⁶⁶ followed by two sets of divine designations ("Lord God Almighty" and "who was and is and is to come"), which likewise are derived from Jewish sources and reflections.⁶⁷ As in other heavenly worship scenes, it is hymnic praise that moves the elders to offer προσκύνησις to God (4:9–10) and to follow with their own hymn of praise (4:11). Their hymn is reflective of both the acclamations of the divine emperor ("our Lord and God") as well as traditional Jewish hymns of praise that celebrate God as the creator of all (Pss 8:3; 33:6–9; 95:5; 102:25; 136:5–9; 146:6). The joining of προσκύνησις with hymnic praise in cultic worship, carried out by both human and heavenly figures, is well attested in the OT and early Jewish literature.⁶⁸ In 4:9–11, the elders' προσκύνησις of God combined with the removal of their crowns certainly evokes an image of political homage, and yet its close association as well with hymn singing suggests it is also an expression of cultic worship.

The second instance of προσκύνησις/prostration is directed to Jesus. When he suddenly emerges as the only one worthy to open the scroll symbolizing God's plan of judgment and redemption for the world, and he takes this scroll from God, the living creatures and the elders immediately prostrate themselves before him (5:8). Once again, the scene involves a mix of political and cultic terms and images. The figure worthy to open the scroll is first described as "the lion of the tribe of Judah, the root of David" (5:5), two messianic titles that have royal and militaristic connotations. But then he appears as a slaughtered lamb (5:6), an image with sacrificial connotations.⁶⁹ Those redeemed by the Lamb are made to be both a kingdom and priests (5:10).

What triggers the reverence of Jesus is his highly significant act of taking the scroll from God (5:7–8). Since it is generally agreed that there is a close connection between

---

⁶⁵ Carnegie, "Worthy," 247; cf. Deichgräber, *Gotteshymnus*, 59; Jörns, *Hymnische Evangelium*, 179.
⁶⁶ The thrice-holy praise (the *trisagion*) appears in many other Jewish and Christian works (*1 En.* 39:12; *2 En.* 21:1 [J]; *3 En.* 1:12; *T. Ab.* 20:12 [A]; *T. Adam* 1:4; 4:8; *Ques. Ezra* 29; *1 Clem.* 34:6) and was also incorporated in Jewish and Christian liturgy (*Apost. Const.* 7.35.3; 8.12.27; Tertullian, *Or.* 3). It is possible then that John's use of the *trisagion* comes more directly from other literary traditions (Jörns, *Hymnische Evangelium*, 24–25) or even from liturgical traditions (Pierre Prigent, *Apocalypse et Liturgie* [CahT 52; Neuchâtel: Delachaux et Niestlé, 1964], 65–66). The latter, however, is particularly difficult to substantiate since clear evidence for liturgical use comes no earlier than the late second century C.E. See discussions in Ardea Caviggiola Russo, "Behind the Heavenly Door: Earthly Liturgy and Heavenly Worship in the Apocalypse of John" (PhD diss., University of Notre Dame, 2009), 67–83; and Jan Fekkes, *Isaiah and Prophetic Traditions in the Book of Revelation: Visionary Antecedents and Their Development* (JSNTSup 93; Sheffield: Sheffield Academic, 1994), 145.
⁶⁷ For the phrase "Lord God Almighty" (κύριος ὁ θεὸς ὁ παντοκράτωρ), see LXX Hos 12:6; Amos 3:13; 4:13; 5:14–16; 9:5; Nah 3:5; Zech 10:3. The phrase "who was and is and is to come" (ὁ ἦν καὶ ὁ ὢν καὶ ὁ ἐρχόμενος) is derived from a paraphrase of the divine name YHWH in Exod 3:14 that developed out of later Jewish interpretations of its significance (Aune, *Revelation*, 1:3033; Beale, *Revelation*, 187–88).
⁶⁸ 2 Chron 29:28–30; Ps 66:4; Sir 50:16–18; 4Q405 20 II–21–22; 7–8; *T. Ab.* 20:12–13 (A); *Apoc. Ab.* 17. Cf. Gen 24:26–27; 1 Macc 4:55; Jdt 13:17; *T. Ab.* 6:8 (A); *Apoc. Mos.* 27:5.
⁶⁹ "The Lamb" has also been understood in political terms as a military ram (cf. *1 En.* 90:9–12; *T. Jos.* 19:8), and it is likely that both political and religious aspects are intended in the overall symbol of the Lamb (Aune, *Revelation*, 1:367–73; Osborne, *Revelation*, 255–56).

the lordship of Jesus and his rightful claim to this unique role of taking the scroll,[70] the prostration of the living creatures and elders may in part be a gesture of homage befitting royalty. This would also be consistent with Jesus's regal status signified by the two messianic titles in 5:5. Yet it is also clear from the hymnic praise that it is Jesus's sacrificial death which brought about the redemption of mankind that is the basis for his worthiness to receive the scroll and thereby to set in motion the final stages of God's redemptive plan. Thus, Jesus's reception of the scroll is also closely associated with his salvific work.

The significance of this event is underscored by the way the praise of Jesus parallels the praise of God. Just as God is hymned as worthy to receive glory, honor, and power for his creative work (4:11), Jesus is hymned as worthy to receive the scroll and thereby also to receive power, wealth, wisdom, might, honor, glory, and blessing[71] (5:12) for his redemptive work (5:9–10). It is even likely that the hymn celebrating Jesus's redemptive work is understood in "new creation" terms so that, like God, Jesus is worthy of worship for his "creative" work.[72] God's worthiness of worship through creating (ἔκτισας) all things (4:11) is paralleled by Jesus's worthiness of worship through making (ἐποίησας) a kingdom and priests (5:10), where ἐποίησας as a parallel to ἔκτισας is likely to be understood in a creative sense (cf. 14:7; 21:5).[73] It is also likely that the hymn sung in praise of Jesus is a "new song" (ᾠδὴν καινὴν) because the new and special thing being celebrated[74] is his redemptive work, which began with his sacrifice and, through his reception and opening of the scroll, culminates in the arrival of the "new" creation (οὐρανὸν καινὸν καὶ γῆν καινήν [21:1]; τὴν πόλιν τὴν ἁγίαν Ἰερουσαλὴμ καινὴν [21:2]; καινὰ πάντα [21:5]).[75] Thus, on account of his key role in God's redemptive and recreative plan, the living creatures and elders respond with cultic worship, as their hymnic "new song" accompanied by cultic musical instruments is sung directly to Jesus.[76] Once again, then, in light of the close

---

[70] There is some debate over whether Jesus's reception of the scroll signifies his enthronement (Traugott Holtz, *Die Christologie der Apokalypse des Johannes* [TUGAL 85; Berlin: Akademie, 1962], 27–29; Ranko Stefanovic, "The Background and Meaning of the Sealed Book of Revelation 5" [PhD diss., Andrews University, 1995], 208–17; Roloff, *Revelation*, 75; Beale, *Revelation*, 311–12, 356–57; Osborne, *Revelation*, 214, 257–58; Boxall, *Revelation*, 99) or his investiture (Matthias Reinhard Hoffmann, *The Destroyer and the Lamb: The Relationship between Angelomorphic and Lamb Christology in the Book of Revelation* [WUNT 2/203; Tübingen: Mohr Siebeck, 2005], 135–36; Aune, *Revelation*, 1:336–38).

[71] Many of these qualities are bestowed on kings by God (cf. Dan 2:37) and properly belong to God himself as Lord of all (cf. 1 Chr 29:11–12). Thus, Jesus's reception of these prerogatives signifies his royal status (cf. Aune, *Revelation*, 1:364–66). Yet it probably also suggests his equal status with God since these same prerogatives are ascribed to God (Rev 7:12) despite minimal, relatively insignificant variation. See Hoffmann, *Destroyer*, 156–63.

[72] Hoffmann, *Destroyer*, 163–66; Thompson, *Revelation*, 58–59; Carnegie, "Worthy," 248–49; Beale, *Revelation*, 358, 369.

[73] Beale, *Revelation*, 364; cf. Carnegie, "Worthy," 248–49.

[74] In the OT and early Jewish literature, a "new song" is introduced to celebrate a very special occasion, typically a saving act of God (Pss 40:1–3; 96:1–2; 98:1–2; 144:9–11; Jdt 16:1–2; *Ps. Sol.* 15:1–3; Philo, *Mos.* 1.255); see Aune, *Revelation*, 1:359–60.

[75] Beale, *Revelation*, 358; cf. Osborne, *Revelation*, 259; Prigent, *Commentary*, 255.

[76] The incense-like prayers associated with the cultic golden bowls in 5:8 are most likely directed to God as prayers for vindication and judgment (cf. 6:9–11; 8:3–4; see Blount, *Revelation*, 113;

association of the heavenly beings' prostration (5:8) with their hymn singing (5:9–10) in the overall depiction of the reverence of Jesus, their prostration is certainly in part an expression of cultic worship.

The final instance of προσκύνησις/prostration in Rev 4–5, though stated intransitively, is directed to both God and Jesus, and is once again, as has been the pattern throughout, closely linked to hymnic praise. Following two hymns and prostration directed to Jesus, which followed two hymns and prostration directed to God, this literary unit concludes with a final hymn in praise of both God and Jesus together as the living creatures and elders respond affirmatively with their respective "amen" and προσκύνησις (5:13–14). Significantly, it is no longer only the living creatures and the elders (4:8–11; 5:8–10), nor the innumerable angels with them (5:11–12), who are involved in worship, but now all creation comes together in praise of God and Jesus (5:13). The universal scope of worship is underscored by the fourfold division of creation (every creature in heaven, on earth, under the earth, and in the sea) and its fourfold ascription of praise (blessing, honor, glory, and might).[77] This final worship scene brings into sharper relief the distinction that has been building up between creation and creator in which Jesus is clearly aligned with the latter. Thus, God is worthy of worship as creator of all things (4:11); no one in all of creation is worthy to open the scroll (5:1–4); Jesus is worthy to open the scroll and to be worshiped as the recreating redeemer (5:5–12); and so all creation worships God and Jesus (5:13).[78]

As noted above, the hymnic sections in Revelation incorporate distinctive elements from Jewish and Christian worship practices, and we see this very clearly here in 5:13–14 where the hymnic praise of God and Jesus takes the form of a doxology. A doxology is a liturgical formula typically consisting of four parts: (1) the recipient of praise, typically addressed in the dative; (2) the word(s) of praise ascribed to the recipient, usually δόξα; (3) an eternity statement (e.g., forever and ever); and (4) a closing "amen."[79] Doxologies appear frequently in the NT and other early Christian literature,[80] and very likely entered Christian writings from the worship practices of the earliest church.[81] Indeed, as Aune observes, "The fact that doxologies are used to conclude a religious text (*1 Clem.* 64:2; *2 Clem.* 20:5) or a unified section of a religious text (Rom 11:36; 1 Tim 1:17; *1 Clem.* 20:12) suggests that they were similarly used

---

Osborne, *Revelation*, 259), though some consider these prayers to be directed to Jesus (Koester, *Revelation*, 379).

[77] Bauckham, *Climax*, 31.
[78] As Carrell rightly states, "The worship of Jesus in Apocalypse 5 is the worship of one who is distinguished from creatures and conjoined with the Creator" (*Jesus*, 114).
[79] Deichgräber, *Gotteshymnus*, 25.
[80] Rom 11:36; 16:25–27; Gal 1:5; Eph 3:20–21; Phil 4:20; 1 Tim 1:17; 6:16; 2 Tim 4:18; Heb 13:21; 1 Pet 4:11; 5:11; 2 Pet 3:18; Jude 24–25; *Did.* 8:2; 9:2, 3, 4; 10:2, 4, 5; *1 Clem.* 20:12; 32:4; 38:4; 43:6; 45:7; 50:7; 58:2; 61:3; 65:2. Doxologies are rare in Jewish literature (Pr Man 15; 4 Macc 18:24), where the functionally equivalent benediction is far more common. Although difficult to trace its development precisely, the doxology certainly has its origin in Jewish tradition (Deichgräber, *Gotteshymnus*, 35–38).
[81] Russo, "Heavenly," 92.

to conclude a liturgical sequence in Christian services of worship."[82] As the evidence indicates, this form of worship is characteristically reserved for God:

> To our God and Father be glory forever and ever. Amen. (Phil 4:20)
>
> To the King of the ages, immortal, invisible, the only God, be honor and glory forever and ever. Amen. (1 Tim 1:17)
>
> To the only God, our Savior, through Jesus Christ our Lord, be glory, majesty, dominion, and authority, before all time and now and forever. Amen. (Jude 25)
>
> Almighty God has justified all men; to whom be glory for ever and ever. Amen. (*I Clem.* 32:4)[83]

For this reason, it is highly significant when this form of worship in the early church that is otherwise exclusively directed to God is in a few cases applied to Jesus:[84]

> The Lord [i.e., Jesus] will rescue me from every evil deed and bring me safely into his heavenly kingdom. To him be the glory forever and ever. Amen. (2 Tim 4:18)
>
> But grow in the grace and knowledge of our Lord and Savior Jesus Christ. To him be the glory both now and to the day of eternity. Amen. (2 Pet 3:18)

Revelation itself contains doxologies directed to God alone (7:12), to Jesus alone (1:5–6), and to God and Jesus together, as seen here in 5:13–14a: "'To him who is seated on the throne and to the Lamb be blessing and honor and glory and might forever and ever!' And the four living creatures said, 'Amen!'"

The final "amen" of the living creatures is combined with the προσκύνησις of the elders as closing affirmations of this doxology (and quite likely of the entire worship scene of Rev 4–5[85]). Thus, while the elders' προσκύνησις in 5:14 may be in part an expression of homage befitting a ruler in line with the two previous instances of prostration which certainly took on this character, what is foregrounded here is the cultic character of this gesture, as it is once again closely linked to liturgical forms of worship.

Throughout Rev 4–5, there is a blend of political and cultic imagery and language permeating the heavenly vision and setting its tone. Accordingly, when both God and Jesus are presented as the ultimate sovereigns of all creation, they are portrayed receiving homage befitting a ruler and worship befitting a deity. Certainly, προσκύνησις/prostration is representative of a type of political homage shown to these figures as it is closely associated with other political gestures and terms (e.g., casting crowns), but it is

---

[82] Aune, "Worship," 6:982.
[83] See also the passages in n. 80 above, with the notable exceptions of 2 Tim 4:18 and 2 Pet 3:18, which are addressed to Christ. Note also a few ambiguous cases of doxologies addressed to either God or Christ (Heb 13:21; 1 Pet 4:11; *1 Clem.* 20:12; 50:7).
[84] Bauckham, *Jesus*, 132–35; Hurtado, *Lord*, 152.
[85] Osborne, *Revelation*, 265–66; Blount, *Revelation*, 120.

also consistently linked with hymnic praise as an expression of cultic worship. Thus, as with God, Jesus receives προσκύνησις as a gesture of both political homage and cultic worship.

F. The significance of the Προσκύνησις of Jesus in Revelation

Most scholars have had little trouble affirming a divine Christology for Revelation, especially in light of this portrayal of Jesus receiving parallel worship alongside God here in Rev 4–5.[86] However, most recently James McGrath has challenged this prevailing view, arguing that the worship offered to Jesus in Revelation is not the kind of worship normally reserved for God and therefore fails as evidence of Jesus's divine status.[87] This assessment is largely due to his judgment that only sacrificial worship counts as the kind of worship reserved for God, which in Revelation is only given to God (7:15; 22:3).[88] The kind of reverence Jesus receives, on the other hand, even as one praised alongside God, is considered comparable to the reverence shown to Israel's king (1 Chron 29:20) and the messianic Son of Man in the *Similitudes of Enoch* (*1 En.* 48:5). These figures are also praised alongside God, yet appear to receive such reverence as God's appointed representatives, not necessarily as divine figures.[89]

McGrath also gives some attention to the use of προσκυνέω in Revelation and here too finds little support for the worship of Jesus as divine. While the term is used to convey cultic worship, as in Rev 13 where sacrificial worship of the emperor is said to be in view,[90] it is also used somewhat broadly to signify prostration before a superior, as in Rev 3:9 where Jews will bow in submission to Christians. It is precisely because the latter is not a form of worship reserved for God that he considers it unlikely that any acts of prostration in Revelation signify divine worship,[91] whether before angels (19:10; 22:8–9), Jesus (1:17; 5:8, 14[?][92]), or even God himself (4:10; 7:11; 11:16; 19:4). Instead, he considers it more appropriate to regard prostration in Revelation as "a sign of submission"[93] rather than an act of divine worship.

There are, however, problems with McGrath's proposal. His contention that sacrificial worship alone is the sole criterion for divine worship is highly problematic.

---

[86] Along with Carrell, *Jesus*, 113–119, and the works cited there (113), see also Hurtado, *Lord*, 591–94; Dunn, *First*, 130–32; Hoffmann, *Destroyer*, 152–68; Stuckenbruck, *Angel*, 261–62; Bauckham, "Worship," 329–31; Osborne, *Revelation*, 35, 46; Beale, *Revelation*, 358; Donald Guthrie, "The Christology of Revelation," in *Jesus of Nazareth, Lord and Christ: Essays on the Historical Jesus and New Testament Christology* (J. B. Green and M. Turner; Grand Rapids: Eerdmans, 1994), 403; John Paul Heil, *The Book of Revelation: Worship for Life in the Spirit of Prophecy* (Eugene, OR: Cascade, 2014), 85.
[87] McGrath, *Only*, 71–80.
[88] McGrath, *Only*, 71–72 (see also pp. 18–19 and 25–37).
[89] McGrath, *Only*, 76, 122, nn. 12 and 13.
[90] McGrath, *Only*, 76–77.
[91] McGrath, *Only*, 75.
[92] McGrath overlooks this passage when he states that there are no instances of Jesus as the object of προσκυνέω (*Only*, 72).
[93] McGrath, *Only*, 75.

He especially frequently distinguishes between prostration/προσκύνησις and sacrifice, arguing that only the latter was the true "make-or-break issue," the one type of worship that Jews and Christians refused to give to any other but God. But this is simply not correct. In some instances, prostration/προσκύνησις is treated as an honor reserved for God which, when given to certain figures, becomes a form of idolatrous worship of false gods. In Dan 3, for example, the three Jews, Shadrach, Meshach, and Abednego clearly demonstrate that they would rather die than engage in idolatrous worship by falling down in προσκύνησις before Nebuchadnezzar's golden image. Jesus regards Satan's request to be reverenced with προσκύνησις through prostration as an arrogation of the worship reserved for God alone (Matt 4:9–10; Luke 4:7–8).[94] McGrath draws attention to some cases where προσκύνησις before a human figure is censured due to what he takes to be the human figure's prideful opposition to God (LXX Add Esth C 5–7; Philo, *Legat.* 116),[95] but this may be saying too little. In some of these cases, such human figures do not merely oppose God, but more specifically they make themselves out to be divine (Philo, *Somn.* 2.123–32; *Legat.* 116–18), making the προσκύνησις attributed to such individuals blasphemous.[96] In certain contexts, then, προσκύνησις through prostration can certainly be regarded as an expression of the kind of worship reserved for God.

There is another problem with the supposition that only sacrifice counts as divine worship. Such a restrictive view would imply that many early Christians did not (and indeed, after the destruction of the Temple, could not) worship God since sacrifice was not a feature of their own distinctive worship gatherings.[97] But Christians certainly saw themselves as truly worshiping God when they came together for such sacral gatherings, so divine worship must include other things besides sacrifice. We noted above that hymn singing was a regular feature of early Christian worship gatherings and that the hymns of Revelation are a reflection of the hymnic praise characteristic of Christian worship. Thus, it is highly significant to find hymns sung not only about and to God alone (4:8, 11; 7:12; 11:17–18; 15:3–4; 16:5–7; 19:1–2) but also hymns sung about God and Jesus (5:13; 7:10; 11:15; 12:10–12; 19:6–8) and hymns sung about and to Jesus alone (5:9–10, 12). Furthermore, the doxologies to God and Jesus together (5:13) and to Jesus alone (1:5–6) are also highly significant, given that this specific form of praise was otherwise exclusively reserved for God. It is rather questionable for McGrath to reduce such material to mere "offering of honor or adulation" simply because it "does not incorporate . . . sacrificial elements."[98]

There are also problems with his suggestion that close parallels to the reverence of Jesus alongside God in Revelation minimize its significance. Perhaps the closest parallel worth mentioning pertains to the reverence of the Son of Man in the *Similitudes of Enoch*. Not only is the reverence of this figure closely linked to the reverence of God (*1 En.* 48:5; cf. Rev 5:13), but he is also a heavenly being (*1 En.* 39:6; 46:1; cf. Rev 1:13–16);

---

[94] See pp. 52 and 83–84 above.
[95] McGrath, *Only*, 50.
[96] For the possibility that LXX Add Esth C 5–7 may be a polemical response to ruler cult, see p. 33 above.
[97] See Larry W. Hurtado, "Early Christian Monotheism," *ExpTim* 122 (2011): 385.
[98] McGrath, *Only*, 73.

he is referred to as "son of man" (*1 En.* 46:2–4; 48:2; 62:5–14; etc.; cf. Rev 1:13; 14:14); he sits on God's own heavenly "throne of glory" (*1 En.* 45:3; 55:4; 61:8; 62:2–5; etc.; cf. Rev 3:21; 22:1, 3); and he is reverenced in similar terms as God (e.g., others "fall down and worship" God [*1 En.* 57:3; 63:1] as well as the Son of Man [*1 En.* 48:5; 62:9]; others "bless, glorify/praise, and extol" God [*1 En.* 39:12; 48:5; 61:11; etc.] as well as the Son of Man [*1 En.* 46:5; 62:6];[99] cf. Rev 4–5). Still, there is an important difference that should be noted. The character of the reverence given to the Enochic Son of Man appears somewhat opaque. In the first clear instance of reverence paid to the Enochic Son of Man, it is said that "all those who dwell upon the earth shall fall and worship before him" (*1 En.* 48:5a). On the one hand, both the allusion to Isa 49:7 where the Servant of the Lord receives homage through prostration from the nations and the contrast with the immediately juxtaposed glorification, blessing, and singing directed to God (48:5b) suggest that here political homage is rendered to the Son of Man while religious worship is directed to God. On the other hand, similar terms used for the praise of God here are also applied to the Son of Man elsewhere. Thus, in the second clear instance, after the Enochic Son of Man takes his seat on the divine throne for judgment, it is said that the kings and the mighty who stand before him "bless, glorify, and extol him who rules over everything, him who has been concealed" (62:6), which clearly refers to the Son of Man (62:7; cf. 48:6). To be sure, this display of reverence should be balanced by the larger context which emphasizes both the terror of these rulers as they stand before the Son of Man (62:4–5) and the obsequious nature of their reverence and prostration which follows as they beg for mercy (62:9). Yet this too should be compared with what follows where these rulers who are ultimately led away to eternal punishment seek respite that they may "fall and worship" before God, and "bless and glorify" him (63:1–2), which parallels their reverence of the Son of Man. Again, there is a sense in which such reverence is perhaps in part self-serving and motivated by a desire to forestall punishment (63:1, 5, 6, 8), but there is also a sense in which the worship they wish to give God now is acknowledged as the worship they should have given him in their earthly lives to avoid judgment (63:4, 7; cf. 46:6–7). The emphasis may be more on the untimely nature of their worship as opposed to its obsequious nature. As a parallel to the reverence of the Son of Man in *1 En.* 62, the implication may be that the same worship acknowledged as due to God here in *1 En.* 63 is also due to the Son of Man.

In the end, however, it should be noted that there is no clear instance of the righteous or angelic figures offering worship to the Son of Man in a liturgical context as they are often depicted doing with respect to God (*1 En.* 39:9–13; 40:3, 6; 47:2; 61:10–13; 69:25; 71:9–12).[100] Instead, in *1 En.* 61:10–11 the Son of Man/Chosen One is depicted joining

---

[99] It is not entirely clear whether God or the Son of Man is the recipient of this similarly phrased praise in *1 En.* 61:7; 69:27.

[100] Contra Charles A. Gieschen, "The Name of the Son of Man in the Parables of Enoch," in *Enoch and the Messiah Son of Man: Revisiting the Book of Parables* (ed. Gabriele Boccaccini; Grand Rapids, MI: Eerdmans, 2007), 238–49, 249; and Steven R. Scott, "The Binitarian Nature of the Book of Similitudes," *JSP* 18 (2008): 55–78, who argue that worship of "the name of the Lord of Spirits" (e.g., *1 En.* 39:9) is not worship of God, but of the Enochic Son of Man since he is given the divine name (48:2–3). But, it is not at all clear that the "name" he receives in 48:2–3 is the divine name. Furthermore, this suggestion produces odd, unlikely readings for some texts, such as the Son of

all the heavenly host in worshiping God. This is a key difference that distinguishes Jesus from the Enochic Son of Man. In Revelation, Jesus is depicted receiving worship from the righteous and from angelic beings in a liturgical setting (Rev 5:8–14; 7:10) and is never said to join these in the worship of God.[101]

Finally, there are problems with McGrath's understanding of the use of προσκυνέω in Revelation. With regard to the προσκύνησις of the beast, McGrath correctly observes that the language and imagery has in view the worship of the Roman emperor, but he seems to assume that only sacrificial worship is in view.[102] Undoubtedly, this is because the worship of the beast is clearly blasphemous, must be resisted at all costs by God's people, and leads to eternal punishment for those who engage in it, which for McGrath means sacrificial worship must be signified. But John does not specify the mode of worship when he mentions the προσκύνησις of the beast. It clearly incorporates some forms of both political homage (13:1–4) and religious worship (13:12), but in the case of the latter, what is represented in 13:12 is the imperial cult in general. Any or all of the phenomena of imperial cult worship discussed previously could have been in view, not just sacrifice. It is possible that a more specific type of worship is in view with the mention of the προσκύνησις of the image of the beast (13:14–15), but again, sacrifice is only one possibility. It certainly should not be overlooked that Rev 13:15 echoes Dan 3 which also threatens death for anyone who does not offer προσκύνησις to the image.[103] The blasphemous act depicted in Dan 3 is προσκύνησις through prostration. It seems best to conclude that the use of προσκυνέω for the worship of the beast is not necessarily meant to point to one specific type of religious worship but to the imperial cult in general and all the ways it blasphemously treats a human ruler as a divine figure.

With regard to the προσκύνησις/prostration of John's angelic guide, since McGrath considers prostration to be a very general form of reverence, he does not consider the angelic refusal of such honor to be significant for the issue of divine worship and its rightful recipients. Instead, he suggests that the angelic refusal with the encouragement for John to see himself as the angel's equal relates to the church's ongoing battle with malevolent celestial forces whose constant targeting of Christians may have led them to regard themselves as inferior to angelic beings.[104] Although there is certainly evidence of this ongoing struggle between the church and spiritual forces (12:17), this is not the issue in the angelic refusal passages. Rather, the context indicates that John is inclined to render προσκύνησις to the angel for his key role as mediator of the heavenly visions. It is not a potentially inferior view of humans that must be corrected but an overly exalted view of angels as mediators of revelation. Since the angel is simply a fellow-servant with John in the role of transmitting divine revelation and not the source of

---

Man/Elect One praising himself, "the name of the Lord of the Spirits" (61:10–11), or the Son of Man being blessed twice, first as "the name of the Lord of the Spirits" and then as "the Elect One" (40:4–5).

[101] This is also where the parallel to the reverence of Israel's king alongside God in 1 Chron 29:20 falls short, for immediately preceding this is the king's own extensive praise of God (1 Chron 29:10–19).

[102] McGrath, *Only*, 76.

[103] Beale, *Revelation*, 711–12. Numerous other allusions to the book of Daniel in Rev 13 make this association likely (see Beale, *Use*, 229–48).

[104] McGrath, *Only*, 78–80.

revelation, he redirects John to worship God, the true source of revelation. So then, in the sense that the προσκύνησις of the angel is portrayed as dangerously reverencing an angelic being for functions that belong properly to God, these passages do indeed have implications for divine worship and the rightful recipients of such.

With regard to the προσκύνησις/prostration of the Philadelphian Christians, this is clearly an instance of submission to or honor of humans *as* humans, and McGrath is right to draw attention to this example. But when he suggests that this instance of προσκύνησις/prostration indicates that this same reverence extended to God and Jesus cannot be a form of divine worship since it is not the kind of reverence reserved for God, he seems to assume that προσκύνησις/prostration signifies the same thing in every situation and context. But we maintain that προσκυνέω is a term capable of expressing various types of reverence/worship, and therefore one must consider various factors to get the sense of reverence/worship implied by the term in any one context. For example, the allusion to human subjection passages from Isaiah in Rev 3:9 is certainly a key indicator that the same idea is in mind when John writes that the Philadelphian Christians' persecutors will do προσκύνησις before them. Although this same gesture is performed before God (and Jesus), the context is very different. This gesture performed before God and Jesus in John's heavenly vision takes place in a temple setting in close connection with cultic activity, where the author uses language and imagery drawn from OT temple worship and early Christian worship. God, Jesus, and Christians may all be depicted as appropriate recipients of προσκύνησις/prostration in Revelation, but it is the context that clarifies the nature of this reverence, and Christians are not depicted receiving this reverence in a cultic context.[105]

Besides the use of the term προσκυνέω, there is little correspondence between Rev 3:9 and Rev 4–5 to suggest the two texts should be closely read in relation to one another. By contrast, numerous parallels between Rev 4–5 and Rev 13 show that the author intended to draw these two units together as the dragon and the beast are clearly depicted as evil counterparts to God and the Lamb.[106] The Lamb receives power and authority from God (5:7, 12), as does the beast from the dragon (13:2). The Lamb was slain (ἐσφαγμένον) and yet lives (5:6), so similarly the beast suffers a fatal blow (ἐσφαγμένην) but recovers (13:3). The Lamb redeems those from every tribe, language, people, and nation (5:9), and the beast exercises authority over every tribe, people, language, and nation (13:7). Finally, and most significantly, just as both God and the Lamb are worshiped with hymns (4:8, 11; 5:9–10, 12, 13) and προσκύνησις

---

[105] The same misunderstanding is apparent when McGrath downplays the significance of Jesus sharing the divine throne in light of 3:21 where Christians are said to share Jesus's throne as Jesus himself shares God's throne (*Only*, 75). But it is not without significance that this throne-sharing idea is ultimately portrayed in different ways for the various figures involved. For Christians, the fulfillment of this text is met in 20:4 (see Laszlo Gallusz, *The Throne Motif in the Book of Revelation* [LNTS 487; London: Bloomsbury T&T Clark, 2014], 195; Koester, *Revelation*, 771), where they reign with Jesus, but on multiple separate thrones. For Jesus, on the other hand, the language of 3:21 is not loosened, as can be seen in 22:1, 3 which speak of the one "throne of God and of the Lamb." Just as with the honor of προσκύνησις, Christians do not share the honor of a throne in precisely the same way that God and Jesus do.

[106] Koester, *Revelation*, 577; Aune, *Revelation*, 2:726; Roloff, *Revelation*, 155.

(4:10; 5:14), so too are the dragon and the beast worshiped with hymn-like praise (13:4) and προσκύνησις (13:4, 8, 12, 15). To suggest, as McGrath does, that the reverence of the evil figures in Rev 13 constitutes divine worship while the reverence of God and Jesus in Rev 4–5 is something less than divine worship is to miss the force and correspondence of the parallels. Both sets of powers are depicted receiving both political homage as well as religious worship through προσκύνησις; one set receives such absolute devotion legitimately, the other receives it blasphemously.

In light of the ongoing, polarizing distinction that continues to be made throughout Revelation between the true worship of God and Jesus and the false worship of Satan, the beast and its image, the dually emphasized angelic refusals of προσκύνησις with the command to give προσκύνησις to God undoubtedly speaks to the issue of true and false worship as well. Neither the blatant idolatrous προσκύνησις of Satan, demons/idols, the Rome-like beast and its image, nor even the seemingly innocent yet potentially dangerous προσκύνησις of God's angelic mediators is tolerated in Revelation.[107] When John depicts Jesus as a recipient of such reverence in a cultic context in close association with other cultic activity, he certainly intends to portray Jesus as a recipient of the kind of worship typically reserved for God alone.

Still, there is one more problem that must be addressed. If Jesus is meant to be included as a recipient of προσκύνησις with God in 5:14, why in 5:8, in contrast to all other instances of heavenly worship of God in which both πίπτω and προσκυνέω appear, is it said that the elders and living creatures only "fall down" (ἔπεσαν) before Jesus with no mention of the key term προσκυνέω? McGrath follows Aune who remarks that the verb προσκυνέω is "conspicuously absent" in this reverence of Jesus and thus suggests "a degree of subordination."[108] This is indeed a potentially significant detail that is generally passed over in commentaries. I suggest, however, that there is a reasonable explanation for the absence of the verb προσκυνέω, one which has nothing to do with Jesus's status.

As discussed above, the general pattern for the use of προσκυνέω in heavenly worship scenes is as follows: a group of worshipers offer hymnic praise, which leads another group of worshipers to respond with προσκύνησις and with their own hymnic praise (4:8–11; 5:13–14; 7:10–12; 11:15–18; 19:1–4).[109] So, for example, in 7:10–12, heavenly saints initiate hymnic praise, crying out, "Salvation belongs to our God who is seated on the throne, and to the Lamb!," which is immediately followed by the angels, the elders, and the living creatures falling down in προσκύνησις and offering their own hymnic praise: "Amen! Blessing and glory and wisdom and thanksgiving and honor and power and might be to our God forever and ever! Amen." The pattern suggests that as a response to another group's hymnic praise, προσκύνησις is intended to function in part as an affirmation of the content of that praise. This is supported by the fact that the affirmatory "amen" often appears with προσκύνησις in heavenly worship as it does here in 7:11–12 (cf. 5:14; 19:4).

---

[107] Bauckham, "Worship," 329.
[108] Aune, *Revelation*, 1:355; McGrath, *Only*, 122, n. 14.
[109] See pp. 141–42 above.

Given this pattern, I propose that the reason the term προσκυνέω does not appear in 5:8 is because the prostration of the elders and living creatures here is not preceded by any hymnic praise, and therefore there is no praise content to affirm with προσκύνησις as elsewhere in the heavenly worship scenes. Instead, what moves them to prostrate themselves before Jesus is the crucial act of Jesus taking the scroll from God, signifying his unique qualification to bring about the final stages of God's plan of judgment and redemption for the world. This prostration, then, is no less an act of worship than the προσκύνησις/prostration extended to God.

G. Conclusion

When J. Lionel North says that there are no instances in the NT in which Jesus is worshiped as divine in his reception of προσκύνησις,[110] he makes no mention at all of Rev 5:14 and thereby overlooks one of the clearest NT passages suggesting otherwise. Notwithstanding the one clear instance where προσκύνησις is rendered to humans with no implications whatsoever for divine worship (3:9), John has otherwise used προσκυνέω to portray the idolatrous worship of Satan, demons/idols, the Rome-like beast and its image, the misguided worship of an angelic mediator, and the true worship of God with Jesus's inclusion in Rev 5:14. In a book such as Revelation which emphatically condemns various types of illegitimate worship along with any hints of association with these, from traditional pagan worship (2:14, 20; 9:20; 21:8; 22:15),[111] to imperial cult worship (13:12, 15; 14:9-11; 16:2; cf. 17:2; 18:3, etc.), to potentially dangerously high views of God's angelic servants (19:10; 22:8-9), the cultic worship of Jesus with God in his heavenly temple through hymnic praise and προσκύνησις is certainly remarkable and undoubtedly signifies the inclusion of Jesus in divine worship.

John is careful to present Jesus not as an alternative recipient of divine worship apart from God but as one who is legitimately included within the worship of the one God.[112] Thus, Jesus is indeed depicted receiving the same kind of worship as God (5:8-12), but only after God himself is worshiped (4:8-11), and in such a way that Jesus's own worship "leads to the joint worship of God and Christ, in a formula in which God retains the primacy"[113] (5:13; cf. 7:10; 11:15; 14:4; etc.). This representation

---

[110] North, "Jesus," 189.
[111] Yet, with some of these texts, there may be some overlap with imperial cult worship (Osborne, *Revelation*, 144).
[112] Bauckham, *Theology*, 60-61; Hurtado, *Lord*, 593-94.
[113] Bauckham, "Worship," 331 (contra Horst, who unconvincingly attempted to downplay Rev 5:13-14 by interpreting it as worship of God in/through Christ [*Proskynein*, 281]). Bauckham also observes that the same concern to represent Jesus as a legitimate recipient of divine worship within the worship of God himself by aligning him closely to God as a unity may be behind the peculiar phenomenon in a few passages where singular pronouns and verbs may very well have their referents in both God and Christ as a unity (e.g., 11:15; 14:1; 21:22; 22:3-4); cf. Holtz, *Christologie*, 201-3. It is possible, then, that one of two passages that McGrath argues alone gives clear evidence of the kind of worship reserved for God (22:3) may actually be applied to God and Christ as a unity: "the throne of God and of the Lamb will be in [the New Jerusalem], and his servants will worship him (οἱ δοῦλοι αὐτοῦ λατρεύσουσιν αὐτῷ)." Also noteworthy is the close link of Jesus to God in the

of Jesus as worthy of divine worship alongside God in Revelation, through hymnic praises containing elements consonant with early Christian worship, is both reflective of Christian devotional attitudes toward God and Jesus,[114] and likely intended as a model for proper worship.[115] Whether or not προσκύνησις/prostration itself was a regular feature of early Christian worship, at the very least, the attitude expressed by this gesture in Revelation is certainly to be imitated. The thrust of Revelation is that Christians are to give complete devotion and allegiance, depicted through both political προσκύνησις and cultic προσκύνησις, to God and to Jesus alone, the only true divine sovereigns.

---

sharing of the divine designations, "Alpha and Omega" and "Beginning and End" (1:8; 21:6; 22:13); see Bauckham, *Theology*, 25–28, 54–58.

[114] Bauckham, "Worship," 331.
[115] Hurtado, *Lord*, 593.

Conclusion

In the introduction to our study, we presented the question of whether the numerous depictions of Jesus as an object of προσκυνέω in the NT might suggest his divine status and/or his worthiness to receive divine worship. This proved to be a much more complex matter than comprehensive treatments of the issue to date (e.g., Johannes Horst, Heinrich Greeven, J. Lionel North, James Dunn), which are largely far too brief and come to very different conclusions, give it credit. In our study, guided by a number of key factors in our exegetical and literary-critical analysis,[1] we aimed to give more detailed attention to the NT προσκύνησις of Jesus passages themselves and to how they are to be interpreted within the particular NT writing in which they appear. In short, we have argued that in their own particular ways, each NT writing ultimately portrays Jesus as one uniquely and closely linked to the God of Israel in his reception of προσκύνησις and in such a way that he is presented as a divine figure included with God as a legitimate recipient of the kind of worship and acknowledgment that is otherwise thought to be reserved for God alone.

A. Summary of findings

In the Gospel of Mark, Jesus's reception of προσκύνησις from the Gerasene demoniac who "takes orders" from Jesus as a mighty sovereign (Mark 5:6) and from the Roman soldiers who make a mockery of Jesus's alleged royal status (15:19) indicate that such reverence is in some sense to be understood in political terms. When other aspects of Mark's larger christological portrait are taken into account, however, it becomes clear that Jesus is not merely considered worthy of such reverence as an ordinary human sovereign but as the transcendent heavenly Son of God, who is uniquely recognized as such by other supernatural beings (1:11; 3:11; 9:7), including the Gerasene demoniac (5:7). Jesus, the Son of God, whom the Gerasene demoniac recognizes and reverences as one who wages cosmic war with Satan (cf. 3:23–27), and whom the Roman soldiers thus ironically reverence more befittingly than they realize, is superior to the angels (13:32) and is destined to share cosmic reign with God in heaven enthroned at his side (14:61–62). What the Jewish authorities regard here as a blasphemous encroachment on God's unique sovereignty (14:63–64), Mark no doubt intends to be understood as Jesus's legitimate claim to divine status as God's Son and thus for his reception of προσκύνησις as the Son of the Most High God to be understood accordingly.

---

[1] See pp. 7–10 above.

In the Gospel of Matthew, Jesus frequently receives προσκύνησις throughout the Gospel narrative, from magi who pay homage to him at his birth as the true King of the Jews (Matt 2:2, 11; cf. 2:8), from various suppliants who approach him reverently with confidence that he can grant their extraordinary requests (8:2; 9:18; 15:25; 20:20), from his disciples who reverence him as the Son of God in response to his Yahweh-like sovereignty over the sea (14:33), and again from his disciples who reverence him at his resurrection appearances where he proclaims his Yahweh-like cosmic sovereignty (28:9, 17). Significantly, in the only other uses of προσκυνέω, προσκύνησις represents a form of reverence that is firmly denied to Satan since it amounts to an idolatrous attempt to receive that which is reserved for God alone (4:9–10; cf. 18:26), making Matthew's frequent depiction of Jesus as a legitimate recipient of προσκύνησις all the more striking. Although it is far from clear that all of Matthew's προσκύνησις of Jesus passages themselves evince cultic connotations, Matthew does give Jesus a central place in the devotional life of the believing community (18:19–20; 23:8–10; 28:19) and hints at Jesus's worthiness to receive cultic worship typically reserved for God (e.g., cries to Jesus evocative of psalmic prayers to God [8:25; 14:30; 15:25; etc.] and praise of Jesus related to psalmic praise of God [21:16]). Some of these instances are closely linked to προσκύνησις of Jesus passages (14:30–33; 15:22–25; 28:17–20). Yet without denying this association, we argued that the primary overarching significance of the Matthean Jesus's reception of προσκύνησις is that he is linked with God as co-sovereign over all creation and through his reception of προσκύνησις is gradually shown to be worthy to be acknowledged as such. Whereas Satan is denied the προσκύνησις that is due to God alone as Lord of all, God's Son, Jesus, who rules over Jews and Gentiles, has authority over disease, demons, death, wind and sea, and ultimately has all authority over heaven and earth, exercises divine lordship and therefore is included as a legitimate recipient of such προσκύνησις otherwise reserved for God alone.

In Luke-Acts, the use of προσκυνέω for cultic worship of God (Luke 4:8; Acts 8:27; 24:11), idolatrous worship of false gods (Luke 4:7; Acts 7:43), and a form of reverence considered inappropriate for mere men (Acts 10:25–26), makes it very likely that the use of the term for the disciples' reverence of the risen and ascended Lord Jesus (Luke 24:52) is likewise to be interpreted in the stronger sense of the term. Indeed, a closer examination of the context of this προσκύνησις of Jesus passage shows Jesus is not only depicted as a supernatural being (Luke 24:15, 31, 36–37) but as one who is closely and uniquely linked to God (Jesus's unprecedented role in the uniquely divine prerogative of bestowing God's Spirit [Luke 24:49]) and who receives προσκύνησις in language drawn from a Jewish text describing the cultic προσκύνησις of Israel's God at his Temple (Luke 24:50–53; cf. Sir 50:20–22). This hint of the risen Lord Jesus as one worthy of the kind of worship reserved for God, most clearly expressed in cultic worship, is substantiated by and more clearly seen in what follows in Acts. The risen and ascended Lord Jesus, enthroned at God's side in heaven (Acts 2:33; 5:31; cf. 7:55–56) from whence he bestows God's Spirit (2:33) and rules as Lord of all (10:36), is the one in whose name the community of believers perform mighty works (3:6–7; 16:18; cf. 4:30), proclaim forgiveness of sins (10:43), baptize converts (2:38; 8:16; 10:48; 19:5), and "call upon" as Lord for salvation (2:21; 22:16; cf. 7:59; 9:14, 21), which is clearly to be understood in the same OT terms of Israel's cultic "call upon the name of the Lord (i.e., Yahweh)."

In the Gospel of John, along with the use of προσκυνέω for cultic worship of God (John 4:20–24; 12:20), one also finds the use of προσκυνέω for the reverence Jesus receives from the formerly blind man (9:38). Although it is unlikely that this individual as a character in the story renders προσκύνησις to Jesus as one whom he takes to be a divine figure and/or as one worthy of the divine worship elsewhere directed to God in John, the reader is in a much better position to discern the deeper significance behind such reverential language. He/She knows very well that the Son of Man Jesus, in whom the formerly blind man puts his faith (9:35–38), has a heavenly origin (3:13; 6:62; cf. 9:39) and has come to, and is able to, make God known (1:51) as one who has a share with God the Father in his identity as θεός (1:1, 18). He/She perceives the significance of one who was once blind but now rather suggestively "sees" keenly acknowledging Jesus better than he realized when he affirms him as one "from God" (9:33), confesses him as κύριε (9:38a), and reverences him with προσκύνησις (9:38b). Since Jesus is the true temple (2:21) not only in the sense of being the true place where God is worshiped as Father in Spirit and truth (4:20–24) but also in the sense of being the true dwelling place of God himself (1:14), he is both one who brings people into true fellowship and worship of God as Father and one who, because of this and because of his share in the θεός identity, is himself worthy to have a share in such worship.

In the Epistle to the Hebrews, Jesus ("the Son") receives προσκύνησις from all the angels at God's command (Heb 1:6). This is not only clearly indicative of Jesus's superiority to the angels, but also, with the support of other key details in the context of Heb 1, ultimately an image of Jesus as a divine figure worthy of the kind of worship typically reserved for God. He who had a role in the uniquely divine act of creation (1:2c, 10–12) and stood to inherit all things (1:2b) is now enthroned in heaven at the right hand of God (1:3d, 13), ascribed divine titles such as "θεός" and "κύριος" (1:8, 10), and receives προσκύνησις from all the angels of God (1:6). Although it is not clear whether or not Hebrews envisages a heavenly sanctuary setting for the angels' προσκύνησις of Jesus, the image nevertheless most closely approximates numerous Jewish and Christian depictions of God enthroned in heaven being worshiped by his heavenly entourage and thus is strongly suggestive of Jesus's worthiness to receive the kind of worship typically reserved for God.

Finally, in the book of Revelation, the frequent use of προσκυνέω is especially (though not entirely [cf. Rev 3:9]) employed for the purpose of distinguishing between true and false worship. Along with what is clearly understood to be idolatrous worship of Satan, demons, and idols (9:20; 13:4), Revelation also condemns the false, idolatrous worship of "the beast and its image" (13:4, 8, 12, 15; 14:9, 11; 16:2; 19:20; 20:4), a symbol of the ultimate eschatological, blasphemous enemy of God, whose power and renown are clearly reflective of the Roman Empire/emperor and the imperial cult. Even the seemingly innocent προσκύνησις of angels (19:10; 22:8) is ultimately rejected since it borders on an overly exalted esteem for their revelatory role, which, as the angels' explanation suggests, likens them more to humans as fellow-transmitters of revelation than to God, who is the source of revelation. By contrast, it is God whom all humanity is called upon to give προσκύνησις (14:7; cf. 15:4; 19:10; 22:9) and who receives such worship and allegiance by his heavenly entourage, who worship him with hymns and προσκύνησις as he is enthroned in his heavenly temple/royal court (4:10; 7:11; 11:16; 19:4; cf. 11:1). Significantly, included alongside God as the only other legitimate recipient of such heavenly worship otherwise reserved for God is Jesus ("the Lamb"), who like God and with God receives hymnic praise (5:9–10, 12, 13; 7:10; 11:15; 12:10–12; 19:6–8; cf. 1:5–6) as well as προσκύνησις (5:14).

Throughout our investigation, we have challenged views, refined analyses, and/or offered new insights, both in our engagement with cursory discussions of the προσκύνησις of Jesus in all the NT writings (e.g., Greeven, North, Dunn) and in our engagement with more detailed and focused discussions of the προσκύνησις of Jesus in individual NT works (e.g., Leim [Gospel of Matthew], Steegen [Gospel of John], Schenck [Epistle to the Hebrews], McGrath [book of Revelation], and esp. Horst) in support of our own argument that each of the NT writings, in their own unique ways, presents the Jesus who receives προσκύνησις as a divine figure uniquely and closely related to God.

B. Significant points of commonality

While each NT writing's christological portrait of Jesus as a recipient of προσκύνησις is ultimately presented in its own distinct ways, there are yet significant points of commonality shared between them. The Jesus who receives προσκύνησις is often presented as a ruler figure. In each case, however, as we have argued, it is clear that he is no ordinary human ruler. He is one who wages cosmic war with Satan and his demonic troops and proves to be the stronger one (Mark); he is one who not only rules over Jews and Gentiles but also has authority over disease, demons, death, wind and sea, and ultimately over everything (Matthew); he is one who is more clearly recognized by his disciples following his resurrection and ascension as Lord of all (Luke-Acts); he is one who reigns in heaven superior to the angels (Hebrews); and in contrast to Satan and the Rome-like beast, it is he who with God reigns in heaven and is worthy of ultimate allegiance from all creation (Revelation).

Jesus is often presented as the messianic, royal Son of God, and yet it is clear that transcendent aspects of Jesus's identity as such show that he is far more than just a human messiah. He is the Son of God who is uniquely recognized as such by other supernatural beings (Mark); he is the Son of God who uniquely exercises Yahweh-like authority over wind and sea as well as over heaven and earth (Matthew); significantly, among a number of the NT writings, he is the Son of God who has the exceptional privilege of sitting at God's right hand enthroned in heaven and of having a share with God in the highly significant designation κύριος (Mark 12:35–37; 14:61–62; Matt 22:41–46; 26:63–64; Luke 20:41–44; 22:69–70; Acts 2:33–36 [as well as θεός (Heb 1:3–13)]). It is this transcendent Son of God destined for cosmic lordship with God in heaven whose exceptional authority is recognized through προσκύνησις by demons (Mark), by Jesus's followers (Matthew, Luke-Acts), and by angels (Hebrews).

In line with this last point, Jesus is frequently portrayed in various ways as one closely and uniquely associated with God, often in ways that surpass what is said of other exalted figures in Jewish literature. Some of the more notable examples include the following: he walks upon and rescues others from the sea as only God does (Matt 14:22–33; cf. Mark 6:45–52; John 6:16–21); he bestows the Spirit of God as only God himself does (Luke 24:49; Acts 2:33; John 16:7; 15:26; 20:22; cf. Mark 1:8 par.); he has OT Yahweh texts applied to him in such a way that he is suggestively named as the κύριος of the OT text (Matt 3:3 par.; Acts 2:21); he is ascribed a role in the uniquely divine act of creation of all things (John 1:3; Heb 1:2, 10); and he is ascribed a place in the uniquely divine exercise of authority and lordship over all things (Matt 28:18; cf. Acts 10:36), undoubtedly symbolically represented by the common motif of Jesus's heavenly enthronement at the right hand of God (along with the passages mentioned above, cf. Rev 3:21; 22:1, 3). Even though not all of these are directly or closely related to προσκύνησις of Jesus passages (a number of them, however, are), they nevertheless certainly enhance the characterization of Jesus as one exceptionally linked to God in ways that signify his divine status and thus give deeper significance to such a one being a worthy recipient of προσκύνησις.

In view of the foregoing, it is not surprising to find that the προσκύνησις Jesus is portrayed receiving is at times either overtly or, more often it seems, suggestively characterized as cultic worship and thus takes on the sense of the most concrete and unambiguous expression of worship that is to be given to God alone. This is most clearly seen in Revelation where Jesus is included with God as a recipient of hymnic praise and προσκύνησις in God's heavenly temple/royal court (5:13–14). In Luke-Acts, an allusion to Sir 50:20–22 at Luke 24:50–53 is highly suggestive of cultic overtones in the disciples' προσκύνησις of the risen and ascended Lord Jesus, this sense being further supported by what follows in Acts as, for example, the heavenly enthroned Lord Jesus is cultically "called upon" for salvation (Acts 2:21; 7:59; 9:14, 21; 22:16). In John's Gospel, the use of προσκυνέω for the reverence of Jesus (John 9:38), a term exclusively used elsewhere in John for what is clearly cultic worship of God (4:20–24; 12:20), may very well be suggestive of Jesus's worthiness to receive cultic worship (cf. prayer in Jesus's name [14:13–14; 15:16; 16:23–24, 26]). In other cases, the προσκύνησις of Jesus may perhaps be suggestive of cultic worship, as in Hebrews, if, as some have argued, a heavenly sanctuary setting is implied in the angels' προσκύνησις of the heavenly enthroned Jesus (Heb 1:6; cf. e.g., 8:1–2) or the προσκύνησις of Jesus is occasionally associated with material suggestive of Jesus as a recipient of cultic worship, as in Matthew's Gospel, when προσκύνησις of Jesus appears alongside cries to Jesus reminiscent of psalmic prayers to God (14:30–33; 15:22–25) and alongside baptism in his name (28:17–20).

Lastly, Jesus's divine status and/or worthiness to receive divine worship are/is ultimately to be understood in terms of his relation to God and in such a way that God retains the primacy. Thus, he is enthroned in heaven reigning over all things, not as an independent deity but as one seated at the right hand of God; he is ascribed a role in the creation of all things, not in contrast to God but as one through whom God created; he shares along with God the divine titles κύριος and θεός, with the distinction that Jesus is Son and God is Father, Jesus is θεός and God is his θεός, God is the sender and Jesus is the one sent, and so on. Similarly, with regard to divine worship, Jesus is worshiped in heaven with hymnic praise and προσκύνησις, not as one who replaces or competes with the worship of God but as one included in the worship of God, who is the first to receive such worship, followed by the worship of Jesus, and culminating in the joint worship of God and Jesus (Rev 4–5); his reception of προσκύνησις by the angels as he is enthroned in heaven beside God, which is reminiscent of the common image in Jewish and Christian literature of God enthroned in heaven as he alone receives such worship from his heavenly entourage, is commanded and thus sanctioned by God himself (Heb 1:6); Sir 50:20–22's depiction of Israel's cultic worship of God with προσκύνησις and blessing is modified to include Jesus, as his disciples give προσκύνησις to him as the risen and ascended Lord and bless God in his Temple (Luke 24:52–53); and Jesus suggestively receives the kind of worship through προσκύνησις that is otherwise understood to be reserved for God (John 9:38; cf. 4:20–24; 12:20), but again, he does not replace or compete with the worship of God, rather it is understood that God's will is for Jesus to be honored, and failure to do so is failure to honor God (cf. 5:23).

C. Final overall assessment

In the only other truly detailed study on the προσκύνησις of Jesus in all the NT writings to date, Johannes Horst by and large concluded that at most Jesus's reception of προσκύνησις is to be understood as worship of God in Jesus. While he was often inclined to acknowledge that the προσκύνησις of Jesus passages have "Anbetungscharakter,"[2] he was clearly disinclined to interpret these passages in such a way that Jesus himself is regarded as a legitimate recipient of the kind of worship reserved for God. In our assessment of the NT material, we have attempted to demonstrate that the evidence by and large suggests otherwise.

It is quite clear in the NT writings examined in our study that the God of Israel alone is truly God (Mark 12:29, 32; John 17:3) and thus he alone is worthy of ultimate allegiance and worship (Matt 4:10; Luke 4:8; John 4:20–24; Rev 14:7; 15:4; cf. Mark 12:30 par.), over against all other so-called gods who receive such reverence as an idolatrous, blasphemous arrogation of that which is reserved for God (Matt 4:9–10; Luke 4:7–8; Acts 7:40–43; 12:22–23; Rev 9:20; 13:1–15; 14:9–11; cf. Acts 14:15; 19:26). And yet, Jesus emerges from these writings as an exceptional figure, as one more closely and uniquely related to God in his godlike characteristics than any other figure and as one to be included with God as a legitimate recipient of divine worship, which is particularly clearly manifested in those instances where he is portrayed as a recipient of the kind of cultic, devotional worship that is otherwise to be reserved for God alone.

Our overall assessment of the προσκύνησις of Jesus in the NT writings is most closely aligned with the views of Richard Bauckham and Larry Hurtado on divine Christology in early Christianity. Both Bauckham and Hurtado agree that the NT

---

[2] Horst, *Proskynein*, 186–87, 236.

writings reflect Christian views of Jesus as a divine being and that his divinity is uniquely conceptualized within the context of Jewish monotheism. Although they differ from one another to some degree over where the weight and emphasis lies in early Christianity's distinctive articulation of Jesus's divinity, both perspectives ultimately mutually reinforce each other in explicating the Christian view of Jesus's unique inclusion with the God of Israel as a divine figure worthy of divine worship. Bauckham stresses that just as Jews distinguished the God of Israel, the one true God, from all other reality, including so-called gods among pagans, particularly by highlighting his unique identity as the sole creator and ruler of all things, so too when Christians uniquely affirm Jesus's inclusion in the creation and rule of all things, they thereby affirm Jesus's unique inclusion in the divine identity.[3] Hurtado emphasizes that just as Jews uniquely distinguished the God of Israel from all other beings by their insistence that cultic, corporate worship is to be reserved for him alone, so too when Christians uniquely include Jesus alongside God as a legitimate recipient of such exclusive worship otherwise reserved for God alone, they thereby acknowledge Jesus's divine status.[4] Much of what we have argued throughout our own focused study of the προσκύνησις of Jesus in the NT is in line with these two interrelated ideas. Jesus is presented as one uniquely and closely linked to God in a number of ways, particularly—as it relates to προσκύνησις—as one who (is destined to) participate(s) with God in cosmic lordship over all things, typically expressed through the potent image of his heavenly enthronement beside God. Jesus is also both suggestively and overtly depicted as a legitimate recipient of cultic worship with God in some instances where he is described as a recipient of προσκύνησις.

In light of the whole of our discussion, προσκυνέω does indeed appear to be quite an apt term for characterizing the worship that Jesus is worthy to receive in these six NT writings. Just as many in antiquity would acknowledge their superiors with προσκύνησις, especially those who rule over them as their kings and lords, so is Jesus aptly depicted as one worthy of προσκύνησις in view of his superior rank as a mighty ruler and one with great power and authority. Yet Jesus's lordship clearly surpasses those of human rulers, and correspondingly the προσκύνησις of which he is portrayed to be a worthy recipient more closely resembles numerous other instances in antiquity where προσκύνησις is given to the most supreme rulers and authorities in the ancient world—the gods. For Christians, it is the God of Israel and his only Son Jesus who are the only true divine sovereigns worthy of divine worship, and the inclusion of Jesus with God as a recipient of προσκύνησις in the NT writings proves to be one significant way in which they affirmed this.

---

[3] Bauckham, *Jesus*, 1–31.
[4] Hurtado, *One*, passim.

Bibliography

Primary sources

The Ante-Nicene Fathers. Edited by A. Roberts and J. Donaldson. 1885–1887. 10 vols. Repr., Peabody, MA: Hendrickson, 1994.

Appian. *Roman History*. Translated by B. McGing. 4 vols. Loeb Classical Library. Cambridge, MA: Harvard University Press, 1912–1913.

Babrius and Phaedrus. *Fables*. Translated by B. E. Perry. Loeb Classical Library. Cambridge, MA: Harvard University Press, 1965.

Chariton. *Callirhoe*. Translated by G. P. Goold. Loeb Classical Library. Cambridge, MA: Harvard University Press, 1995.

The Dead Sea Scrolls: Study Edition. Edited by F. G. Martínez and E. J. C. Tigchelaar. 2 vols. Leiden: Brill, 2000.

Dio Cassius. *Roman History*. Translated by E. Cary and H. B. Foster. 9 vols. Loeb Classical Library. Cambridge, MA: Harvard University Press, 1914–1927.

Diodorus Siculus. *Library of History*. Translated by C. H. Oldfather et al. 12 vols. Loeb Classical Library. London: Heinemann, 1933–1967.

Dionysius of Halicarnassus. *Roman Antiquities*. Translated by E. Carey. 7 vols. Loeb Classical Library. Cambridge, MA: Harvard University Press, 1937–1950.

Epictetus. *The Discourses as Reported by Arrian, the Manual, and Fragments*. Translated by W. A. Oldfather. 2 vols. Loeb Classical Library. London: Heinemann, 1925–1928.

Die Fragmente der griechischen Historiker. Edited by F. Jacoby. Leiden: Brill, 1923–1958.

Herodotus. *The Persian Wars*. Translated by A. D. Godley. 4 vols. Loeb Classical Library. Cambridge, MA: Harvard University Press, 1920–1925.

Josephus. Translated by H. St. J. Thackeray et al. 13 vols. Loeb Classical Library. Cambridge, MA: Harvard University Press, 1926–1965.

"The Letter of Pseudo-Aristeas." Pages 551–606 in *An Introduction to the Old Testament in Greek*. Edited by H. St. J. Thackeray. Repr., New York: Ktav, 1968.

Longus and Xenophon of Ephesus. *Daphnis and Chloe. Anthia and Habrocomes*. Translated by J. Henderson. Loeb Classical Library. Cambridge, MA: Harvard University Press, 2009.

Lucian. Translated by A. M. Harmon et al. 8 vols. Loeb Classical Library. London: Heinemann, 1913–1936.

A New English Translation of the Septuagint: And the Other Greek Translations Traditionally Included under That Title. Edited by A. Pietersma and B. G. Wright. Oxford: Oxford University Press, 2007.

Novum Testamentum Graece. Edited by B. Aland, K. Aland, J. Karavidopoulos, C. M. Martini, and B. M. Metzger. 28th Rev. ed. Stuttgart: Deutsche Bibelgesellschaft, 2012.

The Old Testament Pseudepigrapha. Edited by J. H. Charlesworth. 2 vols. Garden City, NY: Doubleday, 1983–1985.

Ovid. *Metamorphoses*. Translated by F. J. Miller. 2 vols. Loeb Classical Library. Cambridge, MA: Harvard University Press, 1916.

Philo. Translated by F. H. Colson et al. 10 vols. and 2 supplemental vols. Loeb Classical Library. Cambridge, MA: Harvard University Press, 1929–1962.

Plutarch. *Plutarch's Lives*. Translated by B. Perrin. 11 vols. Loeb Classical Library. London: Heinemann, 1914–1926.

Plutarch. *Plutarch's Moralia*. Translated by F. C. Babbitt et al. 17 vols. Loeb Classical Library. London: Heinemann, 1927–1976.

Polyaenus. *Stratagemata*. Edited by E. Woelfflin and J. Melber. Leipzig: Teubner, 1887.

Polybius. *The Histories*. Translated by W. R. Paton. 6 vols. Loeb Classical Library. Cambridge, MA: Harvard University Press, 2010–2012.

Select Papyri. Translated by A. S. Hunt and C. C. Edgar. 3 vols. Loeb Classical Library. London: Heinemann, 1932–1941.

Septuaginta: Id est Vetus Testamentum graece iuxta LXX interpretes. Edited by A. Rahlfs. Rev. ed. 2 vols. in 1. Stuttgart: Deutsche Bibelgesellschaft, 2006.

Strabo. *Geography*. Translated by H. L. Jones. 8 vols. Loeb Classical Library. London: Heinemann, 1917–1932.

The Testament of Abraham. Texts and Studies 2/2. Edited by M. R. James. Cambridge: Cambridge University Press, 1892.

The Testaments of the Twelve Patriarchs: A Critical Edition of the Greek Text. Edited by M. de Jonge. Pseudepigrapha Veteris Testamenti Graece 1/2. Leiden: Brill, 1978.

Testamentum Iobi, Apocalypsis Baruchi Graece. Edited by S. P. Brock and J.-C. Picard. Pseudepigrapha Veteris Testamenti Graece 2. Leiden: Brill, 1967.

Xenophon. *Anabasis*. Translated by C. L. Brownson. Loeb Classical Library. Cambridge, MA: Harvard University Press, 1998.

Secondary sources

Abbott, E. A. *Johannine Vocabulary: A Comparison of the Words of the Fourth Gospel with Those of the Three*. London: A&C Black, 1905.

Adams, E. "The Coming of the Son of Man in Mark's Gospel." *Tyndale Bulletin* 56 (2005): 39–61.

Allen, D. M. *Deuteronomy and Exhortation in Hebrews*. Wissenschaftliche Untersuchungen zum Neuen Testament 2/238. Tübingen: Mohr Siebeck, 2008.

Allen, D. M. "Who, What, and Why? The Worship of the Firstborn in Hebrews 1:6." Pages 159–75 in *Mark, Manuscripts, and Monotheism: Essays in Honor of Larry W. Hurtado*. Edited by C. Keith and D. T. Roth. Library of New Testament Studies 528. London: Bloomsbury T&T Clark, 2015.

Allison, D. C., Jr., *Studies in Matthew: Interpretation Past and Present*. Grand Rapids, MI: Baker, 2005.

Alsup, J. E. *The Post-Resurrection Appearance Stories of the Gospel-Tradition*. Calwer theologische Monographien 5. Stuttgart: Calwer, 1975.

Andriessen, P. C. B. "La teneur judéo-chrétienne de He I 6 et II 14B–III 2." *Novum Testamentum* 18 (1976): 293–313.

Arnold, C. E. *The Colossian Syncretism: The Interface between Christianity and Folk Belief at Colossae*. Wissenschaftliche Untersuchungen zum Neuen Testament 2/77. Tübingen: Mohr Siebeck, 1995.

Attridge, H. W. *The Epistle to the Hebrews: A Commentary on the Epistle to the Hebrews*. Hermeneia. Philadelphia, PA: Fortress, 1989.

Aune, D. E. "The Influence of Roman Imperial Court Ceremonial on the Apocalypse of John." *Biblical Research* 28 (1983): 5–26.

Aune, D. E. "Worship, Early Christian." Pages 973–89 in vol. 6 of *The Anchor Bible Dictionary*. Edited by D. N. Freedman. 6 vols. New York: Doubleday, 1992.

Aune, D. E. *Revelation*. 3 vols. Word Biblical Commentary 52A-C. Dallas, TX: Word Books; Nashville, TN: Thomas Nelson, 1997–1998.

Bacon, B. W. "Heb 1, 10-12 and the Septuagint Rendering of Ps 102, 23." *Zeitschrift für die neutestamentliche Wissenschaft und die Kunde der älteren Kirche* 3 (1902): 280–85.

Badian, E. "Alexander the Great between Two Thrones and Heaven: Variations on an Old Theme." Pages 245–62 in *Alexander the Great: A Reader*. Edited by I. Worthington. 1st ed. London: Routledge, 2003.

Balsdon, J. P. V. D. "The 'Divinity' of Alexander." *Historia: Zeitschrift für Alte Geschichte* 1 (1950): 363–88.

Barker, M. "The High Priest and the Worship of Jesus." Pages 93–111 in *The Jewish Roots of Christological Monotheism: Papers from the St. Andrews Conference on the Historical Origins of the Worship of Jesus*. Edited by C. C. Newman, J. R. Davila, and G. S. Lewis. Supplements to the Journal for the Study of Judaism 63. Leiden: Brill, 1999.

Barnard, J. A. *The Mysticism of Hebrews: Exploring the Role of Jewish Apocalyptic Mysticism in the Epistle to the Hebrews*. Wissenschaftliche Untersuchungen zum Neuen Testament 2/331. Tübingen: Mohr Siebeck, 2012.

Barrett, C. K. *The Gospel According to St. John: An Introduction with Commentary and Notes on the Greek Text*. 2nd ed. Philadelphia, PA: Westminster, 1978.

Barrett, C. K. *A Critical and Exegetical Commentary on the Acts of the Apostles*. 2 vols. International Critical Commentary. Edinburgh: T&T Clark, 1994–1998.

Bateman, H. W. "Psalm 45:6-7 and Its Christological Contributions to Hebrews." *Trinity Journal* 22 (2001): 3–21.

Bateman, H. W. "Defining the Titles 'Christ' and 'Son of God' in Mark's Narrative Presentation of Jesus." *Journal of the Evangelical Theological Society* 50 (2007): 537–59.

Bauckham, R. "The Worship of Jesus in Apocalyptic Christianity." *New Testament Studies* 27 (1981): 322–41.

Bauckham, R. "Jesus, Worship of." Pages 812–19 in vol. 3 of *The Anchor Bible Dictionary*. Edited by D. N. Freedman. 6 vols. New York: Doubleday, 1992.

Bauckham, R. *The Climax of Prophecy: Studies on the Book of Revelation*. Edinburgh: T&T Clark, 1993.

Bauckham, R. *The Theology of the Book of Revelation*. Cambridge: Cambridge University Press, 1993.

Bauckham, R. "The Throne of God and the Worship of Jesus." Pages 43–69 in *The Jewish Roots of Christological Monotheism: Papers from the St. Andrews Conference on the Historical Origins of the Worship of Jesus*. Edited by C. C. Newman, J. R. Davila, and G. S. Lewis. Supplements to the Journal for the Study of Judaism 63. Leiden: Brill, 1999.

Bauckham, R. "Biblical Theology and the Problems of Monotheism." Pages 187–232 in *Out of Egypt: Biblical Theology and Biblical Interpretation*. Edited by C. Bartholomew, M. Healy, K. Möller, and R. Parry. Scripture and Hermeneutics Series 5. Milton Keynes: Paternoster, 2004.

Bauckham, R. "Monotheism and Christology in Hebrews 1." Pages 167–85 in *Early Jewish and Christian Monotheism*. Edited by L. T. Stuckenbruck and W. E. S. North. Journal for the Study of the New Testament Supplement Series 263. London: T&T Clark, 2004.

Bauckham, R. "Monotheism and Christology in the Gospel of John." Pages 148–66 in *Contours of Christology in the New Testament*. Edited by R. N. Longenecker. Grand Rapids, MI: Eerdmans, 2005.

Bauckham, R. *Jesus and the God of Israel: God Crucified and Other Studies on the New Testament's Christology of Divine Identity*. Grand Rapids, MI: Eerdmans, 2008.

Bauckham, R. "The Divinity of Jesus Christ in the Epistle to the Hebrews." Pages 15–36 in *The Epistle to the Hebrews and Christian Theology*. Edited by R. Bauckham, D. R. Driver, T. A. Hart, and N. MacDonald. Grand Rapids, MI: Eerdmans, 2009.

Bauer, D. R. *The Structure of Matthew's Gospel: A Study in Literary Design*. Journal for the Study of the New Testament Supplement Series 31. Sheffield: Almond Press, 1988.

Bauer, D. R. "The Kingship of Jesus in the Matthean Infancy Narrative: A Literary Analysis." *Catholic Biblical Quarterly* 57 (1995): 306–23.

Baumgarten, A. I. *The Phoenician History of Philo of Byblos: A Commentary*. Leiden: Brill, 1981.

Beale, G. K. *The Use of Daniel in Jewish Apocalyptic Literature and in the Revelation of St. John*. Lanham, MD: University Press of America, 1984.

Beale, G. K. *The Book of Revelation: A Commentary on the Greek Text*. New International Greek Testament Commentary. Grand Rapids, MI: Eerdmans, 1999.

Beasley-Murray, G. R. *The Book of Revelation*. New Century Bible. London: Oliphants, 1974.

Beasley-Murray, G. R. *John*. Word Biblical Commentary 36. Nashville, TN: Thomas Nelson, 1999.

Begg, C. T. *Judean Antiquities, Books 5–7*. Vol. 4 of *Flavius Josephus: Translation and Commentary*. Edited by S. Mason. Leiden: Brill, 2004.

Bernhardt, K.-H. *Das Problem der altorientalischen Königsideologie im Alten Testament: unter besonderer Berücksichtigung der Geschichte der Psalmenexegese dargestellt und kritisch gewürdigt*. Supplements to Vetus Testamentum 8. Leiden: Brill, 1961.

Betz, O. "The Concept of the So-Called 'Divine-Man' in Mark's Christology." Pages 229–40 in *Studies in New Testament and Early Christian Literature: Essays in Honor of Allen P. Wikgren*. Edited by D. E. Aune. Supplements to Novum Testamentum 33. Leiden: Brill, 1972.

Beutler, J. "Greeks Come to See Jesus (John 12,20f)." *Biblica* 71 (1990): 333–47.

Bieneck, J. *Sohn Gottes als Christusbezeichnung der Synoptiker*. Abhandlungen zur Theologie des Alten und Neuen Testaments 21. Zurich: Zwingli-Verlag, 1951.

Bieringer, R. "'I am ascending to my Father and your Father, to my God and your God' (John 20:17): Resurrection and Ascension in the Gospel of John." Pages 209–35 in *The Resurrection of Jesus in the Gospel of John*. Edited by C. R. Koester and R. Bieringer. Wissenschaftliche Untersuchungen zum Neuen Testament 222. Tübingen: Mohr Siebeck, 2008.

Biguzzi, G. "Ephesus, Its Artemision, Its Temple to the Flavian Emperors, and Idolatry in Revelation." *Novum Testamentum* 40 (1998): 276–90.

Blount, B. K. *Revelation: A Commentary*. New Testament Library. Louisville: Westminster John Knox, 2009.

Bock, D. L. *Proclamation from Prophecy and Pattern: Lucan Old Testament Christology*. Journal for the Study of the New Testament Supplement Series 12. Sheffield: Sheffield Academic, 1987.

Bock, D. L. *Luke 9:51–24:53*. Baker Exegetical Commentary on the New Testament. Grand Rapids, MI: Baker Academic, 1996.

Bock, D. L. *Blasphemy and Exaltation in Judaism and the Final Examination of Jesus*. Wissenschaftliche Untersuchungen zum Neuen Testament 2/106. Tübingen: Mohr Siebeck, 1998.

Bock, D. L. *Acts*. Baker Exegetical Commentary on the New Testament. Grand Rapids, MI: Baker Academic, 2007.

Boring, M. E., K. Berger, and C. Colpe, eds. *Hellenistic Commentary to the New Testament*. Nashville, TN: Abingdon, 1995.

Bosworth, A. B. *Conquest and Empire: The Reign of Alexander the Great*. Cambridge: Cambridge University Press, 1988.

Bosworth, A. B. *A Historical Commentary on Arrian's History of Alexander*. Vol. 2. Oxford: Oxford University Press, 1995.

Botha, P. J. "God, Emperor Worship and Society: Contemporary Experiences and the Book of Revelation." *Neotestamentica* 22 (1988): 87–102.

Bousset, W. *Die Religion des Judentums im späthellenistischen Zeitalter*. Handbuch zum Neuen Testament 21. Tübingen: Mohr Siebeck, 1926.

Bovon, F. *Luke 3: A Commentary on the Gospel of Luke 19:28–24:53*. Translated by J. E. Crouch. Hermeneia. Minneapolis, MN: Fortress, 2012.

Boxall, I. *The Revelation of Saint John*. Black's New Testament Commentary 19. London: A&C Black, 2006.

Brandon, S. G. F. "The Myth and Ritual Position Critically Considered." Pages 261–91 in *Myth, Ritual, and Kingship: Essays on the Theory and Practice of Kingship in the Ancient Near East and in Israel*. Edited by S. H. Hooke. Oxford: Clarendon, 1958.

Braukämper, U. "Kingship, Divine." Pages 401–3 in vol. 3 of *Encyclopaedia Aethiopica*. Edited by S. Uhlig. 4 vols. Wiesbaden: Harrassowitz, 2003.

Braun, H. *An die Hebräer*. Handbuch zum Neuen Testament 14. Tübingen: Mohr Siebeck, 1984.

Briant, P. *From Cyrus to Alexander: A History of the Persian Empire*. Translated by P. T. Daniels. Winona Lake: Eisenbrauns, 2002.

Brosius, M. *The Persians: An Introduction*. London: Routledge, 2006.

Brown, R. E. "Does the New Testament Call Jesus God?" *Theological Studies* 26 (1965): 545–73.

Brown, R. E. *The Gospel According to John: Introduction, Translation, and Notes*. 2 vols. Anchor Bible 29–29A. Garden City, NY: Doubleday, 1966–1970.

Brown, R. E. *The Birth of the Messiah: A Commentary on the Infancy Narratives in the Gospels of Matthew and Luke*. Rev. ed. Anchor Bible Reference Library. New York: Doubleday, 1993.

Brown, S. "The Greeks: Jesus' Hour and the Weight of the World." Page 397–402 in *Character Studies in the Fourth Gospel: Narrative Approaches to Seventy Figures in John*. Edited by S. A. Hunt, D. F. Tolmie, and R. Zimmermann. Grand Rapids, MI: Eerdmans, 2016.

Bruce, F. F. *The Book of the Acts*. Rev. ed. New International Commentary on the New Testament. Grand Rapids, MI: Eerdmans, 1988.

Bruce, F. F. *The Epistle to the Hebrews*. Rev. ed. New International Commentary on the New Testament. Grand Rapids, MI: Eerdmans, 1990.

Buckwalter, H. D. *The Character and Purpose of Luke's Christology*. Society for New Testament Studies Monograph Series 89. Cambridge: Cambridge University Press, 1996.

Buckwalter, H. D. "The Divine Saviour." Pages 107–23 in *Witness to the Gospel: The Theology of Acts*. Edited by I. H. Marshall and D. Peterson. Grand Rapids, MI: Eerdmans, 1998.

Bultmann, R. *Theology of the New Testament*. Translated by K. Grobel. Vol. 1. London: SCM, 1952.
Bultmann, R. *The Gospel of John: A Commentary*. Translated by G. R. Beasley-Murray, R. W. N. Hoare, and J. K. Riches. Philadelphia, PA: Westminster, 1971.
Burchard, C. *Gesammelte Studien zu Joseph und Aseneth*. Studia in Veteris Testamenti Pseudepigraphica 13. Leiden: Brill, 1996.
Byrskog, S. *Jesus the Only Teacher: Didactic Authority and Transmission in Ancient Israel, Ancient Judaism and the Matthean Community*. Coniectanea Biblica: New Testament Series 24. Stockholm: Almqvist & Wiksell, 1994.
Caird, G. B. *A Commentary on the Revelation of St. John the Divine*. Black's New Testament Commentary. London: A&C Black, 1966.
Caird, G. B. "Son by Appointment." Pages 73–81 in *The New Testament Age: Essays in Honor of Bo Reicke*. Edited by W. C. Weinrich. 2 vols. Macon: Mercer University Press, 1984.
Caneday, A. B. "The Eschatological World Already Subjected to the Son: The Οἰκουμένη of Hebrews 1.6 and the Son's Enthronement." Pages 28–39 in *A Cloud of Witnesses: The Theology of Hebrews in Its Ancient Contexts*. Edited by R. Bauckham, D. Driver, T. Hart, and N. MacDonald. Library of New Testament Studies 387. London: T&T Clark, 2008.
Capes, D. B. *Old Testament Yahweh Texts in Paul's Christology*. Wissenschaftliche Untersuchungen zum Neuen Testament 2/47. Tübingen: Mohr Siebeck, 1992.
Carnegie, D. R. "Worthy Is the Lamb: The Hymns in Revelation." Pages 243–56 in *Christ the Lord: Studies in Christology Presented to Donald Guthrie*. Edited by H. H. Rowdon. Leicester: Inter-Varsity Press, 1982.
Carrell, P. R. *Jesus and the Angels: Angelology and the Christology of the Apocalypse of John*. Society for New Testament Studies Monograph Series 95. Cambridge: Cambridge University Press, 1997.
Carson, D. A. *The Gospel According to John*. Pillar New Testament Commentary. Grand Rapids, MI: Eerdmans, 1991.
Carter, W. "The Prologue and John's Gospel: Function, Symbol and the Definitive Word." *Journal for the Study of the New Testament* 39 (1990): 35–58.
Carter, W. *Matthew and the Margins: A Socio-Political and Religious Reading*. Journal for the Study of the New Testament Supplement Series 204. Sheffield: Sheffield Academic, 2000.
Casey, P. M. "Monotheism, Worship and Christological Developments in the Pauline Churches." Pages 214–33 in *The Jewish Roots of Christological Monotheism: Papers from the St. Andrews Conference on the Historical Origins of the Worship of Jesus*. Edited by C. C. Newman, J. R. Davila, and G. S. Lewis. Supplements to the Journal for the Study of Judaism 63. Leiden: Brill, 1999.
Charles, J. D. "Imperial Pretensions and the Throne-Vision of the Lamb: Observations on the Function of Revelation 5." *Criswell Theological Review* 7 (1993): 85–97.
Charles, R. H. *A Critical and Exegetical Commentary on the Revelation of St. John*. 2 vols. International Critical Commentary. Edinburgh: T&T Clark, 1920.
Chester, A. *Messiah and Exaltation: Jewish Messianic and Visionary Traditions and New Testament Christology*. Wissenschaftliche Untersuchungen zum Neuen Testament 207. Tübingen: Mohr Siebeck, 2007.
Chester, A. "High Christology—Whence, When and Why?" *Early Christianity* 2 (2011): 22–50.

Clines, D. J. A. *On the Way to the Postmodern: Old Testament Essays, 1967–1998*. Vol. 2. Journal for the Study of the Old Testament Supplement Series 293. Sheffield: Sheffield Academic, 1998.

Cockerill, G. L. "Hebrews 1:6: Source and Significance." *Bulletin for Biblical Research* 9 (1999): 51–64.

Cockerill, G. L. *The Epistle to the Hebrews*. New International Commentary on the New Testament. Grand Rapids, MI: Eerdmans, 2012.

Cohen, S. J. D. "Alexander the Great and Jaddus the High Priest According to Josephus." *Association for Jewish Studies Review* 7–8 (1982–1983): 41–68.

Cohen, S. J. D. "Crossing the Boundary and Becoming a Jew." *Harvard Theological Review* 82 (1989): 13–33.

Collins, A. Yarbro. *Crisis and Catharsis: The Power of the Apocalypse*. Philadelphia, PA: Westminster, 1984.

Collins, A. Yarbro. "Rulers, Divine Men, and Walking on the Water (Mark 6:45-52)." Pages 207–27 in *Religious Propaganda and Missionary Competition in the New Testament World*. Edited by L. Bormann, K. D. Tredici, and A. Standhartinger. Supplements to Novum Testamentum 74. Leiden: Brill, 1994.

Collins, A. Yarbro. "Apotheosis and Resurrection." Pages 88–100 in *The New Testament and Hellenistic Judaism*. Edited by P. Borgen and S. Giversen. Peabody, MA: Hendrickson, 1997.

Collins, A. Yarbro. "Mark and His Readers: The Son of God among Jews." *Harvard Theological Review* 92 (1999): 393–408.

Collins, A. Yarbro. "Mark and His Readers: The Son of God among Greeks and Romans." *Harvard Theological Review* 93 (2000): 85–100.

Collins, A. Yarbro. "The Charge of Blasphemy in Mark 14.64." *Journal for the Study of the New Testament* 26 (2004): 379–401.

Collins, A. Yarbro. *Mark: A Commentary*. Hermeneia. Minneapolis, MN: Fortress, 2007.

Collins, A. Yarbro and J. J. Collins. *King and Messiah as Son of God: Divine, Human, and Angelic Messianic Figures in Biblical and Related Literature*. Grand Rapids, MI: Eerdmans, 2008.

Collins, C. J. "John 4:23-24, 'In Spirit and Truth': An Idiomatic Proposal." *Presbyterion* 21 (1995): 118–21.

Collins, J. J. *The Scepter and the Star: Messianism in Light of the Dead Sea Scrolls*. 2nd ed. Grand Rapids, MI: Eerdmans, 2010.

Coloe, M. L. *God Dwells with Us: Temple Symbolism in the Fourth Gospel*. Collegeville, MN: Liturgical Press, 2001.

Compton, J. *Psalm 110 and the Logic of Hebrews*. Library of New Testament Studies 537. London: Bloomsbury T&T Clark, 2015.

Cotter, W. *Miracles in Greco-Roman Antiquity: A Sourcebook for the Study of New Testament Miracle Stories*. London: Routledge, 1999.

Cotter, W. "Greco-Roman Apotheosis Traditions and the Resurrection Appearances in Matthew." Pages 127–53 in *The Gospel of Matthew in Current Study: Studies in Memory of William G. Thompson, S.J*. Edited by D. E. Aune. Grand Rapids, MI: Eerdmans, 2001.

Crump, D. M. *Jesus the Intercessor: Prayer and Christology in Luke-Acts*. Wissenschaftliche Untersuchungen zum Neuen Testament 2/49. Tübingen: Mohr Siebeck, 1992.

Cullmann, O. *The Christology of the New Testament*. Translated by S. C. Guthrie and C. A. M. Hall. Rev. ed. Philadelphia, PA: Westminster, 1963.

Davies, W. D. and D. C. Allison, Jr. *A Critical and Exegetical Commentary on the Gospel according to Saint Matthew*. 3 vols. International Critical Commentary. Edinburgh: T&T Clark, 1988–1997.

Davila, J. R. *The Provenance of the Pseudepigrapha: Jewish, Christian, or Other?* Leiden: Brill, 2005.

Davis, C. J. *The Name and Way of the Lord: Old Testament Themes, New Testament Christology*. Journal for the Study of the New Testament Supplement Series 129. Sheffield: Sheffield Academic, 1996.

Davis, R. D. *The Heavenly Court Judgment of Revelation 4–5*. Lanham, MD: University Press of America, 1992.

Day, J. "The Canaanite Inheritance of the Israelite Monarchy." Pages 72–90 in *King and Messiah in Israel and the Ancient Near East: Proceedings of the Oxford Old Testament Seminar*. Edited by J. Day. Journal for the Study of the Old Testament Supplement Series 270. Sheffield: Sheffield Academic, 1998.

De Boer, M. C. "Ten Thousand Talents? Matthew's Interpretation and Redaction of the Parable of the Unforgiving Servant (Matt 18:23-35)." *Catholic Biblical Quarterly* 50 (1988): 214–32.

Deichgräber, R. *Gotteshymnus und Christushymnus in der frühen Christenheit: Untersuchungen zu Form, Sprache und Stil der frühchristlichen Hymnen*. Studien zur Umwelt des Neuen Testaments 5. Göttingen: Vandenhoeck & Ruprecht, 1967.

Denaux, A. "The Theme of Divine Visits and Human (In)Hospitality in Luke-Acts: Its Old Testament and Graeco-Roman Antecedents." Pages 255–79 in *The Unity of Luke-Acts*. Edited by J. Verheyden. Bibliotheca Ephemeridum Theologicarum Lovaniensium 142. Leuven: Leuven University Press, 1999.

Derrett, J. D. M. "Contributions to the Study of the Gerasene Demoniac." *Journal for the Study of the New Testament* 3 (1979): 2–17.

Derrett, J. D. M. "'Where Two or Three Are Convened in My Name…': A Sad Misunderstanding." *Expository Times* 91 (1979): 83–86.

deSilva, D. A. *Perseverance in Gratitude: A Socio-Rhetorical Commentary on the Epistle "to the Hebrews."* Grand Rapids, MI: Eerdmans, 2000.

Deutsch, C. *Hidden Wisdom and the Easy Yoke: Wisdom, Torah and Discipleship in Matthew 11.25-30*. Journal for the Study of the New Testament Supplement Series 18. Sheffield: Sheffield Academic, 1987.

Dey, L. K. K. *The Intermediary World and Patterns of Perfection in Philo and Hebrews*. Society of Biblical Literature Dissertation Series 25. Missoula, MT: Scholars Press, 1975.

Dillon, R. J. *From Eye-Witnesses to Ministers of the Word*. Analecta Biblica 82. Rome: Biblical Institute Press, 1978.

Docherty, S. E. *The Use of the Old Testament in Hebrews: A Case Study in Early Jewish Bible Interpretation*. Wissenschaftliche Untersuchungen zum Neuen Testament 2/260. Tübingen: Mohr Siebeck, 2009.

Dormandy, R. "The Expulsion of Legion: A Political Reading of Mark 5:1-20." *Expository Times* 111 (2000): 335–37.

Duke, P. D. *Irony in the Fourth Gospel*. Atlanta, GA: John Knox, 1985.

Dunn, J. D. G. "Spirit-and-Fire Baptism." *Novum Testamentum* 14 (1972): 81–92.

Dunn, J. D. G. *Christology in the Making: A New Testament Inquiry into the Origins of the Doctrine of the Incarnation*. 2nd ed. Grand Rapids, MI: Eerdmans, 1996.

Dunn, J. D. G. *Did the First Christians Worship Jesus? The New Testament Evidence*. London: SPCK, 2010.

Edwards, J. R. "The Use of προσέρχεσθαι in the Gospel of Matthew." *Journal of Biblical Literature* 106 (1987): 65–74.
Ego, B. "Mordecai's Refusal of Proskynesis before Haman According to the Septuagint: Traditio-Historical and Literal Aspects." Pages 16–29 in *Deuterocanonical Additions of the Old Testament Books: Selected Studies*. Edited by G. G. Xeravits and J. Zsengellér. Vol. 5 of *Deuterocanonical and Cognate Literature Studies*. Edited by F. V. Reiterer, B. Ego, and T. Nicklas. Berlin: de Gruyter, 2010.
Ehrhardt, A. "The Disciples of Emmaus." *New Testament Studies* 10 (1964): 182–201.
Ehrman, B. D. *The Orthodox Corruption of Scripture: The Effect of Early Christological Controversies on the Text of the New Testament*. Oxford: Oxford University Press, 1993.
Ellingworth, P. *The Epistle to the Hebrews: A Commentary on the Greek Text*. New International Greek Testament Commentary. Grand Rapids, MI: Eerdmans, 1993.
Ellis, I. P. "But Some Doubted." *New Testament Studies* 14 (1968): 574–80.
Engnell, I. *Studies in Divine Kingship in the Ancient Near East*. Uppsala: Almqvist & Wiksell, 1943.
Eskola, T. *Messiah and the Throne: Jewish Merkabah Mysticism and Early Christian Exaltation Discourse*. Wissenschaftliche Untersuchungen zum Neuen Testament 2/142. Tübingen: Mohr Siebeck, 2001.
Evans, C. A. "In What Sense 'Blasphemy'? Jesus before Caiaphas in Mark 14:61-64." Pages 215–34 in *Society of Biblical Literature 1991 Seminar Papers*. Society of Biblical Literature Seminar Papers 30. Atlanta: Scholars Press, 1991.
Evans, C. A. *Mark 8:27–16:20*. Word Biblical Commentary 34B. Nashville, TN: Thomas Nelson, 2001.
Eve, E. *The Jewish Context of Jesus' Miracles*. Journal for the Study of the New Testament Supplement Series 231. Sheffield: Sheffield Academic, 2002.
Fee, G. D. *Pauline Christology: An Exegetical-Theological Study*. Peabody, MA: Hendrickson, 2007.
Fee, G. D. *The First Epistle to the Corinthians*. Rev. ed. New International Commentary on the New Testament. Grand Rapids, MI: Eerdmans, 2014.
Fekkes, J. *Isaiah and Prophetic Traditions in the Book of Revelation: Visionary Antecedents and Their Development*. Journal for the Study of the New Testament Supplement Series 93. Sheffield: Sheffield Academic, 1994.
Fennema, D. A. "John 1.18: 'God the Only Son.'" *New Testament Studies* 31 (1985): 124–35.
Fishwick, D. *The Imperial Cult in the Latin West: Studies in the Ruler Cult of the Western Provinces of the Roman Empire, Volume II, 1*. Leiden: Brill, 1991.
Fitzmyer, J. A. *The Gospel According to Luke X–XXIV: A New Translation with Introduction and Commentary*. Anchor Bible 28A. New York: Doubleday, 1985.
Fitzmyer, J. A. *The Acts of the Apostles: A New Translation with Introduction and Commentary*. Anchor Bible 31. New Haven, CT: Yale University Press, 1998.
Flessen, B. J. *An Exemplary Man: Cornelius and Characterization in Acts 10*. Eugene, OR: Pickwick, 2011.
Fletcher-Louis, C. H. T. "The Worship of Divine Humanity as God's Image and the Worship of Jesus." Pages 112–28 in *The Jewish Roots of Christological Monotheism: Papers from the St. Andrews Conference on the Historical Origins of the Worship of Jesus*. Edited by C. C. Newman, J. R. Davila, and G. S. Lewis. Supplements to the Journal for the Study of Judaism 63. Leiden: Brill, 1999.
Fletcher-Louis, C. H. T. "Alexander the Great's Worship of the High Priest." Pages 71–102 in *Early Jewish and Christian Monotheism*. Edited by L. T. Stuckenbruck and W. E. S.

North. Journal for the Study of the New Testament Supplement Series 263. London: T&T Clark, 2004.

Fossum, J. E. *The Name of God and the Angel of the Lord: Samaritan and Jewish Concepts of Intermediation and the Origin of Gnosticism*. Wissenschaftliche Untersuchungen zum Neuen Testament 36. Tübingen: Mohr Siebeck, 1985.

Fox, M. V. *Character and Ideology in the Book of Esther*. Columbia: University of South Carolina Press, 1991.

Fox, R. L. *Alexander the Great*. London: Allen Lane, 1973.

Fraine, J. de. *L'aspect religieux de la royauté israélite: L'institution monarchique dans l'Ancien Testament et dans les textes mésopotamiens*. Analecta Biblica 3. Rome: Pontificio Istituto Biblico, 1954.

France, R. T. *The Gospel of Mark: A Commentary on the Greek Text*. New International Greek Testament Commentary. Grand Rapids, MI: Eerdmans, 2002.

France, R. T. *The Gospel of Matthew*. New International Commentary on the New Testament. Grand Rapids, MI: Eerdmans, 2007.

Frankfort, H. *Kingship and the Gods: A Study of Ancient Near Eastern Religion as the Integration of Society and Nature*. Chicago, IL: University of Chicago Press, 1948.

Frankfort, H. *The Problem of Similarity in Ancient Near Eastern Religions*. Oxford: Clarendon, 1951.

Fredriksen, P. "Mandatory Retirement: Ideas in the Study of Christian Origins Whose Time Has Come to Go." Pages 25–38 in *Israel's God and Rebecca's Children: Christology and Community in Early Judaism and Christianity. Essays in Honor of Larry W. Hurtado and Alan F. Segal*. Edited by D. B. Capes, A. D. DeConick, H. K. Bond, and T. Miller. Waco, TX: Baylor University Press, 2007.

Friesen, S. J. *Imperial Cults and the Apocalypse of John: Reading Revelation in the Ruins*. Oxford: Oxford University Press, 2001.

Friesen, S. J. "The Beast from the Land: Revelation 13:11-18 and Social Setting." Pages 49–64 in *Reading the Book of Revelation: A Resource for Students*. Edited by D. L. Barr. Resources for Biblical Study 44. Atlanta: Society of Biblical Literature, 2003.

Friesen, S. J. "Myth and Symbolic Resistance in Revelation 13." *Journal of Biblical Literature* 123 (2004): 281–313.

Frye, R. N. "Gestures of Deference to Royalty in Ancient Iran." *Iranica Antiqua* 9 (1972): 102–7.

Gallusz, L. *The Throne Motif in the Book of Revelation*. Library of New Testament Studies 487. London: Bloomsbury T&T Clark, 2014.

Garrett, S. R. *The Demise of the Devil: Magic and the Demonic in Luke's Writings*. Minneapolis, MN: Fortress, 1989.

Garroway, J. "The Invasion of a Mustard Seed: A Reading of Mark 5.1-20." *Journal for the Study of the New Testament* 32 (2009): 57–75.

Gathercole, S. J. *The Preexistent Son: Recovering the Christologies of Matthew, Mark, and Luke*. Grand Rapids, MI: Eerdmans, 2006.

Gheorghita, R. *The Role of the Septuagint in Hebrews: An Investigation of Its Influence with Special Consideration to the Use of Hab 2:3-4 in Heb 10:37-38*. Wissenschaftliche Untersuchungen zum Neuen Testament 2/160. Tübingen: Mohr Siebeck, 2003.

Giblin, C. H. "Structural and Thematic Correlations in the Theology of Revelation 16–22." *Biblica* 55 (1974): 487–504.

Giblin, C. H. "A Note on Doubt and Reassurance in Mt 28:16-20." *Catholic Biblical Quarterly* 37 (1975): 68–75.

Gieschen, C. A. *Angelomorphic Christology: Antecedents and Early Evidence*. Arbeiten zur Geschichte des antiken Judentums und des Urchristentums 42. Leiden: Brill, 1998.

Gieschen, C. A. "The Name of the Son of Man in the Parables of Enoch." Pages 238–49 in *Enoch and the Messiah Son of Man: Revisiting the Book of Parables*. Edited by G. Boccaccini. Grand Rapids, MI: Eerdmans, 2007.

Glasson, T. F. "'Plurality of Divine Persons' and the Quotations in Hebrews 1:6ff." *New Testament Studies* 12 (1966): 270–72.

Gnilka, J. *Das Matthäusevangelium*. 2 vols. Herders theologischer Kommentar zum Neuen Testament. Freiburg: Herder, 1986–1988.

Goodenough, E. R. *Jewish Symbols in the Greco-Roman Period*. 13 vols. Bollingen Series 37. New York: Pantheon, 1953–1968.

Gow, A. S. F. "Notes on the *Persae* of Aeschylus." *Journal of Hellenic Studies* 48 (1928): 133–58.

Grabiner, S. *Revelation's Hymns: Commentary on the Cosmic Conflict*. Library of New Testament Studies 511. London: Bloomsbury T&T Clark, 2015.

Grayston, K. "The Translation of Matthew 28:17." *Journal for the Study of the New Testament* 21 (1984): 105–9.

Green, J. B. *The Gospel of Luke*. New International Commentary on the New Testament. Grand Rapids, MI: Eerdmans, 1997.

Grundmann, W. *Das Evangelium nach Matthäus*. Theologischer Handkommentar zum Neuen Testament. Berlin: Evangelische Verlagsanstalt, 1968.

Gundry, R. H. *Mark: A Commentary on His Apology for the Cross*. Grand Rapids, MI: Eerdmans, 1993.

Gundry, R. H. *Matthew: A Commentary on His Handbook for a Mixed Church under Persecution*. 2nd ed. Grand Rapids, MI: Eerdmans, 1994.

Guthrie, D. "The Christology of Revelation." Pages 397–409 in *Jesus of Nazareth, Lord and Christ: Essays on the Historical Jesus and New Testament Christology*. Edited by J. B. Green and M. Turner. Grand Rapids, MI: Eerdmans, 1994.

Hagner, Donald A. *Matthew*. 2 vols. Word Biblical Commentary 33A–B. Dallas: Word Books, 1993–1995.

Hahn, F. *The Titles of Jesus in Christology: Their History in Early Christianity*. Translated by H. Knight and G. Ogg. London: Lutterworth, 1969.

Hamm, D. "The Tamid Service in Luke-Acts: The Cultic Background behind Luke's Theology of Worship (Luke 1:5-25; 18:9-14; 24:50-53; Acts 3:1; 10:3, 30)." *Catholic Biblical Quarterly* 65 (2003): 215–31.

Hannah, D. D. *Michael and Christ: Michael Traditions and Angel Christology in Early Christianity*. Wissenschaftliche Untersuchungen zum Neuen Testament 2/109. Tübingen: Mohr Siebeck, 1999.

Hannah, D. D. "The Throne of His Glory: The Divine Throne and Heavenly Mediators in Revelation and the Similitudes of Enoch." *Zeitschrift für die neutestamentliche Wissenschaft und die Kunde der älteren Kirche* 94 (2003): 68–96.

Harris, E. *Prologue and Gospel: The Theology of the Fourth Evangelist*. Journal for the Study of the New Testament Supplement Series 107. Sheffield: Sheffield Academic, 1994.

Harris, M. J. "The Translation and Significance of ὁ θεός in Hebrews 1:8-9." *Tyndale Bulletin* 36 (1985): 129–62.

Harris, M. J. *Jesus as God: The New Testament Use of Theos in Reference to Jesus*. Grand Rapids, MI: Baker, 1992.

Hay, L. S. "The Son-of-God Christology in Mark." *Journal of Bible and Religion* 32 (1964): 106–14.

Hayman, P. "Monotheism—A Misused Word in Jewish Studies?" *Journal of Jewish Studies* 42 (1991): 1–15.
Head, P. M. *Christology and the Synoptic Problem: An Argument for Markan Priority*. Society for New Testament Studies Monograph Series 94. Cambridge: Cambridge University Press, 1997.
Heil, J. P. *Jesus Walking on the Sea: Meaning and Gospel Functions of Matt 14:22-33, Mark 6:45-52 and John 6:15b-21*. Analecta Biblica 87. Rome: Biblical Institute Press, 1981.
Heil, J. P. *Worship in the Letter to the Hebrews*. Eugene, OR: Cascade, 2011.
Heil, J. P. *The Book of Revelation: Worship for Life in the Spirit of Prophecy*. Eugene, OR: Cascade, 2014.
Heil, J. P. *The Gospel of John: Worship for Divine Life Eternal*. Eugene, OR: Cascade, 2015.
Held, H. J. "Matthew as Interpreter of the Miracle Stories." Pages 165–299 in *Tradition and Interpretation in Matthew*. Edited by G. Bornkamm, G. Barth, and H. J. Held. Translated by P. Scott. London: SCM, 1963.
Hengel, M. *The Son of God: The Origin of Christology and the History of Jewish-Hellenistic Religion*. Translated by J. Bowden. Philadelphia, PA: Fortress, 1976.
Hengel, M. *Studies in Early Christology*. Edinburgh: T&T Clark, 1995.
Héring, J. *L'Épître aux Hébreux*. Neuchâtel: Delachaux & Niestlé, 1954.
Hoffmann, M. R. *The Destroyer and the Lamb: The Relationship between Angelomorphic and Lamb Christology in the Book of Revelation*. Wissenschaftliche Untersuchungen zum Neuen Testament 2/203. Tübingen: Mohr Siebeck, 2005.
Hofius, O. "'Der in des Vaters Schoß ist' Joh 1,18." *Zeitschrift für die neutestamentliche Wissenschaft und die Kunde der älteren Kirche* 80 (1989): 163–71.
Hofius, O. *Der Christushymnus Philipper 2,6-11: Untersuchungen zu Gestalt und Aussage eines urchristlichen Psalms*. 2nd ed. Wissenschaftliche Untersuchungen zum Neuen Testament 17. Tübingen: Mohr Siebeck, 1991.
Holladay, C. R. *Theios Aner in Hellenistic-Judaism: A Critique of the Use of This Category in New Testament Christology*. Society of Biblical Literature Dissertation Series 40. Missoula, MT: Scholars Press, 1977.
Holleran, J. W. "Seeing the Light: A Narrative Reading of John 9." *Ephemerides Theologicae Lovanienses* 69 (1993): 5–26, 354–82.
Holtz, T. *Die Christologie der Apokalypse des Johannes*. Texte und Untersuchungen zur Geschichte der altchristlichen Literatur 85. Berlin: Akademie, 1962.
Hooke, S. H., ed. *Myth and Ritual: Essays on the Myth and Ritual of the Hebrews in Relation to the Culture Pattern of the Ancient East*. London: Oxford University Press, 1933.
Horsley, R. A. *Hearing the Whole Story: The Politics of Plot in Mark's Gospel*. Louisville, KY: Westminster John Knox, 2001.
Horst, J. *Proskynein: Zur Anbetung im Urchristentum nach ihrer religionsgeschichtlichen Eigenart*. Neutestamentliche Forschungen 3/2. Gütersloh: Bertelsmann, 1932.
Horst, P. W. van der. "Once More: The Translation of οἱ δέ in Matthew 28.17." *Journal for the Study of the New Testament* 27 (1986): 27–30.
Hoskins, P. M. *Jesus as the Fulfillment of the Temple in the Gospel of John*. Paternoster Biblical Monographs. Milton Keynes: Paternoster, 2006.
Howell, J. R. "The Imperial Authority and Benefaction of Centurions and Acts 10.34-43: A Response to C. Kavin Rowe." *Journal for the Study of the New Testament* 31 (2008): 25–51.

Hubbard, B. J. *The Matthean Redaction of a Primitive Apostolic Commissioning: An Exegesis of Matthew 28:16-20*. Society of Biblical Literature Dissertation Series 19. Missoula, MT: Scholars Press, 1974.

Hunter, A. M. "Crux Criticorum—Matt. XI. 25-30—A Re-Appraisal." *New Testament Studies* 8 (1962): 241–49.

Hurst, L. D. "The Christology of Hebrews 1 and 2." Pages 151–64 in *The Glory of Christ in the New Testament: Studies in Christology in Memory of George Bradford Caird*. Edited by L. D. Hurst and N. T. Wright. Oxford: Clarendon, 1987.

Hurst, L. D. *The Epistle to the Hebrews: Its Background of Thought*. Society for New Testament Studies Monograph Series 65. Cambridge: Cambridge University Press, 1990.

Hurtado, L. W. "Revelation 4–5 in the Light of Jewish Apocalyptic Analogies." *Journal for the Study of the New Testament* 25 (1985): 105–24.

Hurtado, L. W. *Mark*. New International Biblical Commentary. Peabody, MA: Hendrickson, 1989.

Hurtado, L. W. *One God, One Lord: Early Christian Devotion and Ancient Jewish Monotheism*. 2nd ed. Edinburgh: T&T Clark, 1998.

Hurtado, L. W. "First-Century Jewish Monotheism." *Journal for the Study of the New Testament* 71 (1998): 3–26.

Hurtado, L. W. "Pre-70 CE Jewish Opposition to Christ-Devotion." *Journal of Theological Studies* 50 (1999): 35–58.

Hurtado, L. W. "The Binitarian Shape of Early Christian Worship." Pages 187–213 in *The Jewish Roots of Christological Monotheism: Papers from the St. Andrews Conference on the Historical Origins of the Worship of Jesus*. Edited by C. C. Newman, J. R. Davila, and G. S. Lewis. Supplements to the Journal for the Study of Judaism 63. Leiden: Brill, 1999.

Hurtado, L. W. *Lord Jesus Christ: Devotion to Jesus in Earliest Christianity*. Grand Rapids, MI: Eerdmans, 2003.

Hurtado, L. W. "Homage to the Historical Jesus and Early Christian Devotion." *Journal for the Study of the Historical Jesus* 1 (2003): 131–46.

Hurtado, L. W. "Early Christian Monotheism." *Expository Times* 122 (2011): 383–86.

Hurtado, L. W. "Christology in Acts: Jesus in Early Christian Belief and Practice." Pages 217–37 in *Issues in Luke-Acts: Selected Essays*. Edited by S. A. Adams and M. Pahl. Gorgias Handbooks 26. Piscataway, NJ: Gorgias, 2012.

Jipp, J. W. "The Son's Entrance into the Heavenly World: The Soteriological Necessity of the Scriptural Catena in Hebrews 1.5-14." *New Testament Studies* 56 (2010): 557–75.

Jobes, K. H. "Distinguishing the Meaning of Greek Verbs in the Semantic Domain for Worship." *Filologia Neotestamentaria* 4 (1991): 183–91.

Johansson, D. "Jesus and God in the Gospel of Mark: Unity and Distinction." Ph.D. diss., University of Edinburgh, 2011.

Johansson, D. "'Who Can Forgive Sins but God Alone?' Human and Angelic Agents, and Divine Forgiveness in Early Judaism." *Journal for the Study of the New Testament* 33 (2011): 351–74.

Johnson, A. R. *Sacral Kingship in Ancient Israel*. Cardiff: University of Wales Press, 1967.

Johnson, L. T. *Hebrews: A Commentary*. New Testament Library. Louisville, KY: Westminster John Knox, 2006.

Jörns, K.-P. *Das hymnische Evangelium: Untersuchungen zu Aufbau, Funktion und Herkunft der hymnischen Stücke in der Johannesoffenbarung*. Gütersloh: Mohn, 1971.

Juel, D. *Messiah and Temple: The Trial of Jesus in the Gospel of Mark*. Society of Biblical Literature Dissertation Series 31. Missoula, MT: Scholars Press, 1977.
Kee, H. C. "The Transfiguration in Mark: Epiphany or Apocalyptic Vision?" Pages 135–52 in *Understanding the Sacred Text*. Edited by J. Reumann. Valley Forge: Judson, 1972.
Keener, C. S. *A Commentary on the Gospel of Matthew*. Grand Rapids, MI: Eerdmans, 1999.
Keener, C. S. *The Gospel of John: A Commentary*. 2 vols. Peabody, MA: Hendrickson, 2003.
Keener, C. S. *Acts: An Exegetical Commentary*. 4 vols. Grand Rapids, MI: Baker, 2012–2015.
Kerr, A. R. *The Temple of Jesus' Body: The Temple Theme in the Gospel of John*. Journal for the Study of the New Testament Supplement Series 220. London: Sheffield Academic, 2002.
Kezbere, I. *Umstrittener Monotheismus: Wahre und falsche Apotheose im lukanischen Doppelwerk*. Novum Testamentum et Orbis Antiquus 60. Göttingen: Vandenhoeck & Ruprecht, 2007.
Kiddle, M. *The Revelation of St. John*. Moffatt New Testament Commentary. London: Hodder & Stoughton, 1940.
Kim, H. C. "The Worship of Jesus in the Gospel of Matthew." *Biblica* 93 (2012): 227–41.
Kingsbury, J. D. "The 'Divine Man' as the Key to Mark's Christology—The End of an Era?" *Interpretation* 35 (1981): 243–57.
Kingsbury, J. D. *The Christology of Mark's Gospel*. Philadelphia, PA: Fortress, 1983.
Kittel, G., and G. Friedrich, eds. *Theological Dictionary of the New Testament*. Translated by G. W. Bromiley. 10 vols. Grand Rapids, MI: Eerdmans, 1964–1976.
Kobelski, P. J. *Melchizedek and Melchiresa*. Catholic Biblical Quarterly Monograph Series 10. Washington DC: Catholic Biblical Association of America, 1981.
Koester, C. R. *Hebrews: A New Translation with Introduction and Commentary*. Anchor Bible 36. New York: Doubleday, 2001.
Koester, C. R. *Revelation: A New Translation with Introduction and Commentary*. Anchor Bible 38A. New Haven, CT: Yale University Press, 2014.
Kossen, H. B. "Who Were the Greeks of John XII 20?" Pages 97–110 in *Studies in John: Presented to Professor Dr. J. N. Sevenster on the Occasion of His Seventieth Birthday*. Supplements to Novum Testamentum 24. Leiden: Brill, 1970.
Köstenberger, A. J. *John*. Baker Exegetical Commentary on the New Testament. Grand Rapids, MI: Baker Academic, 2004.
Kuhrt, A. "The Achaemenid Persian Empire (c. 550–c. 330 BCE): Continuities, Adaptations, Transformations." Pages 93–124 in *Empires: Perspectives from Archaeology and History*. Edited by S. E. Alcock, T. N. D'Altroy, K. D. Morrison, and C. M. Sinopoli. Cambridge: Cambridge University Press, 2001.
Kupp, D. D. *Matthew's Emmanuel: Divine Presence and God's People in the First Gospel*. Society for New Testament Studies Monograph Series 90. Cambridge: Cambridge University Press, 1996.
La Potterie, I. de. "'Nous adorons, nous, ce que nous connaissons, car le salut vient des Juifs': Histoire de l'exégèse et interprétation de Jn 4,22." *Biblica* 64 (1983): 74–115.
Laansma, J. "The Cosmology of Hebrews." Pages 125–43 in *Cosmology and New Testament Theology*. Edited by J. T. Pennington and S. M. McDonough. Library of New Testament Studies 355. New York: T&T Clark, 2008.
Lane, W. L. *Hebrews*. 2 vols. Word Biblical Commentary 47A–B. Dallas, TX: Word Books, 1991.

Lanfranchi, P. "Moses' Vision of the Divine Throne in the *Exagogue* of Ezekiel the Tragedian." Pages 53–59 in *The Book of Ezekiel and Its Influence*. Edited by H. J. de Jonge and J. Tromp. Aldershot: Ashgate, 2007.

Leander, H. *Discourses of Empire: The Gospel of Mark from a Postcolonial Perspective*. Semeia Studies 71. Atlanta, GA: Society of Biblical Literature, 2013.

Lee, A. H. I. *From Messiah to Preexistent Son: Jesus' Self-Consciousness and Early Christian Exegesis of Messianic Psalms*. Wissenschaftliche Untersuchungen zum Neuen Testament 2/192. Tübingen: Mohr Siebeck, 2005.

Leim, J. E. "In the Glory of His Father: Intertextuality and the Apocalyptic Son of Man in the Gospel of Mark." *Journal of Theological Interpretation* 7 (2013): 213–32.

Leim, J. E. *Matthew's Theological Grammar: The Father and the Son*. Wissenschaftliche Untersuchungen zum Neuen Testament 2/402. Tübingen: Mohr Siebeck, 2015.

Lemcio, E. E. *The Past of Jesus in the Gospels*. Society for New Testament Studies Monograph Series 68. Cambridge: Cambridge University Press, 1991.

Levinskaya, I. *The Book of Acts in Its Diaspora Setting*. Vol. 5 of *The Book of Acts in Its First Century Setting*. Grand Rapids, MI: Eerdmans, 1996.

Lierman, J. *The New Testament Moses: Christian Perceptions of Moses and Israel in the Setting of Jewish Religion*. Wissenschaftliche Untersuchungen zum Neuen Testament 2/173. Tübingen: Mohr Siebeck, 2004.

Lincoln, A. T. *The Gospel According to Saint John*. Black's New Testament Commentary 4. Peabody, MA: Hendrickson, 2005.

Lincoln, A. T. *Hebrews: A Guide*. London: T&T Clark, 2006.

Lindars, B. *The Gospel of John*. New Century Bible. London: Oliphants, 1972.

Llewelyn-Jones, L. *King and Court in Ancient Persia 559 to 331 BCE*. Edinburgh: Edinburgh University Press, 2013.

Loader, W. R. G. *Sohn und Hoherpriester: Eine traditionsgeschichtliche Untersuchung zur Christologie des Hebräerbriefes*. Wissenschaftliche Monographien zum Alten und Neuen Testament 53. Neukirchen-Vluyn: Neukirchener Verlag, 1981.

Lohfink, G. *Die Himmelfahrt Jesu: Untersuchungen zu den Himmelfahrts-und Erhöhungstexten bei Lukas*. Studien zum Alten und Neuen Testament 26. Munich: Kösel, 1971.

Lührmann, D. *Das Markusevangelium*. Handbuch zum Neuen Testament 3. Tübingen: Mohr Siebeck, 1987.

Luz, U. *Matthew: A Commentary*. Translated by J. E. Crouch. 3 vols. Hermeneia. Minneapolis, MN: Fortress, 2001–2007.

Mackie, S. D. *Eschatology and Exhortation in the Epistle to the Hebrews*. Wissenschaftliche Untersuchungen zum Neuen Testament 2/223. Tübingen: Mohr Siebeck, 2007.

Manzi, F. *Melchisedek e l'angelologia nell'Epistola agli Ebrei e a Qumran*. Analecta Biblica 136. Rome: Pontificio Istituto Biblico, 1997.

Marcus, J. "Mark 14:61: 'Are You the Messiah-Son-of-God?'" *Novum Testamentum* 31 (1989): 125–41.

Marcus, J. *Mark 1–8: A New Translation with Introduction and Commentary*. Anchor Bible 27. New York: Doubleday, 2000.

Marshall, I. H. *The Gospel of Luke: A Commentary on the Greek Text*. New International Greek Testament Commentary. Exeter: Paternoster, 1978.

Martin, M. W. "Defending the 'Western Non-Interpolations': The Case for an Anti-Separationist *Tendenz* in the Longer Alexandrian Readings." *Journal of Biblical Literature* 124 (2005): 269–94.

Martin, R. P. *Worship in the Early Church*. London: Marshall, Morgan & Scott, 1964.

Mason, E. F. *"You Are a Priest Forever": Second Temple Jewish Messianism and the Priestly Christology of the Epistle to the Hebrews*. Studies on the Texts of the Desert of Judah 74. Leiden: Brill, 2008.

Mason, E. F. "'Sit at My Right Hand': Enthronement and the Heavenly Sanctuary in Hebrews." Pages 901–16 in *A Teacher for All Generations: Essays in Honor of James C. VanderKam*. Supplements to the Journal for the Study of Judaism 153. Leiden: Brill, 2012.

Mastin, B. A. "Daniel 2:46 and the Hellenistic World." *Zeitschrift für die alttestamentliche Wissenschaft* 85 (1973): 80–93.

Mastin, B. A. "A Neglected Feature of the Christology of the Fourth Gospel." *New Testament Studies* 22 (1975): 32–51.

Mathewson, D. L. *Verbal Aspect in the Book of Revelation: The Function of Greek Verb Tenses in John's Apocalypse*. Linguistic Biblical Studies 4. Leiden: Brill, 2010.

McDonough, S. M. *Christ as Creator: Origins of a New Testament Doctrine*. Oxford: Oxford University Press, 2009.

McGrath, J. F. *The Only True God: Early Christian Monotheism in Its Jewish Context*. Chicago: University of Illinois Press, 2009.

McKay, K. L. "The Use of *hoi de* in Matthew 28.17: A Response to K. Grayston." *Journal for the Study of the New Testament* 24 (1985): 71–72.

Meier, J. P. "Structure and Theology in Heb 1,1-14." *Biblica* 66 (1985): 168–89.

Meier, J. P. "Symmetry and Theology in the Old Testament Citations of Heb 1,5-14." *Biblica* 66 (1985): 504–33.

Menken, M. J. J. "The Psalms in Matthew's Gospel." Pages 61–82 in *The Psalms in the New Testament*. Edited by S. Moyise and M. J. J. Menken. New York: T&T Clark, 2004.

Metzger, B. M. *A Textual Commentary on the Greek New Testament: A Companion Volume to the United Bible Societies' Greek New Testament*. 2nd ed. Stuttgart: Deutsche Bibelgesellschaft, 1994.

Michaels, J. R. *The Gospel of John*. New International Commentary on the New Testament. Grand Rapids, MI: Eerdmans, 2010.

Michel, O. *Der Brief an die Hebräer*. 14th ed. Kritisch-exegetischer Kommentar über das Neue Testament 13. Göttingen: Vandenhoeck & Ruprecht, 1984.

Milik, J. T. "*Milkî-ṣedeq* et *Milkî-reša* dans les anciens écrits juifs et chrétiens." *Journal of Jewish Studies* 23 (1972): 95–144.

Moffitt, D. M. *Atonement and the Logic of the Resurrection in the Epistle to the Hebrews*. Supplements to Novum Testamentum 141. Leiden: Brill, 2011.

Moloney, F. J. *The Johannine Son of Man*. 2nd ed. Biblioteca di Scienze Religiose 14. Rome: LAS, 1978.

Montefiore, H. *A Commentary on the Epistle to the Hebrews*. Black's New Testament Commentary. London: A&C Black, 1964.

Moore, C. A. *Esther: Introduction, Translation, and Notes*. Anchor Bible 7B. Garden City: Doubleday, 1971.

Moore, C. A. *Daniel, Esther, and Jeremiah: The Additions. A New Translation with Introduction and Commentary*. Anchor Bible 44. Garden City: Doubleday, 1977.

Moore, S. D. *Empire and Apocalypse: Postcolonialism and the New Testament*. The Bible in the Modern World 12. Sheffield: Sheffield Phoenix, 2006.

Morris, L. *The Gospel According to John*. Rev. ed. New International Commentary on the New Testament. Grand Rapids, MI: Eerdmans, 1995.

Morton, R. S. *One upon the Throne and the Lamb: A Tradition Historical/Theological Analysis of Revelation 4–5*. New York: Lang, 2007.

Motyer, S. "The Psalm Quotations of Hebrews 1: A Hermeneutic-Free Zone?" *Tyndale Bulletin* 50 (1999): 3–22.
Moule, C. F. D. *The Origin of Christology*. Cambridge: Cambridge University Press, 1977.
Mowinckel, S. *He That Cometh: The Messiah Concept in the Old Testament and Later Judaism*. Translated by G. W. Anderson. Grand Rapids, MI: Eerdmans, 2005.
Mowry, L. "Revelation 4–5 and Early Christian Liturgical Usage." *Journal of Biblical Literature* 71 (1952): 75–84.
Müller, E. *Microstructural Analysis of Revelation 4–11*. Andrews University Seminary Doctoral Dissertation Series 21. Berrien Springs, MI: Andrews University, 1996.
Müller, M. "Proskynese und Christologie nach Matthäus." Pages 210–24 in *Kirche und Volk Gottes: Festschrift für Jürgen Roloff zum 70. Geburtstag*. Edited by M. Karrer, W. Kraus, and O. Merk. Neukirchen-Vluyn: Neukirchener Verlag, 2000.
Mussies, G. *The Morphology of Koine Greek as Used in the Apocalypse of St. John: A Study in Bilingualism*. Supplements to Novum Testamentum 27. Leiden: Brill, 1971.
Myers, C. *Binding the Strong Man: A Political Reading of Mark's Story of Jesus*. Maryknoll: Orbis Books, 1988.
Nelson, A. E. "'Who Is This?' Narration of the Divine Identity of Jesus in Matthew 21:10-17." *Journal of Theological Interpretation* 7 (2013): 199–211.
Newsom, C. A. *Songs of the Sabbath Sacrifice: A Critical Edition*. Atlanta, GA: Scholars Press, 1985.
Newsom, C. A. and B. W. Breed. *Daniel: A Commentary*. Old Testament Library. Louisville, KY: Westminster John Knox, 2014.
Neyrey, J. H. *The Gospel of John in Cultural and Rhetorical Perspective*. Grand Rapids, MI: Eerdmans, 2009.
Nickelsburg, G. W. E. and J. C. VanderKam. *1 Enoch 2: A Commentary on the Book of 1 Enoch, Chapters 37–82*. Hermeneia. Minneapolis, MN: Fortress, 2012.
Nolland, J. *Luke 18:35–24:53*. Word Biblical Commentary 35C. Dallas, TX: Word Books, 1993.
Nolland, J. *The Gospel of Matthew: A Commentary on the Greek Text*. New International Greek Testament Commentary. Grand Rapids, MI: Eerdmans, 2005.
North, C. R. "The Religious Aspects of Hebrew Kingship." *Zeitschrift für die alttestamentliche Wissenschaft* 50 (1932): 8–38.
North, J. L. "Jesus and Worship, God and Sacrifice." Pages 186–202 in *Early Jewish and Christian Monotheism*. Edited by L. T. Stuckenbruck and W. E. S. North. Journal for the Study of the New Testament Supplement Series 263. London: T&T Clark, 2004.
Noth, M. "Gott, König, Volk im Alten Testament: Eine methodologische Auseinandersetzung mit einer gegenwärtigen Forschungsrichtung." *Zeitschrift für Theologie und Kirche* 47 (1950): 157–91.
O'Rourke, J. J. "The Hymns of the Apocalypse." *Catholic Biblical Quarterly* 30 (1968): 399–409.
Osborne, G. R. *Revelation*. Baker Exegetical Commentary on the New Testament. Grand Rapids, MI: Baker Academic, 2002.
O'Toole, R. F. "Activity of the Risen Jesus in Luke-Acts." *Biblica* 62 (1981): 471–98.
O'Toole, R. F. *Luke's Presentation of Jesus: A Christology*. Subsidia Biblica 25. Rome: Pontificio Istituto Biblico, 2004.
Painter, J. "John 9 and the Interpretation of the Fourth Gospel." *Journal for the Study of the New Testament* 28 (1986): 31–61.
Parkhurst, L. G. "Matthew 28:16-20 Reconsidered." *Expository Times* 90 (1979): 179–80.

Parsons, M. C. "A Christological Tendency in P^{75}." *Journal of Biblical Literature* 105 (1986): 463-79.

Paulien, J. "The Role of the Hebrew Cultus, Sanctuary and Temple in the Plot and Structure of the Book of Revelation." *Andrews University Seminary Studies* 33 (1995): 245-64.

Peeler, A. L. B. *You Are My Son: The Family of God in the Epistle to the Hebrews*. Library of New Testament Studies 486. London: Bloomsbury T&T Clark, 2014.

Peppard, M. *The Son of God in the Roman World: Divine Sonship in Its Social and Political Context*. Oxford: Oxford University Press, 2011.

Peterson, D. *Engaging with God: A Biblical Theology of Worship*. Grand Rapids, MI: Eerdmans, 1993.

Peterson, D. *The Acts of the Apostles*. Pillar New Testament Commentary. Grand Rapids, MI: Eerdmans, 2009.

Porter, C. L. "John IX. 38, 39*a*: A Liturgical Addition to the Text." *New Testament Studies* 13 (1967): 387-94.

Porter, S. E. "Can Traditional Exegesis Enlighten Literary Analysis of the Fourth Gospel? An Examination of the Old Testament Fulfillment Motif and the Passover Theme." Pages 396-428 in *The Gospels and the Scriptures of Israel*. Edited by C. A. Evans and W. R. Stegner. Journal for the Study of the New Testament Supplement Series 104. Sheffield: Sheffield Academic, 1994.

Porter, S. E. "The Unity of Luke-Acts and the Ascension Narratives." Pages 111-36 in *Ascent into Heaven in Luke-Acts: New Explorations of Luke's Narrative Hinge*. Edited by D. K. Bryan and D. W. Pao. Minneapolis, MN: Fortress, 2016.

Powell, M. A. "A Typology of Worship in the Gospel of Matthew." *Journal for the Study of the New Testament* 57 (1995): 3-17.

Price, S. R. F. *Rituals and Power: The Roman Imperial Cult in Asia Minor*. Cambridge: Cambridge University Press, 1984.

Prigent, P. *Apocalypse et Liturgie*. Cahiers Théologiques 52. Neuchâtel: Delachaux et Niestlé, 1964.

Prigent, P. *Commentary on the Apocalypse of St. John*. Translated by W. Pradels. Tübingen: Mohr Siebeck, 2004.

Puech, É. "Notes sur le manuscrit de XIQMelkîsédeq." *Revue de Qumran* 12 (1987): 483-513.

Rainbow, P. A. "Monotheism and Christology in 1 Corinthians 8.4-6." Ph.D. diss., Oxford University, 1987.

Rainbow, P. A. "Jewish Monotheism as the Matrix for New Testament Christology: A Review Article." *Novum Testamentum* 33 (1991): 78-91.

Rainbow, P. A. "Melchizedek as a Messiah at Qumran." *Bulletin for Biblical Research* 7 (1997): 179-94.

Reeves, K. H. "They Worshipped Him, and They Doubted: Matthew 28.17." *Bible Translator* 49 (1998): 344-49.

Reimer, A. M. "The Man Born Blind: True Disciple of Jesus." Page 428-37 in *Character Studies in the Fourth Gospel: Narrative Approaches to Seventy Figures in John*. Edited by S. A. Hunt, D. F. Tolmie, and R. Zimmermann. Grand Rapids, MI: Eerdmans, 2016.

Resseguie, J. L. "John 9: A Literary-Critical Analysis." Pages 295-303 in *Literary Interpretations of Biblical Narratives*. Edited by K. R. R. Gros Louis. Vol. 2. Nashville: Abingdon, 1982.

Reynolds, B. E. "The Use of the Son of Man Idiom in the Gospel of John." Pages 101-29 in *"Who Is This Son of Man?" The Latest Scholarship on a Puzzling Expression of the*

Historical Jesus. Edited by L. W. Hurtado and P. L. Owen. Library of New Testament Studies 390. London: Bloomsbury T&T Clark, 2011.
Rissi, M. *Die Theologie des Hebräerbriefs: Ihre Verankerung in der Situation des Verfassers und seiner Leser*. Wissenschaftliche Untersuchungen zum Neuen Testament 41. Tübingen: Mohr Siebeck, 1987.
Roloff, J. *The Revelation of John: A Continental Commentary*. Translated by J. E. Alsup. Minneapolis, MN: Fortress, 1993.
Rowe, C. K. *Early Narrative Christology: The Lord in the Gospel of Luke*. Beihefte zur Zeitschrift für die neutestamentliche Wissenschaft 139. Berlin: de Gruyter, 2006.
Rowland, C. *The Open Heaven: A Study of Apocalyptic in Judaism and Early Christianity*. London: SPCK, 1982.
Ruck-Schröder, A. *Der Name Gottes und der Name Jesu: Eine neutestamentliche Studie*. Wissenschaftliche Monographien zum Alten und Neuen Testament 80. Neukirchen-Vluyn: Neukirchener Verlag, 1999.
Russo, A. C. "Behind the Heavenly Door: Earthly Liturgy and Heavenly Worship in the Apocalypse of John." Ph.D. diss., University of Notre Dame, 2009.
Schaberg, J. *The Father, the Son and the Holy Spirit: The Triadic Phrase in Matthew 28:19b*. Society of Biblical Literature Dissertation Series 61. Chico, CA: Scholars Press, 1982.
Schäfer, P. *Rivalität zwischen Engeln und Menschen: Untersuchungen zur rabbinischen Engelvorstellung*. Studia Judaica 8. Berlin: de Gruyter, 1975.
Schenck, K. L. "Keeping His Appointment: Creation and Enthronement in Hebrews." *Journal for the Study of the New Testament* 66 (1997): 91–117.
Schenck, K. L. "A Celebration of the Enthroned Son: The Catena of Hebrews 1." *Journal of Biblical Literature* 120 (2001): 469–85.
Schenck, K. L. *Cosmology and Eschatology in Hebrews: The Settings of the Sacrifice*. Society for New Testament Studies Monograph Series 143. Cambridge: Cambridge University Press, 2007.
Schenck, K. L. "The Worship of Jesus among Early Christians: The Evidence of Hebrews." Pages 114–24 in *Jesus and Paul: Global Perspectives in Honor of James D. G. Dunn for His 70th Birthday*. Edited by B. J. Oropeza, C. K. Robertson, and D. C. Mohrmann. Library of New Testament Studies 414. London: T&T Clark, 2009.
Schnackenburg, R. *The Gospel According to St. John*. Translated by K. Smyth, C. Hastings, F. McDonagh, D. Smith, R. Foley, and G. A. Kon. 3 vols. New York: Herder and Herder, 1968–1982.
Schulz, S. *Die Stunde der Botschaft: Einführung in die Theologie der vier Evangelisten*. Hamburg: Furche, 1967.
Schüssler Fiorenza, E. *Revelation: Vision of a Just World*. Edinburgh: T&T Clark, 1993.
Schwartz, D. R. "On Sacrifice by Gentiles in the Temple of Jerusalem." Pages 102–16 in *Studies in the Jewish Background of Christianity*. Wissenschaftliche Untersuchungen zum Neuen Testament 60. Tübingen: Mohr Siebeck, 1992.
Scott, S. R. "The Binitarian Nature of the Book of Similitudes." *Journal for the Study of the Pseudepigrapha* 18 (2008): 55–78.
Seal, D. "Shouting in the Apocalypse: The Influence of First-Century Acclamations on the Praise Utterances in Revelation 4:8 and 11." *Journal of the Evangelical Theological Society* 51 (2008): 339–52.
Shively, E. E. *Apocalyptic Imagination in the Gospel of Mark: The Literary and Theological Role of Mark 3:22-30*. Beihefte zur Zeitschrift für die neutestamentliche Wissenschaft 189. Berlin: de Gruyter, 2012.

Shively, E. E. "Characterizing the Non-Human: Satan in the Gospel of Mark." Pages 127–51 in *Character Studies and the Gospel of Mark*. Edited by C. W. Skinner and M. R. Hauge. Library of New Testament Studies 483. London: Bloomsbury T&T Clark, 2014.

Silverman, D. P. "The Nature of Egyptian Kingship." Pages 49–92 in *Ancient Egyptian Kingship*. Probleme der Ägyptologie 9. Leiden: Brill, 1995.

Simon, M. *Verus Israel: A Study of the Relations between Christians and Jews in the Roman Empire (135–425)*. Translated by H. McKeating. The Littman Library of Jewish Civilization. Oxford: Oxford University Press, 1986.

Slater, T. B. "On the Social Setting of the Revelation to John." *New Testament Studies* 44 (1998): 232–56.

Smith, D. A. *The Post-Mortem Vindication of Jesus in the Sayings Gospel Q*. Library of New Testament Studies 338. London: T&T Clark, 2006.

Smith, D. A. *Revisiting the Empty Tomb: The Early History of Easter*. Minneapolis, MN: Fortress, 2010.

Son, K. *Zion Symbolism in Hebrews: Hebrews 12:18-24 as a Hermeneutical Key to the Epistle*. Paternoster Biblical Monographs. Milton Keynes: Paternoster, 2005.

Spicq, C. *L'Épître aux Hébreux*. 2 vols. Études bibliques. Paris: Gabalda, 1952–1953.

Spilsbury, P. *The Image of the Jew in Flavius Josephus' Paraphrase of the Bible*. Texte und Studien zum antiken Judentum 69. Tübingen: Mohr Siebeck, 1998.

Staley, J. L. "Stumbling in the Dark, Reaching for the Light: Reading Character in John 5 and 9." *Semeia* 53 (1991): 55–80.

Steegen, M. "To Worship the Johannine 'Son of Man': John 9,38 as Refocusing on the Father." *Biblica* 91 (2010): 534–54.

Stefanovic, R. "The Background and Meaning of the Sealed Book of Revelation 5." Ph.D. diss., Andrews University, 1995.

Stein, R. H. *Mark*. Baker Exegetical Commentary on the New Testament. Grand Rapids, MI: Baker Academic, 2008.

Stempvoort, P. A. van. "Interpretation of the Ascension in Luke and Acts." *New Testament Studies* 5 (1958): 30–42.

Stenschke, C. W. *Luke's Portrait of Gentiles Prior to Their Coming to Faith*. Wissenschaftliche Untersuchungen zum Neuen Testament 2/108. Tübingen: Mohr Siebeck, 1999.

Stolz, L. "Das Einführen des Erstgeborenen in die οἰκουμένη (Hebr 1,6a)." *Biblica* 95 (2014): 405–23.

Stuart, D. K. *Hosea-Jonah*. Word Biblical Commentary 31. Nashville, TN: Thomas Nelson, 1987.

Stuckenbruck, L. T. *Angel Veneration and Christology: A Study in Early Judaism and in the Christology of the Apocalypse of John*. Wissenschaftliche Untersuchungen zum Neuen Testament 2/70. Tübingen: Mohr Siebeck, 1995.

Talbert, C. H. "The Concept of Immortals in Mediterranean Antiquity." *Journal of Biblical Literature* 94 (1975): 419–36.

Tarn, W. W. *Alexander the Great, II: Sources and Studies*. Cambridge: Cambridge University Press, 1948.

Taylor, V. "Does the New Testament Call Jesus God?" *Expository Times* 73 (1962): 116–18.

Theissen, G. *The Gospels in Context: Social and Political History in the Synoptic Tradition*. Edinburgh: T&T Clark, 1992.

Thettayil, B. *In Spirit and Truth: An Exegetical Study of John 4:19-26 and a Theological Investigation of the Replacement Theme in the Fourth Gospel*. Contributions to Biblical Exegesis and Theology 46. Leuven: Peeters, 2007.

Thompson, J. W. "The Structure and Purpose of the Catena in Heb 1:5-13." *Catholic Biblical Quarterly* 38 (1976): 352–63.
Thompson, L. L. *The Book of Revelation: Apocalypse and Empire*. Oxford: Oxford University Press, 1990.
Thompson, M. M. *The God of the Gospel of John*. Grand Rapids, MI: Eerdmans, 2001.
Thompson, M. M. *John: A Commentary*. New Testament Library. Louisville, KY: Westminster John Knox, 2015.
Thyen, H. *Das Johannesevangelium*. Handbuch zum Neuen Testament 6. Tübingen: Mohr Siebeck, 2005.
Tuckett, C. "Seeing and Believing in John 20." Pages 169–85 in *Paul, John, and Apocalyptic Eschatology: Studies in Honour of Martinus C. de Boer*. Edited by J. Krans, B. J. Lietaert Peerbolte, P.-B. Smit, and A. Zwiep. Supplements to Novum Testamentum 149. Leiden: Brill, 2013.
Tuckett, C. "Christ and the Emperor: Some Reflections on Method and Methodological Issues Illustrated from the Gospel of Mark." Pages 185–201 in *Christ and the Emperor: The Gospel Evidence*. Biblical Tools and Studies 20. Leuven: Peeters, 2014.
Turner, M. "The Spirit of Christ and Christology." Pages 168–90 in *Christ the Lord: Studies in Christology Presented to Donald Guthrie*. Edited by H. H. Rowdon. Leicester: Inter-Varsity Press, 1982.
Turner, M. "The Spirit of Christ and 'Divine' Christology." Pages 413–36 in *Jesus of Nazareth, Lord and Christ: Essays on the Historical Jesus and New Testament Christology*. Edited by J. B. Green and M. Turner. Grand Rapids, MI: Eerdmans, 1994.
Turner, N. *A Grammar of New Testament Greek: Volume III: Syntax*. Edinburgh: T&T Clark, 1963.
Twelftree, G. H. *Jesus the Exorcist: A Contribution to the Study of the Historical Jesus*. Wissenschaftliche Untersuchungen zum Neuen Testament 2/54. Tübingen: Mohr Siebeck, 1993.
Twelftree, G. H. *In the Name of Jesus: Exorcism among Early Christians*. Grand Rapids, MI: Baker Academic, 2007.
Ulrichsen, J. H. "Διαφορώτερον ὄνομα in Hebr. 1,4: Christus als Träger des Gottesnamens." *Studia Theologica* 38 (1984): 65–75.
Um, S. T. *The Theme of Temple Christology in John's Gospel*. Library of New Testament Studies 312. London: T&T Clark, 2006.
Van Beek, G. W. "Frankincense and Myrrh." *Biblical Archaeologist* 23 (1960): 70–95.
Vanhoye, A. "L'οἰκουμένη dans l'Épître aux Hébreux." *Biblica* 45 (1964): 248–53.
Waaler, E. *The* Shema *and the First Commandment in First Corinthians: An Intertextual Approach to Paul's Re-reading of Deuteronomy*. Wissenschaftliche Untersuchungen zum Neuen Testament 2/253. Tübingen: Mohr Siebeck, 2008.
Wasserman, T. "The 'Son of God' Was in the Beginning (Mark 1:1)." *Journal of Theological Studies* 62 (2011): 20–50.
Watts, R. E. *Isaiah's New Exodus in Mark*. Grand Rapids, MI: Baker Academic, 2000.
Westcott, B. F. *The Epistle to the Hebrews: The Greek Text*. London: Macmillan, 1903.
Wheaton, G. *The Role of Jewish Feasts in John's Gospel*. Society for New Testament Studies Monograph Series 162. Cambridge: Cambridge University Press, 2015.
Widengren, G. *Sakrales Königtum im Alten Testament und im Judentum*. Stuttgart: Kohlhammer, 1955.
Wiebe, G. D. "The Demonic Phenomena of Mark's 'Legion': Evaluating Postcolonial Understandings of Demon Possession." Pages 186–212 in *Exegesis in the Making:*

Postcolonialism and New Testament Studies. Edited by A. Runesson. Biblical Interpretation Series 103. Leiden: Brill, 2011.

Williams, C. H. *I Am He: The Interpretation of 'Anî Hû' in Jewish and Early Christian Literature*. Wissenschaftliche Untersuchungen zum Neuen Testament 2/113. Tübingen: Mohr Siebeck, 2000.

Williams, C. H. "(Not) Seeing God in the Prologue and Body of John's Gospel." Pages 79–98 in *The Prologue of the Gospel of John: Its Literary, Theological, and Philosophical Contexts*. Edited by J. G. van der Watt, R. A. Culpepper, and U. Schnelle. Wissenschaftliche Untersuchungen zum Neuen Testament 359. Tübingen: Mohr Siebeck, 2016.

Witherington, B. *The Acts of the Apostles: A Socio-Rhetorical Commentary*. Grand Rapids, MI: Eerdmans, 1998.

Witherington, B. *The Gospel of Mark: A Socio-Rhetorical Commentary*. Grand Rapids, MI: Eerdmans, 2001.

Witherington, B. *Revelation*. New Cambridge Bible Commentary. Cambridge: Cambridge University Press, 2003.

Witulski, T. "Jesus und der Kaiser: Das Ritual der *Proskynesis*." Pages 101–46 in *Christ and the Emperor: The Gospel Evidence*. Biblical Tools and Studies 20. Leuven: Peeters, 2014.

Woude, A. S. van der. "Melchisedek als himmlische Erlösergestalt in den neugefundenen eschatologischen Midraschim aus Qumran Höhle XI." *Oudtestamentische Studiën* 14 (1965): 354–73.

Wrede, W. *The Messianic Secret*. Translated by J. C. G. Greig. Cambridge: James Clark, 1971 (1st Germ. ed., 1901).

Young, N. H. "The Gospel According to Hebrews 9." *New Testament Studies* 27 (1981): 198–210.

Ziesler, J. A. "The Name of Jesus in the Acts of the Apostles." *Journal for the Study of the New Testament* 4 (1979): 28–41.

Zwiep, A. W. "The Text of the Ascension Narratives (Luke 24.50-3; Acts 1.1-2, 9-11)." *New Testament Studies* 42 (1996): 219–44.

Zwiep, A. W. *The Ascension of the Messiah in Lukan Christology*. Supplements to Novum Testamentum 87. Leiden: Brill, 1997.

Index of Authors

Abbott, E. A.   102 n.1
Adams, E.   47 n.60
Adams, S. A.   47 n.60, 98 n.45
Alcock, S. E.   15 n.5
Allen, D. M.   119 n.10, 120 n.19,
   122 nn.31, 33, 125, 125 nn.48, 49,
   125 nn.52, 53, 134 n.105, 138 n.127,
   139 n.133
Allison, D. C. Jr.   52 n.4, 53 n.7,
   54 nn.8–10, 57 n.17, 57 n.19, 59 n.59,
   62 n.41, 62 nn.43, 44, 63 n.47, 64 n.50,
   64 n.52, 73 n.102, 74 n.106, 75 n.108,
   77 nn.113, 114, 77 n.117, 78 n.120,
   78 n.124, 79 n.129
Alsup, J. E.   60 n.31, 90 n.15, 151 n.43
Anderson, G. W.   30 n.67
Andriessen, P. C. B.   119 n.10, 120 n.14,
   121 n.24, 121 n.27, 122 n.31
Arnold, C. E.   23 n.38, 90 n.15
Attridge, H. W.   119 n.8, 119 n.11,
   120 nn.12, 13, 121 n.27, 122 n.30,
   123 n.41, 124 n.44, 125 n.54, 126 n.60,
   130 n.85, 133 n.101, 134 n.107,
   139 n.133
Aune, D. E.   41 n.33, 60 n.31, 143 n.3,
   143 nn.5, 6, 145 n.9, 146 n.15, 149 n.32,
   150 nn.33, 34, 150 n.38, 151 nn.40, 41,
   151 n.43, 154 nn.54, 55, 155, 155 n.57,
   155 n.60, 156 n.62, 156 n.64, 157 n.67,
   157 n.69, 158 nn.70, 71, 158 n.74, 159,
   160 n.82, 165 n.106, 166, 166 n.108

Bacon, B. W.   129 n.80, 130 n.83
Badian, E.   20 n.20
Balsdon, J. P. V. D.   20 n.20
Barker, M.   29 n.58
Barnard, J. A.   125, 125 n.47, 125 n.49,
   125 n.51, 125 n.55, 128, 128 n.71,
   128 n.77, 130, 130 n.85, 130 n.87,
   132 n.93, 132 nn.96, 97, 132 n.114,
   133 n.98, 134, 134 nn.106, 107, 135,
   135 n.109, 135 n.112, 136 n.116,
   136 n.118, 138 nn.127, 128

Barr, D. L.   145 n.8
Barrett, C. K.   87 n.8, 94 n.30, 97 n.40,
   98 nn.44, 45, 103 n.6, 103 nn.11, 12,
   104 nn.16, 17, 105 nn.21, 22, 106 n.24,
   107 n.34, 109 n.40, 111 n.58
Bartholomew, C.   6 n.40
Bateman, H. W.   42 n.37, 42 n.39, 44, 45,
   45 n.47, 46, 47, 48, 48 n.63, 48 n.67,
   49 n.71, 127 n.68, 130 n.85
Bauckham, R.   6 nn.40, 41, 45 n.48,
   56 n.15, 66, 67, 67 nn.68, 69, 72 n.93,
   72 n.96, 73 n.99, 114 n.67, 119 n.10,
   124, 124 n.45, 125, 125 n.49, 125 n.51,
   125 n.55, 126, 126 n.57, 126 n.59,
   126 n.60, 127, 127 n.64, 128, 128 n.71,
   128 n.75, 129 n.80, 130, 130 n.81,
   130 n.86, 131, 131 n.90, 133 n.98,
   135 n.114, 136 n.116, 137, 137 n.119,
   138 n.128, 143 n.3, 143 n.5, 145 n.26,
   146 n.15, 146 n.18, 148 n.26, 149,
   149 nn.29, 30, 150 n.34, 150 n.36,
   154 n.50, 159 n.77, 160 n.84,
   161 n.86, 166 n.107, 167 nn.112, 113,
   168 nn.113, 114, 174, 175, 175 n.3
Bauer, D. R.   54 n.11, 62 n.42
Baumgarten, A. I.   18
Beale, G. K.   143 n.2, 143 n.4, 145 n.9,
   146 n.15, 146 n.17, 150 n.38, 151 n.39,
   151 n.43, 153 n.49, 154 n.55, 155 n.60,
   156 n.64, 157 n.67, 158 n.70, 158 nn.72,
   73, 158 n.75, 161 n.86, 164 n.103
Beasley-Murray, G. R.   103 n.9,
   104 n.16, 105 n.21, 107 n.31, 108 n.35,
   108 nn.37, 38, 109 n.41, 110 n.54,
   111 n.54, 111 n.59, 143 n.3, 151 n.43
Begg, C. T.   26 n.48
Berger, K.   61 n.40
Bernhardt, K.-H.   29 n.60, 30 n.67
Betz, O.   41 n.33
Beutler, J.   105 n.22
Bieneck, J.   42 n.34
Bieringer, R.   111 n.57, 111 n.60
Biguzzi, G.   146, 146 n.13

Blount, B. K.   143 n.3, 146 n.15, 153 n.49, 158 n.76, 160 n.85
Boccaccini, G.   163 n.100
Bock, D. L.   44 nn.45, 46, 45 n.49, 46, 46 nn.53, 54, 46 nn.56, 57, 87 n.8, 90 n.16, 95 n.33, 96 n.34, 97 n.40, 98 nn.44, 45
Borgen, P.   60 n.31
Boring, M. E.   61 n.40
Bormann, L.   57 n.18
Bornkamm, G.   56 n.15
Bosworth, A. B.   17 n.12, 20 n.20
Botha, P. J.   146 n.12
Bousset, W.   23 n.37, 149 n.27
Bovon, F.   92 n.22, 93 n.28
Bowden, J.   6 n.40
Boxall, I.   143 n.3, 146 n.15, 153 n.49, 158 n.70
Brandon, S. G. F.   29 n.60
Braukämper, U.   19 n.16
Braun, H.   119 n.9, 123 n.41, 126 n.60
Breed, B. W.   26 n.49
Briant, P.   17 n.10
Brosius, M.   17 n.10
Brown, R. E.   54 n.8, 54 n.10, 103 n.10, 103 n.13, 104 nn.16, 17, 104 n.20, 105 nn.21, 22, 107 n.31, 110 n.54, 111 n.54, 111 nn.58, 59, 113 n.65, 127 n.67
Brown, S.   106 n.28
Bruce, F. F.   86, 86 n.4, 97 n.40, 98 n.45, 119 n.10, 120 nn.19, 20, 122 n.31, 123 n.41, 125 n.54, 126 n.60
Bryan, D. K.   89 n.14
Buckwalter, H. D.   95 n.32, 99 n.47
Bultmann, R.   41, 41 nn.30, 31, 103 n.9, 105 n.22, 110 n.54, 111 n.59
Burchard, C.   22 n.34
Byrskog, S.   73 n.101

Caird, G. B.   128 n.76, 133 n.99, 143 n.3, 151 n.43
Caneday, A. B.   119 n.10, 120 n.14, 120 nn.19, 20, 121 n.27, 122 n.31
Capes, D. B.   6 n.40, 73 n.99
Carey, E.   29 n.57, 32 n.73, 33 n.75
Carnegie, D. R.   155 nn.59, 60, 156 n.64, 157 n.65, 158 nn.72, 73
Carrell, P. R.   23 n.38, 159 n.78, 161 n.86

Carson, D. A.   103 n.8, 103 n.12, 103 n.14, 103 n.16, 104 n.17, 105 nn.21, 22, 107 n.31, 107 n.34, 108 n.35, 108 n.39, 109 n.40, 110 n.54, 111 n.54, 111 n.59, 113 n.64, 115 n.70
Carter, W.   54 n.8, 57 n.19, 58 n.21, 61 n.40, 62 n.43, 63 n.47, 75 n.108, 78 n.120, 79 n.129, 110 n.52
Casey, P. M.   97 n.39
Charles, J. D.   155 n.58
Charles, R. H.   149 n.27, 153, 153 n.49
Charlesworth, J. H.   21 n.22
Chester, A.   6 nn.40, 41, 23 n.37, 24 n.41, 24 n.44, 132 n.93
Clines, D. J. A.   30 n.67
Cockerill, G. L.   119 n.10, 120 n.19, 120 n.21, 121 n.24, 122 n.31, 122 n.33, 122 n.35, 123 n.39, 123 n.41, 125 n.54, 126 nn.60, 61, 132 nn.96, 97, 133 n.104, 134 n.107, 139 n.133
Cohen, S. J. D.   27 nn.52–4, 86 n.5
Collins, A. Yarbro   37 n.8, 39 n.19, 39 n.21, 42 n.37, 42 n.41, 44 nn.45, 46, 46, 46 nn.53, 54, 46 nn.56, 57, 48 n.68, 49 n.71, 57 n.18, 60 n.31, 72 n.93, 145 n.9, 155 n.60
Collins, C. J.   104 n.15
Collins, J. J.   42 n.38, 48 n.68, 72 n.93
Coloe, M. L.   104 n.19, 105 n.23
Colpe, C.   61 n.40
Compton, J.   129, 129 nn.78–80, 130, 130 nn.82, 83, 131, 132 n.92, 133, 133 n.99
Cotter, W.   58 n.25, 60 n.31, 61 n.40
Crouch, J. E.   57 n.18, 92 n.22
Crump, D. M.   97 n.42
Cullmann, O.   126 n.61

Daniels, P. T.   17 n.10
Davies, W. D.   52 n.4, 53 n.7, 54 nn.8–10, 57 nn.18, 19, 59 n.27, 62 n.41, 62 nn.43, 44, 64 n.50, 64 n.52, 73 n.101, 74 n.106, 75 n.108, 77 n.113, 114, 77 n.117, 78 n.120, 78 n.124, 79 n.129
Davila, J. R.   21 n.22, 29 n.58, 45 n.48, 97 n.39
Davis, C. J.   71 n.91, 95 n.33
Davis, R. D.   155 n.56
Day, J.   30, 30 n.66

De Boer, M. C.   52 n.5
Deichgräber, R.   156 n.64, 157 n.65, 159 nn.79, 80
Denaux, A.   90 n.15
Derrett, J. D. M.   38 n.11, 74 n.106
deSilva, D. A.   122, 122 n.32, 125 n.54, 126 n.60, 132 n.97
Deutsch, C.   74 n.108
Dey, L. K. K.   126 n.56
Dillon, R. J.   92 nn.22, 23, 93 n.25
Docherty, S. E.   118 n.7, 121 n.27, 122 n.33, 123 n.37
Dormandy, R.   38 n.13
Duke, P. D.   107 nn.32, 33, 109 n.41
Dunn, J. D. G.   3, 3 nn.20–4, 4, 4 n.28, 9, 9 nn.44, 45, 58 n.26, 91 n.19, 98 n.45, 117, 117 n.1, 124 n.46, 126, 126 n.62, 127 n.63, 131, 132, 132 nn.92–5, 133 n.99, 153 n.49, 161 n.86, 169, 172

Edwards, J. R.   77 n.119
Ego, B.   33 n.74, 33 n.76
Ehrhardt, A.   90 n.15
Ehrman, B. D.   89 n.13
Ellingworth, P.   118 n.4, 119 n.10, 120 n.22, 122 n.31, 122 n.33, 123 nn.36, 37, 126 n.60, 128 n.74, 129 n.80, 130 n.81, 132 n.97, 139 n.133
Ellis, I. P.   63 n.48
Engnell, I.   29 n.59
Eskola, T.   134 n.108
Evans, C. A.   42 n.41, 44 nn.45, 46, 46, 46 nn.55–7, 106 n.25
Eve, E.   58 n.25

Fee, G. D.   73 n.99, 74 n.104
Fekkes, J.   157 n.66
Fennema, D. A.   110 n.54, 111 n.54
Fishwick, D.   147 n.20
Fitzmyer, J. A.   87 n.8, 90 nn.15, 16, 92 n.22, 96 n.34, 98 n.45
Flessen, B. J.   86 nn.6, 7
Fletcher-Louis, C. H. T.   27 nn.51, 52, 28 n.55, 29 n.58, 93 n.27, 136 n.117
Fossum, J. E.   6 n.40
Fox, M. V.   32 n.73
Fox, R. L.   20 n.20
Fraine, J. de.   29 n.60, 30 n.67

France, R. T.   24 n.10, 36 nn.5, 6, 42 n.39, 53 n.7, 54 nn.8, 9, 57 n.19, 58 nn.26, 27, 62 nn.41–3, 63, 63 n.47, 63 n.49, 64 nn.51, 52, 74 nn.105, 106, 75 n.108, 77 n.117, 79 n.130
Frankfort, H.   29, 29 n.60, 30 n.61
Fredriksen, P.   6 n.40
Friesen, S. J.   145 nn.7, 8, 145 nn.10, 11
Frye, R. N.   17 n.11

Gallusz, L.   165 n.105
Garrett, S. R.   94 n.30
Garroway, J.   38 nn.12, 13, 39 nn.14–16
Gathercole, S. J.   47 n.62, 48 n.64, 48 n.66
Gheorghita, R.   118 n.7
Giblin, C. H.   63 n.48, 148 n.23, 150 n.35
Gieschen, C. A.   125 n.55, 132 n.93, 163 n.100
Giversen, S.   60 n.31
Glasson, T. F.   129 n.80, 130 n.81, 130 n.83
Gnilka, J.   57 n.19, 63 n.47, 78 n.120
Goodenough, E. R.   23 n.34
Gow, A. S. F.   17 n.12
Grabiner, S.   142 n.1
Grayston, K.   63 n.48
Green, J. B.   90 n.17, 91 n.19, 92 n.22, 161 n.86
Greeven, H.   2, 2 nn.9–12, 3, 3 n.25, 9, 9 n.47, 22 n.32, 44 n.9, 169, 172
Greig, J. C. G.   41 n.30
Gros Louis, K. R. R.   107 n.32
Grundmann, W.   54 nn.9, 10, 57 n.19, 63 n.47, 64 n.52, 78 n.120
Gundry, R. H.   39 n.19, 52 n.5, 57 n.19, 59 n.27, 78 n.120
Guthrie, D.   161 n.86
Guthrie, S. C.   126 n.61

Hagner, D. A.   53 n.7, 54 nn.9, 10, 57 n.19, 59 n.27, 62 nn.41, 42, 64 n.51, 73 n.101, 78 n.120, 79 n.127, 79 n.129
Hahn, F.   41 nn.30, 31
Hall, C. A. M.   126 n.61
Hamm, D.   92 n.22, 93 n.26
Hannah, D. D.   23 n.38, 136 n.116, 137 n.120
Harris, E.   110 n.52

Harris, M. J. 110 n.54, 111 n.54, 111 n.59, 123 n.40, 126 n.60
Hauge, M. R. 39 n.19
Hay, L. S. 42, 42 nn.34–6, 43 n.42
Hayman, P. 6 n.40
Head, P. M. 65, 65 nn.55–7, 67, 75, 77 n.119
Heil, J. P. 57 nn.17, 18, 57 n.20, 109 n.41, 139 n.133, 161 n.86
Held, H. J. 56 n.15, 67 n.72, 79 n.127
Hengel, M. 6 n.40, 41 n.33, 136 n.116
Héring, J. 119 n.9, 120 n.17
Hoffmann, M. R. 158 nn.70–2, 161 n.86
Hofius, O. 110 n.54, 111 n.54, 133, 133 n.102
Holladay, C. R. 41 n.33
Holleran, J. W. 109 n.41, 113 n.65
Holtz, T. 158 n.70, 167 n.113
Hooke, S. H. 29 nn.59, 60
Horsley, R. A. 38 n.13, 39 n.17
Horst, J. 4, 4 nn.29–32, 5, 5 nn.33–7, 6, 6 nn.38, 39, 9, 9 n.44, 9 n.46, 9 nn.48, 49, 14 n.4, 29 n.57, 37, 37 n.8, 38, 38 n.9, 52 n.5, 53, 53 n.6, 55, 55 n.12, 64 n.50, 66, 66 nn.63–6, 81, 87 n.8, 99, 99 n.48, 102 n.1, 109 n.41, 119 n.9, 147 n.22, 167 n.113, 169, 172, 174, 174 n.2
Horst, P. W. 63 n.48
Hoskins, P. M. 104 n.19, 105 n.23, 114 n.68
Howell, J. R. 86 n.6
Hubbard, B. J. 62 n.43
Hunt, A. S. 106 n.28
Hunt, S. A. 106 n.28, 107 n.33
Hunter, A. M. 74 n.108
Hurst, L. D. 126, 126 n.62, 128, 128 n.76, 133 n.99, 135 n.110, 135 n.112
Hurtado, L. W. 6 nn.40, 41, 23 n.38, 24 nn.42, 43, 29 n.57, 46 n.58, 55, 55 n.13, 56 n.15, 67, 67 nn.70–2, 73 n.99, 74 n.104, 74 n.107, 89 n.12, 95 n.31, 95 n.33, 98 n.43, 98 n.45, 108 n.36, 115 nn.69–70, 132 n.93, 133 n.98, 137 n.124, 152 n.46, 156 n.62, 160 n.84, 161 n.86, 162 n.97, 167 n.112, 168 n.115, 174, 175, 175 n.4

Jipp, J. W. 119 n.10, 120 n.19, 121 n.27, 124 n.44
Jobes, K. H. 3 n.24

Johansson, D. 45 n.52, 46 n.56, 46 n.58, 47 nn.60–2, 48 n.64, 49 n.71, 57 n.18, 58 n.22, 58 n.25, 73 n.99, 91 n.19
Johnson, A. R. 30 n.67
Johnson, L. T. 118 n.4, 119 n.10, 125 n.55, 126 n.60, 130 n.85, 139 n.133
Jonge, H. J. de 137 n.119
Jörns, K.-P. 142 n.1, 156 n.64, 157 nn.65, 66
Juel, D. 42 n.37, 44 n.44

Karrer, M. 66 n.60
Kee, H. C. 47 n.62
Keener, C. S. 54 n.9, 10, 79 n.129, 86 n.6, 90 n.16, 94 n.30, 97 n.40, 98 n.45, 103 n.8, 103 n.14, 104 nn.16, 17, 105 n.22, 106 n.27, 107 n.34, 109 n.40, 110, 110 n.50, 110 n.54, 113 n.65
Keith, C. 125 n.48
Kerr, A. R. 104 nn.19, 20, 105 n.23, 114 n.68
Kezbere, I. 98 n.44
Kiddle, M. 143 n.2, 149 n.27, 151 n.43
Kim, H. C. 67, 67 n.74
Kingsbury, J. D. 41 n.33, 42 n.37, 42 nn.39, 40, 43, 43 n.43, 44, 44 n.44, 47, 47 n.62
Knight, H. 41 n.30
Kobelski, P. J. 72 n.93
Koester, C. R. 111 n.57, 119 n.10, 120 n.14, 120 n.19, 122 n.31, 123 n.38, 123 n.41, 124 n.44, 125 n.54, 126 n.60, 131 n.91, 132 n.97, 139 n.133, 154 n.55, 159 n.76, 165 nn.105, 106
Kossen, H. B. 105 n.22
Köstenberger, A. J. 103 n.5, 104 nn.16, 17, 105 n.22, 107 n.31, 107 n.34, 109 n.40, 110 n.54, 111 n.54, 111 n.58
Krans, J. 111 n.58
Kuhrt, A. 15 n.5
Kupp, D. D. 65, 65 n.58, 66 n.59, 67, 70 n.90, 74 n.106

Laansma, J. 135 n.111
Lane, W. L. 118 n.6, 119 n.10, 120 n.14, 120 n.19, 120 n.23, 122 n.31, 123 n.39, 123 nn.41, 42, 124 n.44, 125 n.54, 131 n.91, 132, 132 n.92, 132 n.97, 133 n.103, 139 n.133

Lanfranchi, P.   137 n.119
La Potterie, I. de.   103 n.4
Leander, H.   38 n.13, 39 nn.14–16
Lee, A. H. I.   132 n.93
Leim, J. E.   47 nn.60–2, 48 n.64, 68, 68 nn.75–7, 69, 69 nn.78–81, 70, 70 nn.82–9, 71, 71 n.91, 72 n.98, 73 nn.100, 101, 74, 74 n.103, 74 n.108, 75, 75 n.108, 76, 76 nn.109–11, 77, 77 n.112, 77 nn.113–15, 77 nn.117–19, 78 n.120, 79, 79 nn.128–31, 80, 80 nn.132, 133, 81, 81 n.135, 82, 172
Lemcio, E. E.   65, 65 nn.53, 54, 67, 75
Levinskaya, I.   86 n.7
Lewis, G. S.   29 n.58, 45 n.48, 97 n.39
Lierman, J.   74 n.104
Lincoln, A. T.   104 n.18, 105 n.22, 106 n.27, 107 n.34, 109 n.40, 110 n.54, 111 n.55, 111 n.58, 113 n.63, 113 n.65, 114 n.66, 122 n.29
Lindars, B.   107 n.31, 107 n.34, 110 n.54, 111 n.58
Llewelyn-Jones, L.   17 n.10
Loader, W. R. G.   119 n.9, 120 n.14, 120 n.16, 125 n.54
Lohfink, G.   91, 92 n.21, 92 n.22
Longenecker, R. n.   114 n.67
Lührmann, D.   42 n.34
Luz, U.   57 n.18, 57 n.19, 62 n.41, 62 nn.43, 44, 63 n.45, 64 n.52, 70 n.90, 74 nn.106, 107, 75 n.108, 78 n.120

McDonough, S. M.   133 n.98, 135 n.111
McGrath, J. F.   3 n.19, 161, 161 nn.87–93, 162, 162 n.95, 162 n.98, 164, 164 n.102, 164 n.104, 165, 165 n.105, 166, 166 n.108, 167 n.113, 172
McKay, K. L.   63 n.48
McKeating, H.   23 n.37
Mackie, S. D.   135 n.110
Manzi, F.   72 n.93
Marcus, J.   31, 36 nn.4–6, 40 n.23, 46 n.59
Marshall, I. H.   90 n.16, 92 n.22, 95 n.32, 156 n.62
Martin, M. W.   89 n.13
Martin, R. P.   156 n.62
Martínez, F. G.   72 n.97
Mason, E. F.   48 n.68, 71 n.92, 72 n.93, 72 n.96, 135 n.110

Mastin, B. A.   27 n.50, 110 n.54, 111, 111 nn.55, 56
Mathewson, D. L.   153 n.49
Meier, J. P.   131, 131 n.91, 133 n.98, 133 n.100
Menken, M. J. J.   78 n.123, 79 n.130
Metzger, B. M.   89 n.14, 107 n.31, 110 n.54
Michaels, J. R.   103 n.8, 104 nn.16, 17, 105 n.22, 107 n.31, 107 n.34, 108 n.39, 109 n.40, 110 n.54, 111 n.61
Michel, O.   119 n.9, 120 n.17, 121 n.27, 139 n.133
Milik, J. T.   72 n.93
Moffitt, D. M.   119 n.10, 120 n.14, 120 nn.19, 20, 122 n.31, 123 n.36, 123 n.38, 136 n.117
Moloney, F. J.   108 nn.38, 39
Montefiore, H.   119 n.8
Moore, C. A.   32 n.73, 33 n.75
Moore, S. D.   38 n.13
Morris, L.   104 n.15, 105 n.22, 109 n.40, 110 n.54, 111 nn.58, 59
Morton, R. S.   152, 152 n.44
Motyer, S.   129 n.80, 130 n.82, 130 n.84, 130 n.88
Moule, C. F. D.   2, 2 nn.13, 14, 9 n.44
Mowinckel, S.   30 n.67
Mowry, L.   156 n.63
Moyise, S.   78 n.123
Müller, E.   152 n.45
Müller, M.   66, 66 n.60, 66 nn.61, 62, 67, 70 n.90
Mussies, G.   153 n.49
Myers, C.   38 n.13, 39 n.17

Nelson, A. E.   79 n.130
Newman, C. C.   29 n.57, 29 n.58, 45 n.48, 97 n.39
Newsom, C. A.   26 n.49, 72 n.94
Neyrey, J. H.   115 n.69
Nickelsburg, G. W. E.   137 nn.121–3, 137 n.125
Nolland, J.   57 n.19, 58 n.26, 62 n.41, 62 n.43, 64 n.50, 75, 78 n.120, 79 n.129, 90 n.15, 90 n.18, 92 n.22, 93 n.28
North, C. R.   30, 30 nn.62–4
North, J. L.   2, 2 nn.15, 16, 3, 3 nn.17, 18, 4, 4 n.27, 8, 8 n.42, 9, 9 nn.43, 44, 9 n.46, 119 n.8, 167, 167 n.110, 169, 172

North, W. E. S.   2 n.15, 27 n.51
Noth, M.   30, 30 n.65

Ogg, G.   41 n.30
Oropeza, B. J.   124 n.46
O'Rourke, J. J.   156 n.63
Osborne, G. R.   143 n.3, 143 n.5, 145 n.9, 146 n.15, 150 n.38, 151 nn.40, 41, 153 nn.48, 49, 155 n.60, 156 n.64, 157 n.69, 158 n.70, 158 n.75, 159 n.76, 160 n.85, 161 n.86, 167 n.111
O'Toole, R. F.   95 n.32, 99 n.47
Owen, P. L.   108 n.36

Pahl, M.   98 n.45
Painter, J.   109 n.41
Pao, D. W.   89 n.14
Parkhurst, L. G.   63 n.48
Parsons, M. C.   89 n.13
Paulien, J.   155 n.56
Peeler, A. L. B.   125 n.55, 132 n.93, 132 n.96, 133 n.98
Pennington, J. T.   135 n.111
Peppard, M.   42 n.41
Perrin, B.   17
Peterson, D.   67, 67 n.73, 87 n.8, 95 n.32, 96 n.34, 97 n.40, 98 n.45
Pietersma, A.   21 n.22
Porter, C. L.   107 n.31
Porter, S. E.   89 n.14, 106 n.25, 106 nn.29, 30
Powell, M. A.   56 n.16, 66, 66 n.67, 67
Price, S. R. F.   19 n.18, 146 n.12, 146 n.14
Prigent, P.   143 n.3, 153 n.49, 155 n.60, 157 n.66, 158 n.75
Puech, É.   72 n.93

Rainbow, P. A.   6 n.40, 72 n.93, 73, 73 nn.101, 102
Reeves, K. H.   63 n.48
Reimer, A. M.   107 n.33, 109 n.41
Reiterer, F. V.   33 n.74
Resseguie, J. L.   107 n.32, 109 n.41
Reumann, J.   47 n.62
Reynolds, B. E.   108 n.36, 110 n.51
Rissi, M.   126 n.56
Roloff, J.   151 n.43, 158 n.70, 165 n.106

Roth, D. T.   125 n.48
Rowdon, H. H.   91 n.19, 155 n.59
Rowe, C. K.   86 n.6, 98 n.46
Rowland, C.   6 n.40
Ruck-Schröder, A.   95 n.32
Runesson, A.   39 n.22
Russo, A. C.   157 n.66, 159 n.81

Schaberg, J.   62 n.41
Schäfer, P.   23 nn.36, 37
Schenck, K. L.   121 n.25, 121 n.27, 123 n.36, 124, 124 n.46, 125, 125 nn.49, 50, 125 n.54, 126 n.62, 128, 128 nn.72, 73, 132 nn.92-4, 133 n.101, 134 n.107, 135, 135 nn.111-13, 136, 136 n.115, 138, 172
Schnackenburg, R.   103 n.8, 103 n.14, 104 n.16, 105 nn.21, 22, 106 n.24, 107 n.31, 107 n.34, 108 n.37, 109 n.41, 110, 110 n.48, 110 n.54
Schulz, S.   41 nn.30, 31
Schüssler Fiorenza, E.   145 n.9, 155 n.58
Schwartz, D. R.   84 n.1
Scott, S. R.   163 n.100
Seal, D.   155 n.58
Shively, E. E.   39 n.19, 39 n.21, 40 n.25, 49 n.69
Silverman, D. P.   19 n.17
Simon, M.   23 n.37
Skinner, C. W.   39 n.19
Slater, T. B.   145 n.9
Smith, D. A.   60 nn.31, 32, 89 n.14
Smyth, K.   103 n.8
Son, K.   124 n.43
Spicq, C.   119 n.8, 119 n.11, 120 nn.12, 13, 126 n.60, 127 n.69, 139 n.133
Spilsbury, P.   27 n.50
Staley, J. L.   109 n.41
Steegen, M.   109, 109 nn.42-6, 110, 110 nn.47-50, 110 n.53, 111, 111 n.57, 111 n.60, 114, 172
Stefanovic, R.   158 n.70
Stegner, W. R.   106 n.25
Stein, R. H.   36 n.3, 39 n.19, 42 n.39, 47 n.62
Stempvoort, P. A. van   92 n.22, 92 n.24
Stenschke, C. W.   87 n.8

Stolz, L.   119 n.9, 120 n.16, 120 n.18, 121, 121 n.28
Stuart, D. K.   96 n.37
Stuckenbruck, L. T.   2 n.15, 24 nn.39, 40, 24 n.44, 27 n.51, 124 n.44, 148 nn.24, 25, 149, 149 n.29, 149 n.31, 150 n.33, 150 nn.36, 37, 161 n.86

Talbert, C. H.   60 n.31
Tarn, W. W.   20 n.20
Taylor, V.   127 n.67, 128 n.70
Theissen, G.   38 n.13, 39 n.15, 52 n.3
Thettayil, B.   104 n.19
Thompson, J. W.   119 n.10, 121 n.26, 125 n.54
Thompson, L. L.   145 n.9, 154 n.55, 155 n.60, 158 n.72
Thompson, M. M.   102 n.2, 103 n.7, 103 n.12, 104 nn.16, 17, 105 nn.21, 22, 106 n.27, 107 n.31, 110 n.54, 111 nn.58, 59
Thyen, H.   109 n.41
Tigchelaar, E. J. C.   72 n.97
Tolmie, D. F.   107 n.33
Tromp, J.   137 n.119
Tuckett, C.   39 n.19, 39 n.21, 111 n.58
Turner, M.   91 n.19, 95 n.33, 161 n.86
Turner, N.   120 n.21
Twelftree, G. H.   39 nn.19, 20, 49 n.70

Ulrichsen, J. H.   125, 125 n.55, 126, 126 n.56, 126 nn.58, 59
Um, S. T.   104 n.19, 114 n.68

Van Beek, G. W.   77 n.117
VanderKam, J. C.   137 nn.121, 122, 137 n.123, 137 n.125
van der Watt, J. G.   111 n.56
Vanhoye, A.   119 n.10
Verheyden, J.   90 n.15

Waaler, E.   73 n.101
Wasserman, T.   41 n.28
Watts, R. E.   40 n.24
Weinrich, W. C.   128 n.76
Westcott, B. F.   119 n.9, 120 nn.17, 18
Wheaton, G.   105 n.23
Widengren, G.   29 n.59
Wiebe, G. D.   39 n.22
Williams, C. H.   57 n.17, 111 n.56
Witherington, B.   37 n.8, 39 n.19, 48 n.64, 88 n.10, 94 n.30, 97 n.40, 98 n.45, 144 n.6
Witulski, T.   39 n.18, 40 n.26, 43 n.41
Worthington, I.   20 n.20
Woude, A. S. van der   72 n.93
Wrede, W.   41, 41 nn.30–2
Wright, B. G.   21 n.22
Wright, N. T.   126 n.62

Xeravits, G. G.   33 n.74

Young, N. H.   135 n.111

Ziesler, J. A.   95 n.32
Zimmermann, R.   107 n.33
Zsengellér, J.   33 n.74
Zwiep, A. W.   89 n.14, 91, 91 n.20, 92 n.22

Index of References

OLD TESTAMENT

Gen
1:1–10	58 n.22
2:2	118 n.6
4:26	96 n.35
5:24	60, 60 n.32
6:2	118
6:4	118
12:8	96 n.35
13:4	96 n.35
15:1	57
18:2	22 n.33
18–19	22 n.33, 90
19:1	22 n.33
22:5	151 n.42
24:12–27	53
24:26–27	157 n.68
24:48	21 n.27
26:24	57
26:25	96 n.35
28:12	104 n.20
28:17	104 n.20
28:19	104 n.20
32:3–8	53
33:1–3	53
33:3–7	151 n.42
37:5–11	31
37:10	77
42:6	25, 77
43:26	25, 77
43:28	25
48:12	24

Exod
3:14	157 n.67
4:31	21 n.27
7:1	127 n.63
11:8	25, 55
12:22	106 n.30
12:46	106 n.30
13:21	45 n.52
14:1–15:21	58 n.23
14:15–31	58 n.25
14:16	58 n.25, 58 n.58
14:26	58 n.25
15:10–11	58 n.24
15:11	147 n.19
18:7	24
20:5	21 n.26, 31 n.69
20:11	58 n.22
21:6	127 n.63
22:8	127 n.63
23:20	72 n.98
24:16	45 n.52
25:40	134
27:3	154 n.55
32:8	21 n.26, 31 n.69
33:10	151 n.42
34:5	45 n.52
34:5–8	59
38:23	154 n.55

Lev
2:1–2	77
16:2	45 n.52
26:1	4 n.26, 31 n.69

Num
4:14	154 n.55
11:25	45 n.52
14:14	45 n.52
16:22	56 n.14
22:31	22, 59, 60 n.30, 148 n.26, 151 n.42
24:17	54
25:2	21 n.26, 31 n.69

Deut
1:33	45 n.52
4:19	21 n.26, 31 n.70
6:5	70
6:13	52, 76 n.111
6:14–15	52
10:20	76 n.111
14:1ff	42
17:3	31 n.70, 77 n.114
23:1	84 n.1
31:1–8	62
31:6	62
31:8	62
31:23	62
32:9	73
32:18–20	42
32:39	57, 130
32:43	4, 22 n.29, 122, 129, 130, 131, 134 n.105
33:1–34:6	61
34:6	60

Josh
1:1–9	62
3:7–4:18	58 n.25
3:8–13	58 n.58
5:14	22, 22 n.32, 148 n.26
7:6–9	56 n.14
7:19	143 n.4
10:4	78 n.121
23:7	21 n.26

Judg
2:2	4 n.26
2:3	4 n.26
3:17–18	77
6	90

6:11–16	62	16:4	26 n.46	2:15	25		
6:19	22 n.33	18:21	25	4:27	56 n.14		
6:23	57	18:28	26 n.46	4:37	25		
7:15	21 n.27	24:20	26 n.46	6:26	78 n.121		
13	90			16:7	78 n.121		
13:20	23 n.35,	1 Kgs		17:35	21 n.26		
	148 n.26	8:10–11	45 n.52	18:22	84		
13:20–22	23 n.35	8:43	96 n.35	19:19	78 n.122		
		10:1–13	54	21:21	21 n.26,		
Ruth		17:21	96 n.36		31 n.69		
2:10	24	18:12	90 n.16				
		18:24	96 n.35,	1 Chr			
1 Sam			96 n.36	16:8	96 n.35		
4:4	134 n.108	18:24–28	96 n.36	16:35	78 n.122		
12:17–18	96 n.35,	19:5–8	75 n.108	21:16	23 n.35, 90,		
	96 n.36	22:19	45 n.50,		148 n.26		
25:32–33	24		138 n.128	21:16–17	56 n.14		
26:19	73		48 n.65,	22:7–16	62		
		22:19–22	154 n.52	22:11	62		
2 Sam				22:16	62		
6:2	134 n.108	2 Kgs		29:10–19	164 n.101		
7:12–13	118	1:8	69	29:11–12	158 n.71		
7:13	127	2:1–18	60	29:20	21 n.27,		
7:14	42, 118, 129	2:8	58 n.25		28, 30, 161,		
7:16	118, 127	2:9–12	61		164 n.101		
22:4	96 n.35	2:13–14	58 n.25				
22:7	96 n.36	2:16	90 n.16	2 Chr			
		5:11	96 n.35,	7:3	21 n.27, 59		
1 Kgdms			96 n.36	20:18–19	21 n.27		
1:19	22 n.28	19:15	128 n.71,	24:17	26		
2:36	25, 55		134 n.108	29:28–30	21 n.27,		
12:18	31 n.68				157 n.68		
15:25	22	3 Kgdms					
15:30–31	22 n.28	1:16	26, 26 n.46,	Neh			
24:9	25		55	9:6	22, 58 n.22,		
28:13	26	1:23	26 n.46		128 n.71,		
28:14	26	1:31	26 n.46		138 n.128		
		1:53	26				
2 Kgdms		2:13	26	Esth			
9:6	26	2:46b	77	3:2	32		
9:7–8	53	19:18	4 n.26,	4:8	96 n.36		
9:8	26 n.46,		14 n.4	5:1	96 n.36		
	151 n.42			8:3	56 n.14		
14:4	26, 55,	4 Kgdms					
	78 n.121	1:13	56 n.14	Job			
14:22	26 n.46	2:8	59	1:6	118 n.3		
14:33	26 n.46	2:9–10	91	1:6–12	48 n.65		
15:1–6	55	2:9–11	91	1:20–21	21 n.27		
15:32	22 n.28	2:14–15	59, 87	2:1	118 n.3		

9:8	57, 58 n.23	29:1	118	70:22	154 n.53
15:8	48 n.65	29:3	58 n.22	71:10	77
17:14 (LXX)	96 n.36	30:10	78 n.122,	71:11	26 n.47,
19:21	78 n.121		78 n.126		28 n.56
26:11–12	58, 58 nn.23, 25	30:17	78 n.122	71:17	28 n.56
		31:18	96 n.35	71:19	147 n.19
33:28	78 n.122	32:2	154 n.53	72:10–11	54, 78 n.123
38:7	118 n.3	33:6–9	157	72:15	54, 78 n.123
38:8–11	58 n.23	33:7	58 n.22	74:12–15	58 n.23
38:16	57, 58 n.23	35:10	147 n.19	77:13–20	58 n.24
		37:11	78 n.123	77:19	57, 58 n.23
Ps		40:1–3	158 n.74	78:2	78 n.123
1:3	78 n.123	40:5	78 n.122,	78:9	78 n.122
2	121		78 n.126	79:6	96 n.35,
2:7	28 n.56, 30 n.66, 42, 118, 129	40:11	78 n.122, 78 n.126	80:1	96 n.36 134 n.108
		42:4	154 n.53	80:1–3	154 n.53
2:8	118	43:27	78 n.122,	80:10	4 n.26
3:8	78 n.122		78 n.126	82:1	48 n.65, 71, 127, 127 n.63, 154 n.52
5:12	93 n.27	44:7–8	28 n.56		
6:3	78 n.122, 78 n.126	44:13	26 n.47, 28 n.56	82:6	127 n.63
6:5	78 n.122	45	121, 126	85:2	78 n.122
7:2	78 n.122	45(LXX 44):7–8		85:3	78 n.122, 78 n.126
8:3	78 n.123, 79, 80, 157	45:7	123 30 n.66, 127	85:9	22 n.31
8:6	127 n.63	45:7–8	126, 127, 129	85:16	78 n.122
9:14	78 n.122, 78 n.126	47:8	133	88:28	28 n.56
		49:15	96–7 n.38	89(LXX 88)	121
11:2	78 n.122, 78 n.126	50:3	78 n.122	89:6–8	147 n.19
		53:3	78 n.122	89:6–9	58 n.24
11:4	138 n.128	53:5	96 n.36	89:7	118
14:4	96 n.35, 96 n.36	55:2	78 n.122, 78 n.126	89:8–9 89:9	58 58 n.23
16:8–11	96	56:2	78 n.122	89:26–27	42
18:7	96 n.36	56:8–9	154 n.53	89:27	121
18:15	58 n.25	58:3	78 n.122	89:28	121
18:16	58, 58 n.23	59:7	78 n.122	89:30	121
19:10	78 n.122, 78 n.126	65:4	21 n.27	91:1–4	154 n.53
		65:7	58, 58 n.23	91:15	96 n.35
20:5	28 n.56	66:4	157 n.68	95:5	58 n.22, 157
21:22	78 n.122	68:2	71, 78 n.122	95:11	118 n.6
21:28	22 n.31	68:2–4	78	96	130
22:8	78 n.123	68:15	78 n.122	96:1–2	158 n.74
24:3–4	78 n.123	68:15–16	78	96:5	128 n.71
24:16	78 n.122	69:1–3	58, 58 n.23	96:7	4 n.26, 22 n.29, 31 n.69, 122, 130
25:11	78 n.122	69:6	78 n.122		
26:7	78 n.122	69:14–15	58, 58 n.23		
27:9	78 n.122	70:2	78 n.122		

97:5	71, 154 n.53	110(LXX 109):1	124	13:6	71
97:7	127 n.63	110:1	45, 96, 129	13:10	71
98:1–2	158 n.74	110:4	127	14:12–15	30
99:1	134 n.108	116:4	96 n.36	19:1	45 n.52
99:6	96 n.36	116:13	96 n.35	24:21–22	49
101	131	117:25	78 n.122, 78 n.126	26:19	69
101:1–16	130			29:18–19	69
101:1–23	130	118:29	78 n.122	31:3	30
101:17–23	130, 130 n.88	118:58	78 n.122	33:2	78 n.122
101:23	130	118:86	78 n.122	35:5–6	69
101:24	130	118:94	78 n.122	37:20	78 n.122
101:24a	130, 131	118:132	78 n.122	40:3	69, 71, 71 n.91, 72, 95
101:24b–29	130, 131	118:146	78 n.122		
101:24b–25a	130	119:176	78 n.123	40:28	128 n.71
101:24–29	130	122:3	78 n.122, 78 n.126	41:4	57
101:26	123 n.37, 130			43:1	58 n.20
		130:8	78 n.123	43:2	58 n.20, 58 n.23
101:26–28	131	135:5–6	58 n.24	43:5	58 n.20
101:27	123 n.37	135:6	58 n.22	43:10	57
102	128	136:5–9	157	43:16	58 n.20, 58 n.23
102(LXX 101):26–28	123, 123 n.37	138:1	127 n.63		
		144:7	58, 58 n.23	43:23	77
102:24	130	144:9–11	158 n.74	44:3	91
102:25	157	145:18	96 n.35	44:5	96 n.36
102:26–28	128, 129, 130	146:6	58 n.22, 157	44:7	147 n.19
102:27–28	128	146:7	154 n.53	44:15–19	4 n.26
103:2	123 n.37	150:3	154 n.53	44:17	21 n.27
103:5	123 n.37			44:23	93 n.27
103:19–21	138 n.128	Prov		44:24	128 n.71
104	123	1:28	96 n.36	45:14	150
104(LXX 103):4	122	2:3	96 n.36	45:18	128 n.71
		8:12	96 n.36	46:5	147 n.19
104:3	45 n.52	8:29	58 n.23	46:6	31 n.69
104:7	58 n.25	18:6 (LXX)	96 n.36	49:3	93 n.27
104:7–9	58 n.23			49:7	163
105:19	4 n.26	Song		49:23	150
105:47	78 n.122, 78 n.126	3:6	77, 77 n.117	50:2	58 n.23, 58 n.25
		4:6	77, 77 n.117		
106:9	58 n.25	4:14	77, 77 n.117	51:10	58 n.23
107:1–3	154 n.53			51:15	58 n.23
107:7	78 n.122	Isa		52:7	71, 71 n.92
107:23–30	58 n.23	1:2	42	55:5–6 (LXX)	96 n.36
107:29	58	2:8	4 n.26, 31 n.69	60:14	150
108:26	78 n.122, 78 n.126			61:1	69
		6:1–13	154 n.52	61:2	71
109:1	28 n.56	6:3	157	64:6	96 n.35, 96 n.36
109:3	129	6:8	48 n.65		
110	68, 69, 121	10:15	93 n.27	66:23	22

Index of References

Jer		7:8	146,	Mic	
1:4–10	62		146 n.16	1:3–4	71
1:16	21 n.26,	7:9	46	5:2	129
	31 n.69	7:9–10	154 n.52	5:12	4 n.26
2:27	78 n.122	7:10	45 n.50	5:13	31 n.69
3:16–17	134 n.108	7:13	45, 129	7:18	147 n.19
3:19	42	7:13–14	62, 62 n.42		
5:22	58 n.23	7:21	146	Nah	
6:20	77	7:24	146	1:3–4	58 n.23
8:2	31 n.70	7:25	146, 146 n.16	1:4	58 n.25
9:22–23	93 n.27	8:15	90	3:5	157 n.67
10:10–12	128 n.71	8:17	23 n.35, 90		
10:25	96 n.36	8:17–18	148 n.26	Hab	
17:14	78 n.122	8:18	148 n.26	3:15	57, 58 n.23
31:35	58 n.23	10:9–10	23 n.35,		
33:2	77 n.114		148 n.26	Zeph	
		10:12	57	1:5	4 n.26
Lam		10:13	40 n.24	2:11	22 n.31
3:55–57	96 n.36	10:20–21	40 n.24	3:9	96 n.35,
		11:36	30, 146		96 n.36
Ezek		11:36–37	146,		
1:4	45 n.52		146 n.16	Zech	
8:16	31 n.70			10:3	157 n.67
9:8	56 n.14	Hos		13:9	96 n.35,
11:24	90 n.16	7:7	96 n.35		96 n.36
28:1–10	30	7:11	96 n.36	14:9	133
36:27	91	12:6	157 n.67	14:16–17	22 n.31, 105
		13:4	128 n.71		
Dan				Mal	
2:19–23	26	Joel		1:6	42
2:26–30	26	2:1	71	3:1	69, 71,
2:37	158 n.71	2:29	91		72 n.98
2:46	26	3:1–5	95	3:19	69
2:46–47	87	3:5	95, 96,	3:23	69, 91
2:47	26 n.49		96 n.35	3:23–24	69
3	26, 162, 164				
3:5	31 n.69	Amos		**NEW TESTAMENT**	
3:12–18	21 n.26	3:13	157 n.67		
3:92	118 n.4	4:13	157 n.67	Matt	
3:95	21 n.26	5:8	58 n.23	1:18–23	67
4	26	5:14–16	157 n.67	1:18–25	54
5:11–12	27	5:25–27	85	1:21	70, 73,
5:17–23	26	9:5	157 n.67		78 n.123
6:3	27			1:21–25	70
6:25–27	26	Jonah		1:23	66, 70, 72
6:27	21 n.26	1:4–16	58 n.23,		n.98, 74
7	146,		58 n.24		n.105, 82
	146 n.17	1:6	96 n.36	1–2	53
7:2–7	146	1:9	58 n.22	2	76, 77, 80

Index of References

2:1–12	77, 81	8:2	1 n.7, 2, 3, 5,	14:30–33	80, 170, 173
2:2	1 n.7, 10, 51,		8, 10, 51, 55,	14:31	65
	54, 65, 67, 77,		76, 77 n.119,	14:32	57, 58
	77 n.119, 82,		82, 170	14:33	1 n.7, 2, 4, 5,
	170	8:3	55, 76		9, 10, 51, 57,
2:4–6	54	8:4	66		58, 65, 67, 69,
2:6	73	8:23–27	58, 79		75 n.108, 76,
2:7	54	8:25	78, 80, 170		82, 107 n.35,
2:8	1 n.7, 10, 51,	8:27	59, 75 n.108		170
	54, 65, 67, 77,	8:29	59 n.29, 69	15:21–28	79
	77 n.119, 82,	9:6	75 n.108	15:22	55, 65, 76, 78,
	170	9:18	1 n.7, 2, 3, 5,		80
2:9	54		8, 10, 51, 55,	15:22ff	66
2:10	54		76, 77 n.119,	15:22–25	80, 170, 173
2:11	1 n.7, 2, 3		82, 170	15:22–26	5
	n.24, 4, 9, 10,	9:25	55, 76	15:25	1 n.7, 2, 3, 8,
	51, 54, 63,	9:27	80		10, 51, 55, 65,
	65, 67, 77,	9:27–28	78		76, 77 n.119,
	77 n.119,	9:27–31	79		78, 80, 82,
	78 n.123, 82,	10:32–33	59 n.29		170
	170	11:1–12:8	69	15:27	76
2:15	69	11:3–5	69, 71	15:28	55
3:1–17	69	11:4–5	75 n.108	15:31	127 n.65
3:3	69, 71	11:10	69, 71,	16:16	69, 107 n.35
3:3 par.	173		72 n.98	16:27	121
3:4	69	11:14	69	17:5	69
3:9–10	69	11:16–24	69	17:7	78 n.119
3:10–12	69	11:25	80, 84	17:14–18	79
3:11	69	11:25–27	69	17:15	78, 80
3:12	73	11:27	59 n.29, 69,	17:24	78 n.119
3:13	69		75 n.108, 82	18:12	78 n.123
3:17	59 n.29, 69	12:1–8	69	18:19	70
4:1–11	52	12:25–29	80	18:19–20	70, 74, 170
4:3	59 n.29, 69	12:26	84	18:20	67, 70, 74
4:6	59 n.29, 69	12:50	59 n.29		n.105, 80
4:8	52	13:35	78 n.123	18:23–35	52, 52 n.5
4:8–10	64, 64 n.52	14:12	78 n.119	18:26	1 n.5, 2, 3,
4:9	1 n.4, 51, 52,	14:22–25	56		51 n.2, 52, 53,
	63	14:22–33	9, 56, 69, 79,		55, 56, 63, 80,
4:9–10	2, 162, 170,		81, 82, 173		82, 170
	174	14:25–26	57, 58 n.20	18:29	53, 56
4:10	1 n.3, 51, 52,	14:26–27	57	18:35	52
	65, 66, 76,	14:27	57, 58 n.20	19:16–17	66
	76 n.111,	14:28	70	20:20	1 n.7, 2, 3, 3
	80, 82,174	14:28–29	58 n.20		n.24, 10, 51,
4:11	75 n.108	14:28–31	57		55, 65, 76, 77
5:5	78 n.123	14:30	70, 78, 80,		n.119, 81, 82,
5:8	78 n.123		170		170
7:21	59 n.29	14:30–31	58	20:20ff	66

20:20–21	65	28:16–18	64 n.52	4:35–41	49 n.71
20:20–23	5	28:17	1 n.7, 2, 3, 4,	4:38	41 n.27
20:21	55		5, 9, 9 n.49,	4:41	59
20:30–31	78, 80		10, 51, 60, 62,	5:3	39
20:30–33	78		63, 65, 67, 76,	5:3–5	36
20:30–34	79		82, 151 n.42,	5:4	39
21:1–11	79		170	5:6	1 n.7, 2, 8, 10,
21:9	79	28:17–20	80, 81, 170,		35, 37, 38, 39,
21:12	79		173		43, 56, 169
21:14	79	28:18	62, 75 n.108,	5:6–7	40
21:14–15	79		78 n.119, 173	5:7	36, 37, 41, 43,
21:15	79	28:18–20	9, 60, 61		169
21:16	78 n.123, 79,	28:19	62, 70, 74, 91,	5:7–12	36
	80, 170		170	5:9	36
21:37–38	69	28:19–20	62, 70	5:10	38
21:41	78 n.123	28:19–20a	62	5:10–12	36
22:34–40	70, 73	28:20	61 n.39, 62,	5:11	38
22:41–46	68, 70, 73,		67, 70,	5:13	36, 38
	172		74 n.105	5:14–20	36
22:42	68			5:22	2, 51, 55
22:45	68	28:20b	62	5:33	35
23:5–7	73			5:34–43	49 n.71
23:8	70	Mark		5:35	41 n.27
23:8–10	70, 73,	1:1	42	6:14–16	41 n.27
	73 n.102, 80,	1:3 par	72	6:45–52	49 n.71,
	170	1:7	40		57 n.18, 173
		1:8 par.	173		
23:9	70	1:10–11	49 n.71	6:50	46 n.58
23:10	70	1:11	41, 42, 44,	7:25	35, 55
24:29–30	71		169	7:28	41 n.27
24:31	73	1:11 par.	118 n.5	8:27–33	44
26:53	75 n.108	1:21–28	36	8:28	41 n.27
26:63–64	172	1:23	36 n.4	8:29	41 n.27
26:69	78 n.119	1:23–27	49 n.71	8:38	41 n.29, 47,
26:73	78 n.119	1:24	8, 36, 38, 41,		47 n.61, 48
27:29	56		49	9:2–3	43
27:43	78 n.123	1:34	8, 38, 41	9:2–8	47 n.62
27:45	62	1:40	2, 35, 51, 55	9:5	41 n.27
27:51	62	1:40–42	49 n.71	9:7	41, 42, 43, 44,
27:54	107 n.35	2:1–12	49 n.71		169
27:58	78 n.119	3:1–6	49 n.71	9:7 par.	118 n.5
28:5	63	3:11	36, 37 n.7, 40,	9:9	42, 43
28:5–6	62		43, 107 n.35,	9:17	41 n.27
28:9	1 n.7, 2, 3, 4,		169	9:38	41 n.27
	5, 9, 10, 51,	3:11–12	8, 38, 41	10:17	35, 41 n.27
	60, 62, 63, 67,	3:22	40	10:17–18	5
	76, 77 n.119,	3:22–27	40, 49	10:18	127 n.65
	81, 82, 170	3:23–27	49, 169	10:20	41 n.27
28:9–10	62	3:24	40	10:35	41 n.27, 55
28:10	63	3:27	39, 49	10:47	41 n.27

10:47–48	44, 47	15:39	41, 42, 44,	20:41–44	96, 172
10:48	41 n.27		107 n.35	22:41	97 n.41
10:51	41 n.27			22:69	99
11:7–10	47	Luke		22:69–70	172
11:21	41 n.27	1:5–25	92 n.22	23:4	88 n.11
12:1–9	42	1:12	90	23:6	88 n.11
12:6	41 n.29	1:13	57	23:14	88 n.11
12:14	41 n.27	1:17	98 n.46	23:34	97
12:19	41 n.27	1:19	45 n.50	23:46	97
12:28–30	6	1:32–35	42 n.38,	23:47	88 n.11
12:29	174		118 n.5	24:1–12	90
12:30 par.	174	1:35	107 n.35	24:5	90
12:32	41 n.27, 174	1:43	98	24:13–35	90
12:35	42	1:46–55	156	24:15	90, 170
12:35–37	44, 47, 172	1:68	127 n.65	24:16	64
13:1	41 n.27	1:68–79	156	24:31	90, 170
13:24–32	47	1:76	98 n.46	24:34	98, 99
13:26	48	2:9	90	24:36	90
13:27a	47 n.61	2:10	57	24:36–37	170
13:28b	47 n.61	2:11	98	24:36–43	63, 64, 90
13:32	41 n.29, 48,	2:13	120	24:37	90
	49, 169	3:4	98 n.46	24:38–43	90
14:45	41 n.27	4:1–13	83	24:44–48	95
14:53–65	44	4:6	84	24:44–49	90
14:61	46 n.59	4:7	1 n.4, 83, 84,	24:47	91
14:61–62	41 n.29, 43,		93, 99, 170	24:49	91, 91 n.19,
	47, 50, 169,	4:7–8	94, 162, 174		93, 95, 96, 99,
	172	4:8	1 n.3, 83, 93,		170, 173
14:61–64	44		94, 99, 170,	24:50	92
14:62	42, 48		174	24:50–53	89, 91, 92,
14:63–64	169	4:19	98 n.46		92 n.22, 93,
14:64–65	43	5:8	89		99, 170, 173
15:1–15	37	5:12	55, 89	24:51	91, 95
15:2	37, 44, 47	7:8	88 n.11	24:51–52	91
15:9	37, 41 n.27	7:34	88 n.11	24:52	1 n.7, 2, 3, 9,
15:12	37, 41 n.27	7:38	89		9 n.49, 10, 83,
15:16–20	37	8:25	59		89, 91, 92, 93,
15:17	37	8:28	89		99 n.48, 170
15:18	37, 41 n.27	8:41	55, 89	24:52–53	174
15:18–19	40	8:47	89	24:53	92, 93, 94
15:19	1 n.7, 2, 3, 5,	10:2	98 n.46		
	10, 35, 37,	10:21	84	John	
	38, 39, 40, 50,	10:39	89	1:1	110, 112, 113,
	56, 97 n.41,	11:18	84		114, 115, 116,
	169	13:16	84		171
15:21–32	37	14:52	4	1:1–18	49 n.71, 116,
15:26	37, 41 n.27, 47	17:16	89		156
15:32	37, 41 n.27,	18:9–14	92 n.22	1:3	173
	42, 47	19:35–40	79	1:6	112

1:12–13	106 n.27	4:20–24	1 n.3, 101,	8:12	105
1:14	104, 110,		104, 109, 113,	8:14	112
	111 n.54, 112,		114, 116, 171,	8:23	112
	114, 115, 171		173, 174	8:28	108
1:17	104	4:21	102 n.1	8:42	112
1:18	110, 111,	4:21–24	102	9:1–7	107
	111 n.56, 112,	4:22	102, 102 n.1	9:8–12	107
	113, 115, 116,	4:23	1 nn.2, 3, 101,	9:11	107
	127 n.67, 171		102 n.1, 103,	9:13–17	107
1:29	106		109	9:13–34	107
1:29–36	106	4:24	102 n.1, 103	9:14	107
1:32–33	49 n.71	4:48	106 n.28	9:15	107
1:33	112	4:49	113 n.63	9:16	107, 112
1:34	107 n.35	5:1	105	9:17	107, 112
1:49	107 n.35	5:7	113 n.63	9:18–23	107
1:50	106 n.28	5:17	115	9:24	107, 112, 115,
1:51	104, 104 n.20,	5:18	115 n.69		143 n.4
	108, 109, 115,	5:19	115	9:24–34	107
	171	5:21	115	9:25	112
2:13	105	5:22	115	9:27–28	107
2:13–22	104, 105	5:23	115, 174	9:29	107, 112
2:13–25	106	5:27	108, 109	9:30	107, 112
2:19–22	105	6:1–14	106	9:31–32	112
2:21	109, 171	6:1–71	105	9:33	107, 112, 113,
3:2	112	6:14	112		116, 171
3:5	103, 104	6:16–21	173	9:34	107
3:6	103, 104	6:22–71	106	9:35	107
3:8	103	6:23	113 n.63	9:35–38	171
3:11	108 n.39	6:27	108, 109	9:35–41	106 n.28
3:11–13	108, 110	6:30	106 n.28	9:36	108, 113 n.63
3:12–13	108 n.39	6:33	112	9:37	108
3:13	108, 112, 113,	6:34	113 n.63	9:38	1 n.7, 2, 5, 10,
	115, 171	6:38	112		101, 107, 108,
3:13–14	109	6:46	112		109, 110, 113,
3:14	108	6:50	112		113 n.63, 116,
3:14–15	108 n.35	6:50–62	110		171, 173, 174
3:17	112	6:51	112	9:38a	116, 171
3:18	107 n.35	6:53	108, 109	9:38b	116, 171
3:19	112	6:58	112	9:39	107, 108, 112,
3:28	112	6:62	108, 109, 112,		113, 113 n.62,
3:31	112		113, 115, 171		171
3:31–32	108 n.39, 110	6:68	113 n.63	9:40–41	107
3:32	108	7:1–8:59	105	10:22–39	105
3:34	105	7:8	105	10:33	115 n.69
4:1	113 n.63	7:10	105	10:36	106, 112
4:10	103, 104	7:29	112	11:2	113 n.63
4:11	113 n.63	7:37–38	105	11:3	113 n.63
4:14	103, 104	7:37–39	104	11:21	113 n.63
4:20	102, 102 n.1	7:38–39	103, 104	11:27	107 n.35, 112

11:32–33	114	19:13–42	106	3:6–7	94, 170		
11:45	106 n.28	19:14	106	3:16	94, 95		
11:47–12:8	106	19:29	106 n.30	4:9–10	95		
11:47–50	106	19:31	106	4:10	94		
11:48	106 n.26	19:33	106 n.30	4:12	95, 97 n.38, 99		
11:51–52	106	19:36	106 n.30				
11:55	105, 106	19:42	106	4:17–18	95		
12:1	105	20:14	64	4:24	84		
12:19	105	20:17	111, 114	4:30	94, 170		
12:20	1 n.3, 101, 105, 109, 116, 171, 173, 174	20:18	113 n.63	5:4	88		
		20:20	113 n.63	5:14	98 n.46		
		20:22	104, 173	5:28	89 n.11, 95		
12:21	105	20:25	64, 113 n.63	5:29	88		
12:23	108	20:25–29	106 n.28	5:31	94, 170		
12:23–32	105, 106	20:28	110, 111, 112, 113 n.63, 114, 116	5:38–39	88		
12:24	106			5:40	95		
12:32	105, 106			5:41	95		
12:34	108	20:31	107 n.35	6:1	105		
12:44–45	106 n.28	21:4	64	7:40–43	174		
12:46	112			7:41–43	85		
13:1	105	Acts		7:42	85		
13:1–17:26	106	1:1–11	91	7:43	1 n.4, 83, 85, 94, 99, 127 n.66, 170		
13:3	112	1:2	91				
13:6	113 n.63	1:2–3	95				
13:13–14	113 n.63	1:3	91	7:49	84		
13:31	108	1:4–5	91, 95	7:55–56	94, 97, 170		
13:37	113 n.63	1:8	91, 95	7:55–60	97, 98		
14:5	113 n.63	1:9	95	7:59	97, 170, 173		
14:6	104	1:11	91	7:59–60	98, 99		
14:8	113 n.63	1:21	98	7:60	97		
14:13–14	173	1:24	99	8:12	95		
14:17	104	1:24–25	98 n.45	8:16	95, 170		
14:22	113 n.63	2:1–4	95	8:25	98 n.46		
15:16	173	2:14–21	95	8:27	1 n.3, 83, 84, 93, 94, 99, 151 n.42, 170		
15:26	104, 173	2:21	72, 95, 97, 99, 170, 173				
16:7	104, 173						
16:13	104			9:4	98 n.44		
16:23–24	173	2:22–32	96	9:14	74 n.107, 98, 99, 170, 173		
16:26	173	2:33	91 n.19, 94, 96, 97, 99, 170, 173				
16:27–28	112			9:15	95		
16:28	112			9:16	95		
16:30	112	2:33–36	96, 98, 99, 172	9:17	98		
17:3	127 n.65, 174			9:20	107 n.35		
17:5	112	2:34	97	9:21	74 n.107, 98, 170, 173		
17:8	112	2:36	94, 97, 98				
17:18	112	2:38	95, 96, 97, 170	9:27–28	95		
18:6	114			9:29	105		
18:37	112	2:47	98 n.46	9:31	98 n.46		
19:7	115 n.69	3:1	92 n.22	9:35	98 n.46		

9:40	97 n.41	16:25	156	14:26	156		
10:1	86	16:29	98 n.44	15:27	120		
10:1–6	85	16:31	98 n.44, 99				
10:2	85	17:23	127 n.66	2 Cor			
10:3	92 n.22	17:24	84	1:19	108 n.35		
10:4	85	17:31	94, 99	4:4	127 n.66		
10:7–23	85	19:5	95, 170				
10:22	85, 87	19:13–20	94	Gal			
10:25	1 n.5, 2, 85, 94	19:26	127 n.66, 174	1:5	159 n.80		
		19:37	127 n.66	2:20	108 n.35		
10:25–26	60 n.30, 83, 88 n.10, 98, 98 n.44, 99, 170	20:28	127 n.67	3:6	127 n.65		
		20:36	97 n.41	4:8	127 n.66		
		21:5	97 n.41				
		21:13	95	Eph			
10:26	85	21:14	98 n.46	3:20–21	159 n.80		
10:30	92 n.22	21:17–26	84 n.1	4:6	127 n.65		
10:31	85	22:7	98 n.44	5:19	156		
10:33	86	22:16	74 n.107, 97, 97 n.38, 99, 170, 173	6:12	40 n.24		
10:36	88, 94, 97 n.38, 98, 99, 170, 173			Phil			
				2:6–11	156		
10:40–43	88	24:11	1 n.3, 83, 84, 93, 94, 99, 105, 151 n.42	2:9–11	115, 126		
10:42	94, 99			3:19	127 n.66		
10:43	94, 95, 170			4:20	159 n.80, 160		
10:48	95, 170	24:14	127 n.65				
11:20	105	24:17	84 n.1	Col			
11:21	98 n.46	26:14	98 n.44	1:15–20	156		
12:21–23	6	26:18	84	2:18	23		
12:22	85, 127 n.66	28:3–6	86, 88, 88 n.10	3:16	156		
12:22–23	88, 88 n.10, 98, 174	28:4	88 n.10	1 Thess			
12:23	127 n.66	28:6	98, 127 n.66	1:9	127 n.65		
13:2	98 n.45, 99			4:17	45 n.51		
13:10	98 n.46	Rom		5:2	72		
13:11	98 n.46	2:17	93 n.27				
13:33	42 n.38, 118 n.5	9:5	127 n.67	2 Thess			
		10:13	72, 96	2:3–4	146 n.16		
13:38–39	94	11:36	159, 159 n.80	2:4	6, 127 n.66		
13:44	98 n.46	16:25–27	159 n.80				
14:11	127 n.66			1 Tim			
14:11–13	85	1 Cor		1:17	159, 159 n.80, 160		
14:11–15	88, 88 n.10, 98	1:2	74, 96				
		1:31	72, 93 n.27	2:5	127 n.65		
14:14–15	127 n.66	5:1–5	74 n.105	6:16	159 n.80		
14:15	174	5:4	74 n.105				
15:26	95	8:4	6	2 Tim			
16:7	91 n.19	8:4–5	127 n.66	2:22	74 n.107		
16:14	98 n.46	8:6	6, 127 n.65	4:18	159 n.80, 160, 160 n.83		
16:18	94, 170	14:25	1 n.3				

Index of References

Titus		1:10	125, 128, 133,	10:28–30	122
2:13	127 n.67		171, 173	10:30	119
		1:10–12	123 n.37, 127,	11:16	122
Heb			128, 129,	11:21	1 n.3, 117 n.2
1	117, 133, 134		131 n.91, 171	12:2	127
1:1	127 n.65	1:11–12	128, 129	12:22	122
1:1–4	118, 131	1:13	118, 121, 124,	12:28	139
1:2	118, 126, 131,		127, 131 n.91,	13:8	127
	133, 173		171	13:14	122
1:2b	131 n.91, 171	1:14	122, 123, 123	13:15–16	139
1:2c	131 n.91, 171		n.38, 124, 135	13:21	139 n.133, 159
1:3	118, 121, 122,		n.114, 136		n.80, 160 n.83
	124, 127, 132,		n.114		
	134,	2:1–18	137	Jas	
	134 n.105	2:3	122	5:13	156
1:3a	131 n.91	2:5	121, 122		
1:3b	131 n.91	2:9	120	1 Pet	
1:3d	131 n.91, 171	2:9–10	122	4:11	159 n.80,
1:3–4	133	2:12–13	119		160 n.83
1:3–13	172	4:1–11	118 n.6	5:11	159 n.80
1:4	125, 126, 133	4:4–5	119		
1:4–5	133	4:16	134	2 Pet	
1:5	42 n.38, 118,	6:5	122	1:1	127 n.67
	119, 121, 124,	6:19–20	134	3:18	159 n.80, 160,
	125, 131 n.91	7:11–28	129		160 n.83
1:5–2:18	23	7:24	127		
1:5–13	133	8:1	127	1 John	
1:5–14	118, 124, 126	8:1–2	134, 136	4:15	108 n.35
	n.56, 129, 131		n.116, 173	5:5	108 n.35
1:6	1 n.7, 2, 3, 4,	8:2	134, 135	5:20	127 n.67
	5, 9, 10, 117,		n.112, 136		
	119, 120, 121,		n.114	Jude	
	122, 124, 129,	8:5	134, 135 n.112	24–25	159 n.80
	134 n.105,	8:6	136 n.114	25	160
	138, 139, 171,	9	134		
	173, 174	9:3	134	Rev	
1:6a	119	9:3–5	134, 136 n.116	1:1	150 n.34
1:7	122, 123,	9:7	134	1:5–6	160, 162,
	123 n.38, 133,	9:11–12	134, 135 n.112		172
	135 n.114	9:13–14	122	1:8	168 n.113
1:7–8	126	9:14	139	1:9–22:9	150
1:7–12	124	9:21	136 n.114	1:13	163
1:8	118, 121, 126,	9:23	135 n.112	1:13–16	162
	127, 171	9:24	134, 135 n.112	1:17	148 n.26,
1:8–9	121, 123, 125,	9:25	134		161
	127, 128,	10:11	136 n.114	2:14	167
	131 n.91	10:11–23	137	2:20	167
1:8–12	123, 129	10:12	127	2–3	145
1:9	126, 126 n.60	10:20	134	3:8	151

3:9	1 n.5, 2, 3, 5, 147 n.21, 150, 151, 161, 165, 167, 171	5:8–10 5:8–12 5:8–14 5:9	152, 159 153 n.49, 167 164 165	9:20 11:1	1 n.4, 143, 144, 147, 167, 171, 174 1 n.3, 143, 147, 151, 172
3:21	163, 165 n.105, 173	5:9–10	152, 158, 159, 162, 165, 172	11:7–13	61 n.38
4	45 n.49	5:9–14	142 n.1	11:12	45 n.51
4:1–5:14	135	5:10	157, 158	11:13	143 n.5
4:2	154, 154 n.51	5:11–12	152, 159	11:15	162, 167, 167 n.113, 172
4:4	154	5:12	158, 162, 165, 172	11:15–16	142
4:5	154				
4:8	152, 157, 162, 165	5:13	143 n.5, 153, 154 n.51, 159, 162, 165, 167, 172	11:15–17 11:15–18 11:15–19 11:16	142 142 n.1, 166 135 1 n.3, 141, 147, 147 n.21, 152 n.47, 153 n.49, 161, 172
4:8–11	138 n.128, 142, 142 n.1, 152, 159, 166, 167	5:13–14	152, 153 n.49, 159, 166, 167 n.113, 173		
4:9	143 n.5, 154 n.51	5:13–14a	160		
4:9–10	157	5:14	1 n.3, 1 n.7, 3, 10, 141, 147, 147 n.21, 151, 151 n.43, 153, 153 n.49, 160, 161, 166, 167, 172	11:16–18 11:17–18 11:18 11:19 12:7–9 12:10–12	138 n.128, 142 162 143 n.5 154 49 142 n.1, 162, 172
4:9–11	152, 153 n.49, 157				
4:10	1 n.3, 141, 147, 147 n.21, 152 n.47, 153, 153 n.49, 154 n.51, 155, 161, 166, 172				
4:10–11	156	6:9–11	158 n.76	12:17	164
4:11	143 n.5, 152, 153, 153 n.49, 155, 157, 158, 159, 162, 165	6:16 7:10 7:10–11 7:10–12	154 n.51 154 n.51, 162, 164, 167, 172 142 142, 142 n.1, 166	13 13:1 13:1–2 13:1–4 13:1–15	144, 145, 161, 165, 166 146 146 164 174
4–5	152, 153, 154, 155, 155 n.56, 159, 160, 161, 163, 165, 166, 174	7:11	1 n.3, 45 n.50, 141, 147, 147 n.21, 152 n.47, 153 n.49, 161, 172	13:1–18 13:2 13:3 13:4	40 n.24, 144 147, 165 165 1 n.4, 144, 144 n.6, 146, 147, 166, 171
5:1	154 n.51				
5:1–2	48 n.65, 152	7:11–12	142, 166	13:5	146
5:1–4	159	7:12	143 n.5, 158 n.71, 160, 162	13:5–6	146
5:5	157, 158			13:7	146, 165
5:5–12	159			13:8	1 n.4, 144, 144 n.6, 146, 147, 166, 171
5:6	157, 165	7:15	154, 154 n.51, 161		
5:7	154 n.51, 165				
5:7–8	157	8:2	45 n.50	13:12	1 n.4, 144, 146, 147, 164, 166, 167, 171
5:8	153, 154, 157, 158 n.76, 159, 161, 166, 167	8:3 8:3–4 9:13	154 158 n.76 154	13:13–14	146

Index of References

13:14	144	19:5	143 n.5	**APOCRYPHA and**	
13:14–15	146, 164	19:6–8	162, 172	**SEPTUAGINT**	
13:15	1 n.4, 144, 147, 164, 166, 167, 171	19:7	143 n.5	Bar	
		19:9–10	149	3:2	78 n.122
		19:10	1 n.3, 1 n.6, 23, 138 n.131, 143, 147, 147 n.21, 148, 149, 149 n.29, 150, 161, 167, 171, 172		
14:1	167 n.113			Bel	
14:4	167			4	31 n.69
14:6–11	147			5	128 n.71
14:7	1 n.3, 143, 147, 158, 172, 174			36	90 n.16
14:9	1 n.4, 144, 144 n.6, 147, 171	19:11–20:3	40 n.24	Add Esth	
		19:14	121	C 5–7	33, 66, 162, 162 n.96
14:9–11	144, 167, 174	19:20	1 n.4, 144, 147, 171	D	33
14:11	1 n.4, 144, 144 n.6, 147, 171	20:4	1 n.4, 144, 144 n.6, 147, 165 n.105, 171	Ep Jer	
				5	4 n.26, 22 n.30, 31 n.69
14:14	163				
14:15–16:17	135	20:7–10	40 n.24		
14:15–17	154	20:11	154 n.51	Jdt	
14:18	154	21:1	158	3:8	96 n.36
15:1	148	21:2	158	5:7–8	22
15:3–4	142 n.1, 162	21:5	154 n.51, 158	6:18–19	21 n.27
15:4	1 n.3, 143, 147, 172, 174			6:19	78 n.122
		21:6	168 n.113	7:26	96 n.36
15:5–8	154	21:8	167	8:17	96 n.36
15:6	149	21:9–22:9	147, 149	8:18	4 n.26, 31 n.69
16:1	154	21:22	167 n.113		
16:2	1 n.4, 144, 147, 167, 171	22:1	163, 165 n.105, 173	9:12	58 n.22
				10:23	25, 77
16:5	58 n.25	22:3	161, 163, 165 n.105, 167 n.113, 173	13:17	21 n.27, 157 n.68
16:5–7	142 n.1, 162				
16:7	154			13:17–18	24
16:9	143			14:7	25
16:13–14	40 n.24	22:3–4	167 n.113	16:1–2	158 n.74
16:17	154	22:6	150, 150 n.34	16:2	96 n.35
17:1–19:10	147, 149	22:6–9	149		
17:2	167	22:8	1 n.6, 147 n.21, 149, 150, 171	1 Macc	
18:3	167			4:54	154 n.53
19:1	143 n.5			4:55	21 n.27, 157 n.68
19:1–2	162	22:8–9	23, 138 n.131, 143, 147, 148, 149, 149 n.29, 150, 161, 167		
19:1–4	142, 166				
19:1–8	142 n.1			2 Macc	
19:4	1 n.3, 141, 142, 147, 147 n.21, 152 n.47, 153 n.49, 154 n.51, 161, 166, 172			1:24	128 n.71
		22:9	1 n.3, 147, 148, 172	2:8	45 n.52
				3:15	96 n.36
		22:13	168 n.113	3:31	96 n.35
		22:15	167	3:34	90 n.16

7:27	78 n.121	5–12	90	4Q400	
8:2	96 n.35	11:14	23, 24	1 I, 1–20	134
10:4	56 n.14	11:17	24	1 I, 20	72
10:25–26	56 n.14	12:16	23 n.35, 90,	1 II, 7	72, 127 n.63
12:15	96 n.35		148 n.26		
		12:16–22	149 n.29	4Q403	
3 Macc		12:17	57	1 I, 30–36	128 n.71
1:16	56 n.14			1 I, 32–33	72, 127 n.63
6:12	78 n.122	Wis		1 I, 41–46	134
		2:12–20	42		
4 Macc		6:21	128	4Q405	
4:10–11	23 n.35, 148 n.26	7:22	131	20 II–21–22	138 n.128, 157 n.68
		7:26	132		
7:18	45 n.50	7:27	128	7–8	157 n.68
18:24	159 n.80	8:13	129		
		9:1	132	4Q511	
Pr Man		9:1–4	128	2 I, 5	73
15	159 n.80	9:2	131		
		9:4	45 n.49	11Q10	72
Sir		9:8	134		
4:10	42	9:10	45 n.49	11Q13	71, 72
18:1	128 n.71	11:4	96 n.36	II, 5	73
18:33	128 n.71	13:17	96 n.36	II, 8	73
18:43	128 n.71	14:1	120 n.20	II, 9	71
36:1	78 n.122	14:1–11	58 n.24	II, 10	71, 72, 72 n.98, 127, 127 n.63
36:11	78 n.122	14:3–7	58 n.23		
43:23	58 n.22				
44:16	60 n.32	**QUMRAN**		II, 12	72
44–50	93			II, 13	48
46:5	96 n.35, 96 n.36	1Q28b		II, 14	72
		V, 20–25	48	II, 15–16	71
48:9	61			II, 23–25	71, 72
48:9–10	91	1QH			
48:12	61	IX, 13–14	58 n.22	**OLD TESTAMENT PSEUDEPIGRAPHA**	
49:14	60 n.32				
50	99	1QM	40 n.24		
50:16–18	157 n.68	I, 5	73	*Apoc. Mos.*	
50:17	93, 93 n.27	I, 10	72	7:2	22 n.29
50:17–18	21 n.27	XIII, 10–11	49	17:1	22 n.29
50:20	92, 93 n.27	XVII, 5–9	49	25:3	78 n.122
50:20–22	92, 93, 94, 99, 170, 173, 174			27:5	22 n.29, 157 n.68
		1QS			
50:21	92, 93, 93 n.27	II, 2	73	33:5	21 n.27, 22 n.29
50:22	92, 93	III, 20ff	40 n.24		
51:10	96 n.35			36:1	56 n.14
		4Q174			
Tob		1 I, 10–12	42 n.38, 118 n.5	*Apoc. Sedr.*	
5:4 (S)	90			14:1	78 n.121
5:14	84, 151 n.42	4Q246	42 n.38	14:2	56 n.14

Apoc. Zeph.		7:29–30	78 n.121	53:6	73, 47 n.61	
6:11–15	23, 138 n.131, 149, 149 n.29	7:30	96 n.36	54:4–6	40 n.24	
				55:4	45 n.49, 49, 137, 163	
6:14–15	66	*1 En.*				
		9:4–5	128 n.71	57:3	137 n.126, 163	
Apoc. Ab.		10:4–6	49	60:2	45 n.50	
7:10	128 n.71	10:11–12	49	61:5	71	
17	138 n.128, 157 n.68	14:8	45 n.51	61:7	163 n.99	
		14:9–23	134	61:8	45 n.49, 47 n.61, 137, 163,	
18:3	138 n.128	14:18–20	138 n.128			
		14:18–23	154 n.52			
Ascen. Isa.		14:22	45 n.50	61:8–9	137 n.125	
4	146	18:16	49	61:10	58 n.25	
4:2–4	146	38:1	47 n.61, 73	61:10–11	163, 164 n.100	
4:6	146, 146 n.16	39:6	162	61:10–13	138 nn.126, 128, 163	
4:7–8	146	39:9	163 n.100			
4:10	146	39:9–13	138 nn.126, 128, 163	61:11	163	
4:11	146			62	163	
6:8	138 n.128	39:12	137 n.126, 157 n.66, 163	62:2–5	45 n.49, 47 n.61, 137, 163	
7:13–10:6	45 n.49					
7:18–23	149 n.29	39:12–40:1	45 n.50			
7:21	23, 138 n.131, 149	40:3	138 n.126, 163	62:3–9	136	
		40:4–5	24, 164 n.100	62:4–5	163	
8:1–5	149 n.29	40:6	138 n.126, 163	62:5–14	163	
8:4–5	149	45:3	45 n.49, 47 n.61, 137, 163	62:6	137, 163	
9:27–32	34			62:7	138 n.132, 163	
9:27–36	138 n.131					
9:37–10:6	138 n.128	45:4–5	137	62:8	47 n.61, 73, 137	
10:20–29	120	46:1	162			
11:32–33	45 n.49, 138 n.131	46:2–4	163	62:9	137, 163	
		46:5	137, 163	62:14–16	137	
		46:6–7	163	63:1	163	
2 Bar.		46:8	47 n.61, 73	63:1–2	163	
4:5	134	47:2	138 n.126, 163	63:1–7	137 n.126	
21:4–7	128 n.71	47:3	45 n.50, 154 n.52	63:4	163	
21:6	45 n.50, 123 n.38, 138 n.128			63:5	163	
		48:2	129, 163	63:6	163	
		48:2–3	163 n.100	63:7	163	
48:10	45 n.50, 154 n.52	48:5	137, 137 n.126, 161, 162, 163	63:8	163	
				66:1–2	58 n.25	
48:23–24	73 n.102			69:25	138 n.126, 163	
72:2	48	48:5a	163			
76	91	48:5b	163	69:27	129, 163 n.99	
		48:6	47 n.61, 138 n.132, 163			
3 Bar.				69:29	45 n.49, 137 154 n.52	
11:6	22, 138 n.131	51:3	45 n.49, 47 n.61	71:5–10		
				71:9–12	138 nn.126, 128, 163	
4 Bar.		52:6	71			

81:3	128 n.71	13:52	42 n.38	193	96 n.35		
84:2–3	45 n.49	14	91				
90:9–12	157 n.69	14:9	42 n.38	*Liv. Pro.*			
101:4–9	58 n.23			3:15	134		
101:6	58 n.22	*Jos. Asen.*					
105:2	42 n.38	5:10	25 n.45	*Pss. Sol.*			
108:12	45 n.49	12:1–2	128 n.71	2:36	96 n.35		
		12:11	78 n.122	6:1	96 n.35		
2 En.		14:3	23, 148 n.26	9:6	96 n.36		
1:7	148 n.26	14:10	23, 148 n.26	15:1	96 n.35		
3:1 (J)	45 n.51	14:11	57	17:1	93 n.27		
17	138 n.128	15:11	22, 23	17:4	118 n.5		
19:4	58 n.25	15:11–12x	21 n.22, 23, 24	17:21–24	118 n.5		
20:1–3	154 n.52	15:12–12x	22	17:21–27	48		
20:1–3 (J)	45 n.49	15:12x	24	17:30–32	48		
20:1–21:1	138 n.128	22:4	25 n.45	18:5–9	48		
21:1	45 n.50	22:7–8	25				
21:1 (J)	157 n.66	24:12	78 n.121	*Ques. Ezra*			
24:1 (J)	45 n.49	28:2–3	78 n.121	29	157 n.66		
24:2–3	128 n.71						
33:3–8	128 n.71	*Jub.*		*Sib. Or.*			
39:1–67:3	61	2:2	123 n.38	2:60	31 n.68		
47:3–4	128 n.71	5:6	49	3:20–35	128 n.71		
67:1–3	60 n.32,	10:1–11	40 n.24	3:30	31 n.71		
	61 n.38	10:7–14	49	3:716–717	56 n.14		
67:2	45 n.49	12:3–5	128 n.71	5:33–34	146 n.16		
		17:15–18	48 n.65				
3 En.		48:1–19	40 n.24	*Sib. Or.*			
1:12	157 n.66	48:15–19	49	frg. 3	128 n.71		
16:1–5	149 n.29						
		L.A.E.		*T. Benj.*			
Ezek. Trag.		4:3	136 n.118	10:7–8	34		
68–82	136	12:1	136				
74–76	45 n.49	13–15	136	*T. Dan*			
74–80	136	13:2	136	5:10–11	40 n.24,		
83–89	136	13:3	136		49 n.70		
101	138 n.132	14:3	138 n.132				
		15:3	45 n.49, 136	*T. Jos.*			
4 Ezra		25:3	136 n.118	13:2	56 n.14		
3:4	128 n.71	27:2	136 n.118,	13:5	25		
6:1–6	128 n.71		138 n.132	19:8	157 n.69		
7:28–29	42 n.38	46:3	138 n.132				
8:20–21	138 n.128	47:3	45 n.49, 136	*T. Levi*			
8:21	45 n.50			3:4–8	45 n.49, 134,		
8:21–22	123 n.38	*Let. Aris.*			138 n.128		
13	45 n.52	42	154	5:1	45 n.49, 134,		
13:4	71	135–137	4 n.26, 31		138 n.128		
13:32	42 n.38	138	31 n.71	5:5	23, 96 n.38		
13:37	42 n.38	177	33 n.77	18:12	49 n.70		

Index of References

T. Naph.		39:8–40:4	61 n.38	2.165	21 n.26,
6:1–10	58 n.23	42:1	45 n.52		31 n.69
				2.288–291	60 n.32, 61
T. Reu.		**PHILO**			
6:12	34			Mut.	
		Conf.		125–129	127 n.63
T. Sim.		49	33 n.77		
6:6	40 n.24			Plant.	
		Contempl.		18	132
T. Zeb.		9	31 n.71		
2:2	78 n.121			Prov.	
3:6–7	25 n.45	Decal.		2.19	33 n.77
9:5	4 n.26, 21 n.24	4–9	33 n.77		
9:8	49 n.70	64	4, 31 n.70	QG	
		76	21 n.24, 31 n.69	1.86	60 n.32
T. Ab. (A)					
3:5–6	59			Sacr.	
3:6	22, 148 n.26	Det.		8	132
6:8	157 n.68	54	131	8–10	60 n.32
7:6	78 n.121			9	127 n.63
7:11	45 n.50	Deus.			
8:1	45 n.50	57	132	Somn.	
9:1	23 n.35, 148 n.26			1.5	120
		Her.		2.78–92	31
9:2–3	56 n.14	199	131	2.78–154	31
9:7	45 n.50			2.110–132	31
10:1	45 n.51	Ios.		2.123–129	32
11–13	45 n.49	164	25 n.45	2.123–132	46, 162
16:9	25			2.130–132	32
18:10	56 n.14	Legat.		2.140	33 n.77
20:12	157 n.66	74–118	32		
20:12–13	21 n.27	116	4, 32, 66, 156, 162	Spec.	
				1.15	31 n.70
T. Ab. (B)		114–116	32	1.24	33 n.77
4:4–6	22 n.29	116–118	162	1.84–87	27
8:3	45 n.51	310	33 n.77	1.93–97	27
10:4	78 n.121	353–357	46	2.199	21 n.27
14:9	34	367–368	46		
				JOSEPHUS	
T. Isaac		Migr.			
6:4–5	138 n.128	6	132	Ag. Ap.	
				2.192	128 n.71
T. Adam		Mos.		2.193	73 n.102
1:4	157 n.66	1.155	61 n.39		
4:8	157 n.66	1.158	127 n.63	Ant.	
		1.276	21 n.24	1.85	60 n.32
T. Job		2.23	5, 33 n.77	1.273	78 n.122
14:1–3	154 n.53	2.40	5, 33 n.77	3.91	4, 21 n.24, 31 n.69
33:3	45 n.49	2.117–135	27		

3.143	154	*J.W.*		9:4	159 n.80
3.150	154 n.54	1.73	151 n.42	10:2	159 n.80
3.151–178	27	2.341	21 n.23	10:4	159 n.80
3.180	27	2.394	96 n.35	10:5	159 n.80
4.50	78 n.122	2.414	21 n.25	16:4	146 n.16
4.201	73 n.102	4.164	28 n.55		
4.320–326	61	4.262	28 n.55,	Ign.	
4.326	60 n.32		33 n.77	*Smyrn.*	
6.285	26 n.47	4.324	28 n.55	9:1	31 n.68
6.333	26 n.48	5.99	21 n.23		
7.95	21 n.27	5.381	33 n.77	Justin	
7.381	31	5.402	5, 33 n.77	*2 Apol.*	
8.118	21 n.25	6.123	33 n.77	13:4	34
8.119	21 n.27				
8.225–228	21 n.23			*Dial.*	
8.248	31 n.69	**EARLY CHRISTIAN**		63–64	34
8.317	4 n.26	**WRITINGS**			
8.343	59	Aristides		*Mart. Pol.*	
9.11	21 n.27	*Apol.*		17:3	34
9.28	60 n.32	13	19		
9.64	78 n.121	14.4	23	Tertullian	
9.135	21 n.26			*Or.*	
9.269	21 n.27	*1 Clem.*		3	157 n.66
10.11	56 n.14	20:12	159, 159 n.80,		
10.29	21 n.23		160 n.83	**RABBINIC**	
10.69	4 n.26, 31	32:4	159 n.80, 160	**LITERATURE**	
	n.69	34:6	157 n.66		
10.211–212	27 n.50	38:4	159 n.80	*b. Sanh.*	
10.213	21 n.24	43:6	159 n.80	38b	46
10.263	22 n.30	45:7	159 n.80		
11.3	22 n.30	50:7	159 n.80,	*j. Ber.*	
11.87	21 n.23		160 n.83	9:13a–b	23
11.231	56 n.14	58:2	159 n.80		
11.327–331	27	61:3	159 n.80	*Pesiq. Rab.*	
11.331	27, 28	64:2	159	36 (161a)	129
11.331–333	26 n.49	65:2	159 n.80		
11.333	28			*t. Hul.*	
11.334–335	27	*2 Clem.*		2:18	23
12.53	154	20:5	159		
12.114	33 n.77			**OTHER SOURCES**	
13.54	21 n.23	Clement of Alexandria			
14.304	155 n.57	*Strom.*		Achilles Tatius	
14.313	155 n.57	6.5.41	23	*Leuc. Clit.*	
17.94	56 n.14			8.8.8	13 n.1
19.2	56 n.14	*Did.*			
20.28	26 n.47	8:2	159 n.80	Antoninus Liberalis	
20.56	26 n.47	9:2	159 n.80	*Metam.*	
20.65	26 n.47	9:3	159 n.80	25.4	91

Index of References

Apollodorus
Bibl.
2.7.7   60 n.33

Apollonius Rhodius
Argon.
1.179–184   57 n.18
4.1330   90 n.16

Apost. Const.
7.35.3   157 n.66
8.12.27   157 n.66

Appian
Hist. rom.
12.104   16

Arrian
Anab.
4.10.5–12.5 20
4.10.7   20
4.11.3   20
4.11.9   16 n.9
7.23.2   155 n.57

Artemidorus
Onir.
2.37   19 n.15

BGU 423.6–7 = SelPap I,
112   57 n.18
BGU 423.11–16 = SelPap I,
112   15 n.7
BGU 615.6–9 15 n.7

Chariton
Chaer.
1.1.5   13 n.1
1.1.16   19
2.2.7   13 n.1, 15
3.2.14   19
3.6.3   13 n.1
3.8.6   14 n.2
3.9.1   19
4.1.9   19
5.2.2   16
5.2.3   15 n.6
5.3.3   16
5.3.9   19
5.3.11   15 n.6
5.4.8   16
5.8.9   16
6.7.3   16
6.7.5   15 n.6, 16
7.5.15   16
8.4.10   13 n.1
8.5.5   16
8.5.12   16

Cicero
Sest.
27   155 n.57

CPR 19.5–8 = *NewDocs* I,
16   15 n.7

Dio Cassius
Hist. rom.
50.5.4   156 n.61
56.46.1–2   61 n.36
59.24.4   156
59.27.1   147 n.20
59.27.5   147 n.20, 156
62.23.3   147 n.20, 156
63.2.4   147 n.20
63.4.3   147 n.20, 156
63.5.2   147 n.20, 156
65.5.2   147 n.20
67.13.4   147 n.20, 156
68.8.6   147 n.20

Dio Chrysostom,
Or.
3.30–31   57 n.18
32.50   18 n.14

Diodorus Siculus
Hist.
1.83.4   15 n.5
1.90.3   19, 28
3.5.1   19, 28, 151 n.42
3.71.5   19 n.15
4.38.4–5   60 n.33
4.43.1–2   57 n.18
4.51.3   13
4.82.6   60 n.34, 61 n.38
18.61.1   20

Diogenes Laertius
Vit. phil.
8.68   60 n.34, 61 n.38

Dionysius of
  Halicarnassus
Ant. rom.
1.64.4–5   60 n.34, 61 n.38
2.63.3–4   60 n.35

Epictetus
Diatr.
1.4.31   14 n.3
4.1.60   19
4.1.103–105 14 n.3

Eratosthenes
frg. 182   57 n.18

Euripides
Hel.
605–606   90 n.16

Galen
Protr.
1.8 K   18 n.14

Herodotus
Hist.
7.56   57 n.18
7.136   17

Hesiod
frg. 148   91
Homeric Hymns
22   57 n.18

Homer
Il.
13.26–30   57 n.18

Od.
1.96–324   90

Livy
Hist.
1.16   60 n.35
1.16.7   62

Longus
Daphn.
2.2.4–5   14 n.2
2.24.1–2   14
3.28.1   14 n.2

Lucian
Cal.
17   19
Cat.
11   16 n.9
Dial. mort.
3(2).2   16 n.9
Gall.
9   15 n.5
14   15 n.5
Nav.
22   15
30   16 n.9
37–38   16 n.9, 17 n.13
Nigr.
21   15 n.5
Sat.
29   15 n.5
Peregr.
39   92
Tim.
5   15
Tyr.
19   20 n.21
Ver. hist.
1.7   20 n.21

Ovid
Fast.
2.475–512   60 n.35
Metam.
8.611–724   90
15.746–50   61 n.38
15.746–51   61 n.36

Pausanias
Descr.
4.27.2   19 n.15
6.9.6–9   60 n.34

P.Giess.
11.12–15 = *SelPap* II,
423   15
17.11–12 = *SelPap* I,
115   15
22.5–6   15 n.7
77.8–9   15 n.7

Philo of Byblos
FGH 790 frg.
1.29   18
2.6   14 n.2
2.10   14

Philostratus
Vit. Apoll.
8.30–31   61 n.37

Plautus
Cas.
50   39 n.20

Pliny
Nat.
2.94   61 n.36
33.26   39 n.20

Plutarch
Ag. Cleom.
18.2   13
Alex.
45.1   20
51.3   20
54.2–4   20
Alex. fort.
328C   14
Amat.
771D–E   14 n.2
Arist.
5.6   16
Art.
11.3   16, 151
                  n.42

13.2   16 n.9
15.5   14 n.2
22.4   17
23.5   13
29.6–7   14 n.2
Cam.
5.6–7   13
Comp. Thes. Rom.
6.4   18 n.14
Crass.
31.1   16 n.8
33.2   16
Exil.
607A   20 n.21
Flam.
21.7   16 n.8
Frat. amor.
488F   16
Gen. Socr.
590B   19 n.15
Luc.
24.5   18
Marc.
6.5–6   14 n.3
Mulier. virt.
258B   13
Num.
2.3   91
14.2   14
14.3–5   14 n.3
Pomp.
27.3   18 n.14
Quaest. rom.
266C   14
266F–267A   14 n.2
270D   14 n.3, 151
                  n.42
Rom.
27.6   62
27.6–28.3   60 n.35
27.7   62
27.7–8   19, 61 n.38, 91
27.8   62, 151 n.42
28.1   62
28.2   62
Sull.
22.5   16 n.8
23.3   16

Superst.
170E	14 n.3

Them.
27.3	17
28.1	16 n.9
29.2	16 n.9

P.Mich.
465.4	15 n.7
465.33	15 n.7
473.4	15 n.7
474.6	15 n.7

Polyaenus
Strat.
7.10.1	16 n.9
8.22	18

Polybius
10.17.8	16
10.38.3	16
10.40.3	16, 151 n.42
18.54.10	14
30.18.5	18
32.15.7	14 n.3

Porphyry
Vit. Pyth.
29	57 n.18

Posidonius
FGH 87 frg.
5	16
15*.5	14 n.3

Ps.-Mt.
3:3	149 n.29

SB
9636.6	15 n.7

Seneca
Herc. fur.
322–324	57 n.18

Strabo
15.3.20	15

Suetonius
Aug.
99.4	61 n.36

Dom.
13.2	155

Tacitus
Ann.
15.29	155 n.57

Theocritus
Id.
22.1–26	57 n.18

Virgil
Aen.
5.800–821	57 n.18

Xenophon
Anab.
3.2.13	17

Xenophon of Ephesus
Anth. Habr.
1.1.3	19
1.2.7	19
1.12.1	19
3.11.4–5	14
5.11.4	14 n.2

www.ingramcontent.com/pod-product-compliance
Lightning Source LLC
Chambersburg PA
CBHW052038300426
44117CB00012B/1868